ASSYRIA

ASSYRIA

THE RISE AND FALL OF THE
WORLD'S FIRST EMPIRE

Eckart Frahm

BASIC BOOKS
New York

Basic Books
Hachette Book Group
1290 Avenue of the Americas, New York, NY 10104
www.basicbooks.com

Printed in the United States of America

First Edition: April 2023

Published by Basic Books, an imprint of Perseus Books, LLC, a subsidiary of Hachette Book
Group, Inc. The Basic Books name and logo is a trademark of the Hachette Book Group.

The Hachette Speakers Bureau provides a wide range of authors for speaking events.
To find out more, go to hachettespeakersbureau.com or email HachetteSpeakers@hbgusa.com.

Basic books may be purchased in bulk for business, educational, or promotional use.
For information, please contact your local bookseller or Hachette Book Group Special
Markets Department at special.markets@hbgusa.com.

The publisher is not responsible for websites (or their content) that are not owned
by the publisher.

Print book interior design by Jeff Williams.

Library of Congress Cataloging-in-Publication Data
Names: Frahm, Eckart, author.
Title: Assyria : the rise and fall of the world's first empire / Eckart Frahm.
Description: First edition. | New York : Basic Books, 2023. | Includes bibliographical
    references and index. |
Identifiers: LCCN 2022035344 | ISBN 9781541674400 (hardcover) |
    ISBN 9781541674394 (ebook)
Subjects: LCSH: Assyria—History. | Assyria—Civilization.
Classification: LCC DS71 .F73 2023 | DDC 935/.03—dc23/eng/20220801
LC record available at https://lccn.loc.gov/2022035344

ISBNs: 9781541674400 (hardcover), 9781541674394 (ebook)

LSC-C

Printing 1, 2023

Contents

CONTENTS

Assyria's Most
Important Rulers

The following list provides the names and regnal years of Assyria's most important rulers in the somewhat simplified rendering, without special characters, that is used for ancient Near Eastern names throughout this book. The number preceding each ruler's name indicates his position within the Assyrian King List (AKL), an Assyrian chronicle known from first-millennium BCE copies. The available manuscripts of the AKL come to an end with Shalmaneser V (no. 109); the numerals preceding the names of the kings following him continue the AKL's numbering system, running from 110 to 117. Ititi and Zarriqum are not mentioned in the AKL but are included in the list below because of their historical importance, while the names of several rulers who feature in the AKL but are otherwise poorly attested are excluded. If known, the names of the principal wives of the Neo-Assyrian kings are mentioned below as well, marked by italics.

The regnal dates of the kings from Tiglath-pileser I (no. 87) onward can be determined with complete accuracy, while there is a certain margin of error for those of the earlier kings. The dates provided for the Old Assyrian rulers follow Gojko Barjamovic, "Assur Before Assyria" (forthcoming).

In accordance with Mesopotamian calendrical practices, the first year given for a specific ruler is not his accession year but his first full year in office. Thus, Shalmaneser III (AKL 102) is said to have ruled from 858 to 824 BCE, even though he actually ascended the throne at some point in 859 BCE.

Third Millennium BCE

00	Ititi	twenty-third century
00	Zarriqum (or Sarriqum)	mid-twenty-first century
27	Sulili/Sulê	ca. 2025?

Old Assyrian Period

30	Puzur-Ashur I	ca. 2020?
31	Shalim-ahum	
32	Ilushumma	
33	Erishum I	ca. 1969–1930
34	Ikunum	ca. 1929–1916
35	Sharrum-ken (Sargon I)	ca. 1915–1876
36	Puzur-Ashur II	ca. 1875–1868
37	Naram-Sîn	ca. 1867–1834/1824
38	Erishum II	ca. 1833/1823–1809
39	Shamshi-Adad I	ca. 1808–1776
40	Ishme-Dagan I	ca. 1775–1736
40a	Mut-Ashkur	
40b	Rimush	
40d	Puzur-Sîn	

Transition Period

41	Ashur-dugul	
47	Adasi	ca. 1730
48	Belum-bani	ca. 1729–1719
54	Kidin-Ninua	ca. 1630–1616
57	Shamshi-Adad II	ca. 1597–1591

58	Ishme-Dagan II	ca. 1590–1574
59	Shamshi-Adad III	ca. 1573–1557
60	Ashur-nirari I	ca. 1556–1530
61	Puzur-Ashur III	ca. 1529–1505
62	Enlil-nasir I	ca. 1504–1491
69	Ashur-bel-nisheshu	ca. 1417–1409

Middle Assyrian Period

73	Ashur-uballit I	ca. 1363–1328
76	Adad-nirari I	ca. 1305–1274
77	Shalmaneser I	ca. 1273–1244
78	Tukulti-Ninurta I	ca. 1243–1207
79	Ashur-nadin-apli	ca. 1206–1203
80	Ashur-nirari III	ca. 1202–1197
81	Enlil-kudurri-usur	ca. 1196–1192
82	Ninurta-apil-Ekur	ca. 1191–1179
83	Ashur-dan I	ca. 1178–1133
84	Ninurta-tukulti-Ashur	ca. 1133?
87	Tiglath-pileser I	1114–1076
89	Ashur-bel-kala	1073–1056
92	Ashurnasirpal I	1049–1031
93	Shalmaneser II	1030–1019
94	Ashur-nirari IV	1018–1013
95	Ashur-rabi II	1012–972
97	Tiglath-pileser II	966–935

Neo-Assyrian Period

98	Ashur-dan II	934–912	
99	Adad-nirari II	911–891	
100	Tukulti-Ninurta II	890–884	
101	Ashurnasirpal II	883–859	∞ *Mullissu-mukannishat-Ninua* *
102	Shalmaneser III	858–824	
103	Shamshi-Adad V	823–811	∞ *Sammu-ramat* (Semiramis)
104	Adad-nirari III	810–783	

---

* The symbol ∞ indicates marriage.

105	Shalmaneser IV	782–773	∞ *Hamâ*
106	Ashur-dan III	772–755	
107	Ashur-nirari V	754–745	
108	Tiglath-pileser III	744–727	∞ *Yabâ*
109	Shalmaneser V	726–722	∞ *Banitu* (?)
110	Sargon II	721–705	∞ 1) *Ra'imâ*
			∞ 2) *Atalya*
111	Sennacherib	704–681	∞ 1) *Tashmetu-sharrat*
			∞ 2) *Naqia*
112	Esarhaddon	680–669	∞ *Esharra-hammat*
113	Ashurbanipal	668–631	∞ *Libbali-sharrat*
114	Ashur-etel-ilani	630–627?	
115	Sîn-shumu-lishir	627?	
116	Sîn-sharru-ishkun	626?–612	
117	Ashur-uballit II	611–609	

A Note on Translations

In translations of Assyrian and Babylonian texts, opening and closing square brackets—as in "[ancient]"—indicate restorations of broken passages, while parentheses—as in "(ancient)"—are used for additions provided to clarify the meaning of a given phrase. In cases in which restorations are not marked, endnotes explicitly say so. Translations draw on the quoted text editions, but where needed with adaptations by the present author. Translations from the Bible are based on the New Revised Standard Version, with occasional adjustments.

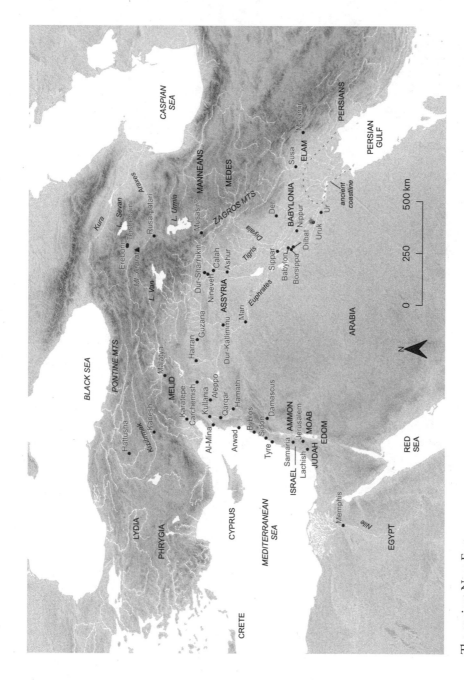

The ancient Near East.
© *Alessio Palmisano*

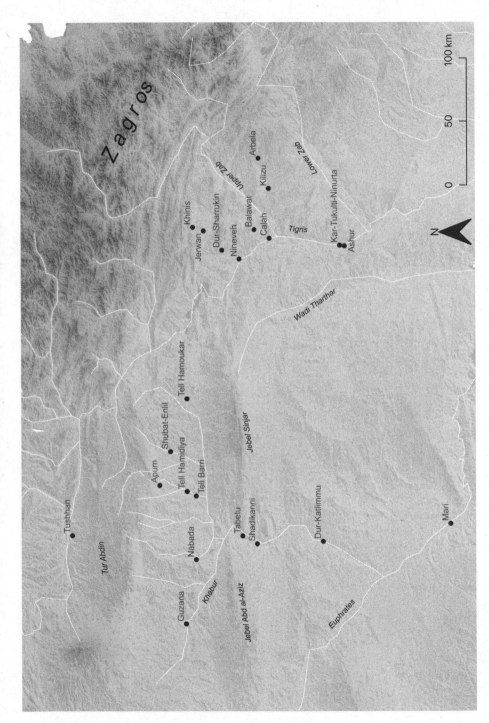

Assyria's heartland on the Tigris and adjoining territories on the Khabur River.

© *Alessio Palmisano*

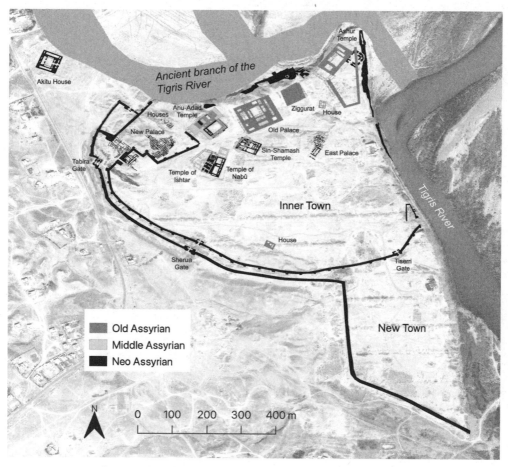

Ashur, Assyria's longtime capital and religious center.
© *Alessio Palmisano*

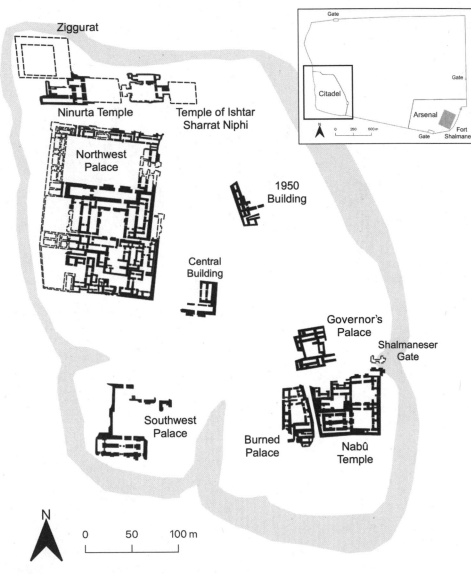

Calah, Assyrian capital in the ninth and eighth centuries BCE, with its citadel.
© *Alessio Palmisano*

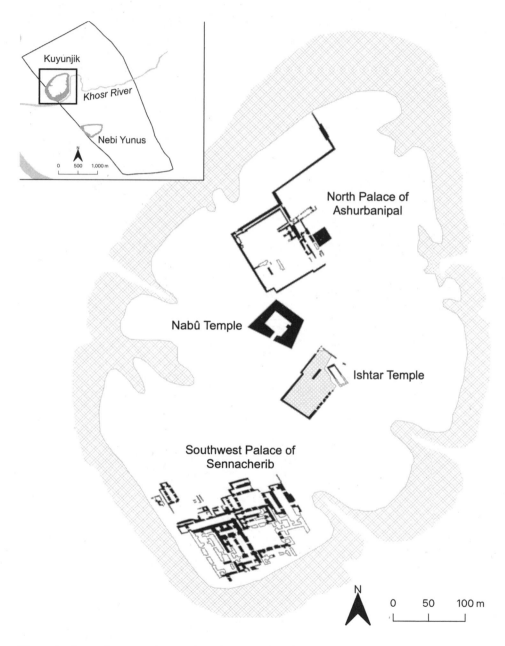

Nineveh, Assyria's imperial capital in the seventh century BCE, with its main citadel.
© *Alessio Palmisano*

Introduction

In the summer of 671 BCE, an army dispatched by the Assyrian king Esarhaddon marched through Western Asia, crossed the Sinai Peninsula, and entered the land of Egypt. Pharaoh Taharqa managed to flee, but his wife, his crown prince, and many of his harem women were captured. Along with enormous amounts of booty and with political hostages, craftsmen, exorcists, and magicians numbering in the hundreds, they were brought to Nineveh, Esarhaddon's mighty capital on the Tigris River in northeastern Iraq.

It was an unprecedented triumph for Assyria. Two years earlier, King Esarhaddon had stated in one of his inscriptions that all his enemies "trembled like reeds in a storm," that their "hearts were pounding," and that "there was no rival whom my weapon could not face." Now, in the wake of his great victory over Egypt, the Assyrian king could make good on his braggadocio. He dispatched letters requesting gifts and professions of respect from rulers of several faraway territories in the Mediterranean—from Cyprus to Greece to what is now modern Spain. When they complied, Esarhaddon had every reason to claim, "I achieved victory over the rulers of the four quarters of the world—and sprinkled the venom of death over all my enemies."[1]

The Assyrian conquest of Egypt represented the culmination of a long historical journey. When that journey began, in the second half of the third millennium BCE, there were few signs that the country would one day achieve hegemony over almost all of Western Asia and some adjoining territories. In fact, Assyria was barely a country at all—in the beginning there was only the city of Ashur (see Plate 1). Located some 100 kilometers (62 miles) south of Nineveh, Ashur was home to a number of important temples—including that of a god likewise named Ashur—but it was not a major political player.

Around 2000 BCE, after spending several centuries under the heel of the powerful kingdoms of southern Mesopotamia, Ashur became politically independent. For the following three hundred years—the so-called Old Assyrian period—it was jointly ruled by a popular assembly and a dynasty of hereditary leaders. The city's role as a hub in the international trade in tin and textiles permitted Ashur to accumulate considerable wealth during this time.

A period of decline starting around 1700 BCE brought the Old Assyrian city-state and many of its institutions to an end, but the journey was not over. When Ashur got back on its feet in the fourteenth century BCE, it assumed a very different role: serving as capital of a territorial state eager to expand its borders through military means. This birth of Assyria in the proper sense of the term—its emergence as a land that included great cities such as Nineveh, Calah, and Arbela, and soon others much farther away—marked the beginning of a new era: the Middle Assyrian period. Now a full-fledged monarchy, Assyrians started to see their land as a peer of the most powerful states of the time, from Babylonia in the south to Egypt in the west.

During the eleventh century BCE, the Assyrian kingdom experienced a new crisis, this one caused by climate change, migrations, and internal tensions. It lost most of its provinces, especially in the west. But when the dust settled, it managed to rise from the ashes faster than any of the other states in the region. A number of energetic and ruthless Assyrian rulers of the Neo-Assyrian period (ca. 934–612 BCE) took advantage of the weakness of their political rivals, embarking on a systematic campaign of subjugation, destruction, and annexation. Their efforts, initially aimed at the reconquest of areas that had been under Assyrian rule before and then moving farther afield, were carried out with unsparing and often violent determination, cruelly epitomized in an aphoristic statement found in another of Esarhaddon's inscriptions: "Before me, cities, behind me, ruins."[2]

Again, there were setbacks. On several occasions—even in the otherwise glorious year of 671—internal and external revolts threatened Assyria's hegemony. In Israel and Judah, resistance to Assyria's military interventions resulted in the emergence of new, anti-imperial forms of religion, with long-term consequences unforeseen at the time. But by the late eighth century, the Assyrians had managed to create a state that transcended all its predecessors in power, size, and organizational complexity.

During the last years of Esarhaddon's reign, Assyria ruled over a territory that reached from northeastern Africa and the Eastern Mediterranean to Western Iran, and from Anatolia in the north to the Persian Gulf in the south. Parks with exotic plants lined Assyrian palaces, newly created universal libraries were the pride of Assyrian kings, and an ethnically diverse mix of people from dozens of foreign lands moved about the streets of Assyrian cities such as Nineveh and Calah. Yet it was not to last. Only half a century after Esarhaddon's reign, the Assyrian state suffered a dramatic collapse, culminating in the conquest and destruction of Nineveh in 612 BCE.

Assyria's fall occurred long before some better-known empires of the ancient world were founded: the Persian Empire, established in 539 BCE by Cyrus II; Alexander the Great's fourth-century BCE Greco-Asian Empire and its successor states; the third-century BCE empires created by the Indian ruler Ashoka and the Chinese emperor

Qin Shi Huang; and the most prominent and influential of these, the Roman Empire, whose beginnings lay in the first century BCE. The Assyrian kingdom may not have the same name recognition. But for more than one hundred years, from about 730 to 620 BCE, it had been a political body so large and so powerful that it can rightly be called the world's first empire.

And so Assyria matters. "World history" does not begin with the Greeks or the Romans—it begins with Assyria. "World religion" took off in Assyria's imperial periphery. Assyria's fall was the result of a first "world war." And the bureaucracies, communication networks, and modes of domination created by the Assyrian elites more than 2,700 years ago served as blueprints for many of the political institutions of subsequent great powers, first directly and then indirectly, up until the present day. This book tells the story of the slow rise and glory days of this remarkable ancient civilization, of its dramatic fall, and its intriguing afterlife.

TWO CENTURIES AGO, FOR A MODERATELY EDUCATED CITIZEN OF the West, Assyria was both much better known and much more poorly understood than it is today. Nineveh was then a household name for most people. They were familiar with it from the Hebrew Bible, which portrayed it as the capital of the state that had sounded the death knell on the Kingdom of Israel. The Book of Jonah, popular and widely read, claimed that Nineveh was so large that it took three days to walk across from one end to the other—and that God had forgiven the Ninevites their sins when they repented. The Book of Nahum painted a much darker picture, comparing Nineveh to a debased prostitute and describing the city's impending destruction, brought about by God to punish Assyria's imperial hubris. In a variety of Greek and Latin texts from classical antiquity, Assyria appeared as the first in a long succession of empires, founded by King Ninus and his colorful wife Semiramis and destroyed by

Babylonians and Medes during the reign of Assyria's last king, Sardanapalus, an effeminate debauchee.

Up to the mid-nineteenth century, most people in the West had a largely negative perception of Assyria. The world of ancient Israel, Greece, and Rome served as models of identity for them. From Jerusalem, they believed, their religious faith had arisen, from Athens, their methods of thinking, and from Rome, their political organization. Nineveh, much like Babylon or Carthage, embodied otherness—in the words of the Book of Nahum, it was "the bloody city, all full of lies and booty." But the Western image of Assyria was not entirely free of ambivalence. Disgust for the "oriental despotism" associated with Assyria was mixed with admiration for the alleged political and military accomplishments of the kingdom, and the imperial ambitions ascribed to King Ninus and his successors resonated with similar aspirations in nineteenth-century Britain and France.[3]

Missing from the picture were the voices of the ancient Assyrians themselves. After the second century CE, no one knew any longer how to read the cuneiform script in which the Assyrians, as well as the Sumerians, Babylonians, and other people of the ancient Near East, had recorded royal inscriptions, literary works, medical treatises, letters, title deeds, and administrative documents. The various languages these people had used, including Assyrian, were all forgotten. The physical traces of Assyrian civilization, from temples and palaces to private houses, had largely disappeared as well; they lay hidden under later settlements or under huge, grass-covered mounds no longer easily recognizable as remains of human habitations. This was to some extent due to the destruction Assyria's main cities had suffered in the late seventh century BCE. But it also resulted from the fact that, much in contrast to ancient Egypt, whose temples and tombs were constructed of stone, all buildings in ancient Mesopotamia were made of mudbrick, which would crumble after a few generations, turning what were once urban centers of massive proportions into heaps of rubble.

THE "REAL" ASSYRIA—RATHER THAN THE DISTORTED IMAGE THE
Bible and the classical texts conveyed of it—began to regain its place
in the historical consciousness of the modern world on April 5, 1843,
when a forty-one-year-old Frenchman by the name of Paul-Émile
Botta sat down at his desk in the city of Mosul to write a letter. Botta
was the French consul in Mosul, at the time a remote provincial
town on the outskirts of the Ottoman Empire, but his letter was not
about politics. Addressed to the secretary of the Société Asiatique in
Paris, it was about a spectacular archaeological find. During the previous days, Botta revealed, some of his workmen had dug up several
strange and intriguing bas-reliefs and inscriptions near the small village of Khorsabad, some 25 kilometers (15 miles) northeast of Mosul.
At the end of his letter, Botta proudly announced, "I believe I am
the first to discover sculptures that may be assumed to belong to the
time when Nineveh was still flourishing."[4]

During the first half of the nineteenth century, several factors had
triggered a renewed interest among Europeans in the lost civilizations
of the ancient Near East. One important element was the Romantic
spirit of the time, which sought escape from the mundanities of the
here and now and indulged in a search for origins. Botta, the French
consul and explorer, was very much under the spell of such yearnings.
Like the famous Romantic poet Lord Byron, he had been in Greece
during the Greek War of Independence. He had later traveled the world
as a ship's doctor, and he was a passionate user of opium, on which he
had written his doctoral dissertation. Man was "forced at all times to
find ways of escaping from his real existence and move into a world
of imagination," Botta had mused in that study, espousing the same
escapist mood that later prompted his quest for Assyrian antiquities.[5]

At the same time, the nineteenth century had also brought to
the fore a strong taste for historical inquiry, aiming at a reconstruction of the past "as it actually happened." Exploring ancient Assyria
promised important insights into the historical truth of the stories

told in the Bible and was thus an endeavor very much in line with the historicist spirit of the age.[6]

Finally, there was for the first time an opportunity to actually study Assyrian and other archaeological sites in the region. The rise of France and Britain to leading imperial powers enabled ambitious and ruthless European men eager to make their mark to travel to and explore faraway places. To be sure, the Ottoman state—unlike substantial swaths of Africa and Southeast Asia—was not an imperial province of any European country. But its political fragility facilitated interventions on the part of the great European powers—including some of a scholarly nature. The most famous of these was the archaeological exploration of Egypt during Napoleon's campaign of the years 1798 to 1801, which eventually led to the decipherment of Egyptian hieroglyphs by Jean-François Champollion in 1822.

Compared to Napoleon's scientific expedition to Egypt, in which a whole army of scholars participated, the rediscovery of Assyrian sites around Mosul in the 1840s and 1850s was a very lonely affair, drawing on the labor of a few European explorers and their local workmen. The results of their efforts, however, were spectacular. The first major breakthrough was owed to Botta, who uncovered at Khorsabad a massive Assyrian palace and parts of a city surrounded by a wall some 7 kilometers (about 4 miles) long. The city, as would eventually transpire, had been called Dur-Sharrukin in Assyrian times and had been built by the Assyrian king Sargon II (r. 721–705 BCE). Luckily for the excavators, the Neo-Assyrian kings had lined the mudbrick walls of their palaces with large stone blocks, or orthostats. This made it possible to easily trace the outline and structure of the buildings, which at Khorsabad were located close to the surface. The images found on the orthostats, and the sculptures of colossal winged bulls uncovered in several palace gates, provided the first glimpses into the world of the ancient Assyrians after the downfall of the Assyrian kingdom some 2,500 years earlier.[7]

In 1845, two years after Botta had initiated excavations at Khorsabad, a young Englishman by the name of Austen Henry Layard, an amateur archaeologist and protégé of the influential British ambassador to Constantinople, Sir Stratford Canning, began exploring another Assyrian site, located some 32 kilometers (20 miles) downstream from Mosul on the eastern bank of the Tigris. Known to local people as Nimrud, it turned out to be a royal city by the name of Kalḫu (or Calah, as it is called in the Hebrew Bible). Within just a few months, Layard and his resourceful assistant Hormuzd Rassam, a Chaldean Christian from Mosul, uncovered on Nimrud's main acropolis hundreds of meters of bas-reliefs depicting royal campaigns, hunting expeditions, and mythological scenes, as well as numerous monumental inscriptions no one was initially able to read. They even found the platform for the throne of the ninth-century BCE Assyrian king Shalmaneser III, with an image of that king and a Babylonian ruler shaking hands, the first known pictorial representation of this widely used gesture.

The archaeological site closest to Mosul, a large area surrounded by massive walls on the other, eastern side of the Tigris, had initially yielded no major finds—even though it seemed from early on likely that it was here that Nineveh, Assyria's most famous city, had once prospered. Nahum's invectives notwithstanding, Nineveh's ancient name had never been entirely forgotten. The site where the city's ruins lay buried under layers and layers of earth and debris was known to the local population as Nuniya. Moreover, a mound by the name of Nebi Yunus on the southwestern edge of the site was the location of a mosque built over what people believed to be the burial place of the biblical prophet Jonah (Yūnus in Arabic), whose life's journey, according to scripture, had ended in Nineveh (see Plate 3).

Western visitors to the Middle East had been interested in the site of Nuniya, and its potential to yield ancient treasures, for quite a while. In 1820, the British resident for the East India Company in Baghdad, Claudius Rich, had spent some time in and around

Mosul. At Nebi Yunus, he was shown relief slabs accessible from an underground kitchen, and he returned from his visit with a number of antiques, including a clay cylinder inscribed all over in a strange, unknown writing system. This created appetite for more. In fact, Botta's assignment to Mosul had originally been motivated by a desire to expand Rich's very limited earlier attempts to explore the area. Between December 1842 and March 1843, the French consul conducted excavations at Kuyunjik, a large mound located about a kilometer (0.62 miles) north of Nebi Yunus. But when his attempts to find noteworthy artifacts at that site led him nowhere, he turned his attention to Khorsabad. It was thus Layard whose name became inextricably linked to the rediscovery of Nineveh. Between 1846 and 1851, Layard's workmen, digging deeper than Botta's and using a network of tunnels, uncovered on the southwestern side of Kuyunjik yet another enormous Assyrian palace, with relief slabs lining walls altogether more than 3 kilometers (1.8 miles) long. Perhaps most importantly, they also unearthed in several rooms of the palace thousands of baked clay tablets inscribed in the same script found on many of the orthostats that lined the palace walls.

In May 1847, the Louvre in Paris became the first European museum to put Assyrian artifacts on public display, astonishing visitors with monumental works created in a completely unfamiliar artistic language. Never keen on playing second fiddle, the British Museum soon followed suit, and eventually other museums in Europe and the United States did so as well. It was the beginning of an "Assyromania" that swept for a few decades across the Western world, influencing fashion, art, and design.

Transporting the often huge objects from their remote locations in the area around Mosul to the capitals of the West was no easy feat. The bull colossi from the palace gates weighed up to 40 or 50 metric tons (44 to 55 US tons), and the methods applied by the excavators to haul them to the Tigris, where they were put on rafts, were no more advanced than those used by the ancient Assyrians themselves.

On one occasion, in 1853, tragedy led to the loss of countless invaluable objects from an Assyrian site: the rafts carrying more than two hundred artifact-filled crates from Khorsabad down to Basra, where they were to be loaded onto a ship headed for France, sank in the marshes south of Baghdad, and everything, including drawings and field notes, was lost.[8]

Today, one may wonder about the wisdom of moving ancient art on such a massive scale from the Middle East to museums and collections in the West. The early excavators and their political backers often had, in fact, considerable difficulty convincing the Ottoman authorities to grant them permission to do so, and occasionally used ruses to deceive them. To be sure, in the mid-nineteenth century, and for quite some time to come, the removal of archaeological finds from their places of origin was common practice. But the fact that the exploration of archaeological sites in the Middle East began as an essentially "Western" project has undoubtedly contributed to the sense of alienation that many local communities in the region feel regarding the pre-Islamic past. This surely was a factor in the looting and deliberate destruction of many Assyrian sites by the Islamic State group in 2015 and 2016.[9]

DURING THE LATE 1840S AND EARLY 1850S, WHILE THE EXCAVAtions at Khorsabad, Nimrud, and Nineveh went on, several scholars in Britain and France began to study the strange writing found on the orthostats, bull colossi, and clay objects that had come to light at these sites. Because of the wedge-shaped nature of the basic elements of individual signs, the script became known as cuneiform, from the Latin word *cuneus*, which means "nail" or "wedge." Not only the script but also the language of these texts was unknown, which made their decipherment extremely challenging. Luckily, a late sixth-century BCE rock inscription from Bisitun in the Kermanshah Province of Iran provided some help. It included three versions of the same text, written in three different "cuneiform" scripts:

Elamite, Babylonian, and Old Persian. The Old Persian version had been deciphered in 1838, and scholars realized early on that the Babylonian writing found at Bisitun was structurally identical with the script found at Assyrian sites farther north. It also helped that Assyrian and Babylonian were Semitic languages, like Hebrew and Arabic. The existence of such well-known cognates facilitated the process of reconstructing their grammar and recognizing the meaning of individual words. But since most of the roughly one thousand signs of the Assyro-Babylonian script have numerous readings and can render, depending on the context, both words and sounds, the decipherment of this writing system still required true genius.

The main breakthrough was owed to a modest but brilliant Irishman by the name of Edward Hincks, a clergyman from Killyleagh in County Down who collaborated closely with Layard. By 1852, Hincks had realized that the cuneiform signs "all represent syllables," with "every vowel definitely expressed." Hincks's correct identification of the values of hundreds of signs allowed Layard, in his 1853 book *Nineveh and Babylon*, to provide remarkably accurate pioneer translations of some of the monumental inscriptions he had uncovered at Nineveh. Sensationally enough, among the events described in these texts was an attack by the army of the Assyrian king Sennacherib on Jerusalem in 701 BCE that was also described in the Bible.[10]

In the mid-1850s, Edwin Norris, secretary of the Royal Asiatic Society in London, thought the time had come to put the results of the work done so far on the Assyro-Babylonian script to a test. Norris asked four scholars involved in the decipherment efforts to provide, independently of each other, transliterations and translations of a long Assyrian royal inscription. The text Norris selected was written on a large clay prism found at Qal'at Sherqat, an Assyrian site located some 50 kilometers (31 miles) south of Nimrud. Apart from Hincks, the scholars invited to participate in the challenge included the British army officer and orientalist Henry C. Rawlinson, who had played a key role in the decipherment of the Persian cuneiform script; the French-German orientalist Jules Oppert; and William H.F. Talbot, a British polymath best known for his work as a photography pioneer. When the translations submitted by the four in 1857 turned out to be largely identical, the decipherment of the Assyro-Babylonian cuneiform script could be considered accomplished, at least for the basics.[11]

The successful decipherment, much like the decoding of Egyptian hieroglyphs some thirty years earlier, opened windows into a past that had been hitherto almost entirely veiled in secrecy—and thus set the stage for nothing less than a "second Renaissance." Whereas the first, the European Renaissance of the fifteenth and sixteenth centuries, had brought back the civilizations of the Greeks and the Romans, the new Renaissance now initiated by Champollion and Hincks allowed deep insights into the preclassical worlds of Egypt and the ancient Near East—and access to what has been aptly called "the first half of history." Some major blank spaces on the map of the past began to be filled in. Botta, Layard, and Hincks had, of course, only established the basis. Others had to follow and engage in the arduous labor of continuing the excavation work and reading and translating the countless cuneiform texts unearthed by the pioneer archaeologists and their successors.[12]

Over the next decades, the study of the texts led to great advances in the understanding of Assyrian civilization. Monumental royal inscriptions on stone orthostats and sculptures provided the foundation for a first outline of Assyria's political and military history. But the clay tablets unearthed on Nineveh's main mound, Kuyunjik, proved even more exciting. Most of them belonged to libraries created by Assyria's last great king, Ashurbanipal (r. 668–631 BCE), who had sought to assemble in his capital copies of all the literary, religious, and scholarly texts available in his age, both from Assyria and Babylonia. That the ancient Mesopotamians had used mudbricks made of clay for construction was a curse for modern explorers, since buildings made of such bricks are difficult to trace. But their use of clay for writing purposes turned out to be an enormous blessing: especially when baked, clay tablets, even though often found broken into pieces, are otherwise almost indestructible, and hundreds of thousands of them have been excavated all over Mesopotamia and neighboring areas up until now.

The tablets from Ashurbanipal's libraries provided highly unexpected insights into Assyria's intellectual, literary, and religious traditions. One of the most spectacular early discoveries was made by a self-taught young scholar by the name of George Smith. Originally a banknote engraver, Smith worked as an assistant in the British Museum, where almost all of the tablets from Ashurbanipal's library had ended up. On a brisk November day in 1872, he looked at a few lines on a recently cleaned tablet and became so excited that he immediately began, in a rather un-Victorian manner, to undress. What Smith had found were parts of a Mesopotamian flood story so similar to the one known from the Hebrew Bible that there could be no doubt that the two traditions were closely related. When on December 3, 1872, Smith gave a lecture about the newly discovered Mesopotamian Noah to the Biblical Archaeology Society, even the British prime minister William Gladstone was in the audience. At least in Britain, it was the apogee of public interest in Assyria.[13]

BY THE END OF THE NINETEENTH CENTURY, EXCAVATORS AND philologists, some of them holders of newly created university chairs, had established an image of Assyria that included numerous details known neither from the Bible nor from classical sources. But in some important respects, this image was still very much in line with the one promoted in those traditions. The bas-reliefs and texts from Nineveh, Khorsabad, and Nimrud, with their focus on the military deeds and construction projects of powerful kings such as Sargon II,

Sennacherib, or Ashurbanipal, confirmed biblical claims about Assyria's unstoppable expansion in the Levant as well as Greek stories of Assyrian empire-building and the founding of cities.

New discoveries made in the twentieth and twenty-first centuries have significantly modified and enhanced the modern understanding of Assyrian civilization, especially with regard to its origins and early history. Excavations at three archaeological sites in particular were instrumental in this respect. First to mention here is Qal'at Sherqat, which had produced the clay prism whose translation in 1857 served as proof for the successful decipherment of cuneiform. Qal'at Sherqat was the site of Assyria's earliest capital and religious center, Ashur, which had given the country its name. Initially largely spurned by excavators because of its failure to yield the same monumental artwork found at other Assyrian sites, Ashur was explored between 1903 and 1914 by a German team directed by Walter Andrae. As soon became evident, the site provided a window into the history of Assyria prior to the great kings of the first millennium BCE and offered important new insights into the social, economic, and religious dimensions of Assyrian civilization. Whereas the focus at other sites had been on excavating royal palaces, Andrae and his team directed most of their efforts to the study of private houses and temples, including that of the Assyrian state god Ashur. Andrae's excavation techniques were highly innovative: he recorded find spots of individual objects, devised new methods to trace walls made of mudbrick, and carefully analyzed the archaeological layers that had accumulated over time to make sense of the complex stratigraphy of the site. Archaeology thus slowly transcended its previous incarnation as a hunt for ancient treasure.[14]

Andrae and those who worked at Ashur after him discovered some ten thousand clay tablets and other inscriptions. But because it proved difficult to reach the site's lowest layers, the excavations produced only limited numbers of texts from the very earliest phases of Assyrian statehood. Quite unexpectedly, information on some of this early history became available through the exploration of a site nearly 1,000 kilometers (about 620 miles) away from Ashur, well outside the area ever fully controlled by any Assyrian king. During the early 1880s, scholars had begun to publish clay tablets written in a peculiar writing style that had been acquired from antiquities dealers in Kayseri in central Turkey. As systematic excavations in 1925 by the Czech researcher Bedřich Hrozný established, the tablets all came from a large mound by the name of Kültepe, located some 20 kilometers (about 12 miles) northeast of Kayseri. Kültepe, it transpired, was the site of the ancient city of Kanesh, where during the first centuries of the second millennium BCE a colony of merchants from Ashur, under the rulership of local kings, had been engaged over several generations in long-distance trade and other mercantile activities. The early excavations at Kültepe, and those conducted since 1948 by Turkish scholars, have produced some twenty-five thousand clay tablets from the archives of these businesspeople. The documents cast light not only on the commercial transactions in which the merchants were involved, but also on the surprisingly complex political organization of their mother city, Ashur, and many aspects of the private lives of the earliest Assyrians who have left us substantial numbers of written records.[15]

A third site whose exploration has significantly enhanced knowledge of Assyrian civilization is Tell Sheikh Hamad, ancient Dur-Katlimmu on the Khabur River in eastern Syria. Likewise located outside the original Assyrian core area, it was excavated between 1978 and the outbreak of the Syrian Civil War in 2011 by a German team led by Hartmut Kühne. Dur-Katlimmu was the urban center from where, beginning in the thirteenth century BCE, a series of Assyrian "viceroys" descending from the Assyrian royal family ruled over the western extension of the Assyrian kingdom—a political arrangement not quite in line with prevailing ideas about Assyrian royal power being undivided and monolithic. The site is, moreover, one of the few places where excavators have been able to apply new archaeological methods such as faunal and floral analysis, landscape archaeology, and advanced forms of pottery studies.[16]

Such techniques have been used only sparingly at Assyrian sites in northern Iraq, where, beginning in the 1980s with the Iran-Iraq War, political instability has made sustained archaeological work difficult. Iraqi and Western teams continued to excavate in this area (see Plate 2), but in the past decades only for short periods of time and with inadequate resources. To compensate for the limited opportunities for fieldwork in Iraq, scholars have recently begun to engage in various forms of "remote" archaeology, analyzing, among other things, declassified photos taken by military satellites. These reveal, often in surprising detail, the courses of ancient Assyrian roads and canals and the locations of otherwise unknown settlements, throwing light on the environment of the great Assyrian capitals and on Assyrian communication networks.[17]

THE STUDY OF ASSYRIA HAS GONE ON FOR MORE THAN 175 YEARS, during which numerous Assyrian voices from the past have begun to speak again. Others may be brought back to life in the future, though many more will remain forever silent. To be sure, new discoveries and fresh analyses of the available evidence will undoubtedly require future reassessments, but at the same time, we have become familiar with Assyrian cities, kings, and political and social institutions about which no biblical or classical author had any clue, and we are probably better informed about the beginnings of Assyrian civilization than were the Assyrians of the imperial period themselves.

The Assyrian civilization we have come to know is one marked by a complex mix of continuity and change, as it wrestled—often more successfully than neighboring kingdoms—with major historical challenges, from attacks by foreign powers to changes in rainfall patterns to major cultural shifts. Over a period of some 1,400 years, until its rapid fall in the late seventh century BCE, the Assyrian state managed to preserve and cultivate a particular identity while at the same time reinventing itself time and again and adapting to ever-changing circumstances. In this and other respects, Assyria has a lot in common with antiquity's most famous and influential political entity: ancient Rome. Similar to the Romans, who owed many features of their culture and religion to another civilization, that of the Greeks, the Assyrians drew heavily on Babylonian models in the spheres of literature, the arts, and cultic affairs. Assyria and Rome experienced, moreover, similar transformations of their systems of governance, with empire as the final outcome. And yet, neither civilization ever lost its strong sense of cohesion. It almost feels as if both Assyrians and Romans had faithfully followed throughout the course of their history the famous adage in Giuseppe Tomasi di Lampedusa's Italian novel *Il Gattopardo*: "For everything to stay the same, everything must change."

Among the continuities in Assyrian history, the Assyrian language holds a prominent place. First attested on clay tablets from the twentieth century BCE, it was still used, although with significant changes in vocabulary, grammar, and pronunciation, during the time of Assyria's fall in the late seventh century. Assyrian never became a major medium of literary expression like the Babylonian language spoken by Assyria's southern neighbors, but it was the vernacular used in everyday life as well as in written documents recording legal and economic affairs, religious rituals, state treaties, royal decrees, and, in certain periods, accounts of military campaigns and other important events.[18]

Worship of the Assyrian state god Ashur also shaped Assyrian civilization through the ages. In fact, the god continued to play an important role even beyond the fall of the empire in 612 BCE—he is mentioned together with his wife Sherua in Aramaic votive inscriptions from as late as the second century CE. Those texts were discovered in the ruins of Ashur, the god's sacred city, which embodies Assyria's *longue durée* more than any other place. It was at Ashur that Assyrian civilization originated and where it later took its last breaths.

More concrete examples of continuity in Assyrian culture and history abound as well. A case in point is provided by the treaty tablets prepared in the name of the Assyrian king Esarhaddon in the spring of 672 BCE in order to secure the succession of Esarhaddon's son Ashurbanipal to the Assyrian throne. The tablets, inscribed with loyalty oaths every Assyrian citizen and vassal had to swear, all feature the same three seal impressions: one from a seal from the time of Esarhaddon's father Sennacherib; one from a seal from the Middle Assyrian period, roughly half a millennium earlier; and a third impression, showing a worshipper introduced by a goddess, from an Old Assyrian seal from the early second millennium, a good 1,200 years before Esarhaddon's treaty tablets were written. As an inscription indicates, the last seal belonged to the god Ashur and the "City Hall," an important civic institution in the early history of Ashur and one still in place, even though stripped of its former political power, in the seventh century BCE. The seal in question was apparently housed in the City Hall for more than a millennium.[19]

Other buildings in Ashur, most prominently the temples, had long histories as well, which, in the case of the temple to Ishtar, the divine patroness of erotic love, stretched back nearly two millennia. Of course, as time went by, temples had to be repeatedly restored and rebuilt. The strong continuity that characterizes Assyria's cultic sphere is also illustrated by the history of a group of minor deities known as the "seven divine judges." An inscription of the twentieth-century BCE king Erishum I mentions that images of them were set up in the so-called Step Gate near the Ashur Temple on the northern edge of the city, a place where legal proceedings took place. Some 1,300 years later, the divine judges reappear in a text known as the Divine Directory of Ashur with only slightly modified names: the god Ṣê-raggu, "Get Out Criminal," for instance, is now called Ḫip-raggu, "Break the Criminal."[20]

Assyria's material culture was marked by certain continuities as well. Several varieties of bread only known from Assyrian but not from Babylonian texts remained in use in Assyria from the fourteenth century BCE—and perhaps even earlier—to the final days of the empire. They include the so-called *ḫuḫḫurtu* bread, a braided or plaited loaf that may have been a forerunner of the challah eaten to this day on Jewish holidays. Bread, the "staff of life," is a particularly important marker of identity, so the longevity of this unique bread type is perhaps not that surprising, and neither is the fact that cuneiform texts from Calah distinguish "Assyrian bakers" from Chaldean, Aramaean, and Suḫaean ones.[21]

Assyrian texts and images of the first millennium BCE place great emphasis on continuity in the political sphere, with a strong focus on kingship. Images of Assyrian rulers, whether in the form of statues or on orthostats or stelae, depict them as an ideal, supra-individual type: a crowned, never-aging, manly and muscular figure with an elaborately coiffed beard, clad in precious robes, and free of emotions even when engaged in deadly battle with enemies or raging lions (see cover image and Plate 7). Although the images undergo stylistic changes over time, no Assyrian king is ever portrayed in the naturalistic manner that characterizes the marble busts of many a Roman emperor. It was the king's "body politic" that Assyrian artists were expected to represent, not his "body natural," burdened with sorrow and marked by sickness. Depictions of enemy leaders, in contrast, do occasionally display individual features.[22]

Middle and Neo-Assyrian royal inscriptions present Assyria's history as an endless series of military conquests, all brought about by the Assyrian kings and the gods supporting them. As time passes, the inscriptions suggest, everything stays essentially the same, only getting "bigger and better." This "cold" model of history writing, which strives to suppress any notion of real historical change as we would understand it, also informs large portions of the Assyrian King List, one of the most important historical documents ever recovered from ancient Assyria. The King List, known from several manuscripts from the first millennium BCE, records the names and genealogical backgrounds of more than one hundred Assyrian rulers, from the beginnings of Assyrian history down to the reign of Shalmaneser V (r. 726–722 BCE). The list promotes the idea that Assyrian kingship never dies—there is just "one damn King after another," as a song by the British a cappella group The King's Singers puts it. The Assyrian King List also stresses that royal power in Assyria was over long stretches of time handed down within one and the same family. This is in stark contrast to the earlier Sumerian King List, on which the Assyrian one was probably originally modeled, where history is presented as a never-ending transfer of power from one city, and one dynasty, to the next.

Based on what is now known, there was indeed a good deal of dynastic continuity in ancient Assyria. For more than a thousand years, it seems that practically all Assyrian rulers were descendants of a certain Adasi, who had lived in the second half of the eighteenth century BCE. But in other respects, things were not quite as stable as the Assyrian King List, and the inscriptions of the Assyrian kings, wanted their readers to believe. Cuneiform chronicles, and especially letters from royal archives, tell stories quite different from those found in the official historical records. These are "hot" stories marked by high drama, with battles being lost, territories seized by the enemy, Assyrian kings murdered, and revolts and epidemics threatening to undermine the very foundations of the Assyrian state. It is, moreover, clear that power structures during the earlier phases of Assyrian history were not quite the same as those of later times. This is, in fact, suggested by the Assyrian King List itself, which mentions in its opening paragraphs "kings who lived in tents" or were "ancestors," and talks in an unusual passage about one king, Shamshi-Adad I (r. ca. 1808–1776 BCE), who "came up" from the south and seized the Assyrian throne by force.

How different Assyrian political culture during the first centuries of the second millennium actually was has become evident through the texts found at Kültepe/Kanesh. For one, we learn from these texts, there was then no "Assyria" yet—there was only a fairly small city, Ashur, and its very limited hinterland. To be sure, while the city's political power was modest, the geographical horizon of its citizens was already quite expansive. The merchants of Ashur traded tin and textiles for silver and other goods over thousands of kilometers and had "colonies" in faraway territories, including at Kanesh. But the Old Assyrian city-state was nonetheless very different from the sprawling territorial state Assyria would become in Middle Assyrian times.[23]

Perhaps equally surprising, the political organization of Ashur at this early time showed few signs of the autocratic cohesiveness that characterized Assyria in later ages. Instead, the city had a "mixed constitution" reminiscent of Republican Rome, with strong popular and aristocratic voices balancing monarchical ones. Remarkably enough, even though a series of hereditary rulers are known to have held office during the Old Assyrian period, these leaders did not yet bear the title used elsewhere all over ancient Mesopotamia to designate kings: šarrum. Instead, they called themselves rubā'um, "Prince," as well as iššiakkum, "Steward (of the god Ashur)," and waklum, "Overseer." The master-narrative of an enlightened and "democratic" West battling an eternally "despotic" Orient, first promoted by the Greek historian Herodotus and later taken up in Hegel's teleological idea that "world history travels from east to west," with Europe being "the absolute end of history" and Asia its beginning, is difficult to sustain in light of Ashur's and Assyria's complicated historical trajectory. Assyria started its journey through the ages as a state that sought to keep autocratic tendencies at bay.[24]

Countering Assyria's reputation for violence, it seems, moreover, that Ashur was initially a remarkably peaceful polity. While many other states of the early second millennium were engaged in almost perpetual warfare, Ashur mostly stayed away from the fray, seeking gain through commerce rather than combat.

Later, from the mid-second millennium onward, this irenic attitude would give way to bellicosity and aggression. Ashur morphed into Assyria, a territorial state whose citizens were still interested in trade, but whose rulers found military assault a more lucrative way to accumulate wealth. To secure their power and stamp out any opposition that might arise, the later Assyrian kings would use a variety of coercive strategies, from targeted killings to mass deportations. The latter became a hallmark of Assyrian politics. During the first millennium, Assyrian armies forcefully moved hundreds of thousands of people to new settlements often hundreds of kilometers away from their original homes, transforming the ethnolinguistic landscape of Western Asia for all times to come. Such measures were not meant to produce only death and destruction. Assyria's elites had an interest in economic development and sought to promote it in various ways, for example, by settling deportees in areas where their labor was needed. But unlike the rulers of the Old Assyrian period, those of later times did take delight in war for war's sake.

Parallel to and interrelated with these political transformations, the character of the Assyrian state god, Ashur, changed as well. In his early days, Ashur was something of a "god without qualities." Most other major deities of the ancient Near East were complex figures with intriguing biographies. As cosmic entities, they represented celestial bodies; in mythology, they appeared as protagonists of stories in which they interacted with other gods and goddesses; and in their "political" capacities—to draw on distinctions established by the Roman polymath Varro—they were associated with specific cities or countries and worshipped in local temples dedicated to them. Ashur initially lacked the first two of these dimensions, in particular the mythological one. He did not have a family and was not celebrated in any grand narrative. Instead, Ashur was a *numen loci*—a deity essentially identical with, and at the same time protecting, the city with which he shared his name. These limitations, however, did not make him any less powerful. In fact, Ashur was considered the actual sovereign of his city. As mentioned above, Ashur's hereditary rulers initially abstained from calling themselves *šarrum*—the royal title was reserved for the god.[25]

The theocratic model established in Ashur in the twenty-first century BCE was never entirely abandoned. More than half a millennium later, the Assyrian priest performing the coronation ritual for the Assyrian ruler would still shout out "Ashur is king! Ashur is king!," and a seventh-century BCE hymn from the reign of Ashurbanipal— who continued to be addressed as "Steward of Ashur"—contains the very same liturgical proclamation. But during the fourteenth century the Assyrian rulers began to claim the royal title, previously held exclusively by the god, also for themselves, while the god, in turn, assumed some of the belligerent qualities those rulers were now expected to possess.

Ashur also acquired a family over the course of Assyrian history. Already during Shamshi-Adad I's "foreign" reign starting in the late nineteenth century BCE, he had been identified with Enlil of Nippur, the Babylonian "king of the gods." This theological association was later revived, and Ashur was coupled with Enlil's wife Ninlil, called Mullissu in Assyrian. The warrior god Ninurta, Enlil's son, became a major figure in Assyrian royal ideology as well. During the early seventh century BCE, in yet another transformation, Ashur assumed the role of the Babylonian god Marduk as heroic vanquisher of Tiamat, the female embodiment of primeval chaos. The Babylonian "Epic of Creation," originally composed to celebrate Marduk, was revised, with Ashur as its new protagonist.[26]

Assyria's history of entwined change and continuity went hand in hand with the kingdom's rise to ever greater power, though this rise was not a steady one. It was interrupted by several major crises. But as in the case of Rome, the final outcome was that Assyria morphed into a war-prone, multiethnic conqueror-state, organized into numerous provinces and geared toward moving resources on a massive scale from the periphery to the political center. In other words, Assyria grew into an empire.

What exactly constitutes an empire hinges, obviously, on how one defines the term. The case of Assyria may be less clear-cut than that of Rome, but from the mid-eighth century onward, the Assyrian state cannot really be described as anything else. After all, it ruled almost all of Western Asia for some 120 years, and for a time even ruled Egypt. Accordingly, many historians in the ancient and medieval worlds were convinced that Assyria should be considered an empire. For the Greek author Ctesias of Cnidus, the Roman Pompeius Trogus, or the Late Antique Christian writer Orosius, Assyria was the first in a linear succession of imperial states that were masters of large portions of the inhabited world. In the same vein, the Italian poet Dante Alighieri, drawing on the medieval concept of *translatio imperii*—the transfer of imperial power—argued that the first ruler to ever "gain the prize" of imperial rule was the Assyrian king Ninus.[27]

Apart from occupying a prominent place in the cultural memory of later civilizations, the Assyrian state also served, first directly and then mediated through more remote successor states, as a model eagerly emulated by the subsequent imperial powers of Western Asia, from the Babylonian and Persian Empires of antiquity to the Abbasid and Ottoman caliphates of the Islamic period and even beyond. Governmental structures and ideological concepts first created in Assyria thus had a long afterlife, one that continues in some respects until today.

NO HISTORY OF ASSYRIA CAN BE FULLY CONTINUOUS, WITH seamless transitions from one period to the next. This is to a significant extent due to the uneven chronological distribution of the available sources. From the three hundred years between 1700 and 1400

BCE, for example, very few ancient records have survived, which makes it hard to identify the root causes of the important changes that took place in Assyria during this time. Other periods in Assyrian history, in contrast, are so richly documented that it would be easy to devote whole books to individual years, and if not books then at least chapters, like the one found in this volume on the year 671 BCE.

History can be written "from above," with a focus on the deeds of "great men" (and women), or "from below," highlighting the gritty lives of the downtrodden. Emphasis can also be placed on the administrative and military elites or the "middle class," if there is one. Which of these paths is taken depends much on the choices the historian makes, but it is also, again, in some measure determined by the available sources. In the case of Assyria, the nature of these sources undergoes major changes over time. Whereas an overwhelming portion of the written documents from Old Assyrian times concerns the economic activities of Ashur's merchant class, most texts and images from Assyria's imperial period are centered on the king and the state apparatus. Just as an illustration, in the house of the Old Assyrian merchant Usur-sha-Ishtar in Kanesh, some 1,600 clay tablets and 400 texts in envelopes have been found, providing ample material for a detailed study of this man and his family. From Neo-Assyrian times, no equally sized archives shedding light on the lives of commoners have survived. But a text corpus even larger than the documentation available for Usur-sha-Ishtar illuminates in often astounding detail the reign of the Assyrian king Ashurbanipal.[28]

A bull colossus from one of the entrance gates into the citadel at Khorsabad nicely emblematizes the "regicentric" imbalance that characterizes the historical record of Neo-Assyrian times. In its arresting monumentality, and through the royal inscription written between its legs, the figure represents in an imposing manner the formidable power of the Neo-Assyrian king who commissioned it, Sargon II. But a careful observer will not fail to notice on the plinth holding the bull some crudely incised interconnected squares, drawing attention to the humble guards who, bored with being stationed in the gate for hours on end, would find some diversion in playing a little board game. In a similar vein, readers of this book will find its focus to lie on politics, stories about kings and queens, monumental cities, and imperial art; but they will also, at least occasionally, come across vignettes depicting the trials and tribulations of common people, as well as deportees, slaves, and other men and women from the bottom of society.[29]

AT FIRST GLANCE, QUITE A FEW ASPECTS OF ASSYRIAN CIVILIZATION appear strange and exotic to the modern observer. Whether it is the faith Assyrian kings placed in liver omens and astrological observations when making political decisions, the idiosyncratic religious rituals and magical practices in which the people of Assyria participated, the aggressive celebration of violence found in Assyrian royal inscriptions, or simply the Assyrian taste for locusts: the Assyrians were engaged in many pursuits that people of the twenty-first century may find at odds with their putatively more advanced and refined intellectual standards, political persuasions, or food preferences. Yet Assyria can also seem remarkably modern. The first "global" state, it combined imperial expropriation with shrewd commercial pursuits, the latter rooted in practices of an earlier period, when the city-state of Ashur was a kind of Singapore of the ancient Near East. Much like modern CEOs run their companies, Assyria's imperial kings governed their state over long stretches of time with a focus on achieving the best possible balance between cost and benefits. The steely determination with which they pursued their goals seems quite in line with the scientific term used to designate the period when Assyria's power climaxed: the Iron Age.

The Assyrian Empire also brought about a new "information age." In their striving to better control the vast territorial expanses they ruled, the Assyrian kings commissioned new roads, way stations, and a postal system that facilitated communication between the center, the provincial capitals, and the kingdom's periphery. Spies stationed in frontier zones would report on a regular basis on political developments and military movements that occurred in enemy territories and among Assyrian vassals. No longer slowed down by borders and seclusive rival states, commodities and ideas circulated more freely, with Assyria's elites eagerly adopting foreign technologies and cultural practices whenever they promised to further their cause. At home, in the meantime, a network of informers sent letter after letter to the court to denounce anyone who seemed even remotely critical of the king and his administration. Besides Assyrian, a new vernacular, Aramaic, was now widely used, eventually taking on a role comparable to that played by English in the modern global world. Obviously, the Assyrians had no Internet, but the speed and frequency with which messages were sent back and forth throughout their empire was nothing short of revolutionary in its time.[30]

One of Assyria's greatest mysteries has a contemporary ring as well: How could an empire as powerful and large as Assyria collapse so utterly and completely within just about a decade? In this regard, Assyria's fate was quite different from that of ancient Rome, whose decline and fall was a long and protracted process. A recent hypothesis links Assyria's fall to climate change, one of the great challenges of our time and a phenomenon that many expect to bring about the collapse of our own civilization. Evidence exists that prolonged drought conditions during the last century of the Assyrian Empire did indeed contribute to slowly decreasing harvests. Man-made ecological changes affected the imperial landscape as well: the intensified agricultural practices promoted by Assyrian governors in the Khabur region, and an endless series of hunting expeditions, led to the extinction of parts of the region's megafauna, most notably its elephants. King Sennacherib decries, moreover, in an early testimony of ecological consciousness, that his royal predecessors had decimated the forests in order to get hold of enough timber for their ambitious building projects.

Whether climate change and the anthropogenic transformation of the biosphere were really the main causes of Assyria's downfall is, however, not so clear. In fact, this book will argue that, paradoxically enough, these phenomena, along with various epidemics that ravaged Assyria around 760 BCE, may have contributed more to the emergence than to the demise of the Assyrian Empire. Although factors such as ecological degradation and foreign invasions probably played a role as well, Assyria's fall may have been above all the result of leadership failures and autocratic delusions of grandeur—phenomena by no means alien to modern times either.

Earlier centuries believed that Assyria represented a barbaric other. But this ancient civilization has actually much more in common with us than one might think. Assyria produced many features that, for better or worse, are still to be found in the modern world: from long-distance trade, sophisticated communication networks, and the state-sponsored promotion of literature, science, and the arts to mass deportations, the practice of engaging in extreme violence in enemy countries, and the widespread use of political surveillance at home. New research has shown that Assyria was affected, much as we are, by the outbreak of pandemics and the vicissitudes of climate change, and by how its rulers reacted to these challenges. Assyria, in other words, has much to teach us—and the time seems ripe to take a new look at this ancient state, which during its heyday morphed into the world's first empire.

THE LONG ROAD
TO GLORY

1

A Small Town on the Tigris

Where to begin? All historians, those studying the civilizations of ancient Mesopotamia no less than others, have to struggle with this question. Clear answers can be found in legend, but legend tends to be unreliable: just as Rome was not founded in 753 by Romulus, Assyria was not founded hundreds of years earlier by Ninus, as the Greeks thought, or by Nimrod or Ashur, as the Hebrew Bible claims, or even by a certain Tudiya, the first ruler mentioned in the Assyrian King List. The story is more complicated. As the German novelist Thomas Mann put it with characteristic literary flair in the introductory sentences of *Joseph and His Brothers*, his renowned epic of ancient Near Eastern history, "Deep is the well of the past. Should not one call it bottomless?"

The roots of Assyrian civilization reach well into prehistoric times. More than ten thousand years ago, the area in northern Iraq that would later see the birth of the Assyrian kingdom played an important part in the emergence of agriculture, animal husbandry, and other technologies of civilization. There is no evidence that the people who produced these developments were early "Assyrians." But between 2500 and 1700 BCE, a tangible Assyrian identity began to take form, with sociopolitical, cultural, and linguistic features that would define Assyrians until the end of the Assyrian kingdom. While frustratingly little is known about the first five hundred years of this period, it is clear that there were now people who spoke the Assyrian language, built Assyrian temples, and believed that the god Ashur, worshipped in the city of the same name, was their true king.

The three centuries after 2000 BCE—the so-called Old Assyrian period—saw the flourishing of the first independent "Assyrian" state. With its rule largely limited to the city of Ashur, its aversion to warfare, and its governmental structures based on civic institutions rather than an all-powerful monarch, the city-state of Ashur was in many respects the opposite of the empire that Assyria would eventually become. Even so, with its wide-ranging commercial interests, it foreshadowed two central features that would define the later empire: its broad geographic horizons, and its acquisitiveness.

NORTHERN IRAQ WAS NOT ONLY THE CRADLE OF ASSYRIAN CIV-ilization; it played an important role in the history of the human species long before Ashur became established. Neanderthal remains have been found in the Shanidar Cave, in the Erbil Governorate, dating back some seventy thousand years. Groups engaged in hunting and gathering inhabited the region for tens of thousands of years. Then, slowly but inexorably, major changes began to occur. From around 10,000 BCE onward, during the so-called Neolithic period, more and more people began to live in settled communities, practicing animal husbandry and agriculture. They domesticated pigs, sheep, and goats and cultivated the native wild emmer and einkorn, ancient varieties of wheat. They also started to produce pottery, an important type of artifact for prehistoric archaeologists, who trace the movement of cultural traditions and the people behind them by analyzing the ceramic styles found at different ancient sites. Some of the earliest known pottery from the Middle East comes from mid-seventh millennium BCE Hassuna, a site some 35 kilometers (about 22 miles) southwest of Nineveh.[1]

The Neolithic Revolution that set humanity, for better or worse, on the path to modernity was forged in a region known as the Fertile Crescent, a semicircular zone spanning from southern Palestine to Anatolia and then onward to the Zagros range in southeastern Turkey, Iraq, and Iran. Throughout this area, rainfall was plentiful enough to allow for settled farming. The region that would later form Assyria's core, a triangle marked by the cities of Nineveh in the north, Arbela in the east, and Ashur in the south, lies in the northeastern segment of the Fertile Crescent. Demarcated by the western fringes of the Zagros Mountains in the east, the southern foothills of the Taurus range in the north, and the Syrian Desert in the west (in antiquity an area less arid than it is today), it is a land of rolling hills and plains, crossed by the southward-flowing Tigris River and its main eastern tributaries, the Upper and Lower Zab.[2]

Ashur lies just barely within the range of 200 millimeters (about 8 inches) of annual precipitation, the minimum amount needed for rain-fed agriculture. The potential of its hinterland for farming was therefore always precarious. This must have prompted Ashur's inhabitants from early on to engage in economic activities other than raising crops, most notably trade.

Downstream from Ashur, farther south toward the Persian Gulf, lay the cradle of another great civilization: Babylonia. Closely intertwined with Assyria in economic, cultural, and eventually political terms, Babylonia exerted, throughout the millennia, a significant influence on its northern neighbor.

In stark contrast to Assyria's geographical setting, the land of Babylonia was a flat alluvial plain, formed and defined by the Euphrates and Tigris Rivers and with too little rainfall to allow for rain-fed agriculture, or so-called dry farming. But as groups of Neolithic people, driven by ever-increasing population pressure, slowly migrated southward from northern Iraq, they discovered that there were other ways to turn the inhospitable Babylonian terrain into a productive agricultural landscape. They established that the alluvial soil carried down by the two big rivers was extremely fertile and, when properly irrigated, capable of producing crop yields significantly higher than anywhere else in the ancient Near East. Getting the water to where it was needed, however, was difficult and required a great amount of manual labor. A network of canals, filled from the Euphrates and the Tigris, had to be created, dams had to be constructed, and fields had to be drained to fend off salinization. This could not be done without an organized workforce. Furthermore, since basic raw materials such as stone and timber were not available in southern Mesopotamia, someone had to make sure they were imported from other regions. All the while, a gradual decrease over time in water levels forced people to live in fewer but larger settlements.

As a response to such challenges, several important milestones commonly associated with the birth of "civilization" were reached in the alluvial plain of southern Iraq during the fourth millennium BCE. One of them was a fully developed urban culture. The world's first real city, Uruk, later famous as the seat of the legendary king Gilgamesh, may have had as many as sixty thousand inhabitants around 3000 BCE. A few centuries earlier, cuneiform, the world's earliest writing system, had been invented in Uruk. Other historical breakthroughs of the era, marking the end of the Neolithic and the beginning of the Bronze Age, include the rise of a new managerial elite, increased social stratification, new patterns of processing and redistributing commodities such as grain and wool, new religious ideas and institutions, and the increased use of bronze rather than stone for implements, weapons, and vessels. All these innovations, perhaps most importantly the invention of writing, would shape the world of the ancient Near East for millennia to come. But this happened gradually, taking centuries in some places, and progress would not be without setbacks.[3]

Northern Mesopotamia had for a long time followed a path of its own. Some (proto-)urban development had already taken place in the region during the Neolithic era, for example at Hamoukar in northeastern Syria, near the Iraqi border. During the fourth millennium, this site harbored a settlement of considerable size. Thousands of clay sealings and substantial quantities of obsidian, imported from regions far away, indicate that Hamoukar, reminiscent of the later city-state of Ashur, was engaged in complex forms of long-distance trade at this time. But around 3500, large parts of Hamoukar were destroyed, perhaps by warriors from Uruk, in what may be the world's earliest example of urban warfare.[4]

While Hamoukar's later history was not particularly noteworthy and of no significance for the eventual rise of Assyria, the opposite is true for another upper Mesopotamian site with Neolithic roots: Nineveh. Located next to an important ford across the Tigris and inhabited from around 6000 BCE onward, Nineveh remained a key regional, and then transregional, center for millennia to come, despite intermittent phases of urban decline. But before the mid-second millennium, Nineveh was not yet an "Assyrian" city, at least if one understands "Assyrian" in an ethnolinguistic sense. It was instead dominated, both in political and cultural terms, by members of an ethnic group known as Hurrians. During the twenty-first century BCE, the main goddess of Nineveh, later identified with the Semitic Ishtar, bore the Hurrian name Shaushka (lit., "the Great [Goddess]"). Ashur, the deity more closely associated with a genuinely Assyrian identity than any other, was not worshipped at Nineveh—his cult center lay elsewhere.[5]

RATHER THAN AT NINEVEH, THE ORIGINS OF ASSYRIAN CIVILIZATION are to be found at Qal'at Sherqat, the site of the aforementioned ancient city of Ashur, which would eventually give the land of Assyria its name. Located some 100 kilometers (62 miles) south of Mosul, on a rocky crag rising some 40 meters (130 feet) above the western bank of the Tigris, Ashur was a natural fortress and, thanks to its position near a river ford on an important trade route, well suited to become a key commercial hub. It linked the southern alluvial plain with resource-rich territories in the north, and the fertile agricultural lands east of the Tigris with the steppe regions crisscrossed by herdsmen farther west.[6]

From around 2700 BCE, the region on the Middle Tigris experienced a phase of increased urbanization, and it is likely that Ashur, too, grew into a town of some significance during this period. The area stretching from Ashur northward to the foothills of the Taurus and Zagros ranges was known as Shubur or Subartu at the time. At least intermittently, it was under southern domination: a stone inscription from the Babylonian city of Kish, probably written between 2750 and 2600 BCE, records the deportation of 6,300 prisoners of war from Shubur/Subartu to the south, where they were apparently forced to work in orchards. Ashur is not yet mentioned in this inscription, but it is included in a mid-third-millennium Babylonian list of geographical names, where it appears together with several cities located along the northern boundary of Babylonia's alluvial plain.[7]

From about the same time the earliest archaeological traces of some significance have been uncovered at Ashur. Near the center of the city, deep below the foundations of several later buildings dedicated to the cult of the goddess Ishtar, excavators found the remains of an earlier sanctuary, undoubtedly built to honor the same deity or an early avatar of her. A "great goddess" was also worshipped from early on in Nineveh, and probably also in Urbil(um), the later Arbela, suggesting that one of the spiritual roots of Assyrian civilization was a strong belief in a powerful female deity. Whether the god Ashur played an equally important role at this early time is unclear—the date of the deepest archaeological layers in the area of the later Ashur Temple, located on the northeastern promontory of the city, cannot yet be established with certainty.[8]

The finds from the "archaic" Ishtar Temple in Ashur also shed some light on the people who lived in the city during this early time. The main room of the temple, about 16 × 6 meters (52 × 20 feet) in size, featured on one of its narrow sides a niche with a pedestal holding the cult image of the goddess. A small basin for blood from sacrificed animals, clay incense holders, and libation vessels provide clues about some of the rituals performed in the temple. But the most remarkable finds made in the sanctuary's debris were fragments of some ninety votive statues, usually less than 50 centimeters (20 inches) high, that had originally been positioned on low mudbrick benches lining the long sides of the inner room. Made of stone, they depict worshippers with folded hands and unnaturally enlarged eyes, undoubtedly set up in the sanctuary to represent members of Ashur's elite families before the goddess in uninterrupted prayer. Some of them were probably dedicated by the political leaders of Ashur, whoever they were at the time. Others depict women, who must have held positions of considerable influence in Ashur's early society (see Plate 4).[9]

The figurines from the Ishtar Temple strongly resemble votive statues from the Babylonian south, at the time inhabited by an ethnic group known as Sumerians. Basing their ideas on such similarities as garments covered with rows of stylized tufts of wool and men with shaved heads, earlier scholars suggested that Ashur's population included a pronounced Sumerian element during the mid-third millennium. But this idea, grounded in a flawed "ethnic" understanding of ancient Near Eastern art, is now widely rejected. It seems more likely that the people of Ashur spoke a Semitic language at the time, possibly an early version of Assyrian. An inscribed stone fragment from Ashur, probably dating to the period between 2500 and 2250 BCE, lists textiles and copper presented to several individuals, at least one of whom, a certain Beli-[. . .], clearly bore a Semitic name, meaning "My lord is [. . .]."[10]

The aforementioned similarities are nonetheless intriguing. They bespeak the strong influence that the culturally more advanced south exerted on Ashur from early on. This influence extended to the political sphere. The powerful southern dynasty of Akkad, founded around 2350 BCE by a king named Sargon and soon in command of large parts of Western Asia, also ruled over Ashur. Akkadian rulers paid their respect to the goddess Ishtar of Ashur through votive gifts, which included a stone mace head with an inscription mentioning the Akkadian king Rimush. The earliest cuneiform tablets from Ashur, economic documents and "school texts" produced by young students, date to the Akkadian period as well. The school texts reflect scribal traditions introduced under the Akkadian kings, perhaps marking the beginnings of the long-lasting fascination that the people of Ashur felt for the political and cultural legacy of Akkad. Later rulers of Ashur would adopt the names of the two most famous Akkadian kings, Sargon and Naram-Sîn, and a legend featuring King Sargon was among the few literary tablets found at the Old Assyrian trade colony of Kültepe/Kanesh.[11]

There are hints that Ashur was already heavily engaged in the overland trade by the time it was ruled by Akkad. The city is mentioned in a few Akkadian period texts from Gasur, an ancient town southwest of the modern city of Kirkuk in eastern Iraq, suggesting that it participated in the commercial exchange with Iran at the time.[12]

The earliest local ruler of Ashur known from textual records is a certain Ititi, son of Inin-labba. According to a votive inscription on a stone plaque from the Ishtar Temple in Ashur, he dedicated to Ishtar a portion of the "booty of Gasur," apparently after conquering that city. Unfortunately, the intriguing text leaves some crucial questions unanswered. Ititi's title is written with a sign that can be interpreted as *waklum*, "Overseer," or as *iššiakkum*, "Steward" or "Governor."

If the former is correct, Ititi would have been an independent ruler, perhaps from shortly after the collapse of the Akkadian state around 2200 BCE, bearing a title later also assumed by the hereditary rulers of the Old Assyrian period and closely linked to Ashur's "City Assembly" (Assyrian *ālum*), a legislative and judicial institution. In this case, the political system in place during Old Assyrian times would have had much earlier antecedents. If instead Ititi's title was that of an *iššiakkum*, one would have to assume that he was a governor who ruled Ashur on behalf of the Akkadian kings. Which of these alternatives is correct remains unclear. That the name of Ititi's father, Inin-labba, means "Ishtar-is-a-Lion" suggests again that it may have been Ishtar rather than the god Ashur who dominated the pantheon of the city of Ashur before the twenty-first century BCE.[13]

If Ashur, in the wake of the Akkadian period, was indeed ruled by sovereign local leaders, then its independence did not last long. Around 2100 BCE, under the so-called Third Dynasty of Ur, another powerful kingdom emerged in Babylonia. Before long Ashur found itself again subjected to southern rule, this time as an outlying military province of the Ur III state. When a military governor of Ashur by the name of Zarriqum (or Sarriqum) built the temple of the goddess Belat-ekallim, he did so on behalf of the Ur III king Amar-Suen (r. ca. 2044–2036 BCE). Zarriqum is attested in Ur III documents from southern Mesopotamia dating from 2048 to 2040 BCE and might have been installed in Ashur by the great Ur III ruler Shulgi (r. ca. 2092–2045 BCE): tellingly, Zarriqum named one of his sons Shulgi-ili, which means "Shulgi-is-my-God." At one point, Zarriqum visited the heartland of the Ur III state with an entourage of no fewer than fifty men, which suggests that Ashur was a city of some significance by now.[14]

As revealed by an economic text from the southern city of Puzrish-Dagan, another visitor to the south was a merchant by the name of Ilshu-rabi, the son of one Puzur-Ashur and therefore clearly a citizen of Ashur. He brought elaborately decorated toggle-pins, one more indication that Ashur's role as a commercial center preceded the subsequent Old Assyrian period. Since other Ur III documents list individuals with names including the divine element Ashur as well, it is, moreover, evident that the god Ashur had become a deity of great importance by this time. Clearly, by the mid-twenty-first century BCE, central elements of Ashur's religious identity were fully formed, and the commercial ambitions of its residents had become a main driving force for the city. Ashur was ready to take on a new role: that of a self-governed economic and religious hub.[15]

IT IS LIKELY THAT ASHUR GAINED ITS INDEPENDENCE NOT MUCH later than 2025 BCE. By then, the Ur III state, exhausted by its hyper-bureaucratic system of economic control and under threat from the seminomadic Semitic Amorites infiltrating it from various directions, entered a final phase of slowly accelerating collapse.

What exactly triggered the transformation that Ashur experienced in the decades around 2000 BCE remains very much a mystery. Unfortunately, the Assyrian King List is not fully reliable when it comes to Ashur's earliest history. It mentions neither Ititi nor Zarriqum, instead claiming that Ashur was initially ruled by seventeen "kings who lived in tents"—the first of whom was named Tudiya—and then by ten "kings who were ancestors." But it is clear that these two groups of rulers are later additions to the list, derived from genealogical traditions popular among the Amorites and originally extrinsic to Assyrian history. They were probably incorporated during the reign of Ashur's conqueror king Shamshi-Adad I (r. ca. 1808–1776 BCE).[16]

We get closer to actual history with the King List's next group of rulers. These comprise "six kings (whose names) are found on bricks but whose eponyms are unknown." "Eponym" (Assyrian *limmum*) is the modern term for the high-ranking officials after whom the Assyrians, starting with the reign of Erishum I (r. ca. 1969–1930 BCE), named individual years of their calendar. As the first of the six rulers who were allegedly in power before this system was put in place, the list names a certain Sulili (or Sulê). He can probably be identified with a "Silulu son of Dakiku," whose name occurs in the inscription of a seal that was found impressed on several later tablets and clay envelopes from Kanesh. The seal inscription claims that Silulu served as "Steward of Ashur," one of the most common titles of Ashur's rulers throughout history, as well as "Herald (*nāgirum*) of the city of Ashur," a more exceptional designation. Based on stylistic criteria, the Silulu seal probably dates to the twenty-first century BCE. While the conclusion that Silulu ruled shortly before the Ur III takeover cannot be ruled out, it seems more likely that he was the first in the long series of independent leaders who held office in Ashur after the city slipped away from the control of the Ur III kingdom. Silulu may have been identical with a certain Ilabasi/ululi(?), "governor of Ashur," who is mentioned in a text from Ur. If so, one can hypothesize that he had initially served as another chief administrator installed in Ashur by the Ur III kings, before cutting ties with his southern overlords. The image on Silulu's seal shows a triumphant hero placing his foot on a prostrate enemy, perhaps an indication that Silulu gained his new position by force.[17]

Most remarkable is that Silulu's seal inscription does not begin with his name and titles, but with the resounding declaration that "Ashur is king." This is the theocratic credo, here found for the first time, that would define Ashur's political identity for centuries to come. A similar ideological model is known from Eshnunna, a city in Babylonia in the Eastern Tigris region, where the god Tishpak was "king," and the ruler, just like in Ashur, his "steward." Eshnunna had close cultural links with Ashur and may have been the place where this political-theological conception originated.[18]

A more elaborate expression of how Ashur's rulers conceived of their god during the Old Assyrian period can be seen in an unusually enigmatic and poetic inscription of King Erishum I, a few decades after Silulu. Originally inscribed on a stela erected near the

Step Gate, the structure in Ashur where justice was administered, the text is known from two copies on clay tablets from Kanesh:

> May justice prevail in my city! Ashur is king! Erishum is Ashur's Steward! Ashur is a swamp that cannot be traversed, ground that cannot be trodden upon, canals that cannot be crossed.
>
> He who tells a lie in the Step Gate, the demon of the ruins will smash his head like a pot that breaks.[19]

Ashur is presented in this text as a deity who cannot really be grasped or visualized (even though he was not completely without mundane cravings, for example for alcohol, as the placement by Erishum of two massive beer vats in the area of the Ashur Temple indicates). Some evidence suggests that the god had bovine qualities: during Erishum's reign, his temple was called "Wild Bull," and a seal impression from eighteenth-century BCE Acemhöyük in Anatolia depicts him as a rock with four legs and a bull's head projecting from its middle. The rock on this image probably represents the elevated northeastern portion of the city of Ashur, but apparently also Mount Ebih, where, according to an inscription of Erishum I's father Ilushumma, Ashur had opened two sources to provide his city with water. A Sumerian myth known from Babylonia links Ebih to the goddess Inanna, the Sumerian counterpart of Ishtar.[20]

In all these texts, Ashur appears as a mysterious deity closely associated with nature—an unusual conceptualization of the divine within the wider Mesopotamian world, where deities were normally worshipped in human form. The Old Assyrian divine seal impressed on Esarhaddon's Succession Treaty from 672 BCE may even represent Ashur in a completely aniconic way: the space where one would expect him to be depicted, between a female deity and a male figure, is empty. But at least occasionally, Ashur was apparently also venerated in anthropomorphic form. This is suggested by a letter found at Kanesh, in which Assyrian traders from Urshu, another Anatolian merchant colony, bitterly complain that "what never happened before (has happened now). Thieves have entered the temple of Ashur, (stealing) the golden sun (disk) on Ashur's breast and Ashur's dagger. They left nothing. We searched for the thieves, but cannot find them."[21]

Besides Ashur, other deities played important roles in Old Assyrian Ashur as well. The Ishtar Temple in particular remained a sanctuary of considerable size and a popular place to leave votive gifts. At some point, a priestess by the name of Abshalim sought to win the goddess's heart by providing her with the model of a vagina made of bronze. Still, the city-state was from now on dominated by Ashur, the god who shared his name with the city.[22]

BY THE TIME OF ERISHUM I (r. ca. 1969–1930 BCE), ASHUR HAD been an independent city-state for several decades. Erishum belonged to a "dynasty" of hereditary rulers who considered a certain Puzur-Ashur (I) to be their ancestor. Later tradition credits Puzur-Ashur, whose reign must have begun in the late twenty-first century BCE, with construction work on the Ashur Temple and the city walls. He is also mentioned in the Assyrian King List, among the "six kings whose eponyms are unknown," where he appears after Sulili/Sulê and two other rulers probably belonging to a different family. How Puzur-Ashur came to assume his position is not known. His immediate successors, Shalim-ahum and Ilushumma, both left inscriptions describing work they did on the temples of Ashur and Ishtar.

Beginning with Erishum I, Ilushumma's son, the Assyrian King List provides information on the lengths of the reigns of the rulers of Ashur. The author who wrote the first version of the King List must have pulled this data from the lists of year eponyms that had been in circulation since Erishum's reign. Such lists have been found in Kanesh and have allowed modern scholars to establish a relative sequence of the thousands of Old Assyrian documents from that site, many of which are dated by eponyms.[23]

The "dynasty" established by Puzur-Ashur I included nine hereditary rulers who remained in charge for about two hundred years, until the reign of Shamshi-Adad I starting in the late nineteenth century BCE. But the term "rulers" and the claim that they were "in charge" are somewhat misleading when describing the political system of the Old Assyrian period. Strictly speaking, Ashur was not "ruled" by Puzur-Ashur and his successors, who were not even allowed to call themselves "kings." Instead, as mentioned earlier, they used the more modest title *rubā'um*, "Prince," along with a few others, most importantly "Steward of Ashur" and "Overseer." Although they apparently were responsible for the cult and the construction and refurbishment of temples, Ashur's hereditary leaders were, in the political and economic arena, *primi inter pares* (first among equals) at best—and not in the sense of the feigned equality the Roman emperors propagated when using the term, but quite literally. They had to share their power with the "City," a democratic body, and with the "aristocratic" *limmum* officials, chosen from Ashur's leading merchant families. Classical political theorists such as Aristotle or Polybius might have described the political structure of the Old Assyrian city-state, with its interconnected but largely autonomous civic institutions, as a "mixed constitution."[24]

The "City" (*ālum*) was a popular assembly, probably headed by a group of "elders," that may have comprised all free male citizens of Ashur. Any private citizen could bring complaints before this body, whose decisions were implemented by the "ruler" in his capacity as overseer. The City Assembly met in an open space (perhaps in the area of the later temple tower of Ashur) near the Step Gate behind the Ashur Temple, where a stone stela inscribed with laws was erected. At least some of these laws dealt with commercial activities, stipulating, among other things, that on penalty of death no citizen of Ashur was to sell gold imported from Anatolia to any Babylonian, Hurrian, or Amorite merchant—an early example of economic protectionism. Assemblies of free citizens also existed in Ashur's trade colonies in Anatolia, most importantly in Kanesh.[25]

The percentage of free citizens within the population of Ashur is difficult to gauge, but it was probably below 50 percent. Many residents of Ashur belonged to various categories of unfree persons, from chattel slaves to better-off servants who conducted business on behalf of their masters. Some of them had been bought, while others had been reduced to their dependent status by debt. Documents from Kanesh indicate that well-to-do merchants could own as many as twenty slaves.[26]

The City Assembly's tasks were primarily of a legal nature; it was the City Hall (Assyrian *bēt ālim*) that served as Ashur's main economic and administrative institution. The City Hall was in charge of taxation, the city's granary and treasury, weights and measures, and other features of Ashur's fiscal and commercial life, and had its own seal. The head of the City Hall was the official known as *limmum*. Recruited, at least most of the time, from the leading families of Ashur, the *limmum* was apparently selected by lot and served for one year. Unlike in later periods, the hereditary rulers of Ashur never held the *limmum* office.[27]

The years of the calendar used in Ashur were named after the *limmum* who was in office at the respective time. This is in stark contrast to the calendrical practices of the Mesopotamian south, where years were named after some great feat the ruling monarch (often considered divine at the beginning of the second millennium) had achieved in the previous year. A typical example, from the city of Larsa, is "Year when King Sumuel defeated the army of Kazallu and its king with his weapons." Year names like this were recorded in thousands of legal and administrative documents and served as an important tool of royal propaganda. That no such southern-style year names were in use in Ashur shows yet again the limited authority claimed by the city's hereditary leaders.

Another indication of the restrictions that applied to the power of these leaders is found in Ashur's urban landscape. During the earlier phases of the Old Assyrian period, there was apparently no palace (*ekallum*) yet in Ashur. In the thousands of Old Assyrian texts from this time, references to such a building are noticeably absent, and clear archaeological evidence for a palace prior to the reign of Shamshi-Adad I is lacking as well. The area of Shamshi-Adad's later palace may instead have been occupied by the City Hall. Most definitely, nothing like an Assyrian "royal court" existed before Shamshi-Adad. While Old Assyrian texts repeatedly refer to "chief cupbearers" or "scepter-bearers" serving the rulers of Kanesh, no such professions are attested with respect to Ashur. Ashur's hereditary rulers, in other words, probably lived in lavish but non-palatial quarters, just like other wealthy citizens. Like these wealthy citizens, texts from Kanesh reveal, the rulers participated in the overland trade, sending their own sons with caravans to Anatolia and following the same rules and regulations that applied to everyone else.[28]

TRADE IS WHAT DEFINED THE OLD ASSYRIAN CITY-STATE, AND being a citizen of Ashur seems to have meant you were a merchant. Long-distance trade in the ancient Near East had roots reaching back well into prehistoric times. Lapis lazuli, for example, was traded as long as eight thousand years ago from eastern Afghanistan to Western Asia and Egypt. The connections with remote resource areas were normally indirect and based on several interlocking circuits of exchange. The Old Assyrian merchants may have been unaware that one of their most important trade goods, tin (a strategical resource needed for the ever more important production of bronze), ultimately came from Central Asia. Besides tin, Ashur's merchants traded primarily in textiles. Some of these were homemade, while others were imported from Babylonia, which not only produced huge amounts of grain but also harbored large flocks of goats and sheep to provide wool.[29]

To sell both tin and textiles for silver and other precious metals and raw materials, Ashur's merchants availed themselves of a complex network of emporia, the most important of which was the city of Kanesh in central Anatolia, 950 kilometers (about 590 miles) northwest of Ashur. Kanesh was a settlement some 150 hectares (about 370 acres) in area and probably home to as many as twenty-five thousand people. It was hence much bigger than Ashur with its 40 hectares (about 100 acres) and five thousand to eight thousand residents. Kanesh's upper town comprised several temples and a local palace, which had been newly built around 2020 BCE. Its lower town included production-related areas and residential quarters, one of which was reserved for the representatives of the merchant families from Ashur involved in the Anatolian long-distance trade. Starting with the reign of Erishum I, many such representatives had settled permanently in Kanesh, where they enjoyed a number of extraterritorial rights and legal autonomy. The local ruler, in return, profited from the import taxes he imposed on the merchants and his right of preemption. Some of the merchants from Ashur traveled to faraway cities such as Durhumit near the Black Sea and Purushhaddum in Western Anatolia, from where goods were transferred into other trading circuits, eventually making their way to Thrace and the Aegean.[30]

The almost twenty-five thousand cuneiform tablets found so far at Kanesh in the houses of Ashur's merchant families provide a detailed picture of their business ventures, typically based on private initiative, entailing considerable risk, and including modern features such as bearer checks (in which payment is made to the person holding the check, which came in the form of a tablet in Kanesh). The merchants from Ashur were allowed by treaty to operate in only one region, central Anatolia, whereas other territories, especially in northwestern Syria and the Levant, were apparently served by other trading networks. Goods were sent with caravans that would take some fifty days for the journey from Ashur to Kanesh. The main means of transportation was the donkey, an animal well suited to navigate different types of terrain and capable of carrying a load of up to 20 percent of its body weight. The donkeys used by the Assyrian merchants would each carry up to 70 kilograms (155 pounds) of tin, plus various types of textiles.[31]

Profits from long-distance trade could be substantial. In Ashur, tin was sold for silver at an average rate of 15 to 1, while the same rate in Anatolia was 7 to 1. The amounts of metal traded were carefully weighed. Since transport costs, tolls, and taxes would markedly reduce the gains merchants hoped to achieve, some of them engaged in the shady business of smuggling. In a letter found at Kanesh, a certain Buzazu writes that he was staying in a place where tin was much in demand and asks that the addressees send him significant quantities of the metal. As the main road toward him cuts through a town that levies heavy tolls, Buzazu suggests that those bringing the tin should either bypass the town on a small smuggler's path or hide at least some of the metal in their undergarments. Another letter shows that the operation was eventually called off. But the case illustrates that merchants had no qualms about using illegal means to maximize profits.[32]

With prices in Anatolia three to four times higher than in Ashur, the trade in textiles was even more lucrative than that in tin. Many of the letters and documents from Kanesh discuss textiles, often in surprising detail. They reveal, for example, that it would take one woman as many as 150 days to produce a standard-sized textile of 4 × 4.5 meters (about 13 × 15 feet). Frequently, correspondents complain about the rotten state of clothes: "We hear that the textiles are infested with moths. Why didn't you examine them, and why hasn't your report come?" a group of traders in Kanesh wrote to a business partner.[33]

Textiles were not only of eminent practical importance, they also marked social rank. Like people today, the ancient Assyrians and Babylonians felt very strongly that "clothes make the man." In a letter from Babylonia from the time of the Assyrian trade colonies, a young man berates his mother in a tone that many a modern parent of moody, brand-conscious teenagers will know only too well:

> From year to year, the clothes of the young gentlemen here become better, but you let my clothes get worse.... At a time when in our house wool is used up like bread, you have made me poor clothes. The son of Adad-iddinam, whose father is only an assistant of my father, (has) two new sets of clothes [...] while you fuss even about a single set of clothes for me. In spite of the fact that you bore me and his mother only adopted him, his mother loves him, while you, you do not love me.[34]

Unlike in this example of an ungrateful son haranguing his mother, in the letters from Kanesh it is often the women and wives who complain to the male members of their families. Left alone at home in Ashur, with their husbands abroad on trade, they had to shoulder a lot of anxiety-inducing responsibilities, from taking care of the children to managing the local side of the business. Many women in Ashur probably also resented that their husbands, when staying for years in some trade colony, were allowed by law to marry another, local woman, even though they had to leave her behind when returning to Ashur. In a typical letter, Taram-Kubi, the wife of the influential merchant Innaya, wrote to her husband, who was staying in Kanesh:

> What about these coils (of silver; see Plate 5) that you allegedly left me (here in Ashur)? When you went away, you did not even leave me a single shekel (ca. 8.4 grams, or 0.3 ounces) of silver. You have picked the house clean and taken out everything. Since you left, a terrible famine has taken place in the city, and you have not left a single liter (1 quart) of grain.... Listen, send me the equivalent of the clothes that I made in the form of silver ... and

I will buy ten *ṣimdu*-measures (ca. 250 liters [about 265 quarts]) of grain.[35]

Despite all her anger and discontent, Taram-Kubi was clearly a very resourceful woman, not only capable of managing her household, dealing with business, and producing textiles, but also literate, as there is little doubt that she wrote her letters herself. Letter-writing in Old Assyrian times required the use of no more than 80 to 120 cuneiform signs, far fewer than in many other periods and places in the ancient Near East. This allowed nearly all free male citizens of Old Assyrian Ashur, and apparently also many of Ashur's women, to read and write with a fair amount of competency.

It seems that almost everything Ashur's merchant families put into writing was business-related. Very few of the thousands of tablets found at Kanesh are inscribed with religious or literary texts. Among these are eleven incantations, some directed against the evil, baby-snatching demoness Lamashtu(m), as well as the aforementioned Old Assyrian Sargon Legend. Several of the feats the legend ascribes to Sargon—for example, his seven-year-long stay with his army in a land of darkness, or his battles against seventy cities in one day—appear so bizarre that some scholars consider the text a parody on royal panegyrics. The jury is still out as to whether this is true.[36]

The literary texts found at Kanesh are written in the Old Assyrian language and orthography, and not in Babylonian. It is hard to gauge the situation at Ashur, where very few texts dating to the Old Assyrian period have been excavated, but it may be that Sumero-Babylonian literary traditions did not yet have that strong an impact on Assyrian civilization at this early point. It was only a matter of time, however, before a conqueror from Babylonia imposed on Ashur cultural and political practices closely linked to the south.

FOR SOME TWO HUNDRED YEARS, FROM PUZUR-ASHUR I IN THE late twenty-first century BCE to Erishum II (r. ca. 1833/1823–1809

BCE), Ashur managed not to become embroiled in any wars. Not that Ashur's citizens were committed to a philosophy of nonviolence—if business required it, harsh punishments could be inflicted. A treaty between Ashur and an unidentified kinglet stipulates, "You shall not allow the Babylonians to come up to you; if they travel overland to your country, you shall hand them over to us and we shall kill them." But large-scale military conflict was something the city-state sought to avoid. Ilushumma's claim that he had "established the freedom" of the Babylonians and several cities in the Eastern Tigris region does not point to an armed intervention, but rather to the abolition of taxes and tolls to facilitate trade with the south.[37]

Around 1809 BCE, however, the repeatedly reinforced city walls of Ashur failed to fend off conquest, and the city found itself at the mercy of a king from the Babylonian south. The events that led to this major turning point are succinctly described in the Assyrian King List: "During the eponymy of Ibni-Adad, Shamshi-Adad (I) came up from Babylonia. He conquered Ekallatum and resided in Ekallatum for three years. During the eponymy of Atamar-Ishtar, Shamshi-Adad came up from Ekallatum and removed Erishum (II), son of Naram-Sîn, from the throne (in Ashur)."[38]

Shamshi-Adad I, the conqueror of Ashur, is one of the ancient Near East's most colorful political figures. A scion of an Amorite dynasty with roots in the Diyala region in eastern Babylonia, and strong ideological ties with the ancient city of Akkad and its famous dynasty, he suffered some major setbacks early in his career, when he was forced by skirmishes with Eshnunna to spend time in exile in Babylon. But he recovered, gathered a strong military force, moved northward, and seized Ekallatum, a city just north of Ashur. Three years later, he conquered Ashur itself and assumed the traditional title "Steward of Ashur." Once firmly established on the Middle Tigris, Shamshi-Adad subjugated the Khabur Triangle farther west and turned a local city, which he renamed Shubat-Enlil, into his new capital. Shamshi-Adad's military success story culminated in his conquest of Mari, an urban center on the Middle Euphrates. In the wake of this victory, he began to use universal titles reminiscent of those of the Akkadian rulers, such as "mighty king," "king of the land of Akkad," and "king of the world."[39]

While not its center, Ashur played an important role in Shamshi-Adad's newly created "Kingdom of Upper Mesopotamia." The ruler adopted the city's practice of dating after eponyms, tore down Erishum I's Ashur Temple to replace it with a new one, and erected west of the temple a massive ziggurat, a pyramid-like stepped temple tower with a base of 60 × 60 meters (about 200 × 200 feet) and a height that was probably 60 meters (200 feet) as well. Next to the ziggurat, he built a large palace, perhaps the first Ashur had ever seen. Agents of Ashur's traditional merchant families continued their activities in Anatolia, and Ashur's City Assembly went on with its regular meetings. But it was clearly Shamshi-Adad who now called the shots. When members of the City Assembly, eager to use Shamshi-Adad's power for their own benefit, sought to lure the king into waging a war against some of Ashur's adversaries in Anatolia, Shamshi-Adad told the representatives in no uncertain terms that they had better leave foreign politics to him: "Since you are merchants, go about your trade as best you can. As for us (the ruler of Harsamna and me), we are mighty kings. Why do you interfere?"[40]

The system of governance that Shamshi-Adad eventually established was very much a family affair. The great king himself coordinated state business from Shubat-Enlil; an older son of his, Ishme-Dagan, served as viceroy in Ekallatum, from where he kept a keen eye on the state's eastern territories; and a younger son, Yasmah-Addu, held the same position in Mari, serving as administrator of the southwestern part of the kingdom. A large cache of cuneiform letters found at Mari suggests that Ishme-Dagan was a far more capable regent than his brother. In one of them Shamshi-Adad berates Yasmah-Addu by stating, "Ishme-Dagan defeated the army of an entire land. While here your brother achieved a great victory, there you lie among your women. Be a man instead!" In another letter, Shamshi-Adad criticizes Yasmah-Addu for having used up far too much gold and silver to manufacture divine images and for having earmarked too many sheep for sacrifices—an interesting example from an ancient world context of political pragmatism prevailing over religious fervor.[41]

In the same message, Shamshi-Adad calls both Mari and Ashur cities "full of gods," an apt description of Ashur. During Shamshi-Adad's reign, Ashur's role was more that of a "holy city" than of a political capital, the latter function being held by the nearby town of Ekallatum. Apart from the temples of Ashur and Ishtar, Ashur also housed sanctuaries for the weather god Adad, the moon god Sîn, the sun god Shamash, the netherworld goddess Ereshkigal, and the god Dagan. Throughout the year, elaborate cultic rituals took place in Ashur. At one point, Ishme-Dagan's wife Lamassi-Ashur—who hailed from Ashur—invited her brother-in-law Yasmah-Addu to join both Shamshi-Adad and Ishme-Dagan for religious festivities held in the city, take pleasure in Ashur's "serene face," and "kiss the god's feet."[42]

Ishme-Dagan's own face and feet were in much poorer shape than his god's at the time. As Lamassi-Ashur's letter reveals, her husband had issues with his mouth, and one of his feet was injured or infected. Since he lacked a physician whom he could trust, his wife asked Yasmah-Addu to send him one from Mari. But Ishme-Dagan's failing health did not prevent him from scoring some major victories during Shamshi-Adad's waning years, among them, most importantly, the conquest of Nineveh.[43]

The city of Nineveh had been part of the independent kingdom of Nurrugum, which along with the lands of Arrapha and Qabra had formed for a while a line of buffer states between Shamshi-Adad's Kingdom of Upper Mesopotamia and the kingdom of Eshnunna farther south. But at some point, Shamshi-Adad forged an alliance with Eshnunna, joined forces with Eshnunna's king, Dadusha, and waged a devastating war against the three lands. Ishme-Dagan played a key role in the events, especially the attack on Nineveh. When the hostilities finally came to an end, Dadusha brought back home rich booty, but Shamshi-Adad got the bigger prize: political control over the whole area. With the cities of Ashur, Nineveh, and Arbela (which was part of the land of Qabra) all ruled by one man, the core region of what would later become the land of Assyria was for the first time politically united.

The unity was short-lived. Shamshi-Adad died around 1776, and much of his Kingdom of Upper Mesopotamia collapsed within a few years. Yasmah-Addu was expelled from the throne in Mari, where after a short transition period an Amorite ruler by the name of Zimrilim seized power. Yasmah-Addu's harem, once the target of his father's biting criticism, was absorbed into the harem of his successor. Ishme-Dagan, not quite so desperate, managed to remain in charge in Ashur, if we are to believe the Assyrian King List, but he suffered numerous setbacks. Attacks by Eshnunna, now no longer an ally but a deadly enemy, and conflicts with the barbarian Turukkaeans (whose leader refused to give his daughter in marriage to Ishme-Dagan's son Mut-Ashkur) forced him several times into exile in Babylonia.

In the meantime, a new king, Hammurapi of Babylon, became Mesopotamia's new strongman. Not only did he eventually seize Mari from Zimrilim and destroy it, but some fourteen years into Ishme-Dagan's reign he also took control of Nineveh and Ashur. In the prologue to his famous law collection, Hammurapi, alluding to an enforced removal of Ashur's divine statue from his city some time earlier, calls himself "the one who returned to Ashur its benevolent protective spirit." Remarkably enough, Ishme-Dagan seems to have survived this latest crisis, too, albeit just barely. A man of continued poor health—at some point, two foreigners called him a cripple, whereupon he burned down their house—and in dire political straits, he probably spent most of his last twenty-five years as a weak puppet king beholden to Babylon. After his death around 1736 BCE, his son Mut-Ashkur ascended to the throne, but he, too, failed in his attempts to consolidate his power. It is possible that his rule was limited to the city of Ekallatum, while other leaders were in charge of Ashur.[44]

The Assyrian King List suggests that a period of chaos ensued in the wake of the final demise of the Shamshi-Adad dynasty a few years after the reign of Mut-Ashkur. Eventually, the system of government that had been in place in Ashur prior to Shamshi-Adad's time was restored. In a highly unusual inscription, a certain Puzur-Sîn, a new ruler who used the traditional title "Steward of Ashur," calls Shamshi-Adad's descendants "a foreign plague, not of the flesh of the city Assur," and claims to have demolished Shamshi-Adad's palace, now apparently considered by many a symbol of an illegitimate type of rule by much-hated non-Assyrians. The ethno-nationalist undertones of the text are something quite extraordinary within the political discourse of the ancient Near East. Tellingly, Puzur-Sîn's inscription is written in the indigenous Old Assyrian language and not in Old Babylonian, the language used in the inscriptions and letters of Shamshi-Adad.[45]

Ashur was now again a city-state. Seventeenth-century BCE letters written by Atal-sharri of Nineveh and Pilah-KUR (reading uncertain) of Ashur show that the two cities were no longer part of the same territorial unit. Ashur's traditional civic bodies regained their authority to determine foreign policy. An economic treaty with the city of Apum, ratified by Ashur's City Assembly some time after 1750, does not mention Ashur's hereditary leader. At the same time, Ashur's commercial involvement in Anatolia seems to have continued, probably until the campaigns conducted between 1630 and 1595 BCE by the Hittite kings Hattushili I and Murshili led to the destruction of many of the commercial facilities that had been used by Ashur's merchant families.[46]

DESPITE THIS REVERSION TO EARLIER OLD ASSYRIAN PRACTICES, the fairly short period during which Shamshi-Adad and his descendants had ruled over Ashur was never entirely forgotten—and not everyone, it seems, shared Puzur-Sîn's negative view of it. During the first half of the sixteenth century BCE, three of Ashur's hereditary leaders assumed the names "Shamshi-Adad" and "Ishme-Dagan." The Assyrian King List, copied well into the first millennium BCE, includes elaborate notes on the reign of Shamshi-Adad. And certain innovations introduced by the Shamshi-Adad dynasty were later taken up again. Among them was the identification of Ashur with the Babylonian god Enlil, patron deity of Nippur and "king of the gods"—an important religious corollary of claims to universal political rule. Shamshi-Adad had officially endorsed this idea when he rebuilt the Ashur Temple not only for Ashur, but also for Enlil.[47]

But the most important legacy left by Shamshi-Adad and his descendants was the idea of having a territorial state ruled by a king, rather than a city-state with civic bodies in charge. When, after a long "Dark Age," Ashur actually turned into such a state, the reign of the great Amorite ruler must have loomed large in the minds of those who brought this transformation about. Shamshi-Adad's Kingdom of Upper Mesopotamia was a prelude to greater things to come.

2

Birth of a Kingdom

Between the seventeenth and fourteenth centuries BCE, the city-state of Ashur, run by merchants and governed by civic bodies, morphed into the territorial state of Assyria, ruled by kings—kings who followed an unabashedly expansionist ideology. "Ashur" was now no longer only the name of a god and a city, it was also the name of a land.

While the root causes of this major political transformation are hard to track, its outcome is clear: after a poorly documented transition period, a new era began. Known as the Middle Assyrian period, it lasted from the fourteenth to the eleventh centuries—and saw the Assyrian state become a major power in Western Asia, occasional crises notwithstanding.

Several key developments during this time, on the political, cultural, and social planes, would shape the Assyrian kingdom up to its very end. Assyria's westward expansion resulted in the formation of a second Assyrian power center in the Khabur region, about 250 kilometers (155 miles) from the Middle Tigris, which was governed by an Assyrian viceroy stationed in the city of Dur-Katlimmu. Assyrian encounters with Babylonia in the south led to a pronounced Babylonization of Assyrian culture and marked the beginning of a strong political rivalry that would characterize the relationship between the two neighbors for centuries to come. And many of the economic structures, royal rituals, and scholarly traditions established in Assyria during Middle Assyrian times would likewise survive well into the first millennium BCE.

THE CENTURIES BETWEEN 1735 AND 1400 BCE ARE SOMETHING OF a "Dark Age," as far as Ashur and Assyria are concerned. Apart from the Assyrian King List, a number of short Assyrian royal inscriptions, and a few other texts, sources shedding light on this period are scarce. To some scholars, this paucity of data suggests an era of decline and chaos, a scenario that may not be entirely off the mark. But the accidents of discovery could play a role as well. The apparent darkness of the age may be more in the eyes of the beholder than in the actual events.[1]

The Assyrian King List is not fully reliable for the centuries in question. Its main version leaves out Mut-Ashkur (Ishme-Dagan I's son) and one or two additional members of the Shamshi-Adad dynasty who may have ruled after him; it also fails to mention Pilah-KUR, who governed Ashur at some point in the seventeenth century BCE. Instead, it claims that Ishme-Dagan I was followed on the throne by a certain Ashur-dugul, "the son of a nobody," and then by six extremely short-lived rulers—who may in truth have been eponyms during Ashur-dugul's six-year reign. The last of these, named Adasi, who probably held his office around 1730, is presented in the list as the founder of the dynasty that stayed in power in Assyria for the rest of its history.

Contemporary information on Adasi, his alleged son and successor Belum-bani, and most of the rulers immediately following them is not available, but the idea of Adasi as a founder was to remain engrained in Assyria's historical memory up to the kingdom's final days. The seventh-century king Esarhaddon still identified Adasi as his forefather. Who this man really was, however, and what he accomplished remains very much a mystery. It is also hard to determine when the city-state of Ashur began to encroach on neighboring territories, and where to look for the origins of the Assyrian provincial system that was in place, fully fledged, by the thirteenth century.

The seventh ruler mentioned in the Assyrian King List after Adasi is a certain Kidin-Ninua, whose reign lasted from about 1630 to 1616 BCE. His name means "(Under)-the-protection-(of-the-goddess?)-of-Nineveh," which might suggest that he, and perhaps already his father, ruled not only over Ashur but also over Nineveh. But this assumption cannot be proven and seems, in fact, contradicted by evidence that points to Nineveh being governed toward the end of the seventeenth century by independent leaders. One of these was Atal-sharri, who is known from a letter. Another may be mentioned in "The Song of Release," a Hurrian poem claiming that a certain "Pizigarra of Nineveh" participated in the destruction of the city of Ebla in northwestern Syria around 1600 BCE. Pizigarra, whose name is Hurrian, plays a prominent, albeit obscure, role in the "Song." In a passage right at the beginning, he is mentioned immediately after the gods: "I shall sing of the god Teshub, the great lord of Kumme.... I shall tell of Pizigarra, who has been brought up [to] Ebla... Pizigarra of Nineveh."[2]

Nineveh, then, was probably still an independent city with a Hurrian cultural profile—and not a dependency of Ashur—when, early in the sixteenth century BCE, the political landscape of Western Asia experienced some dramatic changes. In 1595, the Indo-European Hittites, who had stepped on the stage of history a few decades earlier, emerged from their capital Hattusha in central Anatolia, swept through Syria, and conquered Babylon. This momentous event may not have affected Ashur directly. By all appearances the city was spared the major destruction and political disruption suffered by Babylonia, where Hammurapi's dynasty came to an end and a period of chaos ensued. But it seems that in the wake of the formation of a much-enlarged Hittite state in the west, the many

Hurrian principalities in the territories stretching from northeastern Syria to the Eastern Tigris region slowly began to unite, forming a new state of their own. Ruled by leaders with Indo-Aryan names, this state would eventually be known as Mittani or Hanigalbat—and put enormous pressure on Ashur.

Mittani's ascent, however, was a slowgoing process, and during the sixteenth and much of the fifteenth centuries, Ashur still had considerable room for political maneuvering of its own. Unlike their immediate predecessors, several rulers of this time, from Shamshi-Adad III (r. ca. 1573–1557 BCE) to Enlil-nasir I (r. ca. 1504–1491 BCE), left inscriptions in which they claimed to have rebuilt some of Ashur's most important temples and reinforced the city wall. Ashur-nirari I (r. ca. 1556–1530 BCE) built a new palace, apparently after nearly two hundred years in which there hadn't been one, and his son and successor Puzur-Ashur III, who ruled from about 1529 to 1505, is said in later texts to have added a new suburb, some 15 hectares (37 acres) in size, to the southeastern corner of the city. More importantly still, a later chronicle reports that Puzur-Ashur signed a treaty with Burn-aburiash I, a king of the newly established Kassite Dynasty holding power in Babylonia, to fix the boundary between their respective territories. The Kassites, a people originally from the Zagros Mountains, had gained control of Babylonia a few decades after the Hittite attack of 1595 and eagerly adopted the Babylonian language and culture. If the chronicle is to be trusted—which seems likely, given that inscriptions of Puzur-Ashur III were found in Habuba (Tell Farkha) on the right bank of the Lower Zab—Ashur must have been in control of areas far beyond the city limits during this time. But there is no evidence that Ashur had begun yet to organize these territories as provinces, as it did two centuries later.

As the fifteenth century advanced, the pressure Ashur felt from Mittani began to increase, both from the west, where the Mittani capital, Washukanni (modern Tell Fekheriye), was located, and from the east, where texts from the site of Nuzi, near modern Kirkuk, some 100 kilometers (62 miles) away from Ashur, indicate that the once powerful kingdom of Arrapha had become a vassal state of Mittani. Ashur, too, must have been for decades under Mittani's sway. The clearest evidence for this is found in a Hurrian-Hittite treaty from Hattusha claiming that Shaushtatar, a Mittani king who ruled in the second half of the fifteenth century, had brought a door made of silver and gold from Ashur to his palace in Washukanni (from where it was returned in the mid-fourteenth century BCE).

Mittani's hegemony was not absolute, and the state less centralized than others. The Assyrian King List indicates that Ashur's local dynasty continued to stay in office, and now and then, the city managed to free itself from the grip of its foreign overlords. Under Ashur-bel-nisheshu (r. ca. 1417–1409 BCE), for example, another border treaty with Babylonia was signed. Yet, between 1430 and 1360, Ashur was still very much under Mittani's control. It would take a powerful and visionary new leader to set the Assyrian state on its own feet.

THE RULER WHOSE NAME BECAME INEXTRICABLY LINKED WITH Ashur's final liberation from Mittani dominance was Ashur-uballit I. An outstanding, energetic personality who held power from 1363 to 1328 BCE, Ashur-uballit took advantage of a series of political murders within Mittani's royal family that led to the temporary partition of the Mittani state. Playing the various pretenders to the Mittani throne off against each other, he turned Ashur into a powerful political actor and secured its entrance onto the international stage. Although there is still no unambiguous evidence for the existence of a provincial system during his reign, it is clear that Ashur-uballit also ruled over Nineveh, where he rebuilt parts of the Ishtar Temple. Other key cities in the Eastern Tigris region north of Ashur, such as Calah, Kilizu, and Arbela, may have been under his power as well.[3]

Ashur-uballit's territorial expansion had significant economic consequences for a growing Ashur. Thanks to relatively high amounts of annual rainfall, the areas in question produced much richer harvests than the Ashur region, and shipping grain and other agricultural goods down the Tigris to enhance the Assyrian capital's food supplies was comparatively easy. Some time before 1330, Ashur-uballit destroyed, moreover, the city of Nuzi and took possession of a portion of the kingdom of Arrapha, with the other part now controlled by Babylonia. There can be no doubt: under Ashur-uballit, Ashur metamorphosed from its previous "larval" stage into a powerful territorial state, the "land of Ashur" or "Assyria," as the Greeks would later call it.[4]

Ashur-uballit was not only an effective military leader but also a shrewd diplomat and wielder of "soft power." To create strong bonds with his southern neighbor, Babylonia, he gave his daughter Muballitat-Sherua in marriage to Burnaburiash II, the king of Babylon, while at the same time promoting Babylonian religion and scholarship at home. Marduk, the patron deity of Babylon, received his own cult in Ashur. A priest of the god who hailed from an important Babylonian family of administrators and scholars became Ashur-uballit's chief scribe. His house in Ashur was in close proximity to a "Gate of Marduk" that probably belonged to a newly founded temple of Marduk. Marduk's son Nabû rose to even greater prominence in Assyria as time went by.[5]

This makeover of Ashur's cultural and religious sphere was likely prompted by political considerations. Ashur-uballit wanted to reduce, if not eradicate, the Hurrian influence that had for such a long time shaped the identity of the people north and east of Ashur who now found themselves united in a newly formed Assyrian state. The prestigious, age-old Sumero-Babylonian culture of southern Mesopotamia provided a welcome substitute to this Hurrian heritage.

No less ambitious than his interactions with Babylonia were Ashur-uballit's attempts to engage on an equal footing with Egypt. During the fifteenth century, when the powerful pharaoh Thutmose III made repeated incursions into Syria, Ashur had on several occasions paid tribute to Egypt. Behind these gestures of subservience had been a desire to keep the Egyptians from interfering with Ashur's commercial interests. Now, however, the gift-giving was supposed to be reciprocal. In a cuneiform letter found at Tell el-Amarna in Egypt, the site of the ancient city of Akhetaten founded by the famous "heretic" pharaoh Akhenaten, Ashur-uballit announces that he is sending a royal chariot, white horses, and lapis lazuli to his Egyptian counterpart and then complains about the inadequacy of the gifts he had previously received from him: "Is such a present that of a Great King? Gold in your country is as plentiful as dirt; one simply gathers it up. Why are you so sparing of it? I am engaged in building a new palace. Send me as much gold as is needed for its adornment." Ashur-uballit bolsters this rather immodest request with the claim that one of his predecessors had once received twenty talents of gold from Egypt, an amount so large that one cannot help but wonder whether he had simply made the story up.[6]

What is most notable about the letter, however, is something else: that Ashur-uballit addresses the Egyptian pharaoh as "my brother"—and calls himself "great king." Here, finally, is the title that Ashur's hereditary rulers had up to then eschewed: "king" (*šarru*)—and it appears, tellingly, with an attribute that makes it even more distinguished: "great" (*rabû*). There were only a select few "great kings" at the time of the Amarna correspondence, most importantly those of Egypt, Hatti, Mittani, and Babylonia. Clearly, Ashur-uballit wanted to join this exclusive club, and he signaled his aspirations quite unabashedly to its other members.[7]

At home, in the meantime, Ashur-uballit continued to use in his inscriptions the traditional titles "Steward of Ashur" and "Overseer." But the inscription engraved on his personal seal—which was impressed on numerous official documents—calls him "King of Assyria" (*šar māt Aššur*) as well—and the imagery found on this seal likewise indicates a break with tradition. Whereas seals created in the earlier "Mittani style" usually show freely composed, slightly messy accumulations of fantastic creatures, stylized trees, and abstract symbols, Ashur-uballit's depicts a single group of two winged figures stabbing a lion held upside-down between them. Such visual language conveyed the idea of focused royal power—a concept Ashur-uballit was eager to promote as he sought to forge a new form of governance for Assyria.[8]

IN HIS LETTER TO THE EGYPTIAN PHARAOH, ASHUR-UBALLIT mentions that he was in the process of building a new royal palace. The palace, as an institution, would from now on serve as Ashur's main political, administrative, and economic center. The City Assembly of yore was abolished, and the City Hall's power severely curtailed, to carrying out minor functions such as overseeing weights and measures. The *limmu(m)* official was no longer associated with the City Hall; instead, any official after whom a year was named could now bear the title. Many of Ashur's citizens remained engaged in commercial activities, but others began to pursue new—and potentially more lucrative—careers as royal officials, whether in military or administrative capacities. The wealth of this new elite depended no longer on long-distance trade, but on the ownership of land allotted by the monarch, often in faraway fortified farmsteads called *dunnu*s.

Even though rich and influential, the people who kept the state going were now all "servants of the king" (*urad šarre*). One of the clearest signs of the rise of monarchical power—and the corresponding decline of Ashur's oligarchic and democratic institutions—is the emergence of an Assyrian royal court, with a whole new cadre of officials whose main function was to cater to the needs of the ruler. Among them were numerous eunuchs, whose tasks included guarding the royal harem, another newly created institution that marked the king's exceptional status.

The excavations at Ashur have produced nine fragmentary tablets inscribed with decrees regulating the activities of the palace personnel, and especially how male courtiers and eunuchs were to interact with the king's harem women. The earliest monarch who is said in this collection to have issued such decrees is Ashur-uballit. One of the decrees from a later reign, that of Tiglath-pileser I (r. 1114–1076 BCE), gives a flavor of the rules that were now in place in the palatial quarters of Ashur: "If a woman of the palace has bared her shoulders and is not covered with even a *kindabašše*-garment, and she summons a court attendant, saying: '... [C]ome hither, I wish to give you an order,' and he tarries to speak with her—he shall be struck one-hundred blows, and the eyewitness who denounced him shall take his clothing." Another decree stipulates that if the palace overseer or some other official allowed a non-eunuch to enter the inner quarters of the palace, the official in question was to have his foot cut off, a punishment that mirrors the intruder's "overstepping" into the area where the concubines of the king were to be found.[9]

A more benign aspect of the life led by the royal women of Ashur is illustrated by a large cuneiform tablet that lists the titles of dozens of love songs, including "In the Breeze of the Night," or "He Will Take Me; I Am Ready for My Beloved." We know from the Mari archives that harem women were often accomplished singers and musicians, and it stands to reason that performing the love songs cataloged on this tablet may have been one of the activities the royal concubines at Ashur actually enjoyed. Of course, this does not change the fact that the harems kept by the Middle and Neo-Assyrian kings were just another manifestation of the rulers' unfettered dominance. The harems represented the correlate *in sexualibus* of the kings' political and military power.[10]

THE ROYAL IDEOLOGY THAT PREVAILED IN ASSYRIA FROM THE fourteenth century onward found one of its most prominent expressions in the Assyrian coronation ritual. The clay tablet on which this ritual is recorded was probably written in the twelfth or early eleventh century BCE. It was found in a much later, seventh-century BCE context in the southwestern forecourt of the Ashur Temple, suggesting that the ritual was performed for at least half a millennium. Whether it was already in place during the reign of Ashuruballit is unknown, but it seems likely that rites at least similar to those outlined in the text were carried out at that time.[11]

The coronation ritual began with a procession of the new monarch from his palace to the nearby Ashur Temple, where, upon his arrival, a priest of the god would exclaim, "Ashur is king! Ashur is king!"—a pronouncement reminiscent of the chant "Christus vincit, Christus regnat, Christus imperat" (Christ is victorious, Christ rules, Christ governs) of medieval coronation liturgies. Clearly, the old idea of the supreme rulership of Ashur was still very much alive, and remained so throughout the rest of Assyrian history. But unlike in Old Assyrian times, the divine king, Ashur, was now teamed up with an earthly counterpart who was very close to him—so close, in fact, that the borders between god and king were somewhat blurry. This connection becomes evident as the ritual continues, with the king, after presenting precious stones to various gods, ceremoniously lifting the crown of Ashur and then, immediately thereafter, receiving his own crown from the hands of a priest.[12]

While this happened, the state's most important officials and the royal eunuchs would proclaim a particularly significant blessing: "May Ashur and Mullissu (Ashur's wife), the owners of your crown, put that crown on your head for a hundred years.... May your priesthood and that of your sons be pleasing to Ashur, your god. Expand your land with your just scepter. And may Ashur make sure that your orders be heard and obedience, justice, and peace be with you." Next, the king would be brought back to his palace, where he ascended his throne. After his chief officials and eunuchs paid homage to him and divested themselves of the insignia of their power, the king would address them with the words, "Each and everyone keep his office," making sure that the state apparatus would continue its work seamlessly.

Despite its invocation of "justice and peace," the Assyrian coronation ritual, culminating in the command that the king "expand his land" (*mātka rappiš*), was a theological endorsement of political ruthlessness and military aggression, an ideology of warfare that the Assyrian kings would faithfully put into practice for more than seven hundred years. Given Ashur's comparatively pacific earlier history, this belligerent turn is startling, and it is not easy to determine the factors that actually triggered it. But examples of mercantile-capitalist endeavors leading up to conquest and suppression are also found elsewhere in world history—one that comes to mind is the rise of the East India Company in Southern Asia and how it paved the way for the rule of India by the British crown. It seems that the merchants of Ashur, once their emporia in Anatolia were destroyed and their commercial opportunities severely curtailed, turned their ambitions from trade to territory—a shift in outlook that they were well prepared to undergo by their century-long experience in the logistics of long-distance travel. As far as the technology of warfare was concerned, they probably learned, first and foremost, from their erstwhile overlords, the Hurrians. It is hardly by chance that the title of the leading military officer of the Assyrian army, *turtānu*, originates in the Hurrian language.

Ashur-uballit's Babylonian counterpart Burnaburiash II, who had married the Assyrian king's daughter, was among the first to realize how dangerous the upstart Assyrian state might become. Its ideology of never-ending expansion could be bad news for its neighbors in Western Asia. In a letter to a pharaoh (either Akhenaten or Tutankhamun), Burnaburiash argues that the Assyrians were Babylonian vassals, and asks his Egyptian counterpart, "Why on their own authority have they come to your country? If you love me, they will not conduct any business whatsoever. Send them off to me empty-handed."[13]

But it was too late for such attempts to keep the Assyrians in check. The genie was out of the bottle, and soon, Assyria,

Babylonia's putative vassal, was meddling in Babylon's own internal affairs. After Burnaburiash's death in about 1333 BCE, his son Karaindash—whose mother was the Assyrian princess Muballitat-Sherua—ascended the Babylonian throne. When a group of insurgents removed Karaindash from power—in a rebellion that probably led to Muballitat-Sherua's death—Ashur-uballit dispatched an army to the south and replaced the usurpers with another of Burnaburiash's sons, Kurigalzu II.

The intervention did not have lasting effects. Before long, Kurigalzu II, rather than showing gratitude, embarked on an attack on the cities of Sugaga and Kilizu in the Assyrian heartland, thereby initiating a long series of skirmishes between Assyria and Babylonia, most of which were about control of the Eastern Tigris region. As time went by and each side experienced both victories and defeats, their rivalry intensified. Nothing was ever forgotten or forgiven. A century after Ashur-uballit's reign, the Assyrian author of the Tukulti-Ninurta Epic (on which more later) still invoked Kurigalzu's "betrayal" as the primal scene of Assyro-Babylonian enmity.

DESPITE THIS ONGOING RIVALRY WITH BABYLONIA, ASSYRIA'S most consequential wars during the first half of the thirteenth century occurred elsewhere. They were waged in the west, in the area of the Khabur River, a northern tributary of the Euphrates flowing from sources located in northeastern Syria and southern Turkey. The rich agricultural lands along this watercourse, and especially in the densely populated Upper Khabur Triangle, were an attractive target for an aspiring political power, and over several decades the armies of the Assyrian kings Adad-nirari I (r. ca. 1305–1274 BCE) and Shalmaneser I (r. ca. 1273–1244 BCE) repeatedly invaded the Khabur region to fight what was left there of the once mighty Mittani state. Adad-nirari—the first Assyrian ruler to include in his inscriptions detailed accounts of military events—imposed a hefty annual tribute on Mittani. When the Mittani ruler Wasashatta stopped the payments, Adad-nirari plundered eight of his largest cities, including the Mittani capital Washukanni, and brought the king, his wife and children, and many of his courtiers to Ashur. Bolstered by his success, Adad-nirari started calling himself "strong king" (*šarru dannu*), "king of the land of Ashur" (*šar māt Aššur*), and "king of the world" (*šar kiššati*), titles that would henceforth define the Assyrian monarchy and its territorial ambitions. He also referred to himself as the "extender of borders and boundaries," highlighting the central task the Assyrian coronation ritual imposed on Assyrian rulers.

Some political players still didn't fully recognize the new political status the Assyrians claimed for themselves. The Hittite king Murshili III, annoyed by Adad-nirari's bragging about his military victories, expressed this displeasure in a scathing and somewhat contemptuous letter: "So you have become a 'Great King,' have you? But why do you still continue to speak about 'brotherhood'?...For what reason should I call you 'brother'?...Were you and I born of the same mother?...You should not keep writing to me about being a great king. It displeases me." Yet just as earlier with the Babylonian king Burnaburiash II, Murshili's attempts at questioning Assyria's credentials had little effect. When Adad-nirari's successor, Shalmaneser I, launched a massive attack on the strongholds of Mittani's last king, Shattuara II, the auxiliary troops sent by the Hittites in support of the Mittani ruler proved ineffective. Shattuara suffered a devastating defeat, and the Khabur region became an integral part of the Assyrian state. It was a geopolitical shift of utmost importance.[14]

One of the instruments that Shalmaneser used to consolidate his power in the Khabur area was the deportation of significant portions of the native population. Henceforth a key element of Assyrian foreign politics, such mass deportations helped fracture local identities and provided Assyrian rulers with a large workforce for their building projects and the development of new agricultural lands. While Shalmaneser's claim that he deported no fewer than 14,400 people in the course of his campaign against Shattuara may be exaggerated (the number is four times 3,600, a base number of Mesopotamia's sexagesimal system, and thus suspiciously round), the political, psychological, and economic effects of the deportations ordered by the king were certainly considerable.

Based on the administrative units previously created by the Mittani state, Shalmaneser established several new Assyrian provinces in the Khabur region. His successor, Tukulti-Ninurta I (r. ca. 1243–1207 BCE), created additional provinces farther west, in the territories stretching to the Balikh River, another northern tributary of the Euphrates. Eventually, the Middle Assyrian state would include more than forty provinces and districts, about half of them in the Khabur region and beyond.[15]

Assyria was growing, and it would need to develop new means of governing to flourish. The kingdom now comprised two main areas, which were separated by a steppe region mostly inhabited by migratory pastoralists: on the one hand, the Middle Tigris region, with cities such as Ashur, Nineveh, and Arbela; and, on the other, the territories on the Upper and Lower Khabur and in the far west, likewise home to major cities. This situation posed logistical challenges, and there was a considerable risk that the western territories, removed as they were from the Assyrian core area, might break away from the Assyrian state. To prevent such a scenario from happening and ensure a fast and coordinated response to any active resistance that might arise along the Khabur, Shalmaneser came up with a solution that was similar to Shamshi-Adad I's earlier scheme, of having one of his sons govern the western and another the eastern half of his realm. He placed the western provinces under the command of a member of the Assyrian royal family, a nephew of his by the name of Qibi-Ashur, and conferred upon him the title "Grand Vizier" (*sukkallu rabi'u*), which was later supplemented with a second title, "(Vice)roy of the land of Hanigalbat (or Hanirabbat)" (*šar māt ḪaniGALbat*). The office became hereditary, with its holders primarily residing in the city of Dur-Katlimmu on the Lower Khabur, some distance from the more densely populated—and less Assyrianized—northern Khabur region, where rebels might have more easily disposed of them.[16]

The newly installed grand viziers were entrusted with a broad portfolio of responsibilities. Letters and economic documents from a cuneiform archive found at Dur-Katlimmu reveal that their tasks comprised, among other things, the organization of agricultural work, the capture of robbers and refugees, and the coordination of royal visits. The documents also show that, in sharp contrast to the success stories promoted in the inscriptions of the Middle Assyrian kings, the political, social, and economic order of the area was constantly in jeopardy. Typical is a letter sent by Sîn-mudammeq, a minor official, to the grand vizier Ashur-iddin, Qibi-Ashur's son and successor. It addresses concerns about locusts devouring the harvest, reports the arrival in nearby mountains of some 1,500 enemy troops ready to attack, and then adds, for good measure, that the sender is unable to dispatch 50 soldiers needed for the addressee's personal protection, because all available fighters had run away after receiving their food rations.[17]

Still, despite such intermittent disasters and other challenges, the grand viziers managed to strengthen Assyrian power in the west. Their investment in digging canals to irrigate previously barren plots of land contributed, moreover, to the economic development of the Lower Khabur region, which lay outside the area where rain-fed agriculture was possible.

ONE OF THE MOST REVOLUTIONARY AND MEMORABLE ASSYRIAN rulers of the Middle Assyrian period was Shalmaneser's successor, Tukulti-Ninurta I (see Plate 6). He ascended the Assyrian throne in 1244 and held it for no fewer than thirty-seven years. Early in his reign, Tukulti-Ninurta conquered several districts in the border region between Assyria and Hatti, thus consolidating the northwestern frontier. Then he directed his attention to Babylonia, Assyria's southern neighbor.

Assyria and Babylonia have been described, somewhat like Scotland and England or England and America, as "two countries divided by a common language." The two lands had close linguistic and cultural ties but were often embroiled in conflict. It seems as if the cultural indebtedness the Assyrians felt vis-à-vis Babylonia gradually produced in them a deep-seated minority complex, which prompted them throughout the centuries to engage again and again in aggressive raids on the southern land. A particularly brutal one—which would set the stage for many of the others that followed—took place a few years into Tukulti-Ninurta's reign. It turned Babylonia for an extended period of time into a theater of war and political unrest, with tragic consequences for the Babylonians and Assyrians alike.[18]

According to the Tukulti-Ninurta Epic, a poem composed in honor of the Assyrian king, it was the treachery of the Babylonian ruler Kashtiliash IV that provoked the former's military actions. A man of Kassite stock, Kashtiliash had allegedly broken a bilateral treaty sworn in the name of the sun god, plundered Assyrian lands, and engaged in acts of violence against civilians and deities. The main bone of contention, it seems, was control over territories in the Eastern Tigris region. After initially avoiding open battle, the Babylonian troops were eventually defeated. Kashtiliash was captured and, along with numerous other prisoners and much booty, brought to Ashur. Administrative texts indicate that the returning Assyrian troops were starved when they came back from the campaign, a clear sign of the strenuous character of the fighting and the logistical challenges involved.

In an inscription from about this time, Tukulti-Ninurta calls himself ruler of "Sumer and Akkad," claiming power over all of southern Mesopotamia. He also asserts that he had conquered areas farther west along the Middle Euphrates. But his actual hold on both these regions was probably rather tenuous. Two vassal rulers installed by the Assyrians in Babylon proved ineffective. They were eventually replaced, in the wake of another Assyrian military campaign, by a third puppet king, Adad-shuma-iddina.

After visiting Babylon in person to sacrifice to the city's gods, Tukulti-Ninurta seems to have taken his new Babylonian vassal on a tour of various cities of his realm. We know about this remarkable trip from a cuneiform letter from Dur-Katlimmu in which the grand vizier, Ashur-iddin, is ordered to secure provisions for a visit by the Assyrian king and his Babylonian counterpart. The two rulers were joined on their journey by their respective wives and various other male and female members of their courts, with the women, "ours as well as the Kassite ones," traveling in six carriages. Middle Assyrian kings seem to have inspected their lands often, but that a Babylonian ruler participated in such a tour was highly unusual. It shows, yet again, the love-hate relationship between Assyria and its southern neighbor.[19]

After only six years, Tukulti-Ninurta deposed Adad-shuma-iddina, who along with his Babylonian subjects must have turned against him. Assyrian troops entered Babylon and went on an extended looting spree. Most traumatically for the city's residents, they abducted the statue of Babylon's patron god, Marduk, an act of "godnapping" that became engrained in historical memory. In a literary-religious composition from later times, the so-called Marduk Prophecy, the episode is described from the perspective of Marduk himself, who claims that he had undertaken the journey to Assyria—and two additional ones of a similar kind to Hatti and Elam—of his own accord.

Administrative texts reveal that shortly after Tukulti-Ninurta had reconquered Babylon, several international missions visited the Assyrian king in Ashur, presumably anxious to find out what the great warrior planned to do next. The emissaries included delegates from Egypt, Hatti, the western country of Amurru, and the Mediterranean coastal city of Sidon. The Hittite delegation comprised sixteen men, four chariots, three mule-drawn wagons, and six donkeys.[20]

In the meantime, perhaps prompted by increasingly poor harvests in the Assyrian heartland, Tukulti-Ninurta intensified the economic exploitation of Babylonia, ordering cargo ships to transport large amounts of barley from southern Mesopotamia to Assyria. The king used the new resources derived from his wars for some ambitious building projects. In Ashur, he built a new Ishtar Temple—remarkably enough, not in its traditional location—and a double temple dedicated to the moon god Sin and the sun god Shamash. He also embarked on the construction of a new royal palace in the northwestern part of the city.

The king did something even more unprecedented as well: some 4 kilometers (2.5 miles) upstream from Ashur, on the eastern side of the Tigris, Assyrian workmen, along with Hurrian and Kassite prisoners of war, set out to build a completely new city, named Kar-Tukulti-Ninurta, that is, "Emporium of Tukulti-Ninurta." With a size of at least 240 (and perhaps as many as 480) hectares (or 590 to 1,186 acres), it was much larger than Ashur, which covered only some 70 hectares (172 acres) at this time. Kar-Tukulti-Ninurta was protected by a wall some 7 meters (23 feet) thick and irrigated by means of newly created canals. Most remarkably, it also included a palace, a temple of Ashur, and a ziggurat in honor of the Assyrian god, who up until then had only been worshipped in the city of Ashur.

It was a time of heroic efforts, and this is reflected in the ever more ambitious royal titles Tukulti-Ninurta now used, among them "king of the four corners (of the world)," "king of kings," "lord of lords," and "ruler of rulers." Here was a king with an imperial mission, if not yet with an empire. The historical epic that celebrated Tukulti-Ninurta's Babylonian adventures praised him in even more extravagant ways:

Through the destiny of (the creator-god) Nudimmud, he is reckoned as flesh godly in his limbs.

By fiat of the (divine) lord of the world, he was cast sublimely from the womb of the gods. It is he who is the eternal image of the god Enlil.[21]

No future Assyrian ruler would ever present himself in such godlike terms. A remarkable trajectory had reached its climax: the Assyrian head of state was no longer only a modest "Prince," as in the Old Assyrian period, or even a "great king," as from the time of Ashuruballit onward, but rather someone with well-nigh divine qualities. Yet, as the saying goes, "Pride goes before destruction, a haughty spirit before a fall."[22]

Tukulti-Ninurta's last years were marked by a slowly worsening political crisis that eventually led to a terrible finale for the king. The problems began in Babylonia. While the Assyrians managed for several more years to stay in power in Babylon, the regions farther south and on the Middle Euphrates, conquered at great cost, were before long lost again. A certain Adad-shumu-usur, who was either a son of Kashtiliash IV or a political upstart from the Middle Euphrates region, took control of these areas, driving the Assyrians and their supporters out. As a consequence, Tukulti-Ninurta's megalomania and self-confidence slowly gave way to intimations of impending doom. In a letter to the Hittite court, the king worried about the possibility that he might soon die, and a Sumero-Akkadian bilingual prayer to the god Ashur paints a dark picture of anonymous enemies closing in on the Assyrian capital: "The lands of one accord have surrounded your (the god's) city Ashur with a noose of evil. All of them have come to hate the shepherd whom you named (i.e., Tukulti-Ninurta), and who administers your peoples."[23]

What Tukulti-Ninurta may not have fully realized is that members of Ashur's elite and even his own family had begun to hate him too. The building of Kar-Tukulti-Ninurta cannot have been met with widespread approval in Ashur—many must have considered it an assault on the city's role as Assyria's uncontested capital. The construction in Kar-Tukulti-Ninurta of a temple of the god Ashur, although probably not meant to fully replace the one in Ashur, must have deeply upset Ashur's religious establishment. The same applies to the king's new Ishtar Temple in Ashur, erected away from its previous location—later, when the sanctuary fell into ruin, it was abandoned rather than rebuilt. The enormous costs in lives and money that the endless campaigning in Babylonia created may also have been met with increasing apprehension.[24]

Whatever exactly the reasons, in 1207 BCE some members of Tukulti-Ninurta's inner circle instigated a coup against him. A Babylonian chronicle from later times reveals that the king's own son, Ashur-nadin-apli, together with a number of Assyrian high officials, "removed him from his throne, shut him up in a building in Kar-Tukulti-Ninurta, and killed him with a weapon." It was a miserable end for a king who had once set himself next to the gods.[25]

DESPITE BEING TARNISHED BY HAVING COMMITTED BOTH REGI-cide and parricide, Ashur-nadin-apli followed his murdered father Tukulti-Ninurta on the throne, but for only a few years (ca. 1206–1203 BCE). Ashur-nadin-apli's position was much weaker than Tukulti-Ninurta's, and he had to share some of his power, it seems, with a newly emerging éminence grise, a man by the name of Ili-pada, who may have been the brother of the grand vizier, Salmanu-mushabshi. Ili-pada soon became grand vizier himself.

Ashur-nadin-apli was followed on the Assyrian throne by his son Ashur-nirari III (r. ca. 1202–1197 BCE), under whose short reign Assyrian power further declined. The new ruler suffered considerable humiliation from Assyria's archnemesis, the Babylonian king Adad-shuma-usur, who sent a letter to Assyria that addressed not only Ashur-nirari, but also Ili-pada, as "King." Given that Ili-pada held the title of a "King of Hanigalbat," this was, from a formal point of view, not completely inaccurate, but it was nonetheless embarrassing for Ashur-nirari, as it put into question the traditional preeminence the "King of Assyria" could claim over his grand vizier. The letter begins, moreover, with some extraordinary insults directed at Assyria's two leading men: "[Through] lack of self-control, constant drunkenness, and indecision, you have lost your minds. There is no one of sense or reason among you." Despite its strong anti-Assyrian bias, copies of the letter continued to circulate in Assyria for centuries—perhaps to keep alive the Assyrian hatred of Babylonian rulers meddling in Assyrian affairs.[26]

THE ROUGHLY ONE HUNDRED YEARS FROM THE ACCESSION OF Adad-nirari I in 1306 BCE to the death of Tukulti-Ninurta I in 1207 BCE saw the introduction and consolidation of some new economic and cultural patterns. They largely stayed in place up until the crisis that befell Assyria in the mid-eleventh century BCE—and to some extent even beyond this time. In line with Old Assyrian practices, long-distance trade remained an important feature of Assyrian economic life, but the Assyrian merchants engaged in it would now often operate on behalf of the crown rather than on their own account. Administrative texts from the royal archives in Ashur indicate that traders received funds from the palace to travel to Nairi in southeastern Anatolia to acquire horses, which, along with chariots, played an increasingly important role in warfare. Large quantities of timber and metals—mostly from the Taurus—were likewise imported in this way. The Mediterranean coast provided not only luxury goods such as textiles and jewels, but also wood. At the local level, lead or tin had replaced silver as the main currency for most everyday transactions, but for long-distance business trips, it was often preferable to pay with the more valuable bronze, which was easier to transport because smaller amounts of it were needed.[27]

Local production now played a considerable role in the Assyrian economy. Carpentry, metalworking, and stonecutting techniques were gradually refined. Craftsmen toiling in palace workshops or in workspaces in their homes processed raw materials, brought to the city from outside in the form of tribute, booty, merchandise, or gifts, to produce finished goods that were consumed locally or sold to others for profit. Agrarian estates across the kingdom provided the Assyrian elites with additional economic resources. The owners of such estates had to pay taxes and provide labor for state-run construction projects and soldiers for military campaigns, but they were free to sell their land or bequeath it to an heir. There were also state farms, primarily known from documents from Dur-Katlimmu, where dependent farmers received fields amounting to multiples of 100 *iku* (about 36 hectares, or 88 acres) to grow grain.[28]

The collection of taxes was largely in the hands of the provincial authorities. The duties imposed on each province included the delivery, on an annual basis, of grain, honey, sesame oil, and fruit to the temple of the god Ashur. The amounts to be sent were small, but the practice conveyed an important ideological message: the whole land of Ashur provided sustenance for the god who embodied the land.[29]

The houses in which the citizens of Ashur dwelled during Middle Assyrian times varied in size from some 70 to 240 square meters (750 to 2,600 square feet) and usually included a reception room, a courtyard, a bathroom, toilet facilities, and a main living room. Many people lived with "skeletons in their closets," burying their deceased family members below the floors of their living rooms in vaulted brick chambers accessible by stairs; there, they communicated with and sacrificed to their ancestors. The grave goods found in some of these Middle Assyrian tombs indicate that many residents of Ashur must have been quite wealthy. The artifacts from one of the richest of the tombs, that of the family of a highly placed Assyrian official by the name of Babu-aha-iddina, include ornaments made of gold and semiprecious stones, combs made of ivory, and alabaster vessels. The objects show features of an "international" artistic style popular throughout Western Asia at the time, while also displaying some pronounced Assyrian features.[30]

Families tended to be small, with more affluent households often also including a number of slaves. Slaves in Middle Assyrian times were not entirely without agency. We know, for example, of a female slave who adopted and brought up a foundling whom she had rescued from the river; tellingly, the child received the name Naru-eriba, which means "The river has replaced (an earlier, dead child)." The slave woman's legal claim to be acknowledged as the mother of the child is documented in a cuneiform text inscribed, rather peculiarly, on a clay model of a leg with an attached foot, probably to reflect the Mesopotamian custom of publicizing adoptions of foundlings by imprinting one of the child's feet on a piece of clay. The text illustrates the widespread—and apparently legal—practice in the ancient Near East of exposing unwanted children in a variety of outdoor locations.[31]

Middle Assyrian society was a patriarchal one. Most women lived their lives under the authority first of their fathers and then of their husbands. They had to follow a strict dress code: married women were expected to wear a veil, whereas unmarried ones and prostitutes were prohibited from covering their faces. A large Middle Assyrian law tablet provides insights into the often cruel punishments women faced if they overstepped the boundaries that were laid out for them. If a wife had sexual intercourse with another man, for example, both the adulterous woman and the man were to be killed. Unlike the Bible, which has nothing to say about the matter, the Middle Assyrian laws also criminalized abortion: "If a woman aborts her fetus by her own action..., they shall impale her, they shall not bury her." "Mirror punishments" could have terrible consequences for women: if a married man raped a virgin, for example, his own wife was to be raped. On the other hand, several provisions in the Middle Assyrian laws protected women against sexual assault by punishing the perpetrators more directly: "If a man lays a hand upon a woman, attacking her like a rutting bull(?), and they prove the charges against him and find him guilty, they shall cut off one of his fingers. If he should kiss her, they shall draw his lower lip across the blade(?) of an ax and cut it off."[32]

Not all Middle Assyrian women were housewives. Some engaged in a variety of professions, from midwife to tavern-keeper to prostitute. A certain Tapputi-belat-ekallim served as a perfume-maker. The procedures she used to produce specific scents were recorded on a clay tablet found at Ashur.[33]

In general, however, scribal culture in Middle Assyrian times was largely a male affair, with much of it rooted in Babylonian traditions. The Tukulti-Ninurta Epic provides a list of clay tablets that the conqueror-king seized in the course of his Babylonian campaign and brought to Assyria; they included "exorcistic texts, prayers to appease the gods, divination texts, and medical texts" as well as administrative records. Scribes in Ashur copied many of the literary and scholarly works arriving from Babylonia on tablets and applied a whitish paste of diluted clay—a so-called slip—on their surfaces to enhance their visual appeal.[34]

One of the largest and most beautiful clay tablets ever found in ancient Mesopotamia is a copy by the late-thirteenth-century BCE Ashur scribe Kidin-Sîn of two Babylonian lists of gods. The tablet, measuring 30 × 40 centimeters (about 12 × 16 inches), records the names, functions, and family ties of more than two thousand deities, their spouses, and the divine personnel working for them, providing detailed insights into the complexities of the Assyro-Babylonian pantheon. Scholars from Ashur also copied a wide variety of Sumero-Akkadian "dictionaries," so-called lexical lists, that had been composed in Babylonia, occasionally interspersing them with Assyrian "commentary." Their studies enabled them to write royal inscriptions with archaizing Babylonian sign forms, as well as author prayers in the venerable Sumerian language for Assyrian kings such as Tukulti-Ninurta I.[35]

Middle Assyrian tablets with medical prescriptions provide information on the advanced healing practices in use at the time. One of the texts was ascribed to a famous physician by the name of Rabâ-sha-Marduk, who had begun his career in the Babylonian city of Nippur and later became a doctor in the Hittite capital Hattusha, where he may have married a princess. Clearly, accomplished professionals were in high demand at the courts of the great kings of the Late Bronze Age. A cuneiform letter from the city of Tabetu on the Khabur River throws additional light on the care high-ranking political figures received in case of sickness. In the letter, a healer reports that Ili-pada, Assyria's well-known grand vizier, had fallen ill while traveling. The healer asks a woman in Tabetu to send him various plants, which were apparently meant to be used as ingredients for a potion to be administered to the patient. He points out that the treatment would only begin on a propitious day and after liver divination had established a successful outcome, a fine example of how medical and magical practices were inextricably intertwined in Assyria—and in ancient Mesopotamia in general.[36]

ILI-PADA, THE PROMINENT PATIENT FROM THE TABETU LETTER, became more and more powerful during the years that followed Tukulti-Ninurta's death in 1207 BCE. This led to political tensions. While Ili-pada himself never became king, one of his sons, Ninurta-apil-Ekur, did eventually ascend the Assyrian throne (r. ca. 1191–1179 BCE). After having been forced to spend some time in exile in Babylonia, he marched to Assyria with a private army and moved his predecessor, Enlil-kudurri-usur (r. ca. 1196–1192 BCE), out of the way. The office of "King of Hanigalbat" (albeit not that of the grand vizier) was abolished, and with Ninurta-apil-Ekur a cadet branch of the Assyrian royal family took over power in Ashur.[37]

The decades following these events were marked by repeated altercations between Assyria and Babylonia, with each kingdom occasionally, but never permanently, gaining the upper hand. In between, the two sides buried the hatchet: in a conciliatory gesture, the Assyrian king Ninurta-tukulti-Ashur (r. ca. 1133) returned the statue of Marduk, which had been "godnapped" under Tukulti-Ninurta by Assyrian troops.

Despite some territorial losses in the west, especially in the area of the Balikh River, Assyria's provincial system remained intact until the mid-eleventh century. On the surface, things were calm and stable, and under Tiglath-pileser I (r. 1114–1076 BCE), Assyrian armies marched farther west than ever before. But this was only possible because a storm that had been brewing for quite some time in the Levant had eliminated or weakened many of Assyria's most ambitious political competitors. Before long, this storm would also wreak havoc in territories long ruled by Assyrian kings.

3

Disruption and Recovery

A ssyria's rise to imperial preeminence did not proceed without
fits and starts. Between the fourteenth and twelfth centuries BCE, the kingdom had experienced a period of growth and consolidation. Even the internal troubles at the end of the reign of Tukulti-Ninurta I and the decades that followed had not substantially compromised Assyria's status as a major political power. The provinces in the west remained firmly in Assyrian hands, and under Tiglath-pileser I (r. 1114–1076 BCE) Assyrian troops reached, for the first time ever, the Mediterranean Sea. Shortly thereafter, though, Assyria's fortunes took a turn for the worse. Between the mid-eleventh and mid-tenth centuries, the country suffered a massive crisis, the seeds of which had been sown by events in the western Levant more than a hundred years earlier. Assyria's very existence was at stake.

But unlike some other states in the region, the kingdom recovered. Under the leadership of several energetic and ruthless kings, most notably Ashurnasirpal II, who ruled from 883 to 859 BCE, Assyria regained its former size—and began to accumulate greater power and wealth than at any time before. It was only now, in the ninth century BCE, that many of the features that would define Assyria for the rest of its history came into being: royal cities so

massive that they dwarfed all previous urban foundations, monumental art in the form of bull and lion colossi and reliefs lining the
walls of palaces, and a relentless cycle of annual military campaigns.
Assyria was not yet an empire—but it now had the prerequisites to
become one.

DURING THE LATE THIRTEENTH CENTURY BCE, MOST PEOPLE IN
the Near East saw their communities as unchanging and permanent. There was little to suggest the impending collapse of the political system they were used to. A few large states—Egypt, the Hittite
kingdom, Assyria, Babylonia, and the eastern kingdom of Elam—
and many smaller ones, all organized around palatial centers ruled
by more or less powerful kings, coexisted in what must have looked
to everyone like a fairly well-balanced equilibrium. But as it turned
out, such notions of stability were mistaken. A series of disasters
were about to turn the world as people knew it upside-down.

Around 1200 BCE, seemingly out of nowhere, groups of warriors began to attack large and small states in the Eastern Mediterranean and beyond. The most famous of these groups were the "Sea
Peoples," as they have been called in modern times. According to
ancient Egyptian sources, they included the Shekeleh and Sherden,
ethnic groups possibly originating in Sicily and Sardinia, as well as
the Peleset, whose name would live on with the Philistines and the
geographic region of Palestine. Claims in Egyptian inscriptions that
the Sea Peoples first attacked territories on the Eastern Mediterranean coast are confirmed by written and archaeological evidence. A
cuneiform letter from the coastal city of Ugarit, written by the city's
last king and addressed to the ruler of Cyprus, states, in unequivocal terms, "Now the ships of the enemy have come. They have been
setting fire to my cities and have done harm to my land." Soon thereafter, Ugarit was in ruins, and the marauders moved farther south,
both by land and by sea. Around 1177 BCE, they fought a cataclysmic naval battle with Egyptian troops in the Nile Delta. Pharaoh

Ramses III claimed to have defeated the intruders—and Egypt remained a state of considerable power for centuries to come—but in the course of the events it lost almost all of its influence in Western Asia. Other kingdoms in the region suffered even greater harm. Many cities and palaces of Mycenean Greece were destroyed, and the Hittite state in Anatolia experienced a catastrophic breakdown, with its capital, Hattusha, left devastated and abandoned.[1]

The arrival of the Sea Peoples was part of a broader pattern of disruption, probably triggered to some extent (like the refugee crisis hitting Europe in recent years) by climate change. It seems that around 1200 BCE the Near East entered a period of significantly increased aridity. This put ever greater pressure on local village farmers, many already in dire straits owing to the massive amount of taxes and the labor requirements imposed on them by their kings. As a consequence, many farmers decided to abandon their land and to roam the countryside, causing widespread famine and political chaos.

The precise details of what happened during the first decades of the twelfth century remain obscure, but the general outcome of the events is clear: a large number of palace states (so called because palatial centers absorbed much of their revenue) ceased to exist, their internationally minded elites were wiped out, and new players, mostly organized along tribal or ethnic lines, appeared on the scene, from the Hebrews and Philistines in Canaan to the Arabs on the Arabian Peninsula, the Neo-Hittite Luwians in Anatolia and northern Syria, and the Semitic Aramaeans farther south in Syria. The new groups tended to dwell in places much more modest than the previous palace cities, and their political organization was less hierarchical than that of their predecessors. Cuneiform, the complex writing system used during the Late Bronze Age by the rulers of the region to communicate with one another, was abandoned in the Levant (but not in Mesopotamia) and slowly and haphazardly replaced by simpler and more "democratic" alphabetic writing systems.

WHEN THESE DISRUPTIONS AND DEVELOPMENTS BEGAN, ASSYRIA was far from the center of the storm. Throughout the twelfth century BCE, most of Assyria's western provinces along the Khabur and Balikh Rivers remained firmly in Assyrian hands, and Assyria's kings were able to focus on their repeated altercations with Babylonia. Cuneiform documents suggest that not only the citizens of Ashur, but also those of small, faraway provincial towns, such as Dunnu-sha-Uzibi (modern Giricano near the Turkish city of Diarbakır), continued well into the eleventh century to go about their business, borrowing money, buying slaves and real estate, and engaging in other commercial activities.[2]

In fact, Assyria may at first have profited from the political chaos in the Levant. The fall of the Hittite kingdom and the pressure placed by Aramaean tribes on many of the cities and states of northern Syria facilitated Assyrian incursions into areas farther away than any reached by Assyrian armies before. Tiglath-pileser I in the late twelfth and early eleventh centuries BCE fought successfully against remote peoples such as the Mushku in Phrygia (the ancestors of the legendary Midas), and he was the first Assyrian ruler to repeatedly cross the Euphrates River and operate in the Levant. He even marched with his army to the Mediterranean coast, where he received tribute from the cities of Arwad, Sidon, and Byblos and killed a mysterious sea-creature—perhaps a hippopotamus—a replica of which was erected in one of the gates of his palace in Ashur. An unnamed Egyptian pharaoh sent the king additional animals, including a crocodile and a large female monkey, gifts that clearly appealed to Tiglath-pileser's exotic tastes. Tiglath-pileser is also the first Assyrian ruler whose inscriptions talk about the planting of trees from foreign countries in newly created parks in the Assyrian heartland. Tiglath-pileser's son Ashur-bel-kala (r. 1073–1056 BCE) undertook some ambitious military campaigns as well.[3]

But Tiglath-pileser's and Ashur-bel-kala's official accounts do not tell the whole story. The two kings may have managed to cross large swaths of land devastated by the incursions of the Aramaean tribes that had moved into the region in previous decades. Yet despite Assyrian boasts of having again and again successfully attacked those tribes, the royal armies proved unable to score a decisive victory. When confronted, the tribes, employing guerrilla tactics, simply withdrew into difficult terrain, avoiding the "chivalrous" fights, sometimes conducted from chariots, that Assyrians expected their enemies to engage in. Even worse, as time went by the tribes began, slowly but steadily, to infiltrate areas closer and closer to the Assyrian heartland, wreaking havoc wherever they appeared. A chronicle about Tiglath-pileser's later years paints a devastating picture of the situation: "The (Assyrian) people ate one another's flesh.... The Aramaean clans increased, plundered [the crops(?) of Assyria], conquered and took [many fortified cities of] Assyria. People fled towards the mountains of Habruri to save their lives. They (the Aramaeans) took their gold, their silver, and their possessions.... All the harvest of Assyria was ruined." The situation alluded to in this passage was somewhat paradoxical: while Assyrian soldiers operated many hundreds of kilometers away from their homeland, Aramaean raiders were busy plundering their villages and towns in Assyria.[4]

By the mid-eleventh century, the Assyrian state was in the grips of crisis. An Assyrian chronicle and a poorly preserved text inscribed on a monument known as the "White Obelisk" indicate that under Ashurnasirpal I, who ruled from 1049 to 1031, the Assyrians were still able to conduct occasional campaigns. But the geographic radius of the military activities of this king had dramatically shrunk in comparison to previous times. The districts and towns targeted by him were so insignificant that most of their names are otherwise unknown.[5]

Ashurnasirpal I expressed his desperation in a prayer to the goddess Ishtar of Nineveh, in which he lamented:

You have covered me with sickness. Why am I at
*   death's door?*

> *Like one who committed sins and sacrilege, I*
>   *endure (the penalty).*
> *I am constantly apprehensive; (I dwell) in*
>   *darkness.*
> *I have stopped sexual activity(?)...*
> *I cannot even approach the meal I am supposed*
>   *to eat.*[6]

To be sure, to some extent Ashurnasirpal's grievances may have been clichés. Mesopotamian appeals to the gods often followed the un-spoken rule that only the squeaky wheel gets the grease. Even the great seventh-century king Ashurbanipal—perhaps inspired by a late copy of Ashurnasirpal's prayer housed in his library in Nineveh—complained bitterly in a prayer to another Ishtar, the patron deity of Arbela, about his wretched health and poor mental state. But by all appearances, Ashurnasirpal I did indeed have reasons to feel deeply depressed. His kingdom, Assyria, was under siege. Migratory groups of Aramaean marauders were attacking Assyrian towns and cities, and large swaths of Assyrian territory had been lost.

The kings who followed Ashurnasirpal I seem to have been un-able to conduct any military campaigns at all. From the roughly one hundred years between 1030 and 935 BCE, not a single royal inscription dealing with military action is known. This state of af-fairs cannot be ascribed to the accidents of discovery alone. Remarks in inscriptions from the reigns of later kings leave no doubt about how deep Assyria had sunk during the decades around 1000 BCE. Ashur-dan II (r. 934–912 BCE) mentions that, "from the time of Shalmaneser (II) onwards"—that is, beginning in 1030—Aramaeans had been "murdering" the citizens of Assyria and selling their sons and daughters. Shalmaneser III (r. 858–824 BCE) describes the loss of Assyrian cities located on the Middle Euphrates in the course of Aramaean raids during the long and unglamorous reign of Ashur-rabi II (r. 1012–972 BCE). Other Assyrians, famished and exhausted, had been forced to abandon their cities and towns and escaped into mountains and remote regions where their bloodthirsty Aramaean enemies proved unable to follow them; they were later repatriated by kings such as Ashur-dan II and Ashurnasirpal II and settled in newly built or restored cities. At the turn of the millennium, in other words, Assyria's situation was extremely precarious. Never in its long history as a territorial state had the country suffered a greater crisis.[7]

THE STORY OF ANCIENT ASSYRIA COULD WELL HAVE ENDED here. But in contrast to what happened to the Hittites, the Assyrian crisis remained a temporary one. A combination of tenacity, resilience, and political acumen kept the state moving forward, even at its lowest ebb. Assyria recovered: "When everything was over," to quote the German writer Jörg Fauser, "everything went on."[8]

Assyria's survival was to a significant extent due to the fact that the very core of the Assyrian heartland remained by and large firmly in Assyrian hands. Most importantly, the Aramaeans never managed to conquer the city of Ashur, Assyria's political and cultural heart. The royal dynasty founded in Ashur hundreds of years earlier by Adasi remained in office, and even though the Assyrian kings who ran the Assyrian rump state during the crisis years were weak, their ongoing rule guaranteed some much-needed continuity. It seems, moreover, that despite the destruction of quite a few Middle Assyrian administrative centers in the west, a few Assyrian strongholds in that area withstood the storm. Altogether, the situation in Assyria was less desperate than in Babylonia, where earlier Assyrian attacks, under Tiglath-pileser I, and subsequent invasions by Aramaeans and "Chaldeans" (an ethnic group linguistically related to the Aramaeans, but more cohesive and organized) had created a political landscape marked by total disintegration and the quick succession of short-lived royal dynasties that had little power.

Starting in the second half of the tenth century, a series of strong and ruthless Assyrian kings opened a new chapter in Assyrian history. The new policies they initiated were facilitated by two main factors. The first was that several of the Aramaean tribes that had caused so much damage in Assyria's western territories during the previous decades had begun to settle down in a number of proto-states along the Euphrates and its tributaries, thus diminishing the pressure Assyria had long felt from them. At the same time, Aramaeans who had moved to the Assyrian core area began to assimilate to a more traditional Assyrian lifestyle. No less importantly, the drought conditions that had persisted in the region for the previous three hundred years slowly came to an end. The years around 925 BCE saw the beginnings of the so-called Assyrian megapluvial, a period of slowly increasing amounts of annual rainfall that helped enhance agricultural production in Assyria's core area and beyond.[9]

The Assyrian rulers could have responded to these circumstances by turning inward. They might have followed the example of Egypt in the first millennium, focusing their efforts on redeveloping their home territories. But this was not the path Assyria's kings would take. Quite the opposite: from the earliest possible moment onward, they put all their energy into restoring the large and expansive state that Assyria had been in the Middle Assyrian period. To do so, the Assyrian rulers now in power had to readopt the aggressive militarism of their Middle Assyrian forebears. Every year, usually during the summer months, they would go on campaigns aimed at regaining their kingdom's former lands. Drawing an analogy with the Christian retaking of the territories of Spain from Muslims, one can call their modus operandi a "Reconquista."[10]

The Assyrian Reconquista seems to have started with the aforementioned Ashur-dan II, the first king in more than a century to provide detailed accounts of his military operations. They were mainly directed against areas to the northeast and northwest of Assyria's core territory and included a campaign against the small kingdom of Katmuhu, which had once been an Assyrian province. Rather than reannexing this land, Ashur-dan, whose twenty-two-year reign began in 934 BCE, plundered it and turned it into a vassal state forced to pay a regular tribute and provide troops. This approach exemplifies the "Grand Strategy" the Assyrian rulers pursued during the early phase of the Reconquista in general. To save resources, only places of great strategic importance and hotbeds of opposition were placed by them under direct Assyrian administration.[11]

Making sure that local dignitaries in newly conquered areas remained loyal under such circumstances required a high threat level. The Katmuhu campaign provides a good example of the acts of psychological warfare the Assyrians employed. The kingdom's deposed ruler, Kundibhalê, was taken to Arbela, where he was flayed and executed. His skin was brought back to Katmuhu and draped across the wall of one his former cities, to serve as a warning for other potential troublemakers. The Assyrian inscriptions of the Reconquista period are full of similar accounts, as well as reports of conquered cities being destroyed, ravaged, and burned, divine statues being "godnapped" and brought to Ashur, and enemies being blinded or mutilated in other ways. This grim record of terror and torture has strongly influenced the modern perception of Assyrian civilization. Yet although notably prone to open discussion of such practices, the Assyrians were not alone among the people of the ancient world in engaging in acts of extreme violence. Even in ancient Egypt, often considered a more peace-loving place than Assyria, soldiers heaping up the severed hands (and penises) of slaughtered enemies to celebrate successful military campaigns are frequently shown on temple reliefs and mentioned in texts.

To their credit, the Assyrian kings of the Reconquista era did not only expand their power by implementing state-run protection rackets against foreign rulers; they also rebuilt cities and towns and enhanced the agricultural base of newly reconquered territories. A passage from an inscription of Ashur-dan II—which reappeared in similar form in the inscriptions of several other rulers of the tenth and ninth centuries—provides a good idea of how the Assyrian kings sought to redevelop their territories: "I brought back the exhausted people of Assyria who had abandoned their cities and houses in the face of want, hunger, and famine and had gone up to other lands. I settled them in cities and houses that were suitable, and they dwelt in peace. I constructed palaces in the various districts of my land, hitched up plows in the various districts of my land, and piled up more grain than ever before."[12]

Modern historians call this new era of conquest and development that began with Ashur-dan II the Neo-Assyrian period. Of course, not all the innovations that shaped it can be ascribed precisely to the late tenth century. Among the less clearly datable ones are changes to the Assyrian language, which absorbed new words and underwent a number of phonological and grammatical shifts. There were also modifications to the format of contracts and conveyance tablets. The changes in the legal terminology found in these documents, and in the way they were sealed, may reflect a breakdown of well-established patterns of economic exchange in the decades around 1000 BCE, especially in the relations between the cities and the countryside.[13]

There were some pronounced continuities between the Middle Assyrian and the Neo-Assyrian periods as well—continuities rooted to some extent in the deliberate efforts by later kings to follow in the footsteps of their predecessors. Assyrian throne names provide a good example. All Assyrian kings who ruled after Ashurnasirpal I took on names previously held by some Middle Assyrian ruler, calling themselves Shalmaneser (II) or Ashur-nirari (IV). This name-giving pattern remained in place until the reign of Shalmaneser V in the second half of the eighth century. Many of the royal titles that Neo-Assyrian rulers chose harked back to their Middle Assyrian forebears as well. When Ashur-dan II calls himself "king of the world" (šar kiššati), a title far too ambitious for his still fairly small dominion, this can almost certainly be seen as an attempt to imitate the titulary of earlier kings, such as Tiglath-pileser I. The use of Babylonian rather than Assyrian month names in Neo-Assyrian royal inscriptions, too, can be traced back to the time of Tiglath-pileser I. Rather than a clear break with the past, the transition from the Middle Assyrian to the Neo-Assyrian period was in many respects a gradual process.[14]

FROM THE REIGN OF ASHUR-DAN II ONWARD AND UP TO THE seventh century BCE, Neo-Assyrian royal inscriptions describe hundreds of military campaigns, often in great detail. Few civilizations of the ancient world have left richer sources for a careful study of military history than the Neo-Assyrian age, vividly illustrating how the Assyrian war machine actually worked.

The campaign accounts of Ashur-dan II's two successors, Adad-nirari II (r. 911–891 BCE) and Tukulti-Ninurta II (r. 890–884 BCE), are particularly informative with regard to Assyrian military tactics, which were often aimed at avoiding open battle. Both kings describe in great detail, and almost on a day-to-day basis, how their soldiers moved through enemy territory and what tribute they collected. Under Adad-nirari II, the Assyrians reestablished their dominance in areas to the southeast of Ashur, seizing the strategically important town of Arrapha (modern Kirkuk); in the years that followed, Assyrian armies would often use this location as a launching pad for campaigns to the east. Adad-nirari signed a peace treaty with the Babylonian king Nabû-shumu-ukin, and a new border between Babylonia and Assyria was drawn. To seal the deal, the two kings married each other's daughters. Farther west, in the Khabur Triangle, several local kings became Assyrian vassals or were replaced by puppet rulers.

Both Ashur-dan II and Tukulti-Ninurta II undertook lengthy campaigns along the Euphrates and Khabur Rivers, the former counterclockwise and the latter clockwise. The expeditions were aimed at collecting tribute and securing the loyalty of the many local strongmen, often of Aramaean stock, who at the time ruled small stretches of land along the two rivers. The Assyrian inscriptions allow us to closely follow the itinerary of the Assyrian armies:

> On the twenty-sixth day of the month of Nisannu in the eponymy of Na'id-ili (i.e., 885 BCE), I (Tukulti-Ninurta II) moved out from Ashur.... I crossed the Wadi Tharthar, pitched camp, and spent the night there. By midday, all the water was drawn, (after) I had drawn water from four hundred and seventy wells in the environs.... For four days, I followed the banks of the Wadi Tharthar..., killing eight wild bulls.... (Later, on the Euphrates River), I moved on from the plain and approached the city of Sirqu. I received as tribute from Mudada of Sirqu three minas (about 1.5 kilograms, or 3.3 pounds) of gold, seven minas (about 3.5 kilograms, or 7.7 pounds) of refined silver, eight talents (about 240 kilograms, or 529 pounds) of tin, forty bronze casseroles, one talent (about 30 kilograms, or 66 pounds) of myrrh, [...] hundred sheep, [...] hundred-and-forty oxen, twenty donkeys, twenty large birds, as well as bread, beer, grain, straw, and fodder.[15]

The amounts of goods that Tukulti-Ninurta II received from Mudada were small, but since the Assyrian king was able to force dozens of petty rulers to provide him with tribute, he accumulated over time significant wealth.

It was usually enough for the Assyrian armies to just pass by to make local rulers pay. Only places that failed to comply were attacked. This happened, for example, to a number of cities in Phrygia that were plundered and burned down, and where Tukulti-Ninurta II massacred parts of the local population and destroyed the harvest in the surrounding fields. The indiscriminate killing of civilians was not the rule, however. The Assyrians used it occasionally as a deterrent for other possible rebels, but they had no interest in genocidal campaigns. In view of the constant labor shortages that marked the economic realities of the ancient Near East, Assyrian kings needed subjects who were alive rather than dead. As Tukulti-Ninurta II put it in his own inscriptions, quoting a credo already found in texts written in the name of Tiglath-pileser I, "To Assyria I added land and to her people I added people."[16]

Little is known about Assyria's literary and scholarly culture during the early Reconquista period, but it is noteworthy that Tukulti-Ninurta II is the first Assyrian ruler to employ a "chief scholar," a certain Gabbi-ilani-eresh, who became the ancestor of an extremely influential family of "court intellectuals." The royal inscriptions composed in Tukulti-Ninurta's name—perhaps by Gabbi-ilani-eresh himself—are written in a strongly Assyrianizing idiom rather than in the generally more prestigious Babylonian dialect. Linguistically closely related to Assyrian, Babylonian was used in many Middle Assyrian and later Neo-Assyrian inscriptions, but during the early Reconquista period, Assyria's kings apparently considered it vital to cultivate an identity that was ostentatiously Assyrian.

THE REIGN OF TUKULTI-NINURTA II'S SON AND SUCCESSOR Ashurnasirpal II (r. 883–859 BCE) marked a dramatic turning point, both for Assyrian culture and Assyrian politics. Late in his reign, in 864 BCE, the king showcased the changes he had brought about to an audience of 69,574 people, both Assyrians and foreign dignitaries, whom he had invited to the city of Calah. Being summoned to the Assyrian court was normally not a reason for much rejoicing. But this time, things were different. The king was throwing a party, with no expenses spared. According to his so-called Banquet Stela, Ashurnasirpal served his guests "one hundred fat oxen, one thousand calves and sheep of the stable, ten thousand pigeons, ten thousand turtle doves, ten thousand fish, ten thousand eggs, ten thousand loaves of bread," and equally massive quantities of grapes, onions, honey, dates, fruit, and many other foodstuffs, not to mention a large number of alcoholic beverages. Perhaps the revelers also received skewers with roasted locusts, an Assyrian delicacy depicted on Assyrian wall reliefs from Nineveh, and "Elamite blood broth," as a cuneiform recipe book somewhat gruesomely calls a popular stew. The official occasion for this extraordinary feast was the inauguration of Ashurnasirpal's monumental "Northwest Palace," which was to become the king's new residence in Calah.[17]

Ashurnasirpal had relocated the seat of power from Ashur to Calah in 879, four years into his reign. Calah, located close to the convergence of the Greater Zab River and the Tigris, was not a new foundation; it had a nearly one-thousand-year-long history by the time of Ashurnasirpal's rise to power and had served for centuries as the center of a small inner-Assyrian province. But despite this distinction, the city had never attained a status comparable to that of Ashur or Nineveh. Now, suddenly, it found itself in the process of becoming the glorious new capital of the Assyrian kingdom.

Moving the royal court away from Ashur, seat of the Assyrian state god and the kingdom's traditional capital, was a risky endeavor. Some 350 years earlier, Tukulti-Ninurta I may have paid with his life for a similar attempt at creating a new capital: his plans to relocate his residence to Kar-Tukulti-Ninurta on the other side of the Tigris was probably a main reason for one of his own sons to kill him. But Ashurnasirpal's move to Calah proved successful, and the city would remain the main dwelling place of the Assyrian kings for more than a century and a half. It may have helped that Ashurnasirpal also undertook construction work at Ashur. By restoring Ashur's so-called Old Palace, as well as various temples, he sent a clear message that Ashur would remain a place of vital importance for the Assyrian kingdom, thus defusing any inclination on the part of Ashur's elites to start a revolt. During the winter and early spring, Ashurnasirpal and the Assyrian rulers who followed him would, moreover, regularly spend time in Ashur to participate in some of the state's most significant cultic rituals. They would also continue to be buried in Ashur, in subterranean vaults beneath the Old Palace, where they resided during their stays in the city. Finally, to emphasize that the god Ashur would remain the kingdom's preeminent deity, Ashurnasirpal claimed to have dedicated the city of Calah to him, even though the exact significance of this act remains unclear.[18]

Ashurnasirpal's move to Calah, and the city's transformation into a dazzling metropolis, were bolstered by an influx of enormous amounts of booty and tribute secured through new conquests. But why did the king relocate the court to Calah in the first place? One reason, it seems, was that Ashur had become too small—once Ashurnasirpal had completed the 15-meter (50-foot) wall of Calah's lower town, his new capital, some 380 hectares (940 acres) in size, covered an area about six times as large as Ashur's. Another advantageous feature of Calah was a tall mound on the southeastern end of the city. This mound provided not only security for the king, but also ample space to accommodate the kind of monumental temples and palaces that befitted Assyria's new status as the increasingly uncontested hegemon of much of Western Asia. And whereas Ashur was located on the southern edge of the Assyrian core area, in a peripheral region not particularly suited for agricultural activity, Calah was strategically positioned in the center of the "Assyrian triangle," an area marked by Ashur in the south, Nineveh in the north, and Arbela in the east. It was also surrounded by Assyria's fertile northern plain.[19]

Last but not least, Ashurnasirpal may have moved the court to Calah for political reasons. He may have sought to weaken the power of the old "aristocracy" of Ashur (and perhaps also of Nineveh and Arbela) by relocating his administration to a city whose inhabitants had been handpicked from among the king's most loyal supporters from all over the state, and even beyond. Finding such people had been one of the central tasks that Nergal-apil-kumu'a, Calah's newly chosen governor, had to carry out on Ashurnasirpal's behalf. A royal edict about his appointment lists some of the originating locations for the new citizens of Calah as well as the professions they held—there were bakers, brewers, architects, engravers, bow-makers, weavers, and fullers; goldsmiths, coppersmiths, and ironsmiths; oxherds, bird keepers, farmers, gardeners, and cooks; boatmen and reed-workers; merchants and prostitutes; diviners and exorcists; and many others. Eunuchs, loyal to the king rather than their own families, played an ever-increasing role in the royal administration, and soon also within the officer ranks of the army.[20]

Under Ashurnasirpal and his successors, thousands of construction workers and craftsmen turned Calah and its surroundings into an urban center ready to inspire awe and wonder in its many visitors. Among other things, an artificial watercourse, called the "Canal of Abundance," was dug out from the Upper Zab to irrigate a luscious park with numerous exotic plants, including beautiful pomegranates. "Streams of water (luminous) as the stars of heaven" flowed into the "pleasure garden," the earliest known of the many palatial parks and gardens that would become central features of the imperial landscapes of the Middle East— from the *paridaida* of the Persian kings in Pasargadae and Persepolis (from which the word "paradise" derives) to the palace gardens of the Abbasids in medieval Baghdad and Samarra. The tradition would also spread eastward to India and westward to Rome. In addition, Ashurnasirpal collected exotic animals, including wild bulls, lions, ostriches, and monkeys from his expedition to the Mediterranean, and put them on display in what seems to have been an early kind of zoo.[21]

On Calah's citadel, the king's construction crews erected nine temples, four of which have been at least partly excavated; they were dedicated to the warrior god Ninurta, Marduk's son Nabû, Ishtar of Kidmuri, and another Ishtar-like goddess by the name of Sharrat-niphi. But Ashurnasirpal's most ambitious building project was the so-called Northwest Palace, his new residence, whose inauguration was celebrated with the king's gigantic party. Situated in the northwestern quarter of the citadel, the palace's excavated portions measure some 200 × 120 meters (about 650 × 390 feet). Its actual size must have been considerably larger.

The most impressive part of the palace was the throne-room suite, located next to a huge northern courtyard and adjoined farther south by a complex of large state apartments built around another courtyard. All the walls in this palace wing were lined with bas-reliefs made of limestone and decorated with depictions of military campaigns, hunting expeditions, protective deities, stylized palm trees, and ritual scenes. Some of them were inscribed with texts summarizing the outcome of Ashurnasirpal's military campaigns, and all were originally painted (see Plates 7 and 8). Some of the paint was still intact when the reliefs were excavated—traces of the black paint for the carefully curated beards of the Assyrian kings proved particularly resistant to the ravages of time. Wall paintings and glazed brick panels adorned the walls above the reliefs, enhancing the overpowering multisensory nature of the experience for visitors who were admitted to the inner rooms of the palace. Trees from the Amanus and Lebanon mountains provided the timber used for the large roofs of these rooms.[22]

Ashurnasirpal's wall reliefs are the earliest extant Assyrian examples of this artifact group, soon considered emblematic of Assyrian art. Certain indications suggest that prototypes of them existed already during the reign of Tiglath-pileser I, more than two hundred years earlier. But it seems that the main model for the relief cycles of the Northwest Palace were the stone orthostats decorating the palaces and temples of the central cities of the "Neo-Hittite" and Aramaean states of northern Syria. The "Long Wall of Sculpture" at Carchemish, created in the tenth century BCE, may have served as a particularly important inspiration for Ashurnasirpal's artists. It was characteristic of the Neo-Assyrian elites that they had no qualms about adopting foreign artistic styles and technologies, often transforming them in such a way that they became genuinely Assyrian. The depictions of human beings and protective deities on the Assyrian bas-reliefs, taller, more accomplished, and more elegant than the somewhat stunted figures found on their Neo-Hittite and Aramaean forerunners, provide a good example of this kind of cross-cultural emulation.[23]

Also introduced under Ashurnasirpal, and before long another defining element of Assyrian art and architecture, were the massive sculptures of human-headed winged bulls and sphinx-like lions erected in the main entrance gates of Assyrian palaces and temples. Five of them were positioned along the northern façade of Ashurnasirpal's throne-room suite. Like the Assyrian bas-reliefs, these colossal figures had forerunners in the sculpture of the Neo-Hittite and Aramaean kingdoms of northern Syria, but surpassed their models in execution and size, with the largest of the Assyrian winged bulls measuring up to 5 meters (16 feet) in height and weighing up to 50 metric tons (55 US tons). Exuding strength and potency, the colossi were considered supernatural beings capable of guarding palaces and temples against malevolent intruders. Combining the qualities of different species—the body of a bull or a lion, the head of a human being, and the wings of a bird—their power came from their alleged roots in a primeval past when human and animal forms were not yet fully differentiated. To emphasize that they dominated not only the domains of land and air, but also the sea, some of the colossi even had fish-related features: the belly and breast of two of the winged bulls from Ashurnasirpal's throne-room façade are shaped like a fish torso, with scales, and their heads sport a fish-shaped cap.[24]

THE ASSYRIAN KINGS SEEM TO HAVE BELIEVED THAT THE WINGED bulls and lions represented by the sculptures in their palaces and temples had been among the many monsters that, according to tradition, the Mesopotamian warrior god Ninurta had defeated at the beginning of time and brought home as captives. Once they were removed from the mythological world of chaos they had come from, the domesticated monsters were repurposed as benevolent protectors.

Stories about Ninurta's heroic fights against various wicked adversaries also provided a mythological template for Assyria's expansionist ideology. One of these stories recounts Ninurta's victory over the monstrous, eagle-like Anzû bird. At the beginning, Anzû, brought from his place of origin in the northern periphery to the home of the gods, serves as guardian of the private quarters of Enlil, the king of the gods and Ninurta's father. But Anzû abuses his position by stealing the "Tablet of Destinies" while Enlil is taking a bath. Without that tablet, the gods are unable to maintain the cosmic order. After several other deities, fearful of the encounter with the colossal bird, have refused to retrieve the object, Ninurta steps up and expresses his willingness to face Anzû in battle. Initially, his attack is repulsed: with the help of the Tablet of Destinies, Anzû turns Ninurta's arrows back into their original elements, with the shaft becoming again a reed and the feathers at the ends of the arrows being reunited with the birds that produced them. But then the god Ea tells Ninurta about a trick: he could cut off Anzû's wing feathers. Ninurta does so, and when Anzû uses a magic spell to bring the feathers back, the feathered arrows reach him, too, and bring about his defeat. Ninurta returns with the Tablet of Destinies and is received in triumph by the other gods.[25]

The story of Ninurta and the evil Anzû bird, the chaos monster that had been under control before but had defected and needed to be defeated a second time, provided a particularly good model for the Assyrian "Reconquista" efforts, imbuing them with a cosmological dimension. The Assyrian kings recognized themselves in Ninurta. Just as that god, in primeval times, had fought chaos by defeating monstrous creatures that threatened to undermine the peace and tranquility of the emerging world, Assyria's rulers considered it their "civilizing mission" to create—or re-create—order by defeating their human enemies along the ever-expanding borders of their state.[26]

Needless to say, those very enemies must have had a very different perception of Assyria's aggressive policies, not least because these were often accompanied by acts of extreme violence. One of the most gruesome testimonies to the brutality of the Assyrian armies appears in a long text inscribed in Ashurnasirpal II's name on stone orthostats lining the walls and floor of the newly built Ninurta Temple, located north of his royal palace. The text begins with an invocation of the god Ninurta and a celebration of the king that includes some fifty titles and epithets culminating in a self-predication: "I am king, I am lord, I am praiseworthy, I am exalted, I am important, I am magnificent, I am foremost, I am a hero, I am a warrior, I am a lion, and I am a man." Clearly, modesty was not a quality Assyrian monarchs cultivated much. Then follows a detailed account of the campaigns undertaken during Ashurnasirpal's first five years in office. When describing the conquest of the city of Tela on the Upper Tigris, the king reports, "I captured many troops alive. From some I cut off their arms and hands; from others I cut off their noses, ears, and extremities. I gouged out the eyes of many troops. I hung their heads on trees around the city. I burned many of their adolescent boys and girls. I razed, destroyed, burned, and consumed the city."[27]

The primary purpose of this and other, similar episodes in the Ninurta Temple inscription was probably not to cause fear among Assyria's enemies. None of those who were likely to resist Assyria's relentless expansion would have had the opportunity to read the text. Ostensibly, the inscription was instead directed to Ninurta himself, in an attempt to please him by showing that the Assyrian king had continued the belligerent mission that the god had initiated in mythological times. But its real addressees, we may assume, were later Assyrian kings and the leading circles of Assyria's political and religious establishment. Exposing this inner audience to explicit accounts of violence was an effective way to reinforce among them the aggressive ideology on which the Assyrian state was founded.

Other Assyrian texts are equally obsessed with violence. One disturbing poem says about an Assyrian king, perhaps Tiglath-pileser I, "He slits the wombs of pregnant women; he blinds the infants; he cuts the throats of their strong ones." Even by the standards of the ancient world, these were acts that could be considered war crimes—after all, the biblical prophet Amos predicted that God would punish the Ammonites "because they have ripped open pregnant women in Gilead in order to enlarge their territory." If Assyrian texts glorified such atrocities, this should probably be regarded as an exercise in self-indoctrination, aimed at dissipating the two great fears that tend to compromise an army's performance: the fear of being killed and, perhaps more importantly still, remorse for killing.[28]

Assyrians could actually be quite anxious about violence and its consequences. The Erra Epic, a ninth- or eighth-century BCE literary text that was popular in Assyria, offered a powerful critique of violence and war. In the epic's first scene, Erra, the text's protagonist, a god of combat, mayhem, and plague, lounges lazily with his wife in his bedchamber. His leisure time is rudely disrupted when he is mocked by the Sebetti, a group of seven belligerent deities who extol to him the pleasures of war:

> *Why have you been sitting in the city like a feeble*
> *   old man,*
> *Shall we eat woman food, like non-combatants?*
> *However well developed is the strength of a city*
> *   dweller,*
> *How could he possibly best a campaigner?*
> *However toothsome city bread, it holds nothing to*
> *   the campfire loaf,*
> *However sweet fine beer, it holds nothing to water*
> *   from a skin.*[29]

Erra, his masculinity put into question, immediately springs into action, but with disastrous results: the warfare in which he engages brings the world to the brink of extinction. In an indiscriminate killing spree, he puts "the righteous person to death and the unrighteous person to death." It is only when his faithful adviser Ishum intervenes—talking to his unbalanced master like an experienced psychotherapist—that Erra eventually relents and ends the senseless slaughter. Clearly, as warlike as Assyria's political culture may have been, within the broader cultural landscape, much more nuanced views of the merits of violence existed.[30]

ASHURNASIRPAL, THOUGH, WAS UNLIKELY TO FOLLOW ANYONE who might counsel pacifism. During his reign he conducted at least fourteen military campaigns. He fought in all directions, sparing only Babylonia. In the east he marched three times to the land of Zamua and seized the pass of Babitu (modern Bazian), which provided access to the Iranian plateau. In the north he attacked Nairi and the land of Urartu, which was to become a formidable enemy of Assyria over the following decades. In the west he fought against several Aramaean and Neo-Hittite states located on the eastern bank of the Euphrates, most prominently the kingdom of Bit-Adini, whose ruler, Ahuni, submitted to him several times, although never for good.[31]

Ashurnasirpal's principal strategic goal in all these endeavors was the completion of the "Reconquista"—the restoration of the Assyrian kingdom in its Middle Assyrian borders—that his predecessors had initiated. But unlike Adad-nirari II and Tukulti-Ninurta II, who had often been content with receiving tribute from the petty rulers who had established themselves in the former Assyrian territories, Ashurnasirpal was eager to annex the areas they controlled, turn them into provinces, and transform their main cities into Assyrian administrative centers. With regard to the city of Tushhan, for instance, located on the Upper Tigris, Ashurnasirpal reported, "I took Tushhan in hand for renovation....I founded a palace for my royal residence inside....I took over this city for myself and stored therein barley and straw from the land Nirbu....I resettled (the people of Nirbu) in their abandoned cities and houses and imposed upon their cities more tribute and tax and more corvée than ever before." Elsewhere he noted, "I appointed governors in all the lands and highlands over which I gained dominion; they performed servitude, and I imposed upon them tribute and tax."[32]

By the end of Ashurnasirpal's reign, Assyria had for the most part regained its old borders between the Zagros Mountains in the east and the Euphrates in the west. Outside this area, Ashurnasirpal intervened only once, when he conducted a campaign to the Mediterranean, washed his weapons in the sea, and received presents from various rulers of the kingdoms along the way, including Carchemish, Patina, and Tyre. This unique show of strength, very much in line with a similar campaign conducted during the reign of Tiglathpileser I, apparently did not have any lasting consequences, except for the fact that Ashurnasirpal settled a number of Assyrians in the city of Aribua on the Orontes River in western Syria. But it anticipated the completely new strategic approach that would characterize the foreign policy of Ashurnasirpal's son and successor Shalmaneser III. Under him, military forays into faraway regions would become much more common—with some unforeseen results.

4

The Crown in Crisis

In the 850s and 840s BCE, Assyrian armies began to campaign in territories farther away than ever before. From beyond the Zagros Mountains in the east to central Anatolia in the west, local populations saw themselves confronted with the seemingly unstoppable advance of Assyrian forces. It appeared as though the Assyrian kingdom were finally on its way to gaining uncontested predominance.

But the time was not yet ripe for Assyria to pass the imperial threshold. The far-flung conquests were not consolidated—and, over time, the officers in charge of the Assyrian troops developed a taste for power of their own, weakening that of the crown. Internal unrest and a civil war in the 820s introduced a decades-long period during which Assyria's monarchs were sidelined by other influential figures. By the mid-eighth century, the kingdom would enter a period of crisis and unrest. But this troublesome period was also a turning point for Assyria and a launching pad for greater things to come.

ASHURNASIRPAL II'S SON SHALMANESER III (r. 858–824 BCE) brought new energy to the Assyrian cause when he ascended the throne after his father's death. Over the course of more than three decades, his armies conducted more than thirty military campaigns. Some of the early ones—which usually departed from Nineveh rather than Calah—put the final touches on the restoration of Assyria's traditional territory, a project that had begun less than a century earlier. In 856 BCE, Shalmaneser annexed the kingdom of Bit-Adini and seized its capital, Til-Barsip. Located on an important river ford on the route to the Mediterranean, Til-Barsip was the last major center of Aramaean opposition against Assyria east of the Euphrates. Shalmaneser renamed the city after himself, calling it Kar-Salmanu-ashared, or "Emporium of Shalmaneser"; built a large new palace, which was also used by later Assyrian kings; and relocated a population of native Assyrians into the city. Other cities in the territory of Bit-Adini were likewise renamed and settled with Assyrian colonists, a program of deliberate Assyrianization that was probably a bid to solidify control over a strategically important territory.[1]

One of the cities thus transformed was Nappigi, located a few kilometers west of the Euphrates, which Shalmaneser renamed Lita-Ashur (Power of Ashur). Nappigi can be identified with the later Greco-Syrian town of Bambyke, today's Manbij in the Syrian Arab Republic. In classical antiquity, when it was better known under the name of Hierapolis, the "Holy City," Bambyke was the site of a famous sanctuary dedicated to a powerful deity known as the "Syrian Goddess." A Greek account by the second-century CE rhetorician and satirist Lucian describes the temple and the cult of the goddess in often colorful detail; it refers, for example, to gigantic pillars in the shape of penises standing in the entranceway and scaled twice a year, in memory of mankind's escape from the great flood, by a priest who stayed on top of them for seven days. Particularly noteworthy is the emphasis Lucian puts on the temple's many allegedly "Assyrian" features. Unless Lucian's claims are entirely fictitious, it would seem that Shalmaneser's project of thoroughly Assyrianizing the city of Nappigi had indeed long-lasting consequences.[2]

Shalmaneser's treatment of Bit-Adini and its cities was somewhat atypical of his approach, however. Creating cultural and political homogeneity within a well-defined territory under full Assyrian control would not be a central focus for most of his reign. Very much in contrast to his father, Ashurnasirpal II, Shalmaneser led numerous military campaigns into areas far outside Assyria's traditional borders. The king operated in the Upper Euphrates River valley, in western Syria; in the Van and Urmia basins in the north; and even in places beyond the central Zagros. In 836 BCE, an Assyrian army advanced as far as Hubushna north of the Cilician Gates, one of the westernmost points ever reached by Assyrian troops.[3]

All the while, Shalmaneser showed little interest in annexing any of the remote territories crossed by his armies. Instead, he sought to establish tributary relationships with the states he confronted while allowing them to stay formally independent. At least some of the new Assyrian client rulers seem to have endorsed the relationships thus established, even within their own spheres of power. Luwian, Phoenician, and Aramaic inscriptions from the ninth and eighth centuries written in the names of the kings of Sam'al in the Anti-Taurus Mountains and of Hiyawa/Que in Cilicia speak favorably of the Assyrian overlords to whom these rulers felt beholden. They invoke the parental care, and even the love, putatively shown by the Assyrians, and praise the merging of the local dynasties with the Assyrian royal house. Bar-rakib of Sam'al goes so far as to proclaim, with ostentatious pride, that he had been "running at the wheel" of the Assyrian king's chariot "along with many other kings."[4]

Most of Shalmaneser's campaigns were directed against the Levant. His armies crossed the Euphrates on a regular basis and received the tribute of powerful and prosperous kingdoms such as Sam'al, Patina, Bit-Agusi, Aleppo, and Carchemish. If Shalmaneser's inscriptions are to be trusted, this tribute was often extremely large. King Qalparunda of Patina sent the king, along with other things, "three talents of gold, one hundred talents of silver, and one thousand casseroles of bronze," which is about sixty times the gold, eight hundred and fifty-five times the silver, and twenty-five times the number of casseroles that Shalmaneser's grandfather Tukulti-Ninurta II had once received from Mudada of Sirqu.[5]

But not all the Assyrian actions in the Levant were as success-ful. In 853 BCE, the influential Hadad-ezer, king of Damascus, along with the ruler of Hamath (modern Hama in Syria), brought together an alliance of twelve leading political powers in the Levant and fought a pitched battle against Assyrian troops at Qarqar on the Orontes River. In a famous inscription, Shalmaneser claims that he scored a great victory on this occasion, "damming the Orontes River with the bodies" of the slain enemies. In the following years, however, Assyrian troops had at least six additional altercations with Hadad-ezer, a clear sign that the Battle of Qarqar had not fully es-tablished Assyrian hegemony in the region.[6]

The anti-Assyrian coalition at Qarqar included Ahab, the king of Israel, and Gindibu', king of the Arabs. According to Shalmaneser, the former added two hundred chariots and ten thousand soldiers to the allied troops, the latter one thousand camels. These are the earliest references to named Israelite and Arab rulers in history, and it is worth noting, considering the modern-day tensions between the state of Israel and the Arab world, that in their first joint appearance on the historical stage, we find them fighting side by side. Years after Qarqar, Jehu, a new king of Israel who had ascended the throne in the wake of a bloody coup, brought Shalmaneser gold, silver, and various valuable vessels as tribute. The depiction on Shalmaneser's "Black Obelisk" from Calah of Jehu prostrating himself before the Assyrian king is another "historical first": the earliest known picto-rial representation of an Israelite king. With payments and gestures of submission like the one shown on the Black Obelisk, not only Israel but also many other states in the Levant tried to forestall fu-ture Assyrian attacks.[7]

In line with his propensity to venture beyond Assyria's tradi-tional borders, Shalmaneser also meddled in Babylonian politics.

He intervened on the side of the local king, Marduk-zakir-shumi, helping him quell a rebellion instigated by one of his brothers. Shalmaneser visited a number of Babylonian temples and fought some of Marduk-zakir-shumi's Chaldean enemies in the Mesopotamian south. Back home in Calah, he commemorated his good relations with his Babylonian counterpart in the form of a bas-relief carved on the stone base of his own throne. It shows the two kings shaking hands with each other. For a while at least, the tensions that existed between Assyria and Babylonia were diffused.

ALTHOUGH SHALMANESER WAS NOT PARTICULARLY INTERESTED in—and perhaps also incapable of—placing much additional territory under direct Assyrian rule, his long reign dramatically expanded Assyria's geographic horizons. Assyrian troops were now regularly marching to exotic, faraway places that no Assyrian soldier had ever reached before. The logistical adaptations these campaigns required had significant, and to some extent unanticipated, repercussions. The Assyrian army, previously composed of conscripts recruited on an ad hoc basis during the summer months, began to include special units of professional soldiers, often foreigners who excelled in the use of specific types of weapons. Some of these units were stationed in the capital, at Calah, where Shalmaneser built a gigantic new arsenal, the so-called Review Palace, to store military equipment and house some of the ever more important cavalry horses. But many of the new army units had their headquarters distant from the kingdom's center. They were posted, for instance, in newly created provinces on the northwestern and northeastern edges of the Assyrian kingdom.[8]

These "border marches" were governed by four Assyrian officials whose positions became more and more influential in the course of Shalmaneser's reign. The traditional titles they held do not properly convey their increasingly extensive responsibilities. The Assyrian "field marshal" (turtānu) was in charge of the province that had been created along the Euphrates in the territory of the former kingdom of Bit-Adini and farther north. From here, the Assyrians set off to attack the wealthy lands of northern Syria. The "treasurer" administered a province located north of the modern Iraqi city of Dohuk, and the "chief cupbearer" and "palace herald" operated from provinces adjoining that of the treasurer in a southeastern direction, along the upper valley of the Greater Zab. From there they faced Urartu and various small principalities in the Zagros Mountains.[9]

By providing these officials with well-equipped army units and assigning them "border marches," Shalmaneser was able to react quickly to any kind of disturbance on the Assyrian frontier and launch attacks on lands in all directions. Yet empowering these officials also carried certain risks. The field marshal and his three colleagues were extremely influential. Their elevated position among Assyria's highest civilian and military authorities can be gauged from the new sequence of eponym holders established under Shalmaneser III: the four directly followed the king, preceding the other regular governors of the Assyrian provinces. To be sure, the new masters of the border marches were often eunuchs, who were believed to have little reason to defy the crown, as they had no way to found "dynasties" of their own. But the king's confidence in their undivided loyalty proved to be somewhat deceptive.

As time passed, some of Assyria's highest officials started to develop a dangerous appetite for expanding their political portfolios. The result of their quest for ever more power was a period of instability where several Assyrian kings seem to have been only nominally in charge. As a matter of fact, in some respects the new oligarchy actually reinvigorated the Assyrian state, as many high officials worked hard to develop the regions under their control and enhance their economic productivity. This was a prerequisite for Assyria's eventual rise to imperial glory. But at the same time, to paraphrase William Butler Yeats, "things fell apart—the center could not hold."

THE CRISIS BEGAN DURING THE LAST YEARS OF SHALMANESER'S long reign. The king was an old man by this time, probably in increasingly poor health, and it became impossible for him to lead the annual campaigns of his armies in person. In his stead, his field marshal, an experienced old hand by the name of Dayyan-Ashur, now accompanied the troops as their commander in chief. This alone would not have been that unusual. Truly remarkable, however, is the fact that the royal inscriptions from this period openly refer to Dayyan-Ashur. Up to then, Assyrian royal inscriptions had tended to ascribe all agency to the king, who was by and large the only Assyrian they ever mentioned. Now, however, a report about the Assyrian campaign of 830 BCE against the northern kingdom of Urartu acknowledged the marshal: "In my twenty-seventh regnal year, I (Shalmaneser) mustered my chariots and troops. I issued orders and sent Dayyan-Ashur, the field marshal, chief of my extensive army, to lead my army to Urartu. He went down to Bit-Zamani, entered the pass of Ammash, and crossed the River Arsania." The text then shifts somewhat uneasily between the first-person singular—for the king—and the third-person singular—for Dayyan-Ashur. But the reader is left in no doubt that the credit for leading every Assyrian military campaign undertaken between 830 and 826 BCE actually belonged to the latter.[10]

Even more striking is another text inscribed on a broken statue found during the early years of the Syrian Civil War by villagers at Tell Ajaja, a large mound on the Khabur River in eastern Syria and the site of the ancient city of Shadikanni. The inscription provides a first-person singular account of the last six military campaigns of Shalmaneser's reign. The person speaking, however, is clearly not the king. Even though his name is not preserved, it seems instead that it is Dayyan-Ashur who claims to have led the military activities outlined in the text. A typical passage, introducing, in slightly idiosyncratic orthography, the aforementioned 830 BCE campaign against Urartu, reads, "On my second campaign...I (Dayyan-Ashur) went...to the inner regions of Ulartu." Previously, the king had been the only one allowed to take credit for Assyria's military exploits. The usurpation of the royal "I" by someone else was unprecedented and a clear signal of Shalmaneser's waning authority.[11]

Although Dayyan-Ashur assumed certain prerogatives traditionally reserved for the king, however, he seems not to have openly conspired against Shalmaneser; in fact, he mentions him in the Tell Ajaja inscription as his "lord." But by 826 BCE, other Assyrian officials—and also members of Shalmaneser's own family—had begun to defy the king more openly and even fight against him. The main cause of the unrest was uncertainty about who was to succeed Shalmaneser on the Assyrian throne. While the exact circumstances remain murky, it seems that Shalmaneser had rather suddenly decided to make a younger son of his, the later king Shamshi-Adad V, his crown prince. Understandably, the previously nominated heir apparent, Ashur-da"in-aplu, was not amused by this move and initiated an insurgency. With prominent support from twenty-seven of Assyria's most powerful cities and provinces, including Nineveh, Ashur, Arrapha, and Arbela, he sought to move his younger brother—who operated from his base in the capital, Calah—out of his way. In the end, Ashur-da"in-aplu's rebellion was crushed. When Shalmaneser, in 824, finally died, it was Shamshi-Adad who became king of Assyria.[12]

As the Assyrian Eponym Chronicle candidly notes, Shamshi-Adad's accession did not mark the end of his worries. It took him another long four years of fighting against his internal enemies before the new monarch, backed by various high officials and the Babylonian ruler Marduk-zakir-shumi, finally found himself firmly established as Assyria's uncontested king. By now, however, things were no longer as they had been before. The crown had proven to be weak, and the generals, governors, and court officials at the helm of Assyria's government wanted a larger and more visible role for themselves.[13]

THUS BEGAN THE "AGE OF THE MAGNATES," AS IT HAS OFTEN BEEN called. While Shamshi-Adad V (r. 823–811 BCE) tried to settle in as the new king, his field marshal, Yahalu, and a provincial governor by the name of Nergal-ila'i, who later also became a field marshal, made many of the important decisions. As freely acknowledged in one of Shamshi-Adad's inscriptions, the king's second campaign, to the Nairi lands in the northwest, was led by his chief eunuch, a newly created rank. And many high officials kept their positions much longer now than they had before.

Until around 815 BCE, Shamshi-Adad struggled a great deal and suffered several setbacks. His third campaign to areas in the Zagros Mountains seems to have ended with a defeat. Most of the rulers of the northern Syrian kingdoms withheld their tribute. And in 817 and 816, a revolt in the city of Tillê, located east of the Khabur Triangle and thus alarmingly close to Assyria's core area, raised the specter of renewed chaos. It was only during the last four years of Shamshi-Adad's reign that the overall situation slowly improved. Brazenly disregarding an earlier treaty he had concluded with his Babylonian counterpart Marduk-zakir-shumi, Shamshi-Adad attacked areas under Babylonian control east of the Tigris, conquered the city of Der on the Babylonian-Elamite border, and brought several divine statues from Der to Assyria. Marduk-balassu-iqbi, the new Babylonian king, was sent into captivity in Nineveh. In 812, Shamshi-Adad moved into central Babylonia, where he fought against Marduk-balassu-iqbi's successor while also sacrificing to the gods of Babylon, Borsippa, and Cutha. In the end, Babylonia had been turned upside-down, and the Babylonian throne remained vacant for quite some time.

If all these actions against Assyria's still prestigious, albeit thoroughly exhausted, southern neighbor had restored some of the kingdom's political weight, Shamshi-Adad's death in 811 BCE pitched the kingdom yet again into a state of disarray. Shamshi-Adad's successor, Adad-nirari III (r. 810–783 BCE), was probably still a minor when he ascended the throne, and for several years he would have therefore been unable to take full control of the state. During this time, the actual power seems to have been concentrated in the hands of two other members of the Assyrian elite: the aforementioned "magnate" Nergal-ila'i, and, more remarkably, and with greater long-term repercussions, Adad-nirari's mother, Sammu-ramat.

Sammu-ramat's background and the circumstances that led to her marriage with Shamshi-Adad V are shrouded in mystery. But during the long civil war from 826 to 820 BCE, when her husband, cooped up in Calah, faced a host of deadly enemies bent on destroying him, she must have learned how to be fearless and resilient in the eye of a storm. Whatever the exact circumstances, when Shamshi-Adad died and the young Adad-nirari ascended the throne, Sammu-ramat was ready to take the reins of power.[14]

That Sammu-ramat acted for several years as a kind of "regent" for her son did not find expression in her titles. A stela erected in her honor in Ashur calls her "Palace Woman of Shamshi-Adad, mother of Adad-nirari, and daughter-in-law of Shalmaneser," all conventional designations for the main wife of an Assyrian king and mother of another. But the fact that such a stela was dedicated to her in the first place—and set up with dozens of similar stelae commemorating Assyrian kings and high officials—does show that Sammu-ramat's position was considered unusual. Even more noteworthy is another stela mentioning her, one that was erected, probably in 805 BCE, not in the Assyrian heartland but near the modern city of Maraş in southern Turkey. Reflecting confusion about who was actually in charge, the inscription on the stela uses the first-person singular "I" for Adad-nirari as well as names him in the third person, refers to his mother by name, and also uses "they," third-person plural, for both of them. It reports that "when Ushpilulume, king of the Kummuhites, prompted Adad-nirari, king of Assyria, and Sammu-ramat, the Palace Woman, to cross the Euphrates, I fought a pitched battle with…Atarshumki…of Arpad and with eight kings who were with him at Paqarahubunu.…In the same year, they erected this boundary stone between (the territories of) Ushpilulume, king of the Kummuhites, and Qalparuda…, king of the Gurgumites."[15]

The text describes how the Assyrian leadership, both through diplomacy and by means of war, resolved a border conflict in northern Syria after an Assyrian ally, Ushpilulume of Kummuh, had asked for its intervention. But the many unpronounceable names and the complicated details of the whole affair are not of major concern here. Of greater relevance is the important role the text ascribes to Sammu-ramat: Adad-nirari's mother had accompanied her son on a military campaign across the Euphrates, and she had helped redraw the borders between two powerful states in the Levant. Since no other Assyrian royal inscription from earlier or later times ever credited an Assyrian royal woman with such deeds, there can be no doubt that Sammu-ramat wielded enormous power during Adad-nirari's early years in office.

It probably did not take long for the king to find it somewhat embarrassing that his mother had been so prominent during his early years on the throne. In his later inscriptions, written after Sammu-ramat's death around 800 BCE, he no longer mentions her. And even in the aforementioned stela inscription, one can sense a certain unease about the situation, manifest in the change between the first-person singular in the description of the battle and the third-person plural in the passage about drawing the new border. It was simply contrary to the patriarchal standards of Assyrian public life that a woman should have been so much in the limelight.

In the popular imagination of the time, however, Sammu-ramat's deeds were not forgotten. On the contrary, they became the stuff of legend, with Sammu-ramat morphing into the semifictional, all-powerful, exotic—and erotic—Assyrian queen whom the classical historians of ancient Greece and Rome called Semiramis. The legendary image of Sammu-ramat/Semiramis would shape the perception of Assyria both in Europe and in the Middle East for more than two millennia.[16]

ADAD-NIRARI MAY HAVE BEEN FREED FROM THE INFLUENCE OF his mother once she died, but this did not mean he was fully in command of his kingdom. The "magnates" continued to put limits on the authority of the crown. From about 787 BCE onward, a eunuch by the name of Palil-eresh was the strongman who informally wielded power, governing much of the Assyrian territory on the Middle Euphrates and the Khabur River. The king, in the meantime, was mostly preoccupied with campaigns against the east and the consolidation of Assyria's hold on Western Iran.

A few years before the end of his reign, Adad-nirari installed a new field marshal, a certain Shamshi-ilu, whose family background, like that of almost all the magnates, remains unknown. He soon became even more influential than Palil-eresh. For some forty years, throughout the reigns of the three rather unimpressive kings who successively ruled Assyria after Adad-nirari's death, Shamshi-ilu seems to have been the principal wielder of power in Assyria. Whereas longer inscriptions written in the names of those monarchs are remarkably rare, several texts are known that celebrate the deeds of Shamshi-ilu. Some of them still acknowledge the role of the king. An inscription from the last years of Adad-nirari III, found near Antakya on the Orontes River, is quite similar to the Sammu-ramat stela from the Maraş region: it claims that both the king and his field marshal had been instrumental in the resolution of a local border conflict in the region. The same applies to another border-stone inscription from the time of Adad-nirari's successor, Shalmaneser IV (r. 782–773 BCE). But in a third text, composed toward the end of Shalmaneser IV's reign and inscribed on two colossal stone lions erected in his headquarters at Til-Barsip, Shamshi-ilu takes all the credit for a significant military victory over the troops of the Urartian king Argishti for himself. Claiming to have acted on behalf not of the king, but of "Ashur, the father, the great lord, and the lofty mother of (the temple) Esharra, the goddess Mullissu," the field marshal, writing in third person, proudly declares that he "rushed forth like a terrible storm with the roar of weapons at the ready, which reverberate terrifyingly. Like the Anzû bird, he let fly against him (Argishti) the furious steeds harnessed to his chariot and defeated him. Frightened by the fighting, he (Argishti) escaped like a thief."[17]

No other inscription from this period uses such a well-stocked arsenal of rhetorical figures. Shamshi-ilu clearly presents himself here in almost every respect like a king, with the one exception that he does not claim the royal title. Early on in the text, however, he calls himself "governor of the land of Hatti and the land of Guti and all the land of Namri," indicating that his dominion stretched from the Euphrates River in the west to regions in the Iranian east, and thus far beyond the confines of a single province.

During Shamshi-ilu's years in office, Assyria's political and military fortunes shifted, slowly turning for the worse as disease and climate change began to affect the kingdom. On the one hand, there were significant successes, including a victory against the northern kingdom of Urartu in 774 BCE and Shamshi-ilu's 773 campaign against Damascus, which resulted in the acquisition of rich tribute and prompted Damascus's ruler to send the Assyrian king one of his daughters as a prospective wife. In 754, shortly after the accession of Ashur-nirari V (r. 754–745 BCE), the Assyrian army carried out another victorious campaign against the powerful city-state of Arpad north of Aleppo, forcing its king, Mati'ilu, to sign a treaty acknowledging Ashur-nirari V as his master. A cuneiform copy of the treaty was found among the tablets from Ashurbanipal's libraries at Nineveh. Stipulating that, for Mati'ilu, "our death must be your death and our life your life," it includes a number of grim, sexually charged curses against Mati'ilu should he "sin" against the treaty; in that case, he was to "become a prostitute and his soldiers were to become women."[18]

But the successful campaign against Arpad was an exception. Beginning in the 760s, Assyrian victories became rare, and the kingdom suffered several serious setbacks. There were plagues—the first one possibly brought to Assyria by soldiers who had fought in 765 in the swampy, mosquito-infested marshes of the Orontes estuary in western Syria—and repeated rebellions in various provinces. Under Ashur-nirari V, the Assyrian army lost an important battle against the Urartian king Sarduri II, an event celebrated in one of Sarduri's inscriptions. The local "governors" of Suhu and Mari on the Middle Euphrates, who left inscriptions as well, were apparently able to direct their affairs without any Assyrian interference. And for many years, as the Assyrian Eponym Chronicle records, the king and his troops stayed "in the land," a clear indication that Assyria lacked the means to assert its role as the region's preeminent political power.[19]

MODERN HISTORIANS HAVE STRUGGLED TO ASSESS THE EIGHTY-five years of rule by magnates under a weak crown. Some have argued that the years in question were by and large a period of decline, one that saw a contraction of Assyrian power on almost every front. The "age of the magnates" has been compared to other episodes in world history during which generals, court officials, eunuchs, or harem women usurped power and ushered in "decadent" regimes. The role that the military commander Flavius Stilicho played in bringing about the crisis of the Western Roman Empire at the turn of the fourth to fifth centuries CE, and the impact the "empress dowager" Cixi had on the fall of the Qing Dynasty in China in the early twentieth century, have been cited as historical analogies to the ways in which Shamshi-ilu or Sammu-ramat influenced the course of Assyria's history.[20]

Much in contrast to these cases, however, Assyria's "age of the magnates" did not herald the kingdom's final collapse, but rather its rise to unprecedented imperial dominance. The magnates, it seems, made good use of the autonomy they possessed—for example, by expanding the economic base of the provinces they controlled. Archaeological surveys have shown that the area between the Khabur, Euphrates, and Tigris Rivers saw a substantial increase in settlements from the late ninth century onward, which may have been the result of attempts on the part of regional officials to convert parts of the steppe into agricultural land to grow more crops. The officials were able to do so because the period of increased rainfall that had started around 925 BCE continued—and actually reached new peaks—during the first half of the eighth century.[21]

As far as we know, none of the magnates, not even the most ambitious ones, ever tried to become king. The Assyrian monarchs were weak, but they remained throughout this period the formal heads of the Assyrian state. There were rebellions, but they seem not to have undermined the legitimacy of the ruling dynasty: the man who led an insurrection in Ashur in 763/762 BCE was a member of the royal family. In fact, the role of officials such as Palil-eresh or Shamshi-ilu resembles in many respects that of the Middle Assyrian "grand viziers" who served as viceroys of the kingdom's western territories, a political arrangement from which the Assyrian state profited a great deal.[22]

Even so, it is hard to deny that the last twenty years of the "age of the magnates" were marked by several very serious crises. The key question is how it happened that the phoenix of empire rose from the ashes of these *anni horribiles*.

EMPIRE

5

The Great Expansion

Many historical polities reached universal recognition as empires following long periods of growth. Eventually, after a gradual ramping up, they crossed a threshold that marked the difference between a state and an empire, shifting from a well-defined core territory to sustained centralized power exercised over numerous faraway countries and peoples. This was the story of the Roman and also of the British Empire.

Assyria's story is different—and less straightforward. Immediately before the Assyrian kingdom crossed the imperial threshold, it passed through two decades of political disarray and decline. In an almost ironic twist, it was apparently the traumatic experience of these very years that prompted Assyria's subsequent imperial expansion. The Assyrian Empire was born out of crisis.

Assyria's imperial transformation was brought about between 745 and 705 BCE by Tiglath-pileser III and his two immediate successors, Shalmaneser V and Sargon II, who all ruled over their dominion with an iron fist. The political structures these kings created, from Assyria's far-flung provinces to the state's highly efficient communication networks, would define the Assyrian Empire up to its final days.

THE HISTORICAL NOTES THE ASSYRIAN EPONYM CHRONICLE provides for the years between 765 and 746 BCE are laconic, but there is no ambiguity about the fact that things were not going well. It started off, in 765 and 759 BCE, with two waves of plague ravaging the kingdom. It is hard to establish how grave the situation really was, but earlier Hittite prayers and cuneiform letters from eighteenth-century BCE Mari show how catastrophic and terrifying the outbreak of contagious diseases could be among the people of the ancient Near East. As if a large death toll wasn't enough of a blow to these societies, the measures taken to curb the spread of epidemics could have disastrous consequences of their own.[1]

Mesopotamian authorities attempted to deal with epidemics in part through travel bans. As a letter from Mari states, "Inhabitants of the towns, as soon as they have been touched (by plague), must not enter into untouched towns. Otherwise, it could well happen that they touch the whole country." If similar measures were implemented in eighth-century Assyria, which seems likely, one can easily imagine how they must have paralyzed the kingdom's economy and military readiness.[2]

The hardships caused by the ongoing epidemics in various regions of the Assyrian kingdom were probably instrumental in the outbreak of a number of revolts. In 763 and 762 the city of Ashur seems to have been the center of one of them, and for a while, the head of the insurgents who had taken control of Assyria's religious center claimed the kingship for himself. Additional revolts took place in 761 and 760 in the eastern city of Arrapha, and also in Guzana in the western Khabur Triangle during the plague year of 759. The Eponym Chronicle tells us that the Guzana insurrection was crushed in 758 and that peace was restored, but it was a very uneasy one: the chronicle notes that the Assyrian army stayed "in the land" during seven of the following eleven years. Babylonia was in turmoil during this time as well. A solar eclipse in 763 added to the general sense of doom that must have permeated these years.[3]

Unsettled, racked by disease and unrest, Assyria seemed on the verge of a complete breakdown. But the country was about to experience a dramatic turnaround instead. The restive situation prompted a certain Pulu, in 746 BCE, to embark on yet another re-volt, from which he would emerge under the throne name Tiglath-pileser (III) as Assyria's new king. We know very little about Pulu's background. Like his three predecessors, he may have been a son of Adad-nirari III, but only one of his many inscriptions claims that he descended from that king. Because his name, Pulu, bears some similarity to that of Bit-Pa'alla, an alternative name of the kingdom of Gurgum in northern Syria, it has been suggested that his mother might have been a princess from there, brought by Adad-nirari III to Assyria in the wake of the early campaign he had undertaken with Sammu-ramat, but this is far from certain. Equally speculative is, for the time being, that he was involved in the revolt in Ashur in 763 and 762.[4]

As for the revolt of 746, centered in the capital, Calah, little is known other than its outcome. King Ashur-nirari V disappeared from the scene and, as the Eponym Chronicle puts it, Pulu, or rather Tiglath-pileser, "took the throne on the thirteenth day of the month of Ayyaru" in the year 745 BCE. Few might have expected it at the time, but as it would soon turn out, it was the beginning of a new era.

GIVEN THE DIRE CONDITIONS HE FACED AT THE START OF HIS reign, it is astonishing how much Tiglath-pileser III (r. 744–727 BCE) managed to transform and expand his kingdom within just eighteen years. He fundamentally altered the political landscape of Western Asia.[5]

One of the most sweeping changes he implemented in the do-mestic sphere was to centralize authority by cutting back the power of the "magnates." Of course, the king could not have succeeded in his quest for the throne and his later military endeavors without the help of leading army commanders and administrators. But he made sure that those men would not keep their offices for too long. The particularly significant positions of field marshal, chief cupbearer, and treasurer were given to *homines novi* (that is, men not previously part of the elite class). Those appointed to these influential positions were now no longer allowed to compose inscriptions in royal style, as Shamshi-ilu and other previous magnates had done; indeed, some of those earlier inscriptions, including texts written in the names of Shamshi-ilu and Palil-eresh, were partially erased in an act reminiscent of the Roman practice of *damnatio memoriae* (the elimination of certain individuals from public memory). And from the mid-eighth century onward, the habit of setting up stelae in honor of high officials in the city of Ashur was gradually abandoned. In other words, Tiglath-pileser III's rise to power initiated a period in which more than ever before everything was centered around the monarch.[6]

Almost immediately, Tiglath-pileser also began to resume conducting annual campaigns against foreign enemies—and he did so with a vengeance. Already in his accession year, only three months into his reign, he led his armies to northern and eastern Babylonia, routed several unruly Aramaean tribes close to the Assyrian border, and deported many of their people. One year later, he created the new provinces of Parsua and Bit-Hamban in the Zagros region, establishing a pattern of annexation that would become a defining feature of his reign.[7]

A second phase of Tiglath-pileser's campaigning, in the years from 743 to 738, focused on the kingdom of Urartu and the city-states of northern Syria. In 743, the Assyrian army defeated the Urartian king Sarduri II, forcing him to shamefully flee at night. One of Sarduri's most important allies on this occasion was Mati'ilu of Arpad, whose renewed hostility toward Assyria flagrantly breached the treaty he had concluded with Ashur-nirari V in 754. Tiglath-pileser spent three years besieging Arpad and in 740 finally conquered the city, turning it into the center of another new Assyrian province.

The fall of Arpad triggered a chain reaction, with other states in the region submitting to Tiglath-pileser as well. In 738, the powerful kingdom of Patina (also known as Unqi), as well as Hatarikka and Simirra farther west, were annexed and transformed into provinces. Assyria's direct control now stretched to cities close to or on the Mediterranean—for example, Gabala, modern Jableh near Latakia, and Kashpuna in the area of the modern Lebanese city of Tripolis. Terrified by the rapid expansion of Assyria's power, numerous rulers of other western states, including Rezin of Damascus and Menahem of Israel, brought Tiglath-pileser tribute.

From 737 to 734, Assyrian troops fought again against Urartu, reaching its capital Turushpa, and against regions in Media. Then Tiglath-pileser was back in the Levant. This time, his army marched as far as Philistia and the Egyptian border. Judah, Moab, Edom, and the Arabs sent the king tribute. In the following two years, the Assyrians fought against the forces of Peqah of Israel and Rezin of Damascus, whose alliance is also described in the Bible (from the point of view of Judah, which remained loyal to Tiglath-pileser). The Assyrian intervention ended with the conquest and annexation of Damascus and the partition of the Kingdom of Israel into smaller units, some turned into Assyrian provinces. The remaining rump state of Israel, cut off from the sea, was handed over to a puppet king, Hoshea.

Tiglath-pileser's final years were devoted to the conquest of Babylonia. In 732, a certain Nabû-mukin-zeri, leader of the Chaldean proto-state of Bit-Amukani in the Mesopotamian south, had seized the throne in Babylon. Tiglath-pileser defeated him and in 729 became king of Babylon himself. In additional campaigns against Chaldean strongholds he consolidated his power over the region. Twice in a row, the king participated in Babylon's famous New Year's Festival, which was of preeminent significance for the city's religious identity. Gaining control over the south, and especially the city of Babylon with its enormous cultural prestige, was the crowning achievement of Tiglath-pileser's reign.

WHEN TIGLATH-PILESER III DIED IN THE WINTER OF 727 BCE, Assyria was more than twice as large as it had been at the beginning of his reign. The country's new western border was no longer the Euphrates River but the Mediterranean Sea, and in all other directions the king had made enormous territorial gains as well.[8]

This turn of fortune is nothing but amazing, especially given that the years of plague and internal unrest prior to Tiglath-pileser's reign had been joined by other mounting problems. From the mid-eighth century onward, the "Assyrian megapluvial"—the period of significantly augmented rainfall levels that had started around 925 BCE—slowly came to an end. Annual precipitation decreased substantially, and even though no massive droughts were yet in sight, this must have had an adverse effect on Assyria's agricultural base. Man-made ecological degradation added to the environmental stress placed upon the Assyrian countryside. A craze for ivory on the part of the Assyrian elites led to countless hunting expeditions, which decimated the elephant herds that used to be at home in Syria. Meanwhile, the gigantic building projects sponsored by the crown, as well as the ever-increasing need for firewood as fuel for smelting iron ore, resulted in a depletion of the region's forests.[9]

Based on conventional wisdom, Assyria should have experienced rising political chaos under such circumstances. After all, were not the Antonine Plague of 165–180 CE, the Plague of Cyprian some seventy years later, the Justinian Plague in 541 BCE, and the Late Antique "Little Ice Age" major factors in the decline of the Roman Empire? It is also widely acknowledged that the fall of the Maya civilization around 900 CE and of the Khmer Empire in the fifteenth century, as well as the political crises faced in recent years by countries such as Syria, are in some way related to the effects of climate change. And yet circumstances that led other polities to the point of collapse vaulted Assyria to unprecedented heights.[10]

The apparent paradox disappears if one accepts that history is not governed by deterministic rules. Challenges can be met by adapting to the changes taking place. And that is exactly what Tiglath-pileser did. Taking stock of the loss of life caused by the epidemics of the 760s and 750s in the Assyrian heartland, and realizing that it was hard to boost crop production under increasingly unfavorable ecological conditions, the king decided to implement a new political strategy. He focused on the conquest and annexation of foreign lands, the extraction of their wealth for the greater good of the Assyrian center, and the deportation of hundreds of thousands of people from all areas of the newly expanded realm to replenish the workforce needed to keep the state running. In addition, to make government processes more efficient, the king dismantled the decentralized power structure that had been in place under his predecessors, reserving important decisions for himself.

It was, all in all, a remarkable feat of political and demographic reengineering, though Tiglath-pileser's way out of the crisis can hardly be considered a model for our own time. His violent campaign of imperial expansion and centralization, in fact, might be conceived as a warning about the ways in which "bad actors" can take advantage of the natural disasters that tend to befall humanity. But for better or perhaps worse, it cannot be denied that Tiglath-pileser's new regime secured Assyria's place in the sun for more than a century.

THE TWO KINGS WHO FOLLOWED TIGLATH-PILESER ON THE AS-syrian throne continued the expansionist politics of their influential predecessor. The first, Tiglath-pileser's son Shalmaneser V (r. 726–722 BCE), was originally named Ululayu, after the month Ululu in which he was born. He learned the craft of governing during his time as crown prince, and a number of cuneiform letters that he wrote to his father survive from that time. One of them reveals that he dealt with foreign delegations when the king was out of the country. But the crown prince was also in charge of more mundane matters, including the transportation of ice—needed to cool food and wine stored in underground chambers—with the help of rafts of inflated skins. As this episode incidentally reveals, refrigeration was not an invention of the nineteenth or twentieth century but an age-old technology.[11]

Shalmaneser's accession apparently went smoothly, and even though not a single more elaborate royal inscription from the king's short reign has been recovered, it is clear that he conducted a number of military campaigns. Indirect evidence suggests that he added large territories in northern Syria, Cilicia, and central Anatolia to the Assyrian state and put pressure on the city of Tyre. It is very likely that he also besieged, conquered, and annexed the city of Samaria, capital of what had been left of the Kingdom of Israel after Tiglath-pileser's 732 campaign. That it was Shalmaneser who thus brought an end to Israel's independence is suggested both by the Bible and the Babylonian Chronicle.

In 722 BCE, the year of Samaria's conquest, a new king, Sargon II (r. 721–705 BCE), ascended the Assyrian throne. This time, the transfer of power was apparently much bumpier. In a text from early in his reign, Sargon accuses his predecessor of having imposed taxes and forced labor on the citizens of Ashur, who were traditionally exempt from such obligations, thus angering the god Ashur. Since open criticism of earlier rulers is atypical for Assyrian royal inscriptions, it can be safely assumed that Sargon had ousted Shalmaneser in a coup and now needed reasons to justify this move. Sargon's claim that he resettled "6,300 Assyrians who had committed crimes" to the land of Hamath indicates internal trouble as well—the "criminals" were probably opponents of his power grab whom the king sent to a distant region to have them out of his way.[12]

Like Shalmaneser V, Sargon II seems to have been a son of Tiglath-pileser, but probably from a different wife. In contrast to his (half) brother, Sargon had never served as crown prince. His name, Sharru-ukin ("Sargon" is the biblical version), must have reminded people of the name of the great Sargon (Sharru-kinu) of Akkad, the founder of the first transregional kingdom in Mesopotamian history and a widely celebrated legendary figure. The names of several members of Sargon II's family allude to the moon god Sîn, whose religious center was in the Assyrian-controlled western city of Harran, where Sargon may have grown up or held some important military office prior to becoming king.[13]

The domestic troubles Sargon faced early in his reign were just the beginning of his worries. Many people outside the kingdom's core area had used the period of unrest that followed Sargon's power grab to cast off the Assyrian yoke. In Babylonia, a Chaldean chieftain, Marduk-aplu-iddina (II), had seized the throne, and in the west, a strongman from Hamath by the name of Yaubi'di had assembled a powerful anti-Assyrian coalition of a number of provinces, many of them only recently created by Tiglath-pileser III and Shalmaneser V, including Arpad, Simirra, Damascus, and Samaria.

In 720, more than a year after ascending the throne, Sargon was finally ready to turn his attention to the restoration of Assyrian power over the rebel regions. An Assyrian attack on Babylonia failed to achieve the desired results because Marduk-aplu-iddina received military assistance from Elam. In the west, however, the Assyrians prevailed: Sargon's troops defeated the united enemy troops in a bloody battle on the Orontes River. The rebellious provinces were re-annexed and significant portions of the people of Samaria deported to various places in the Assyrian Empire. Yaubi'di, who had spent the previous two years killing off every Assyrian who happened to fall into his hands, was brought to Ashur and flayed. His skin was preserved with salt and publicly displayed, and the scene was depicted in grisly detail on an Assyrian relief.[14]

Sargon's triumph over the western alliance restored stability and enabled the king over the following years to further expand his realm. After campaigning for two years in Anatolia and Western Iran—home of the ever more important warhorses—Sargon achieved one of his greatest victories in 717, when he conquered the affluent Neo-Hittite city of Carchemish, a commercial hub on the Euphrates River near the modern Turkish-Syrian border. The looting of Carchemish's state treasury funneled so much silver into Assyria's coffers that the copper standard that had previously been in use in the kingdom was gradually replaced by a silver standard. Sargon settled native Assyrians in Carchemish and built a new palace in the city.[15]

In 714, Sargon scored another important victory when he defeated the troops of the Urartian king Rusa I in a surprise attack in the mountainous terrain near Lake Urmia. Sargon celebrated the campaign—which culminated in the plundering of the temple of the Urartian state god Haldi in Musasir—in a long "letter" to the god Ashur that includes some of the most elaborate descriptions of nature to be found in any ancient Near Eastern text. Mount Simirria, for example, is said in the text to "point upward like the blade of a spear" and to be "higher than the mountains where the goddess Belet-ili dwells," with its summit "touching the sky above" and "gorges of the outflows of the mountains deeply cutting into its flank." Clearly, Sargon was deeply in awe of the sublime power of the rugged landscape he and his troops encountered while campaigning in this region.[16]

Between 716 and 713, Assyrian troops also fought against Median principalities in the east, Arab tribes in the southwest, and the Phrygian king Mita—known to the Greeks as Midas and credited with a legendary "golden touch"—in central Anatolia. It'amra, a ruler of the fabled land of Sheba in southern Arabia, and Osorkon IV, the ruler of Tanis in Lower Egypt, brought Sargon presents. Never before had Assyria's geographical horizons been broader.

Sargon's last great triumph was the reconquest of Babylonia in 710, ten years after his botched first attempt at retaking the country. Marduk-aplu-iddina fled to Bit-Yakin, his ancestral homeland in the Mesopotamian south, and then farther on to Elam, which granted him exile. The citizens of Babylon opened their gates to the Assyrian troops, and Sargon was so enchanted by the welcome he received, ostensibly with great enthusiasm, and his encounter with the city's venerable culture and religious traditions that he stayed in Babylon until 707, participating in the New Year's Festival and receiving emissaries from faraway places such as Yadnana (modern Cyprus) in the Mediterranean and Dilmun (modern Bahrain) in the Persian Gulf. During this time, his son and crown prince, Sennacherib, was in charge of government affairs in Assyria.

In 707, Sargon returned to Assyria. According to the Babylonian Chronicle, Assyria was ravaged by plague during this year, which makes the king's decision to return at that moment somewhat surprising. But Sargon knew he would soon be living in a place where he could expect to be safe from the illness wrecking his country. In 706, he moved together with his court to a new capital, named Dur-Sharrukin, or "Fort Sargon." Royal construction crews, including thousands of deportees, had built it from scratch over the previous ten years at the site of the small village of Magganubba, some 16 kilometers (10 miles) northeast of Nineveh. The owners of the land on which the new city rose received monetary compensation for their lost fields or were offered parcels of land in other regions.[17]

One reason for Sargon's decision to relocate to a new capital may have been fear on his part that members of the Calah elite continued to harbor ill feelings toward him. As a usurper, he had to assume that not everyone in the old capital saw him as the legitimate ruler. His lack of trust in Assyria's leading officials may also explain why he relied so heavily on family members for important state business—not only his son Sennacherib, but also his brother Sîn-ahu-usur, for whom Sargon revived the Middle Assyrian office of grand vizier. In this capacity, Sîn-ahu-usur commanded his own military troops, gathered intelligence, and corresponded with other officials about important matters of state. Between 707 and 705, he represented the crown in Babylonia. In Dur-Sharrukin, next to Sargon's massive new residence, Sîn-ahu-usur owned a large palace of his own.[18]

IN THE COURSE OF THE FORTY YEARS FROM THE ACCESSION OF Tiglath-pileser III in 745 to the death of Sargon II in 705, Assyria morphed into a political entity of unprecedented power, size, and complexity. It can be argued that it became the first empire in world history.

This designation is in line with the view of most historians from ancient Greece and Rome, but in modern times it has become a matter of debate. For many more recent scholars, the history of empire begins either much earlier—for example, with the Akkadian kingdom, which was centered in Lower Mesopotamia and lasted from about 2350 to 2150 BCE—or later, with ancient Rome. Others have questioned whether there were any ancient empires at all, and have reserved the term for the "modern" empires that began to emerge around the year 1500, most prominently the British Empire.

Needless to say, the discussion hinges fundamentally on the question of what "empire" actually means. There have been many attempts to define the term. A fairly recent one is by the historian and political scientist Stephen Howe:

> An empire is a large political body which rules over territories outside its original borders. It has a central power or core territory—whose inhabitants usually continue to form the dominant ethnic or national group in the entire system—and an extensive periphery of dominated areas. . . . Diversity—ethnic, national, cultural, often religious—is [an empire's] essence. . . . Empires always

involve a mixture of direct and indirect rule. The central power has ultimate sovereignty, and exercises some direct control, especially over military force and money-raising powers, in all parts of its domain. But there will usually be some kind of decentralized, "colonial," or "provincial" government in each of the empire's major parts, with subordinate but not trivial powers of its own.[19]

This definition lists many of the main features that characterize an empire, but it also leaves some important questions open. It remains unclear, for example, what Howe has in mind when he calls empire "a large political body." How large is large enough—where exactly is the turning point from quantitative to qualitative change that Hegel considered so crucial? And for how long does a powerful hegemonic state have to survive to qualify as an empire—a political entity, that is, that has transitioned from an unstable phase of expansion to a more extended phase of political consolidation?[20]

Though unequivocal answers to these questions are hard to come by, it does seem that the Assyrian kingdom, in the form it assumed during the "Late Assyrian" period—the time from the reign of Tiglath-pileser III onward—fits Howe's definition better than the other candidates for history's first empire. The Akkadian state, for instance, and Egypt's New Kingdom, and the Middle Assyrian kingdom of the thirteenth century can all be seen as "aspirational empires." They had an imperial mission that found expression in ideological declarations—such as the divine command in the Middle Assyrian "Coronation Ritual" that the Assyrian king "expand his land." But they fall short in terms of being large, cohesive, or diverse enough to be considered actual empires. On the other hand, claiming that no premodern state—not even Rome—lived up to the standards required of a true empire reveals a certain modernist bias—and is perhaps more the result of ignorance about ancient civilizations than of analytical acuity.[21]

It is true, of course, that when compared to Rome or the British Empire the Late Assyrian state is not an exact analogue. During the phase of its greatest expansion in the mid-seventh century BCE, the Assyrian kingdom covered a surface of some 822,700 square kilometers (318,000 square miles)—about one and a half times that of modern France. The Roman Empire under Trajan was roughly eight times, and the British Empire, the biggest in history, forty-six times as large. Assyria seems to fall somewhat short in chronological terms as well. It ruled most of Western Asia for no more than about 120 years. The Achaemenid Empire, not to speak of the Roman or the British Empire, lasted much longer.[22]

But despite such limitations, it cannot be denied that beginning with the reign of Tiglath-pileser III, Assyrian statehood possessed many of the hallmarks of empire: a powerful center represented by a strong king; a complex, wide-ranging provincial system; a well-equipped army; mass deportations as a means of breaking up centers of opposition and optimizing the distribution of the labor force; a highly developed communication network based on well-kept roads and routinized information flows; and a great deal of diversity with regard to the cultures, languages, and religions found throughout the state. And the linchpin figure of the whole system was a powerful monarch wielding centralized power.[23]

WITH THE SIDELINING OF THE "MAGNATES," THE ASSYRIAN KING had again become the uncontested center of the Assyrian state. He was head of government and supreme commander of the army, owned a disproportionate share of the state's wealth, served as the final authority on legal matters, and was the high priest of the state god Ashur. To be sure, the actual execution of the decisions the king made lay in the hands of administrative officials, generals, and priests, all personally appointed by him. But beginning with Tiglath-pileser III—and in strong contrast to the previous decades—all public statements about military campaigns, construction work, and other government-sponsored activities were made in the name of the king alone. The only fame high officials were still able to gain was by serving as eponyms—that is, having a year named after them—an age-old practice that remained in place until the very end of the Assyrian kingdom.[24]

The Assyrian monarchs of the imperial period commissioned thousands of inscriptions, many of them long and detailed. But studying these "autohagiographies" of sorts can only reveal so much. To grasp the enormous power the kings held, and the fear their demands instilled in their own officials, it is more instructive to look instead at some of the terse cuneiform letters they wrote. In one of them, Sargon II orders the governor of Ashur—not an unimportant man in the hierarchy of the state—to send seven hundred bales of straw and seven hundred bundles of reeds to Dur-Sharrukin. He declares that the materials must be at hand by the first day of the month of Kislimu, and then continues, "Should even one day pass by, you will die." The statement conveys with somewhat shocking aphoristic brevity that in imperial Assyria, deadlines set by the king were quite literally what the term implies. Another letter is even more graphic. In it, Sargon asks the addressees to bring cavalry horses to a collection point by a specific time, only to add, "Whoever is late will be impaled in his own house, and his sons and daughters too will be slaughtered."[25]

Unlike the monarchs of other periods of Mesopotamian history, Assyrian kings never claimed that they were actual gods. Their written names are not preceded by the divine determinative, and there were no temples specifically dedicated to their cult. But because of their power, the kings were very much perceived as godlike. Comparisons with the sun god Shamash, the paragon of justice, were particularly common, and many Assyrian texts use Shamash's sacred number, twenty, to write the title "king." In 669 BCE, Adad-shumu-usur, a prominent scholar, wrote to King Esarhaddon, "The king, the lord of the lands, is the very image of Shamash"—a statement reminiscent of the Christian motto *Rex imago dei* (The king is the image of God), which defined the political theology of the Middle Ages. In another letter, the same Adad-shumu-usur establishes an interesting tripartite hierarchy that places the king at the intersection between the world of the gods and that of ordinary human beings: "They say thus: 'Man is the shadow of god.' But man is nothing but the shadow of man. The king, he indeed is the true likeness of god." A Mesopotamian myth that distinguishes the creation of the king from that of man seems to point in the same direction. And a royal reinvestiture ritual, performed in the sixth month of the year, applied to the garments and the throne of the king some of the same sacred procedures that were used when a new divine statue was made, bringing about—in the minds of the participants—a eucharist-like transformation of those objects.[26]

Images of Assyrian kings were set up in sanctuaries in central Assyria and in the capitals of Assyrian vassal states and provinces. How exactly they were treated and whether they received regular offerings are not entirely clear, but it is hard to imagine that their presence did not intrigue—and occasionally trouble—those confronted with them. Even without such images, though, the persona of the Assyrian king must have loomed large in the minds of most of the people who lived in the vast Assyrian Empire. In Judah, the traumatic encounter with the Assyrian state machinery may have led to a transfer of qualities of the Assyrian king onto the Israelite god, a crucial milestone in the genesis of biblical monotheism.[27]

WHILE THE KING, IN HIS PALACE IN THE ASSYRIAN CAPITAL, REPresented the center of the Assyrian Empire, its provinces were the units that constituted its larger political fabric. The division of the Assyrian state into provinces went back to Middle Assyrian times. After the crisis years at the turn of the millennium, the rulers of the Reconquista period had restored Assyrian power over the territories lost during the previous decades and reorganized the provincial structure of that region. Shalmaneser had created new "border marches" and assigned them to a number of particularly influential magnates. With Tiglath-pileser III's accession to the throne, some of the larger provinces—for example, Rasappa on the Middle Euphrates and the province of the field marshal—were split up into smaller units. At the same time, Tiglath-pileser massively expanded the Assyrian kingdom by creating new provinces in the east, the north, and especially the west—a process that continued under the kings who followed him. In 670 BCE, the Assyrian kingdom had some seventy-five provinces. Since Assyria was a classical land empire, made up of contiguous territories, none of them were isolated places outside Western Asia.[28]

Prior to Tiglath-pileser, booty acquired during military campaigns, tribute received from vassal kings, and "presents" sent by political allies contributed to a significant extent to Assyria's wealth. These sources of income never entirely dried up, but with the creation of so many new provinces Assyria's government began to rely more and more on the "routinized plunder" of taxes, which were levied on people, livestock, crops, and trade and collected by the provincial governors. Predation morphed into governance. The new system reduced the need for constant military intervention and the use of extreme violence, but led to increased administrative costs.[29]

Provincial governors bore the Assyrian title *pāḫutu* or *bēl pāḫete*, which means "proxy" and indicates that they acted on behalf of the king. The palaces in the provincial centers in which they resided were small replicas of the royal palaces in the Assyrian capitals. To minimize the risk that provinces might become breeding grounds for local dynasties, the position of governor was not hereditary, and many governors of the imperial age were eunuchs. A treaty found at Tell Tayinat on the Orontes, the site of the provincial capital of Kullania, provides a long list of the military and administrative staff that served under the governor of a typical Assyrian province. It mentions "the deputy (of the governor), the majordomo, scribes, chariot drivers, third men (on a chariot), village managers, information officers, prefects, cohort commanders, charioteers, cavalrymen..., outriders, specialists (in various trades), shield bearers, craftsmen, and (other) men (under the governor's authority)."[30]

One of the most important tasks of provincial governors, apart from levying taxes, was to maintain the so-called Royal Road (*ḫūl šarri*); another was to provide road stations (*bēt mardēti*) located within their provinces with personnel, food and water, and transport animals. The Royal Road, specifically designed for the needs of the state, was the empire's main artery for long-distance communication and an early avatar of the famous road system of the Persian period, which is described, and greatly admired, in the writings of the Greek historians Herodotus and Xenophon, among others. In Assyrian times, the Royal Road was for the most part an unpaved, albeit well-kept trail, but where it entered a city, it could take on more representative forms, reminiscent of the wide boulevards used in modern states for political and military parades. A number of stelae that King Sennacherib set up along the stretch of the Royal Road that passed through Nineveh claim that the road in this area was some 25 meters (80 feet) wide—and warn that anyone whose house encroached onto it would be impaled.[31]

The Royal Road enabled the Assyrian king to stay in regular contact with provincial governors and other Assyrian officials in the various parts of the empire. Messages were either entrusted to envoys who traveled all the way from the sender to the addressee, or they were delivered in the form of letters that were handed on in a relay system from one post station to the next. Their carriers traveled on mules, which are sturdy, reliable pack animals and capable of swimming across small rivers. It has been estimated that it would have taken no more than five days during Assyria's imperial period to deliver a letter from Que in the Adana region in modern Turkey to Calah or Nineveh some 700 kilometers (435 miles) farther east.

Not until the advent of the telegraph in the nineteenth century was there a way to communicate with greater speed.[32]

Luckily for modern historians, some 3,000 cuneiform letters from the "state archives" of the Assyrian Empire have been excavated, mostly in Nineveh, but also in Calah. Some 1,200 of them date to the reign of Sargon II; smaller numbers are known from the reigns of the other kings of the imperial period, beginning with Tiglath-pileser III. Altogether, they cover no more than about thirty years, which suggests that only a small fraction of all the state letters ever written have been recovered. The letters have a standardized oblong format. When delivered, they were protected by a sealed clay envelope to make sure no unauthorized person would read them.

The letters can be divided into two major groups: those exchanged between the king and a variety of administrators, army officers, and royal delegates, stationed throughout the empire and charged with political, economic, or military tasks; and a second group of some 400 letters exchanged between the seventh-century kings Esarhaddon and Ashurbanipal and several dozen scholars, priests, exorcists, and physicians, who were physically closer to the rulers and responsible for their health and spiritual well-being. The letters of this second group tend to be more "baroque"—but also more intimate—than the usually terse and businesslike letters of the first type.[33]

Most of the "political" letters deal with serious problems and challenges, such as the strength and movements of enemy troops, economic trouble in the provinces, the management of deportees, or the procurement of building materials. That no one was to bother the king and his high officials with routine affairs and trivial matters is made abundantly clear by one of the few letters that were found with their envelopes still intact. When opened in the British Museum, the letter turned out to be a whining plea from a man who wanted his lost job back. "Why is my lord silent while I keep wagging my tail and run about like a dog?" he complains. "(And this after) I have already sent three letters to my lord." Clearly, by the time the poor fellow was writing for a fourth time, the addressee, a deputy governor, had lost every desire to even open the document.[34]

DURING THE IMPERIAL PERIOD, WITH THE HELP OF WELL-KEPT roads and communication networks, the Assyrian army grew into the most formidable military machine the world had yet seen. Its core was formed by professional soldiers who were organized in units posted all over the empire. Some received their orders from governors and were stationed in provincial capitals, while others were under the direct command of the king and had their headquarters in the Review Palaces of Calah, Dur-Sharrukin, and Nineveh in the Assyrian heartland. Among them were specialized elite troops that had been recruited from particular ethnic groups, similar to the Sikhs in the British army in India. The Aramaean Itu'eans, for example, were used for policing and to suppress revolts, Samarians from Israel provided chariot troops, and Phoenicians and Greeks were in charge of naval operations. The standing armies were supplemented by seasonally levied troops, and Assyrian vassal kings had to provide reinforcements as well. Soldiers received a share of the booty and could expect that the king would take care of them should they be wounded or become permanently handicapped.[35]

Assyria's armed forces specialized in different types of weapons and military equipment. Two-wheeled chariots, the tanks of the ancient world, were used to smash into enemy formations and create holes in the defense line. Initially drawn by two or three and later by four horses, they were manned with a driver, an archer—who also served as commander of the chariot—and one or two shield bearers, who would protect the crew against attacks. Cavalry troops brought speed and mobility to the fray. By the eighth century BCE, mounted archers were able to control their horses without the help of another horseman riding next to them, which greatly enhanced the cavalry's effectiveness. Bowmen operating on foot as long-range fighters and spearmen for close combat played important roles as well. Textual references to commanders who were in charge of ten or fifty soldiers suggest the existence of Assyrian army units of standardized strengths.

Bas-reliefs from Assyrian palaces show that armies on campaign were often accompanied by scribes, who would use their bookkeeping skills, inherited from the long-gone days of the Old Assyrian merchants, for the grim task of recording the number of cut-off heads and the amount of booty. Scouts explored what happened behind enemy lines. Priests and diviners provided spiritual support for the troops, and even the gods, in the form of divine standards set up in ceremonial chariots, were present when an Assyrian army operated far from home.

Military campaigns usually took place during the summer months—after the spring harvest and before the sowing season in the fall. Provincial capitals served as supply depots. Outside the borders of the kingdom, troops often had to go foraging in the countryside. Fortified camps provided soldiers with a safe space to eat and rest. On most occasions, it was enough for the Assyrian army, as large, well equipped, and well trained as it was, to simply arrive on the scene to force enemies into submission or prompt them to escape. Pitched battles with enemy forces seem to have been fairly rare. Sieges of enemy cities were costly in life and resources, but sometimes deemed necessary by the leaders of the Assyrian army, even if they took several years. Troops charged with besieging a city used siege towers, ladders, battering rams, and tunnels to achieve their goals.

Formally, the king was the commander of the army, and in their inscriptions Assyrian rulers often depict themselves as dashing heroes fearlessly throwing themselves against the forces of the other side. Describing a battle in 691 BCE, for example, Sennacherib claims that he "put on armor," "blew like the onset of a severe storm against the enemy on their flanks and front lines," and "filled the plains with their corpses." The reality was considerably less dramatic. In a letter to Sennacherib's son and successor Esarhaddon, a highly placed official writes, "The king my lord should not get close to the fighting. Just as your royal fathers have done, stay on the hill and let your magnates do the fighting." The actual execution of military operations, in other words, lay in the hands of specialists, not the Assyrian king. When the latter participated in a campaign, he was well protected and kept away from the heat of battle.[36]

ONE OF THE MOST SIGNIFICANT CONSEQUENCES OF AN ASSYRIAN army conquering enemy territory was the deportation of significant portions of its local population. The practice of forced population movements is attested since the earliest days of Mesopotamian history, and in Assyria since the thirteenth century BCE. But with the accession of Tiglath-pileser III, it reached unprecedented dimensions. The inscriptions of this king describe some fifty military operations during which people were deported, with a total of nearly 600,000 deportees.[37]

This last number may be somewhat exaggerated, but probably not by that much. Letters from Tiglath-pileser's reign leave no doubt that managing the logistics of deportations loomed large in the minds of many royal officials. In one of these letters, the governor of Arrapha in eastern Assyria acknowledges that he had received an order from the king to "feed the 6,000 captives" he was overseeing. The governor points out that he had told the king earlier that he did not have sufficient provisions at hand, and that keeping them fed would be impossible: "For how long? (They are) 6,000!" But he is willing to work on a solution. He asks that he be supplied with "6,000 (or) 3,000 (ass-loads, that is, possibly ca. 300,000–600,000 liters, or 315,000–635,000 quarts) of barley" and proposes to share the burden of taking care of the captives with other leading officials.[38]

Tiglath-pileser III not only deported more individuals than any king before him but also implemented a crucial change: repopulation. When people from a specific region were relocated to another, they were now often replaced by deportees from somewhere else. This occurred, as a rule, in cases where a conquered territory had been turned into a province, clearly with the objective of securing its continued economic flourishing. Otherwise, deportations had the same main goals as in earlier times: to weaken the identity of recently defeated polities in order to reduce the risk of future resistance; and to add to the labor force wherever this seemed most beneficial, whether on construction sites and workshops in the Assyrian capitals or in the countryside, where relocated people served as tenant farmers on unused or underused land. Unsurprisingly, skilled craftsmen and experts in magic and divination were particularly valued targets of Assyrian deportations. Some deportees were also integrated into the Assyrian army.

Modern scholars have painted sharply different pictures of the Assyrian practice of deportation. Some have focused on its punitive and violent aspects, while others have argued for a more benign interpretation, stressing that people sent by the Assyrians to places far from their homelands were usually allowed to take their families, belongings, and farm animals with them; that they received food, waterskins, and clothes for the journey; and that they became slaves only rarely. Occasionally, as a letter written to Tiglath-pileser by an Assyrian official demonstrates, the Assyrian state even provided newly settled deportees with spouses: "As for the Aramaeans about whom the king has said, 'They are to have wives!'—[we] found numerous (suitable) women, but their fathers refuse to give [them] in marriage, saying, 'Not until they will pay us money (as a bride price).' Let them be paid so that they (the Aramaeans) can get married." To be sure, the women in question clearly had no say in the affair. Yet because of statements like this, it has been suggested that the population transfers implemented by the Assyrians should be labeled "resettlements" rather than "deportations," especially given the associations the latter term has acquired in modern times with ethnic cleansing and genocide.[39]

This view might be overly generous—after all, it cannot be denied that the Assyrians essentially engaged in acts of "bodysnatching" when sending conquered people to locations hundreds of kilometers away from home—and some of their captives did die on the long journeys forced upon them. But it is true that the Assyrian authorities invested significant resources in keeping the deportees alive, apparently because they wanted them to eventually become loyal Assyrian subjects and taxpayers. As the biblical Book of Proverbs puts it, "The glory of a king is a multitude of people; without people a prince is ruined."[40]

To get a better idea of how the Assyrians treated the people they resettled, it is instructive to look at the most famous mass deportation ever carried out in Neo-Assyrian times: that of the people of Israel after the conquest of Samaria in 722 BCE. The episode looms large in the cultural memory of later times because its description in the Bible—in 2 Kings 17—gave rise to the legend of the "ten lost tribes of Israel," told in countless versions and with very different claims about the tribes' eventual whereabouts. The fictional fourteenth-century memoir *The Travels of Sir John Mandeville*, for example, considers the people of Gog and Magog, as well as other nations allegedly confined behind a large wall built in the Caucasus by Alexander the Great, to be descendants of the "lost tribes," and associates their eventual reemergence in the future with the end of days. After the discovery of the Americas, it was argued that the very same tribes were the ancestors of the native populations of the New World. And even in modern times, many people—from the Jews of Cochin, Kashmir, and Ethiopia to the Pashtuns of Afghanistan to a group of African Americans in the United States who identify as "Black Hebrew Israelites"—have claimed descent from the "lost tribes of Israel."[41]

In actual fact, the idea that the Israelite tribes deported by the Assyrians all vanished into thin air, only to turn up again in some fantastically faraway location, is unfounded. The Bible itself specifies their final destinations. As 2 Kings 17:6 states, "The king of Assyria...carried the Israelites away to Assyria. He placed them in Halah, on the Habor, the river of Gozan, and in the cities of the Medes." Assyrian sources confirm this account and provide additional information on the situation in which the deportees found themselves. Halah—or Halahhu, as the Assyrians called it—was the region where Sargon's new capital, Dur-Sharrukin, was located. It is easy to imagine that many of the Israelites who were resettled there worked on the construction of the city. Samarians are also attested in cuneiform documents from Guzana—biblical Gozan—on the Khabur (Habor) River. A legal document from 700 BCE records the sale of a bathhouse by a Samarian from Guzana, and a letter from the late 670s presents testimony by another one against a corrupt scribe and his family. From the "cities of the Medes" in the far east, no written evidence is available, but since it is known that, in 716, Sargon II created two new provinces in the region, there is no reason to question that some Israelites were resettled there shortly thereafter, apparently after having been kept in some other location before. Samarians were also among the highly prestigious chariotry troops stationed in Calah. On balance, it seems that the deported Israelites fared quite well in their new environments.[42]

While the Samarians were transferred to a variety of locations in the heart of the Assyrian Empire and on its eastern borders, people from other areas were newly settled in Samaria and the emptied lands of the former Kingdom of Israel. In 715 BCE, as noted in his inscriptions, Sargon brought to Samaria a number of Arab tribes from the margins of the Syro-Arabian desert. According to the

Bible, Samaria was also resettled with people from Babylon, Cutha, Hamath, and a few other cities, and even though neither Sargon nor any later Assyrian king mentions these population transfers, they may well have happened. To what extent this redevelopment program really led to an economic revival of the region remains unclear. Based on archaeological surveys, it has been argued that Samaria and its hinterland actually suffered a significant decline after the Assyrian conquest of 722. Judah and other polities farther south that became Assyrian client states but were not annexed appear to have fared much better.[43]

WHEN TALKING ABOUT THE SOCIAL AND ECONOMIC INTEGRA-tion of specific groups of deportees, Assyrian kings often claimed that they "counted them with the people of Assyria" and imposed upon them taxes and corvée work "as upon the Assyrians." Such statements indicate that deportees, those from Israel as well as all others, had the same rights and duties as other subjects of the Assyrian kings—and that the term "Assyrian" largely lost its ethnic connotations during Assyria's imperial period. As personal names and other data reveal, the people who lived within Assyria's borders spoke a variety of different languages at this point, including Semitic ones, such as Assyrian, Babylonian, Aramaic, Phoenician, Hebrew, and Arabic; Indo-European ones, such as Luwian and Median; the Afro-Asiatic Egyptian language; and isolates such as Shubrian, Urartian, and Elamite. They also continued to worship their traditional gods. And yet, as long as they paid their taxes, showed up for military duty, and completed the work assignments periodically imposed on them by the state, they were all regarded as bona fide "Assyrians." Cultural reeducation programs and religious indoctrination were not among the defining features of Assyria's imperial ideology.[44]

Of course, where people from very diverse backgrounds come together, as they did in the cities, towns, and villages of imperial

Assyria, they must find a common language in which to communicate. Sargon II acknowledges this necessity when claiming that he made all the different people of his realm "of one mouth." Perhaps his main point here was that his subjects, whatever their origins, now all acted in concert; but the expression also has a linguistic dimension. Remarkably enough, the language that eventually prevailed—and would be spoken by nearly every Assyrian citizen—was not Assyrian. An "Assyrianization" analogous to the "Romanization" of newly incorporated populations in Roman times never took place in Western Asia. Instead, the idiom that became the lingua franca in the Assyrian Empire—and survived its fall—was Aramaic, a humble tongue that carried, at least initially, little cultural prestige. Written in an alphabetic script on leather or papyrus—and increasingly also used within the empire's administration—it would remain the "common language" of the Middle East for nearly one and a half millennia, until the seventh and eighth centuries CE, when Arabic slowly replaced it.[45]

In the mid-seventh century, the Assyrian king Ashurbanipal would claim that the god Ashur "has placed at my disposal all the languages that are spoken from sunrise to sunset." And yet, many people and places remained beyond the umbrella of the Assyrian Empire. Powerful as the empire was, there were still insurmountable roadblocks capable of impeding the Assyrian quest for world domination.[46]

6

On the Edges of Empire

Empire is defined by the space it occupies. In their inscriptions, Assyrian monarchs often called themselves "king of the four corners (of the universe)" or "king of the world." But even during the imperial period, they ruled only a small portion of the Eurasian landmass. True global domination was out of reach for them. The outer periphery of the empire marked a space beyond which Assyria would never venture.

Still, one of the ways in which the Assyrians cast a long shadow on world history is through their neighbors—those who lived on the edges of their empire. Some of these neighbors—Phoenicians, Greeks, Arabs, and Persians—were prompted by their encounters with Assyria to create new forms of political organization, and in time went on to dominate the region themselves.

ALTHOUGH NOT EAGER TO ACKNOWLEDGE IT, THE ASSYRIAN kings knew the limits of their power. They understood that there were regions beyond the area under their immediate control, remote places such as Tarsisi (Tartessus) in modern Spain, Luddi (Lydia) in western Asia Minor, Yaman (Ionia) in the Aegean, Guriana east of Urartu, Qadê in modern Oman, Saba' (Sheba) in modern Yemen, Tema (Tayma) in northern Arabia, or Kusu (Kush) in Nubia on the

Upper Nile. All of these cities and lands are mentioned in Assyrian texts, even though they were separated from the empire by high mountains, deep oceans, and seemingly endless deserts that Assyrian armies were unable to cross.[1]

Assyrian military expeditions would occasionally make forays into the no-go zones on the margins of the empire, but such endeavors were fraught with difficulties. Mountains represented a relatively moderate hindrance for Assyrian troops, but only if they were not too high. In the foothills of the Taurus and the Zagros ranges, the Assyrians managed to exercise political control over extended periods of time. In the rugged territories beyond, however, in Tabal in central Anatolia or Media in the east, they never established their power for long. A short text from the reign of Sargon II's son Sennacherib (r. 704–681 BCE), probably about a military campaign into the Zagros Mountains in 702 BCE, demonstrates how anxious Assyrian kings felt when they found themselves in regions lying at a high altitude: "Across the mighty mountains, ... wherein even the tough trunks of *e'ru*-trees grow flat on the ground and between which a perpetual strong wind never ceases to blow ... where no other living man had ever brought a tent, I myself, together with my troops, travelled with great difficulty."[2]

The desert was far worse. When King Esarhaddon, in 676 BCE, sought to gain control over the land of Bazu on the northeastern flank of the Arabian Peninsula, he had to pass through a region that one of his inscriptions describes as "a district in a remote place, a forgotten place of dry land and saline ground, a place of thirst, one hundred and twenty leagues of desert, thistles, and gazelle-tooth stones, where snakes and scorpions fill the plain like ants."[3]

Crossing the ocean was an adventure the Assyrians were not well prepared for either. In 694 BCE, Sennacherib sent a fleet built by specialists from northern Syria across the Persian Gulf in pursuit of his Babylonian arch-enemy Marduk-aplu-iddina II, who tried to flee to Elam. Sennacherib himself stayed back on the shore. That the king was clearly not ready for a more sustained encounter with the sea is illustrated by his description of how he and his troops pitched camp near the coastal town of Bab-Salimeti: "The high tide of the sea rose mightily, entered my tent, and completely surrounded my entire camp. For five days and nights, on account of the strong water, all of my soldiers had to sit curled up as though they were in cages."[4]

The episode also shows something else, though—that the Assyrians sometimes found ways to overcome the limitations of their own logistical abilities, usually with the help of others. For the naval expedition of 694, Sennacherib tapped the expertise of Syrian shipwrights and Phoenician and Greek sailors, who were put in charge of the operation. Similarly, on the various occasions when Assyrian armies ventured into the desert, they would be guided by Arab tribes familiar with the terrain and capable of organizing the necessary caravans.

Phoenicians and Arabs, and to a lesser extent also Greeks, were peoples in the interstitial realm between the Assyrian Empire and the outer periphery who were useful to the Assyrians for facilitating contacts and economic exchanges with places even farther away. As a reward for these services, the Assyrian kings allowed them to remain engaged in commercial activities of their own, whether in the Mediterranean Sea or along the "Incense Routes" of the Arabian Desert. But the relations between Assyria, on the one hand, and Phoenician city-states and Arab tribes, on the other, were never fully symbiotic, and the partners not entirely equal. The Assyrians siphoned off significant portions of the wealth generated by the long-distance trade the Phoenicians and Arabs conducted, and, especially during the seventh century, tried repeatedly to take full control of Phoenician island-cities, defeat Arab tribes, and conquer remote Arab desert towns.

THE SEMITIC-SPEAKING PHOENICIANS ARE AMONG THE MOST FAmous peoples of the ancient world. Credited by the Greeks with the

ASSYRIA

invention of the alphabet, and renowned for the purple dye drawn from sea snails that they traded far and wide, from the second half of the ninth century BCE onward they colonized large swaths of coastal land in northern Africa and Spain. The founding of the city of Carthage near modern Tunis marked the culmination of their expansion. Throughout the Mediterranean and the Levant, they also traded metals, timber, and a variety of luxury products.[5]

The most important Phoenician cities, located on a narrow strip of coastland on the Eastern Mediterranean shore, were, from north to south, Arwad, Byblos, Sidon, and Tyre. Equipped with natural harbors and flanked on the east by high mountains, each of them developed over time a pronounced maritime culture and a strong sense of independence. In fact, the unifying term "Phoenicians" was never used by the people of Sidon or Tyre themselves—and also not by the Assyrians. Based on the word *phoinix*, which designates the color purple, it was a name applied to them by the Greeks.

Unlike Ugarit, the Phoenician cities managed to survive the crisis brought about by the onslaught of the Sea Peoples in the twelfth century BCE. Largely unscathed by the events, they slowly began to expand their commercial enterprises again and to rebuild their wealth—which attracted the interest of the Assyrians. It was under Tiglath-pileser I (r. 1114–1076 BCE) that Assyria interfered in Phoenicia for the first time. The king received tribute from Byblos, Sidon, and Arwad—and killed a hippopotamus while participating in a boat trip off the coast of Arwad.

When the Assyrians tried to regain influence in the region in the ninth century BCE, they followed the precedent set by Tiglath-pileser: in exchange for substantial payments, they would refrain from attacking Phoenician cities and interfering in their commercial activities. The first time this happened was during the ninth campaign of Ashurnasirpal II (r. 883–859 BCE). The mere presence of his troops was enough to prompt the leaders of various Phoenician cities to send him precious metals, multicolored garments, and other luxury goods, including hippopotamus ivory. Envoys from Tyre and Sidon traveled to Assyria to participate in the great feast held in Calah on the occasion of the inauguration of Ashurnasirpal's new palace.

Under Ashurnasirpal's successor, Shalmaneser III (r. 858–824 BCE), Assyrian raids across the Euphrates became more frequent, which led initially to growing resistance in the region. Byblos was a member of the western coalition that fought against the Assyrians in 853 at Qarqar. But as Assyrian attacks continued—and with them the threat of Assyrian troops blocking land routes, mountain passes, and river valleys that served as arteries of the Phoenician overland trade—the Phoenicians realized that it might be wiser to give in, and to increase the tribute they sent to Assyria. A scene found on one of the bronze bands attached to a gate set up under Shalmaneser's reign in the Assyrian city of Balawat illustrates the new routine: it shows harbor service vessels bringing cauldrons and other valuable items from Tyre, depicted as a walled city in the sea, to carriers waiting on the shore. Phoenician efforts at this time to colonize additional territories in the Western Mediterranean may have been prompted by the need to find new sources of income to compensate for the large payments the Assyrians demanded as protection money.

A NEW, MORE FRACTIOUS CHAPTER IN ASSYRO-PHOENICIAN RE-lations began with the creation of several Assyrian provinces in the western Levant during the reign of Tiglath-pileser III (r. 744–727 BCE). For the first time in history, Assyrian troops and civil administrators were to be permanently stationed in close proximity to Phoenicia's coastal cities—allowing Assyria to interfere in Phoenician affairs more directly. Henceforth, sending tribute to Calah would no longer suffice for Tyre and Sidon and other nearby cities; they also had to pay taxes on their commercial activities. In addition, the

Assyrians created ports of trade of their own—so-called *kārus*—on the Mediterranean shore and manned them with royal merchants.

Under Tiglath-pileser, a certain Qurdi-Ashur-lamur served as governor of Simirra, a new Assyrian province west of the Orontes River and thus close to the Phoenician coast. A cuneiform letter he sent to his royal master at Calah provides a glimpse into Assyria's new strategy toward Phoenicia. In it, the governor tells the king what he had done to keep good relations with the ruler of Tyre while also making sure Assyria would profit from them: "All (his) ports of trade have been released to him; his servants go in and out of these ports of trade and sell and buy as they wish. Mount Lebanon is at his disposal, and they go up and down as they wish and bring down timber. But I collect taxes from anyone who brings down timber, and I have appointed tax collectors over the ports of trade all over Mount Lebanon."[6]

The Tyrians, appreciative of the privileges bestowed on them, were willing to comply with the Assyrian tax demands, but the people of Sidon were apparently less docile. As Qurdi-Ashur-lamur indignantly notes, they had chased the Assyrian tax collectors away. This prompted the governor to send the dreaded Itu'eans against them, special forces entrusted with the suppression of revolts. The frightened Sidonians thereupon gave up their resistance and allowed the Assyrian tax man into their city.

As all this shows, the Assyrians continued under Tiglath-pileser to grant Tyre, Sidon, and other Phoenician merchant cities a significant degree of autonomy so they could send their ships to distant places in the west and engage in the timber trade in the Levant. But the empire wanted a substantial share of the profits. This practice led, before long, to a series of revolts on the part of the Phoenicians, followed by Assyrian attempts to rule the region more directly. In 677, after Sidon had conspired with a number of towns in Cilicia to throw off the Assyrian yoke, the Assyrian king Esarhaddon finally conquered the city. He renamed it after himself, as "Kar-Ashur-ahu-iddina" (Trading Post of Esarhaddon), and turned Sidon and its hinterland into an Assyrian province. Shortly thereafter, he signed a treaty with Sidon's sister city Tyre to secure its compliance.

The treaty, known from a poorly preserved clay tablet found at Nineveh, is not one among equals, but it does acknowledge that the Tyrians continued to hold certain rights. Most importantly, they were allowed to use several Assyrian-controlled harbors along the seacoast, from Akko in the south to Byblos in the north. The treaty's stipulations about the cargo and crews of marooned Tyrian vessels are likewise geared toward the interests of both parties: "If there is a ship of Ba'al (the king of Tyre) or the people of Tyre that is shipwrecked off the land of the Philistines or within Assyrian territory, everything that is on the ship belongs to Esarhaddon, king of Assyria; yet one must not do any harm to any person on board the ship but one must return them all to their country."[7]

While formally acknowledging Tyre's independence, the Assyrians interfered heavily in the city's government affairs. The treaty decrees that an Assyrian "royal delegate" (qēpu) stationed in Tyre had to be consulted every time the Tyrian king or "the elders of your country"—an allusion to the Phoenician-Punic institution of "suffetes," or "judges"—made important decisions. The Assyrians, as this passage indicates, were apparently well aware of the oligarchic system of government that was in place in Tyre.

To dissuade the Tyrians from violating any of its clauses, Esarhaddon's treaty with them ends with a series of curses. One curse in particular, invoking several Phoenician gods, shows again the central importance of Tyre's seabound trade: "May the gods Ba'al Shamaim, Ba'al Malagê, and Ba'al Saphon raise an evil wind against your ships to undo their moorings and tear out their mooring pole, may a strong wave sink them in the sea and a violent tide rise against you!"

King Ba'al, it seems, was not impressed by this threat. In 671 and then again in 663/662, he rebelled against the Assyrians, who defeated him on both occasions but left him on the throne—probably because they knew full well that without any naval expertise of their own, ruling Tyre directly was not, in fact, in their very best interest.

THE LETTERS OF QURDI-ASHUR-LAMUR NOT ONLY PROVIDE IN-formation on the Phoenicians, but are also the earliest Assyrian documents to mention the Greeks. The term used for them by the governor—and also in other Assyrian texts—is Yamnaya or Yawnaya, that is "Ionians," a name from which the designation for Greeks in modern Arabic and Persian, Yūnāni, is derived as well.[8]

Credited with the "invention" of Western civilization, Greeks tend to feature in modern debates as pathbreaking philosophers, powerful poets, or accomplished artists. From the perspective of Qurdi-Ashur-lamur, though, they were little more than raiders and looters, similar to the Sea Peoples some 450 years earlier. In one of his letters, probably from shortly after 738 BCE, Qurdi-Ashur-lamur describes how the "Yawnaya" had launched a naval attack on the cities of Samsimuruna and Harisu on the Eastern Mediterranean coast, but had returned to their boats empty-handed when he arrived with his troops. Inscriptions from the reign of Sargon II paint a similarly negative picture. In a poorly preserved passage in his "Annals," the Assyrian king talks about a naval battle, in 715 BCE, against Greek pirates who had pestered Tyre as well as Que in Cilicia, now an Assyrian province: "In order to vanquish the Ionians, whose abode is in the middle of the sea, and who since the distant past had killed the people of the city of Tyre and the land of Que and had interrupted commercial traffic, I went down towards them to the sea with ships from the land of Hatti (northern Syria) and struck them down with the sword, both young and old."[9]

But Assyria also collaborated with some of the Greeks—who at the time busily colonized large swaths of the coastline of Anatolia and other regions in the Mediterranean. In 738, Tiglath-pileser III conquered "the city of Ahtâ, a port of trade on the seashore and a royal 'storehouse.'" "Ahtâ" could very well be the Assyrian rendering of the Greek word *akte*, which means "headland" or "cape," and may have been the ancient name of the site of Al-Mina, located in the Orontes estuary close to the Mediterranean shoreline. Abundant amounts of Greek pottery found at Al-Mina suggest that the site was home to a colony of Greeks, many of them probably traders. Al-Mina was connected through the Amuq plain with the land of Patina/Pattin and from there, via Carchemish, with northern Mesopotamia and the Assyrian core territory. The city was hence well suited to serve as a commercial hub linking the Aegean world with the Assyrian Empire. In a similar way, Tiglath-pileser later turned the city of Gaza, on the southern end of the Eastern Mediterranean shore, into a port of trade for commerce with Egypt and the Arabian Peninsula.[10]

THE LAST DECADES OF THE EIGHTH CENTURY MARK THE BEGINNING, in ancient Greece, of the so-called Orientalizing Period. Animals and monsters depicted on Greek vases—and many other features of Greek civilization—were now characterized by a strong eastern influence. In all likelihood, Al-Mina was one of the places that facilitated this cultural transfer from east to west.

As material goods and artistic styles from the East started to circulate more widely at this time, so did Near Eastern religious ideas and literary motifs. Some may even have reached the great poet Homer, who is believed to have lived around 700 BCE. A case in point is a reference in Homer's *Iliad* to "Oceanus, from whom the gods are sprung, and mother Tethys." As first recognized in 1890 by the British prime minister William Gladstone, an enthusiastic amateur classicist, the watery genealogy charted in this line is reminiscent of the beginning of the Babylonian Epic of Creation, popular also in Assyria, which portrays Apsû, the cosmic underground water, and

Tiamat, the primeval sea, as the parents of all the other gods. The name "Tethys" may even be derived from "Tiamat." Several phrases in a poetic account by the Assyrian king Sennacherib of a battle fought in 691 BCE at Halulê near Samarra have been compared to verses in the *Iliad* as well. Sennacherib states, for example, that "the swift thoroughbreds harnessed to my chariot plunged into floods of (my enemies') blood," so that its wheels "were bathed in blood and gore"—which brings to mind an equally graphic passage in the *Iliad* about Hector's horses trampling the corpses of the fallen and spattering his chariot "with gobs of blood thrown up from horses' hooves and chariot wheels."[11]

A direct link between Sennacherib's Annals and the *Iliad* is difficult to prove, of course, and one must beware of the temptations of "parallelomania." Homer was hardly an Assyrian eunuch living in Cilicia, despite recent attempts to substantiate such a scenario. That the Assyrians had some influence on the Greek world, undoubtedly, for the most part, through intermediaries, is nonetheless plausible. At the same time, the Greeks began to make their mark in regions east of the Mediterranean, including Assyria. Sennacherib manned the boats he sent across the Persian Gulf in 694 BCE with Greek sailors, and an apparently Greek mercenary by the name of "Addikritushu," that is, Antikritos, served in eastern Mesopotamia during the reign of Sennacherib's successor, Esarhaddon. A Phoenician silver bowl found at Amathus on Cyprus depicts Greek hoplite fighters along with soldiers with a pronounced Assyrian look in the act of attacking a Near Eastern city. As all these cases show, the practice of using Greek mercenaries as reinforcements for eastern armies clearly goes back to Assyrian times, even though it is better known in connection with the Neo-Babylonian and Achaemenid Empires—with the ten thousand fighters serving under the Greek general Xenophon in the army of Cyrus the Younger being the most famous example.[12]

UNLIKE THE PERSIAN KINGS DARIUS I AND XERXES WHO WOULD later rule over an empire of their own, the Assyrians never tried to conquer any of the more remote Greek islands or any part of the Greek mainland. From the reign of Sargon II onward, they showed, however, great interest in the island of Cyprus—or Yadnana, as they called it—an important center of the copper trade located not far from the Levantine coast in the Eastern Mediterranean. Cyprus, it seems, was at this point under the (indirect) control of the Phoenician city of Tyre. In 707 BCE, while residing in Babylon, Sargon II received gold, silver, and other precious gifts from a delegation of seven unnamed kings from "Ya', a region of (Y)adnana, whose abodes are situated at a distance of seven days' journey in the middle of the sea." The emissaries had arrived in the wake of a military intervention in Cyprus by Shilta, king of Tyre, who probably had some Assyrian support on the occasion.[13]

In 1845, local workmen discovered a large stone stela with a cuneiform inscription of Sargon at Kition, not far from the Cypriot city of Larnaca—the westernmost point that has ever produced an Assyrian monumental inscription. The stela seems to have been erected to mark the oversight Assyria claimed over Cyprus and may have been brought there by the very Cypriotes who visited Sargon in 707. Given the considerable weight of the monument, transporting it to its final destination must have been an extremely arduous task. Even though Cyprus's local population was unable to read it, encounters with the stela may have triggered the emergence in Cyprus of a tradition of monumental inscriptions in the local syllabic script, whose beginnings can be traced back to the end of the eighth century.[14]

Over the next decades, the Assyrians became better acquainted with Cyprus's complicated political landscape. An inscription from the later years of Esarhaddon mentions the names of ten "kings of Yadnana" who had supplied building materials for the construction of Esarhaddon's new armory at Nineveh. Two of them were

Phoenicians, but the others, including Ekishtura (Akestor) of Idalion, Pilagurâ (Philagoras) of Chytroi, Ituandar (Eteanthros) of Paphos, and Ereshu (Aretos) of Soloi, clearly had a Greek background. Along with that of the aforementioned Antikritos, theirs are the earliest Greek personal names attested in cuneiform.[15]

It was during this time that Assyria's political elites looked farther west than ever before or after. In one of his latest inscriptions, Esarhaddon proudly proclaims, "I wrote to all of the kings who are in the midst of the sea, from Yadnana (Cyprus) and Yaman (Greece) to Tarsisi (Tartessos in modern Spain), and they bowed down at my feet. I received their heavy tribute. I achieved victory over the rulers of the four quarters (of the world)." Esarhaddon clearly exaggerates the influence he exerted on the remote places mentioned in this passage, and Assyrian hopes to control the entire Mediterranean would never come to fruition. But for a short moment in history, it seemed as though there might be a chance for Assyria to reinvent itself one more time—as an enormous maritime empire.[16]

IN NOVEMBER 656 CE, AISHA, THE WIDOW OF THE PROPHET MUhammad, directed a small army from the back of her camel against the troops of her opponent, Muhammad's son-in-law Ali ibn Abi Talib. The "Battle of the Camel" near Basra, which ended with a defeat for Aisha, would become a fabled event in Islamic historiography.

Some 1,400 years earlier, in 733 BCE, the barren region south of Damascus had seen a battle that seems in some respects almost like a prefiguration of Aisha's military adventure at Basra. Tiglathpileser III, one of the combatants, describes it in his Annals as follows: "(When fighting with) Samsi, queen of the Arabs, at Mount Saqurri, I defeated 9,400 (of her people). I took away from her 1,000 people, 30,000 camels, 5,000 (pouches) of all types of aromatics, her military equipment, and the staffs of her goddesses. To save her life, she set out like a female onager (a kind of wild ass) to the desert, a place of thirst. I set the rest of her possessions and her tents within her camp on fire." The parallels between the two events are striking. In both instances, an Arab woman led armed men on the northern edges of the Arabian Desert into combat against the troops of a powerful male opponent. And a bas-relief from Tiglath-pileser's palace in Calah seems to show that Samsi, just like Aisha, was riding a camel when she eventually fled the scene.[17]

The Assyrian kings of the Neo-Assyrian period repeatedly interacted with the Arabs, who lived like the Phoenicians and the Greeks on the imperial periphery. They appeared in many ways to the Assyrians to be strange and exotic—not least because most of their leaders at the time were, in fact, women. To be sure, the first Arab ruler to be mentioned in an Assyrian text—a certain Gindibu' (from Arabic *ğundub*, "locust"), who fought alongside the Israelites against Shalmaneser III in 853 BCE at Qarqar—had been a man. But by the second half of the eighth century, ruling "queens," as they were called by the Assyrians, had become the linchpins of the system of government employed by the leading Arab tribes. Assyrian royal inscriptions provide information on several of them. There were Zabibe and Samsi, Arab queens during the reigns of Tiglath-pileser III and Sargon II; Yati'e and Te'elhunu, active in the time of Sennacherib, the latter attacked by Sennacherib's troops near Adummatu (modern Dumat al-Jandal in northern Arabia) and brought to Nineveh as a captive; Tabu'a, an Arab hostage at the royal court at Nineveh who was sent back to her homeland by Esarhaddon to rule over the Arabs with Assyrian interests in mind; Yapa' and Baslu, the respective rulers, under Esarhaddon, of the cities of Diḫranu (modern Dhahran) and Ihilum in eastern Arabia; and finally, Adia, an Arab queen during the reign of Ashurbanipal, who accompanied her husband Yauta' on at least one campaign.

By the time of Ashurbanipal, the taste of the Arabs for female leaders seems to have waned a bit, and most of their political and military leaders were now men. Altogether, though, the role of powerful women in the Arab world of the eighth and seventh centuries

BCE is nothing but astonishing. The Assyrian title ascribed to them, *šarratu*, that is, "queen," was otherwise used only for goddesses—even the influential Sammu-ramat, wife of Shamshi-Adad V and mother of Adad-nirari III in the ninth century BCE, did not bear it.

How exactly the Arab queens governed is largely unknown. There are no texts from the Arabian Peninsula that provide first-hand information on Samsi and the other female leaders. Te'elhunu appears in Assyrian texts with religious titles, but as the presence of several Arab queens on the battlefield shows, it would be wrong to consider the role of these women as merely ceremonial. For the Assyrians, who lived in an environment largely ruled by patriarchal norms, being confronted with a society in which so much power lay in the hands of females must have been a source of endless fascination. Encounters with Arabs are the topic of a great many Assyrian royal inscriptions and even a letter to the god Ashur.

But there are also signs that the Arab "gynocracy" prompted strong resentment among some Assyrians. This is most apparent from a bas-relief prominently placed in the throne-room suite of Ashurbanipal's North Palace in Nineveh. The relief shows an attack by Assyrian troops on an Arab camp and depicts several Arab women being killed or tortured by the raiders next to their tents. In a particularly gruesome scene, initially interpreted as a rape, it seems as if two Assyrian soldiers are ripping open the body of an Arab woman to kill her fetus. Assaults on women must have occurred in ancient Near Eastern warfare on a regular basis—a curse against oath breakers in Esarhaddon's Succession Treaty asks that the goddess Ishtar "make your wives lie in the lap of your enemy before your eyes." Nowhere else on Assyrian reliefs, however, are acts of violence against the female population depicted. If an exception was made in the case of Arab women, then this can hardly be separated from the fact that women played so central a role in the political affairs of the Arab tribes.[18]

THE ARABS WERE EXOTIC IN THE EYES OF THE ASSYRIANS IN other respects as well. Like the Phoenicians and the Greeks, they were a people on the margins of the empire that possessed the ability to connect with even more remote areas. But rather than crossing the ocean with ships, as the Phoenicians and Greeks did, the Arabs crossed the vast arid regions of southern Syria and the Arabian Peninsula with their camels—the "ships of the desert."

Camels are closely associated with the emergence of the Arabs as a people. Indeed, it was the large-scale introduction of domesticated dromedary camels around the turn of the millennium that catapulted the Arabs onto the world stage. Capable of traveling some 30 kilometers (18 miles) per day through desolate tracts of land without needing food or water, while carrying loads weighing up to some 100 kilograms (220 pounds), camels enabled the Arabs to traverse previously impassable stretches of desert over distances of sometimes more than 2,000 kilometers (1,250 miles). They were thus used to transport incense, spices, precious stones, and other valuable items from locations in the southern part of the Arabian Peninsula to the Mediterranean and Mesopotamia. The trade was enormously lucrative and made those engaged in it fabulously rich.[19]

The earliest reference to the Arab caravan trade is found in an inscription of Ninurta-kudurri-usur, an independent mid-eighth-century BCE ruler of the small state of Suhu on the Middle Euphrates. The ruler mentions a raid he launched against a caravan organized by the people of Tayma in the Hejaz and Sheba in modern Yemen. The intercepted caravan may well have been on its way to (or returning from) Assyria, which, as time went by, became an ever more important destination for the luxury goods procured by the Arabs. It is telling that when Sennacherib, in the 690s, built a new wall around the city of Nineveh, one of its monumental gates, the "Desert Gate," received the ceremonial name "The gifts of the people of Sumu'il and Tayma enter through it."

Sumu'il was the name of an Arab tribal confederation led by the Qedarites. Its center was the aforementioned city of Adummatu, an oasis town in the Wadi Sirhan in northern Arabia. In the Hebrew Bible, Sumu'il is represented by Ishmael, Abraham's unloved son, who was sent away to the desert together with his mother, Hagar. Material evidence for the goods traded by Sumu'il is available in the form of several onyx and agate beads found in Sennacherib's palace at Nineveh. The cylinder-shaped objects are inscribed with cuneiform texts indicating that they were "booty from Adummatu," where Assyrian troops must have seized them when conquering the city in 690 BCE.[20]

These were not the only beads that reached Sennacherib from the Arabian Peninsula. Others were brought to him as "audience gifts" by Karib'il Watar, a powerful Sabean ruler known from an inscription left by him near modern Marib in Yemen. Direct contacts between Assyria and Sheba had been initiated under Sennacherib's father, Sargon II, who claims to have received presents from Karib'il's uncle Yita"amar Watar. Both Sabean rulers sought to be on good terms with the Assyrians to make sure they would not interfere in their long-distance trade, as Sheba's economic well-being depended on it.[21]

HOWEVER PROFITABLE THE COMMERCIAL EXCHANGE BETWEEN the Arab world and Assyria may have been, relations between the two sides were far from cordial. From early on, the Assyrians were troubled by the freedom the Arabs enjoyed. Sargon regarded them as people "who know neither overseer nor governor," and was annoyed by their repeated acts of insubordination, which included a raid on the Babylonian city of Sippar and another on a caravan that carried booty from Damascus to Assyria. As a result, Sargon strictly forbade the sale of iron to the Arabs—an early attempt to prevent the proliferation of materials for producing weapons.[22]

During the eighth century, the Assyrians repeatedly attacked Arab caravans and temporary camps that Arabs had set up in southern Syria and Babylonia, but did little to interfere in Arab affairs more directly. Tiglath-pileser III tried to place a royal delegate at the court of Queen Samsi, but it seems unlikely that the delegate had much influence there. In the early seventh century BCE, however, a notable shift took place in Assyria's attitudes and "Grand Strategy." The kings became more interventionist toward both the Arabs on their southern flank and the Phoenicians. All of a sudden, Assyrian armies began to operate deep inside the Arabian Peninsula.

One result of this new policy was the conquest of the oasis town of Adummatu under Sennacherib and the subsequent capture of the Arab queen Te'elhunu. Never before had an Assyrian army penetrated so far south. The measures Sennacherib took to subdue the Arabs included the removal of the statues of six Arabian deities, among them Attarsamayin, a celestial goddess probably identical with Al-Lat (of *Satanic Verses* fame); Nuhay, a solar deity; and "Ruda," that is, Orotalt, whom Herodotus identified with Dionysus. They were all brought to Assyria.

Transforming the Arab territories into Assyrian provinces proved impossible, however, and Esarhaddon, Sennacherib's successor, thought it wise during his first years in office to return to the use of more indirect means to control the region. In a gesture of goodwill, he repatriated all the divine statues his father had "godnapped"— albeit only after having put on each of them an inscription praising the god Ashur and the power of the Assyrian king. Along with the statues, he sent the Arabs of Adummatu a new queen, an Arab woman by the name of Tabu'a, who had grown up as a hostage at the court of Nineveh.

For a little while, this arrangement seems to have worked to everyone's satisfaction. A new leader, by the name of Haza'il, and then his son Ya(u)ta, joined Tabu'a as rulers of Adummatu and the surrounding areas, and the Assyrians received from them rich tribute in the form of camels, donkeys, gold, precious stones, and aromatics. But before long, the Arabs threw off the Assyrian yoke again, and warfare resumed. On more than one occasion, first under Esarhaddon and then under Ashurbanipal, Assyrian armies attacked Arab towns and camps, pursued fleeing enemies, and replaced hostile Arab leaders with putatively more congenial ones. At one point, Ashurbanipal claims, he made so many Arabs prisoners and captured so many camels that gardeners, brewers, and tavern-keepers in Assyria were paid with camels and captives—a statement that, while clearly hyperbolic, displays a keen sense of the phenomenon of inflation. Diplomacy was used as well to pacify the Arabs. A cuneiform treaty between Ashurbanipal and the Qedarites, known from a fragmentary clay tablet from Nineveh, can be seen as an attempt to "domesticate" the members of this tribe by integrating them into established systems of international security.

In the end, these military operations and diplomatic efforts produced little result. At no point during the seventh century BCE did the Assyrians ever manage to take full control of large swaths of the Arabian Peninsula, and the constant campaigns in far-off desert regions proved a drain on their resources. Arabs supported Ashurbanipal's faithless brother Shamash-shumu-ukin, the king of Babylon, when he sought to gain independence from Assyria in 652, and participated—if later Greek historians are to be believed—in the final attack that brought the Assyrian Empire down.[23]

EVEN THOUGH THE TERRITORIES OF THE ARABS WERE NEVER incorporated into the Assyrian Empire, it seems as if the repeated encounters between the two sides had a profound effect on Arab material and political culture. Recent excavations at Dumat al-Jandal, ancient Adummatu, have unearthed a substantial quantity of ceramics that imitate Assyrian wares, and the iconography and style of a number of bas-reliefs from Tayma and Sheba display Assyrian features as well. Assyrian influence can also be detected in the inscriptions the Sabean leaders Yita''amar Watar and Karib'il Watar left at Sirwah in modern Yemen, more than 2,000 kilometers (1,240 miles) away from Calah and Nineveh. Contemporaries of Sargon II and Sennacherib, respectively, both rulers had sent emissaries to the Assyrian court, who, while staying in the Assyrian capitals, must have seen the monumental sculptures and inscriptions celebrating Assyrian kings. Apparently, this left such an impression on them that attempts were made to extol the Sabean kings in comparable ways. It can hardly be considered a coincidence that both the late royal inscriptions of Sennacherib and Karib'il's Sirwah inscription include the same basic elements: an introduction naming the ruler and his titles; a report about his military campaigns, in both instances numbering exactly eight; and an account of building work completed. In Karib'il's case, this last section includes improvements to the local irrigation system, a topic also covered in several inscriptions from the reign of Sennacherib.[24]

The repeated confrontations with Assyria seem to have prompted some Arab tribes to also make changes to their system of government. During the reigns of Esarhaddon and Ashurbanipal, the female leaders of the Qedarites were gradually replaced with male leaders—a shift that can most likely be seen as an attempt on the part of the Qedarite Arabs to adopt ruling structures more compatible with the male-dominated character of Assyrian kingship. One cannot help but notice the irony that at the same time, Assyria's political landscape was experiencing changes of its own that went very much in the opposite direction: royal women suddenly began to play much more important roles in government affairs than in previous decades. Is it possible that female agency within Assyria's leading circles increased around 690 BCE because of Assyrian encounters with Arab queens? If so, this would be another example of the complex interdependencies that exist within empires between the inner and outer spheres. The imperial center tends to reshape the periphery—but every so often it also mimics it.

THE WESTERN AND SOUTHERN EDGES OF THE ASSYRIAN EMPIRE traced the Mediterranean Sea and the Arabian Desert, hundreds of kilometers away from the Assyrian capitals of Calah, Nineveh, and Dur-Sharrukin. In the northeast and southeast, however, Assyrian imperial control did not extend nearly so far. The military campaign that Tiglath-pileser III led in 739 BCE against the land of Ulluba was directed against a region located not much more than 70 kilometers (40 miles) north of Nineveh. The barrier that blocked Assyria's eastward expansion into the vast stretches of the Iranian highlands was the Zagros range, a mountain chain whose highest elevations run along the modern border between Iraq and Iran. Crossing these mountains represented a major challenge to Assyrian armies.[25]

The people living in the valleys of the Zagros Mountains raised cattle and bred horses, the latter urgently needed by the Assyrians for their military. Due to the rugged nature of the region, for a long time its political landscape remained extremely fragmented. The most famous people with roots in the Zagros were the Persians, who have dominated Iranian culture and politics for the past two and a half millennia. The Medes, another ethnic group originating in this region, were destined for fame on the world stage as well, eventually playing a decisive role in the fall of the Assyrian Empire. But their unification under Cyaxares happened at a very late point, probably not prior to the last decades of the seventh century BCE. Before that, their vast territories were split into numerous small units ruled by local strongmen.[26]

At least initially, Assyria's interventions in the Zagros region were centered on a far less prominent polity: the kingdom of Mannea with its capital Izirtu, a buffer state between Assyria and Urartu to Mannea's north, in what is today Iranian Kurdistan. The material culture of Mannea was less sophisticated than that of the Assyrian core area or of the cities and kingdoms of the Levant. Still, Mannea was home not only to villages but also to a number of larger towns, and there is evidence that the people living in some of them made great strides in adopting the artistic and scribal traditions of their western neighbors. This is most prominently demonstrated by archaeological finds from the 1970s at Qalaichi Tepe in Bukan County in Iran, a site that has been identified by some scholars with the Mannean capital Izirtu. A fragmentary stela from Qalaichi, inscribed in Aramaic and referring to a treaty concluded with an unknown partner, exemplifies Mannea's participation in the system of international relations of the time. Images of winged bulls and lions found on a number of glazed bricks once belonging to a columned hall are testimony to the impact of Assyrian artistic conventions on Mannea's visual culture.[27]

Unsurprisingly, the cultural influence that Mannea, and the Zagros region in general, exerted in turn on Assyria was far more limited. But it is noteworthy that Ahura Mazda, the supreme deity in early Iranian religion—a god prominently mentioned in the royal inscriptions of the Persian kings of the late sixth and fifth centuries BCE as well as the holy writings of Zoroastrianism—is first attested in seventh-century Assyria. According to an administrative text from the reign of Ashurbanipal, he received regular food offerings in the city of Ashur, along with numerous other deities from Assyria and abroad.[28]

Some of the early Persians who worshipped Ahura Mazda seem to have lived in a territory the Assyrians called Parsua, which was located between Mannea in the north and the Great Khorasan Road that connected Mesopotamia with central Iran. The earliest reference to Parsua is found in inscriptions of Shalmaneser III, who campaigned in the region in 843 and then again in 834, when he received the tribute of no fewer than twenty-seven "kings." In 744, Tiglath-pileser III turned Parsua into an Assyrian province, ruled by a governor who resided in the town of Nikkur. In 714, Sargon II added territories to the province that had previously belonged to the neighboring land of Gizilbunda. Briefly threatened under Esarhaddon by raids undertaken by Cimmerians and Scythians, Parsua remained an integral part of the Assyrian Empire at least until the reign of Ashurbanipal, when it is attested for the last time. In 2008, the discovery of an Iron Age cemetery in the region of modern Sanandaj—which might have been part of Parsua—cast some light on the province's material culture. The grave goods found in the tombs included fibulae (clasps or brooches), seals, and vessels for the consumption of wine, items the local elites may have cherished because they wanted to imitate Assyrian practices.[29]

But were the inhabitants of the land of Parsua in the central Zagros really the ancestors of the later Persians? The two names are strikingly similar, but questions remain. Most notably, as linguistic analysis reveals, only a few of the names of the cities and rulers of Parsua mentioned in the Assyrian sources include elements clearly identifiable as Iranian. Parsua seems to have had a multiethnic population that included speakers of both Iranian and non-Iranian languages. The region where the Persians, probably after prolonged migrations, really entered the world stage lay elsewhere: in the land east of the kingdom of Elam that was later known to the Greeks as Persis, and subsequently as Farsistan or Fars.[30]

Even though Assyrian troops never reached this distant country, it is again Assyrian texts that provide us with some of the earliest glimpses into its history. Apparently, the region was known to the Assyrians as Parsumash, a name that occurs for the first time in a fragmentary cuneiform letter from 707 BCE. The letter reports that the king of Elam had tried to recruit military units from Parsumash to attack an unknown enemy, perhaps Assyria. A few years later, in 691, soldiers from Parsumash fought alongside Elamite, Babylonian, and other troops against Sennacherib's army at Halulê near Samarra.

The breakup of Elam under Ashurbanipal in the 640s facilitated the establishment of more direct contacts between Parsumash and Assyria. Sometime around 640 BCE, a king of Parsumash by the name of Kurash sent his son Arukku to Nineveh to pay his respects to the Assyrian monarch. This Kurash must have been an ancestor of the renowned Persian king Kurash (or Cyrus) II, who, in the 530s—almost exactly one hundred years after Arukku's visit—established the Persian Empire and became famous in Western historiography as Cyrus the Great. It may well be that Arukku learned something about empire-building while staying at Ashurbanipal's imperial court at Nineveh—and passed it on to his descendants.

THE ASSYRIAN KING SENNACHERIB WAS THE PROUD RECIPIENT of a good number of onyx and agate beads from Adummatu in northern Arabia and Sheba in modern Yemen, and had them inscribed with the names of the places from where they originated. Similarly inscribed beads found in Sennacherib's palace at Nineveh had come from the Phoenician city of Samsimurruna in the west and from the Sealand on the Persian Gulf. Since almost all these beads were perforated when they were discovered, it is evident that they were originally strung on cords or chains. We do not know what the purpose of these chains may have been. They might have served as necklaces and been worn by royal wives, or even by the Assyrian king himself; as amulets attached to chariots or thrones in need of magical protection; or as offerings to the gods placed in foundation deposits located under the floors of Assyrian palaces or temples. But whatever their exact function, one thing is clear: the chains represented the circle of lands found on the edges of the Assyrian Empire, and thus symbolized the unlimited power the Assyrian monarchs claimed for themselves over the known world. As King Esarhaddon later put it in one of his inscriptions, "The one who fled into the sea to save his life did not escape my net. The swift runner who took to the stepped ridges of the mountains, I caught him like a bird. I ripped out the roots of the Suteans who live in tents in remote places (in the desert). From the midst of the sea, my enemies spoke thus: 'Where can the fox go to get away from the sun?'"[31]

In truth, the foxes of the Neo-Assyrian period were actually not entirely without shadowy dens where they could hide. Imperial Assyria was powerful, but not so powerful as Esarhaddon would have liked. The desert, the sea, and the mountains represented obstacles that Assyrian armies, despite Esarhaddon's protestations to the contrary, were often unable to overcome. Conditions at home, too, were not always as rosy as Assyrian royal propaganda would have it.

7

A Ghost Story

From the reign of Tiglath-pileser III onward, power in Assyria was concentrated in the hands of one person: the Assyrian monarch. When rulers were up to the task, this centralized leadership system had the potential to strengthen the empire's cohesion and prevent it from fracturing. But the system also had certain structural weaknesses, chief among them the issue of succession. The moment when power transitioned from one king to the next resulted in chaos and instability in the empire on several occasions.

One such crisis broke out after the untimely death of King Sargon II (r. 721–705 BCE), an event that led to a great deal of anxiety in the kingdom, shattering, at least temporarily, the belief of Assyrian elites in their divinely mandated imperial mission. What happened in the wake of this dramatic episode is a story worth telling, not only because of its effect on the collective psyche of Assyria's leading circles, but also in light of the strange way in which it is reflected in the Bible—and even, indirectly, in later Christian traditions.

SARGON II WAS ONE OF ASSYRIA'S MOST SUCCESSFUL CONQUER-ors. Once he had quelled the rebellions that had broken out after his accession, his reign saw triumph after triumph. Under his leadership, the Assyrian Empire became richer and more powerful than it had ever been before. But the king's sad end nearly negated every one of these achievements.

We will probably never know exactly what happened when Sargon II embarked with his army in the summer of 705 BCE on a campaign from which he was not to return. Normally filled with lengthy accounts about military endeavors undertaken by their kings, Assyrian royal inscriptions in this case are silent. No detailed account of the campaign has ever been found, and probably none was ever written: official Assyrian sources, eager to stress seamless continuity from one Assyrian king to the next, as a rule avoid any reference to the death of the ruler.

What is known is that Sargon's 705 campaign was directed against Tabal, a large, mountainous, and unruly region in central Anatolia. Earlier in Sargon's reign, Tabal had been an Assyrian vassal, first under a king by the name of Hulli and then under Hulli's son Ambaris. Getting a foothold in Tabal seemed so important to Sargon that he gave one of his daughters, Ahat-abisha, to Ambaris in marriage. A few years later, however, to Sargon's great chagrin, his brother-in-law threw off the Assyrian yoke. Assyrian troops eventually defeated Ambaris and forced his ally Mita (known from Greek tradition as Midas) into submission. But the political situation in Tabal remained volatile. A ruler called Gurdi or Kurti continued the fight against the Assyrian aggressor, and Sargon decided, in 705 BCE, to attack the region again.[1]

Only one year earlier, Sargon had moved the royal court from Calah to Dur-Sharrukin, the new capital he had built at enormous expense on the site of the small village of Maganuba northeast of Nineveh. The new foundation covered almost 300 hectares (740 acres) and was surrounded by a massive wall 7 kilometers (4.3 miles) long. The king took up residence in Dur-Sharrukin in a gigantic new palace that stood alongside several large temples on a terrace 12 meters (40 feet) high overlooking the northern part of the city wall.

Sargon was some sixty years old at this point. He could have left military operations in the hands of his generals and stayed in his new home, enjoying the fruits of his impressive previous campaigns. But for reasons about which one can only speculate—perhaps lack of trust in the military leadership or an undying sense of adventure—the king decided to lead the campaign against Gurdi himself. This turned out to be a fatal mistake.

Whether by means of a nightly attack, like the one undertaken a few decades later by the Mannean king Ahsheri against Sargon's great-grandson Ashurbanipal, or in some other fashion, Gurdi's troops managed to seize the Assyrian camp. The Assyrian ruler was killed—but that was not all. An Assyrian text probably written more than twenty-five years after the event, during the reign of Sargon's grandson Esarhaddon, adds a devastating detail. The remaining Assyrian troops were unable to recover Sargon's body and so the king remained unburied.

This was a major calamity. In one of his inscriptions, Sargon himself, deeply horrified, had bemoaned a similar case in 714 BCE in the area of Mount Waush, near Lake Urmia, when the insurgent Bagdatti of Wishdish had left the body of the Assyrian ally Aza of Mannea unburied on the battlefield. In retribution, Sargon had ordered Bagdatti flayed on the spot where the crime occurred. Now the Assyrian king himself had met the same fate as Aza.

BURIAL PRACTICES IN ASSYRIA AND BABYLONIA VARIED SIGNIFI-cantly, but it was an almost universal belief that the dead had to be interred underground. In the case of the kings of Assyria, burial was commonly in large stone sarcophagi deposited within vaulted subterranean tombs in the Old Palace in Ashur, a practice that continued even after that city had lost its status as Assyria's political capital. Modern archaeologists have uncovered several of these sarcophagi. All had been plundered in ancient times, but a cuneiform text from Nineveh describes in some detail the original richness of these royal burials. Probably composed on the death of King Esarhaddon, the text begins with a lament, stressing that even nature was upset by the demise of the ruler: "The ditches wail, the canals respond, all trees and fruit-bearing plants are mourning." It then lists a variety of grave goods destined for the king's tomb, including a bed of ivory and silver, ten horses, a chariot with golden trappings, thirty oxen, three hundred sheep, and numerous precious garments. Once the king had been laid to rest, the text adds, his coffin was carefully closed and sealed.[2]

There were many reasons, practical and spiritual, for these traditions. By sealing the coffin the Assyrians sought to prevent people from tampering with the earthly remains of the king and stealing the grave goods deposited inside. But they also wanted to guarantee that the royal body would not be able to leave its final resting place and haunt the living. If they were not properly buried, Assyrians believed, the dead—especially if they had been abandoned on the battlefield after being killed there—would do just that: find their way back to those they had known in life and punish them with sickness, misery, or death. Numerous ritual texts against the ghosts of the dead are known, both from Assyria and from Babylonia, and if these ghosts were the spectral remains of a powerful ruler, the dangers for the living were, of course, particularly great. A Jewish legend with possible roots in Mesopotamian folklore reports that to make sure his dead father, Nebuchadnezzar II, would not return, the Babylonian king Amel-Marduk (r. 561–560 BCE) cut the body into three hundred pieces and fed them to three hundred vultures.[3]

When news of Sargon's disastrous death reached Assyria and his body was not brought home for burial in one of the vaulted tombs in Ashur's Old Palace, it appears that many members of the Assyrian elite were gripped by anxieties. One member of this elite was Nabû-zuqup-kenu, a scholar and diviner from Calah, who bore the title of scribe (tupšarru) but clearly had more political influence than this modest appellation suggests. He hailed from an important family of royal advisers, one of whom, Gabbi-ilani-eresh, had been chief scribe of the Assyrian kings Tukulti-Ninurta II and Ashurnasirpal II in the ninth century. Nabû-zuqup-kenu himself had a son and grandson who later successively held the same position at the courts of Esarhaddon and his son, Ashurbanipal. As part of such a lineage, Nabû-zuqup-kenu was likely a close adviser to the crown during the reigns of the preceding two kings, Sargon II and his son and successor Sennacherib. That Nabû-zuqup-kenu was the author of a number of royal inscriptions of these two kings is suggested by a clay tablet from his library that lists uncommon words included in some of these inscriptions.[4]

On the twenty-seventh day of the month of Du'uzu (IV), 705 BCE, Nabû-zuqup-kenu copied the twelfth and final tablet of the Epic of Gilgamesh, the most famous literary text known from ancient Mesopotamia. The epic recounts the deeds of Gilgamesh, king of Uruk, who starts off as a tyrant oppressing the men and women of his city, but who later turns into a hero, defeating, together with his friend Enkidu, the monstrous Humbaba, guardian of the cedar forest. Eventually, after Enkidu's death and a long pilgrimage to the edges of the world, Gilgamesh becomes a sage, receiving antediluvian knowledge from the only survivor of a great deluge, a man named Utanapishti.[5]

The twelfth tablet of the epic, the one Nabû-zuqup-kenu was interested in, is a somewhat awkward appendix to this compelling story. It reports how Enkidu goes down to the netherworld to retrieve two of Gilgamesh's playthings, a stick and a ball, that had fallen into the abode of the dead through a hole. Enkidu's plan to return with them from his infernal journey is thwarted when, in defiance of Gilgamesh's advice to keep a low profile, he draws attention to himself by wearing beautiful clothes and making a lot of noise. Ereshkigal, the pale-faced and bare-breasted queen of the netherworld, forces Enkidu to stay in her realm. But the gods grant

Gilgamesh a final encounter with his friend, who is briefly allowed to depart from his infernal abode to speak to the king of Uruk about the rules of the netherworld. The final lines of the tablet—and the last ones copied by Nabû-zuqup-kenu on this summer day in 705—recount the conclusion of this conversation, with Enkidu outlining the fates of anonymous individuals who met unfortunate ends:

> (GILGAMESH): Did you see the one who was killed in battle?
> (ENKIDU): I saw him. His father and mother honor his memory,
>   and his wife weeps over him.
> (GILGAMESH): Did you see the one whose corpse was left lying in
>   the open countryside?
> (ENKIDU): I saw him. His ghost does not rest in the Netherworld.
> (GILGAMESH): Did you see the one whose ghost has no provider
>   of funerary offerings?
> (ENKIDU): I saw him. He eats the scrapings from the pot and
>   crusts of bread that are thrown away in the street.[6]

The death scenarios sketched out here read very much like a description of the fate of Sargon. It seems extremely likely that Nabû-zuqup-kenu studied the passage—and probably all of Tablet XII of the Gilgamesh Epic—to explore what the death of his king actually meant. News of the event, or at least rumors about it, must have reached him in Calah a short time before. The conclusions Nabû-zuqup-kenu drew from his study of Enkidu's final words cannot have been pretty. That the ghost of his royal master, just a few days earlier the most powerful man on earth, seemed now to be roaming the streets in search of discarded food was a scenario that must have deeply troubled the scribe.

Every year during the last few days of the month of Du'uzu, the people of Assyria and Babylonia celebrated the dead by performing rituals in honor of Tammuz, a deity who had died but for those days was allowed to return from the netherworld. The news of Sargon's death had reached Nabû-zuqup-kenu just a few days before these rituals culminated in the so-called release of Tammuz. Most likely, Nabû-zuqup-kenu and the chief priests of Assyria used the Tammuz ceremonies that year to appease the ghost of their deceased ruler. It is clear, however, that this was not enough to cope with the terrible fate that had befallen the king—a fate that threatened to affect his heir and successor as well.

This heir, Sargon's son and crown prince, was Sennacherib, between thirty-five and forty years old at the time. Sennacherib was deeply disturbed by his father's sudden inauspicious death. Indeed, he may initially have refused to believe the news. This would explain references to Sargon rather than Sennacherib in a number of short clay-cone inscriptions dated slightly later than Nabû-zuqup-kenu's copy of Gilgamesh XII—that is, after news of Sargon's death became widely known. The inscriptions record new building work on the temple of the god Ashur:

> For Ashur, father of the gods..., Sargon, king of the world, king of Assyria..., renovated Ehursaggalkurkura, the temple of Ashur, plastering the walls of the towers of the whole building, and creating friezes, pedestals, and glazed clay cones for those towers.... He did this...to preserve his life, to enjoy long days, to rule firmly, and to defeat his enemies. Month of Abu (V), eponymate of Nashir-Bel, governor of Sinabu (i.e., 705 BCE).[7]

The text seems to reflect a desperate hope on the part of Sennacherib and certain members of Assyria's political and religious elites that Sargon might yet return from his ill-fated campaign against Tabal. But soon enough, any faith in such an outcome had to be abandoned. On the twelfth day of Abu, the same month listed in the inscription, Sennacherib ascended the Assyrian throne.

SHOCKED AND TRAUMATIZED BY SARGON'S FATE, SENNACHERIB seems to have felt a strong need to distance himself from his fallen father and predecessor—whose end he considered a cruel punishment inflicted by the gods. Most tellingly, he never moved to Dur-Sharrukin. The gigantic new city was not entirely abandoned, but its short spell as Assyria's capital was over. Instead, Sennacherib relocated the royal court to Nineveh, where over the next fifteen years he pursued an ambitious building program that turned the city into the largest urban center ever created in ancient Near Eastern history—even larger than Dur-Sharrukin.

Positioned near a ford across the Tigris, Nineveh had been an important city for centuries, and it is possible that Sennacherib also had strategic reasons for residing there. But the king must have been primarily motivated by the fear that the ghost of his dead father would continue to haunt Dur-Sharrukin. His move guaranteed that he would avoid contamination from whatever Sargon had touched there. When writing about the construction work in Nineveh, Sennacherib's scribes plagiarized elements of Sargon's inscriptions, yet they never mentioned his name. Even a stela from Ashur that Sennacherib dedicated to his mother, Ra'ima, includes no reference to her husband, Sargon.[8]

Sennacherib tried to erase the memory of his father in other ways too. In the course of restoration work in the Ashur Temple, Sargon's workmen had used glazed bricks to produce images of some of the king's military campaigns along one of the temple's terraces. When Sennacherib renovated these terrace walls, his own construction workers proceeded randomly and sloppily when reassembling the bricks, and eventually raised the temple forecourt in such a way that it concealed the images of Sargon's military endeavors altogether. Sennacherib did not want them displayed in the empire's holy of holies.

Early in his reign, in 702 BCE, Sennacherib was involved in another building project: the reconstruction of the temple of Nergal in the city of Tarbisu, a few kilometers north of Nineveh. As the god of war, death, and destruction, and the husband of Ereshkigal, the terrifying queen of the netherworld, Nergal was the deity with the closest links to the fate of Sennacherib's dead father. A long inscription that commemorates Sennacherib's work on this sanctuary—apparently composed by none other than Nabû-zuqup-kenu—does not mention Sargon by name, but Sennacherib must have had him in mind, and may have hoped for some kind of redemption, when he inaugurated the newly restored temple. He sacrificed "massive bulls and fat sheep" to regain Nergal's favor.

Sennacherib also sought revenge. In an attempt to penalize Gurdi, the Kulummaean leader responsible for Sargon's death, in 704 BCE an Assyrian army headed back to Tabal. Since yet another royal death in battle would have thrown the Assyrian state into complete disarray, Sennacherib chose not to participate in this campaign. The expedition seems to have ended in failure, for it is not mentioned in any royal inscriptions, and its only record is in a poorly preserved note in the Assyrian Eponym Chronicle. Nine years later, in 695, another Assyrian army, again led by generals and not the king, was more successful. It conquered the city of Til-Garimmu, possibly modern Gürün in Turkey's Sivas Province, which was governed by a ruler named Gurdi—likely the same man who had defeated Sargon. Parts of Til-Garimmu's population were deported, and the divine statues of the city's temples were brought to Assyria. Gurdi, however, escaped for good—and thus the devastating blow he had dealt to the Assyrians ten years earlier remained forever unpunished.

Based on the available evidence, it appears that Sennacherib felt unable to openly acknowledge and process what had happened to Sargon. The anxieties produced by the traumatic experience of the events of 705 BCE seem to have stayed with the king and over time triggered certain psychotic syndromes. A letter from the reign of his son and successor Esarhaddon mentions that Sennacherib was frequently so enraged that none of his diviners dared tell him of any untoward sign they had observed, and adds that the king struggled with the "*alû* demon," often mentioned in cuneiform texts alongside spirits of the dead. Though not entirely clear, the supposed affliction caused by this demon appears to have been some mental disturbance. It does not require too much of a stretch of the imagination to connect this to Sennacherib's inability to cope with Sargon's death.

DESPITE ALL HIS ATTEMPTS TO DISTANCE HIMSELF FROM THE negative aura of his father, Sennacherib met a violent end as well: he was killed in 681 BCE by a group of insurgents that included one or more of his own sons. His successor, Esarhaddon, who was probably not involved in the plot, was now left with the burden of having to deal with the brutal and inauspicious deaths of not just one but two kings: his father, Sennacherib, and his grandfather Sargon.

Consulting with his scholarly and scribal advisers, Esarhaddon took a strategy diametrically opposed to Sennacherib's to face this situation. Rather than repressing the past, he addressed it relatively openly. Esarhaddon's inscriptions regularly mention the names of his immediate forebears, referring to himself as "son of Sennacherib" and "grandson of Sargon." Later inscriptions even include an account of the murder of Sennacherib, although what had actually happened remains somewhat vague.

It is another text, however, called by modern scholars "The Sin of Sargon," and known from a fragmentary clay tablet from Nineveh, that offers the most intriguing insights into Esarhaddon's efforts to explain the violent deaths of his two predecessors. In it, a dead Sennacherib addresses the reader from the Great Beyond to explain what had happened to him and his father. The scene thus echoes the famous episode two centuries later in Aeschylus's *Persians*, the earliest preserved Greek tragedy, in which the ghost of the Persian king Darius is conjured up to explain the causes of the humiliating defeat of his son Xerxes against the Greeks in the Battle of Salamis.[9]

In *The Persians*, Darius suggests that Xerxes had triggered the fiasco by neglecting the god Poseidon, destroying foreign sanctuaries, and carrying off their divine statues. The text about the "Sin of Sargon" similarly identifies religious offenses as prompting the disasters that had befallen Esarhaddon's predecessors. It begins with Sennacherib pronouncing that, while he was pondering the deeds of the gods, "the death of Sargon, my father, who was slain in the enemy country and who was not interred in his house occurred to my mind." Sennacherib goes on to assemble a number of haruspices, splits them into groups, and asks them to perform liver divination to investigate "the sin of Sargon, my father." The text is badly broken in this section, but the haruspices apparently determine that it was Sargon's neglect of the Assyrian gods and his exaggerated enthusiasm for the gods of Babylonia that had brought about his fate. Sargon had indeed shown great admiration for Babylonian culture, so the charge was not without merit. Sennacherib then claims that he sought to rectify the imbalance identified by the diviners as the cause of Sargon's death, but that his own scribes prevented him from proceeding with his plans, whereupon he, too, had to die.

With this story, Esarhaddon had furnished an intriguing historical-theological explanation for the violent deaths of his two predecessors. Each had failed in his own way to show proper respect to the gods. At the same time, Esarhaddon had found an excellent justification for his own new religious politics of maintaining a balance of power between Ashur and Marduk of Babylon.

The tale of Sargon's and Sennacherib's religious mistakes was apparently put to use in a more practical way as well, as suggested by a poorly preserved clay tablet from Nineveh inscribed with a text similar to the "Sin of Sargon." A subscript explains that the text had been copied from stone slabs laid out in the temple of Ashur on which the king, most likely Esarhaddon, used to prostrate himself to kiss the ground before the Assyrian state god. All this suggests that Esarshaddon had left an inscription recounting the fates of Sargon and Sennacherib in the very heart of Assyrian statehood—the Ashur Temple in Ashur—and had embraced what had happened to his predecessors in the most literal sense possible. It is hard to imagine a more powerful effort to exorcise the past than this newly invented ritual of repentance, clearly aimed at breaking the fatal cycle of violent royal deaths.

THE DEATH OF SARGON TROUBLED AND DISTRESSED ASSYRIAN rulers, priests, and scholars for decades. Outside Assyria, reactions were understandably quite different. The people who had suffered from Assyria's aggressive expansionism had little reason to mourn their chief tormentor. How they viewed the monarch's downfall is most impressively illustrated by a mocking dirge on an unnamed "king of Babylon" found in Chapter 14 of the biblical Book of Isaiah. While it is not entirely certain that Isaiah's Babylonian king is to be identified with Sargon, compelling arguments support this assumption: the biblical prophet Isaiah was a contemporary of Sargon and Sennacherib; Sargon was not only king of Assyria but also of Babylonia; and, most importantly, Isaiah claims—immediately bringing to mind the dire fate of Sargon—that the king mocked by him had died violently without proper burial: "All the kings of the nations lie in glory, each in his own tomb; but you are cast out, away from your grave, like loathsome carrion, clothed with the dead, those pierced by the sword."[10]

For Isaiah, the fall of the enemy ruler is a reason not for sadness but for jubilation: "How the oppressor has ceased! How his insolence has ceased!" In sharp contrast to the Assyrian text that claims that even the trees were in mourning when a king died, in Isaiah they do just the opposite: "The whole earth is at rest and quiet; they break forth into singing. The cypresses exult over you, the cedars of Lebanon, saying: 'Since you were laid low, no one comes to cut us down.'"[11]

Not only because of its poetic qualities, one section of Isaiah's indictment of royal hubris deserves particular attention. In verse 12, the prophet exclaims, "How you are fallen from heaven, Bright one, Son of Dawn (Hebrew *hêlēl ben šāḥar*); how you are cut down to the earth, you who laid the nations low." Given the enormous power the Assyrian kings of the eighth and seventh centuries BCE possessed, Isaiah's use of a cosmological metaphor to characterize the taunted, ill-fated monarch does not come as a great surprise. Several Christian interpreters of Isaiah 14, however, were unwilling to consider this metaphor as a mere trope—they took it literally. The most important of them was the early Christian scholar Origen of Alexandria (ca. 184–ca. 253 CE). He read the whole passage through the lens of a famous verse in the gospel of Luke (10:18), which refers to "Satan falling from heaven like a flash of lightning." Isaiah's *hêlēl ben šāḥar*—translated as Heosphoros (Dawn-Bringer) in the Septuagint, the Greek translation of the Hebrew Bible, and as Lucifer (Light-Bringer) in St. Jerome's Latin Vulgate—thus became one of the archetypes of a new, highly influential Christian reconceptualization of the forces of evil, in which Satan, a minor nuisance in ancient Israel, was promoted to the status of a fallen angel of enormous power.

This image of Satan has been planted in the minds of Christians ever since. The history of religious thought is full of strange turns, but few new ideas in this sphere have been as serendipitous as the emergence of the devil from a dubious interpretation of a cosmological metaphor used in the Hebrew Bible to characterize an unlucky ancient Near Eastern king killed on the battlefield—a king who, in all likelihood, was none other than Sargon II.

THE ASSYRIANS AND THEIR KINGDOM LEFT AN INDELIBLE MARK on foundational biblical stories. While Sargon remains anonymous in Isaiah's mocking condemnation of an oppressive king, another episode in Isaiah, also known from 2 Kings and from Chronicles, talks about an Assyrian king much more openly. That king is Sargon's ill-fated son and successor Sennacherib. In 701 BCE, twenty years prior to his violent death, Sennacherib had invaded the Kingdom of Judah and threatened to seize the city of Jerusalem. It was also the time when the two foremost powers of the age, Assyria and Egypt, met each other for the first time in a major battle.

For the biblical authors, these were events of great importance, and the stories they had to tell about them—stories to which we now turn—would for centuries shape how the Assyrians were remembered in East and West alike.

8

At the Gates of Jerusalem

On a fateful day in the late summer or fall of 701 BCE, an Assyrian general known as the "Rabshakeh" was standing by the conduit of the upper pool near the northern part of Jerusalem's city wall. He was waiting for envoys from the city. The Rabshakeh had a message to convey—a message that would deeply disturb Eliakim, Hilkiah, and Shebnah, the three high officials whom Hezekiah, the king of Judah, had sent outside to negotiate with him. What the Rabshakeh had to say to them meant that Jerusalem was facing its last days as the capital of an independent kingdom. King Sennacherib of Assyria would take over, and resistance was futile.

The Rabshakeh's message was vivid with menace. If Hezekiah thought he could rely on Egypt, the Rabshakeh noted, he would be making a grave mistake. Egypt was a "broken reed of a staff, which will pierce the hand of anyone who leans on it"—it would certainly not be able to help the Judean king. And if Hezekiah hoped that a divine intervention would save him, he was mistaken as well. "Is it without the LORD that I myself have come up against this place to destroy it?," the Rabshakeh says, quoting Sennacherib, his royal master, and invoking the biblical god. Using another rhetorical question, and alluding to the Assyrian practice of "godnapping," he then asks, "Has any of the gods of the nations ever delivered its land out of the

191

hands of the king of Assyria? Where are the gods of Hamath and Arpad?" And finally, in the rhetorically most ambitious part of his speech, the Rabshakeh points out why the people of Jerusalem need not be afraid of submitting to Assyria, even though this might lead to their eventual deportation: "Thus says the king of Assyria: 'Make your peace with me and come out to me; then every one of you will eat from your own vine and your own fig tree, and drink water from your own cistern, until I come and take you away to a land like your land, a land of grain and wine, a land of bread and vineyards, a land of olive oil and honey, that you may live and not die.'"[1]

The Rabshakeh's speech is a master class in psychological warfare, and Hezekiah's negotiators were aware of the potential ramifications if word got out about what he had said. Worried that the Assyrian general might persuade the people of Jerusalem with his eloquent reasoning, grounded in realpolitik as well as theology, the Judean officials beg him not to conduct the negotiation so openly: "Please speak to your servants in the Aramaic language, for we understand it; do not speak to us in the language of Judah within the hearing of the people who are on the wall." But the Rabshakeh declines this request. His use of "the language of Judah," that is, Hebrew, rather than Aramaic—at the time the language of international diplomacy in the Levant—is quite deliberate. The Rabshakeh wants to communicate directly with "the people sitting on the wall," who, he says—addressing the officials but also speaking to everyone else—would be "doomed with you to eat their own dung and to drink their own urine" if they were confined in Jerusalem for much longer.

The words of the Rabshakeh are from one of the many stories that were told about the Assyrian attack on Judah in 701 BCE: the biblical account found both in 2 Kings 18–19 and Isaiah 36–37. The different reports—the ones in the Bible and those from other sources—reflect a wide variety of different perspectives and were written down at different times. Separating facts from fiction and establishing what really happened at Jerusalem in 701 BCE has proven to be a puzzle, and scholars to this day continue to squabble about it.

SENNACHERIB'S ATTACK ON JUDAH IN 701 BCE CAN IN SOME REspects be called "the first world event." In addition to Assyrians and Judeans, it involved Egyptians, Nubians, Phoenicians, Philistines, the Transjordanian kingdoms, and possibly even Babylonians and Arabs. It is described in Assyrian sources, in several books of the Hebrew Bible, and in the work of the Greek historian Herodotus. But the most important reason for dwelling on the campaign of 701 in some detail is that it had a significant impact on Assyria's later reputation. As time went by, the conflict between Sennacherib and the Judean king Hezekiah became part of the cultural memory of a wide range of premodern—and even modern—civilizations, far beyond the Middle East and the Mediterranean.[2]

For modern historians, the availability of so many sources is in many respects a blessing. Where else in their study of the ancient Near East can they draw on equally abundant documentation? But this embarrassment of riches also holds its challenges, because the available texts often contradict one another. The greatest contradiction of all is that whereas the Bible claims the Assyrians ended up suffering a major defeat at Jerusalem, the Assyrian sources present the campaign as a great Assyrian triumph.

Since the mid-nineteenth century, historians and religious scholars have tried to resolve such tensions. Because the reliability of the Bible was in the balance, the stakes were high. Many researchers were guided to an unusual degree by the agendas of their times or their personal beliefs. Taking a closer look at Sennacherib's attack on Judah therefore not only brings into sharper focus an important moment in Assyrian history—one that decisively shaped the memory of Assyria in later tradition—but also teaches some important lessons about the writing of history in general and the extrinsic factors that tend to influence it.[3]

SENNACHERIB, SARGON II'S SUCCESSOR, HAD ASCENDED THE AS-syrian throne in 705 BCE. His reign was in several regards remark-able, with many achievements. Under Sennacherib, the city of Nineveh, Assyria's new capital, was transformed into a metropolis of spectacular splendor. Eventually covering some 750 hectares (1,850 acres)—more than twice the size of Calah or Dur-Sharrukin—it became the largest and possibly the wealthiest city the world had ever seen. By the end of Sennacherib's reign, Nineveh featured sev-eral massive new palaces, temples, and arsenals, as well as gigantic boulevards well suited for triumphal processions and military pa-rades, all within a wall 12 kilometers (7.5 miles) long equipped with towers, buttresses, and eighteen colossal gates. New metalworking techniques were invented, allegedly by none other than Sennacherib himself, to facilitate the production of monumental bronze statues of winged bulls and lions, among other things. And it was mostly during the reign of Sennacherib that, in response to slowly dimin-ishing amounts of annual precipitation, a network of interconnected canals, aqueducts, and navigable waterways was constructed in the hilly northern sectors of Assyria's core territory to irrigate previously barren land. Among the farmers and gardeners recruited to work the new fields and orchards now blanketing the region were thousands of resettled deportees.[4]

But there was also trouble. The shadow of Sargon's violent end loomed large over Sennacherib's time in power. Apart from affect-ing the king and his entourage psychologically, it had major politi-cal implications. When news of Sargon's untimely death had spread across the empire, it encouraged recently conquered areas and vassal kingdoms on almost every front to seek to regain their indepen-dence. As a result, from his earliest days in power Sennacherib found himself forced to devote much of his time and energy to fighting against rebels rather than further expanding the empire's geographic horizons.

The majority of Sennacherib's military campaigns were directed against Babylonia, where opposition against his rule was particularly fierce. The north and the east were occasional targets of Assyrian attacks as well. But the king's most widely discussed military operation, counted in his Annals as his "third campaign," was aimed at the pacification of the western Levant, where dozens of political leaders had united in yet another attempt to cast off the Assyrian yoke.

Sennacherib's earliest account of his third campaign dates to the second month of the year 700 BCE, a few months after the bulk of the Assyrian army had returned home. It was inscribed on clay cylinders that were buried in the foundations of various buildings in Nineveh and Ashur, where later kings were expected to find and study them. Excavators have uncovered no fewer than eight complete exemplars of these cylinders and some eighty fragments of them, which establishes beyond doubt that Sennacherib and his "court historians" must have attributed considerable importance to the events they describe.[5]

Sennacherib presents his third campaign as a sequence of several episodes: the flight of the king of Sidon, the submission of unfaithful vassals, the punishment of Ashkelon, an armed conflict with the Philistine city of Ekron and its Egyptian allies, and finally, as the climax of the whole operation, the Assyrian attack on the Kingdom of Judah. It is clear that these episodes were actually interrelated and included events that must have happened simultaneously, but an exact timeline for them is hard to establish.

The Assyrian troops had made their way to the western Levant in the summer of 701 without facing much opposition. If we are to believe Sennacherib's Annals—and there is no reason not to in this case—their arrival in the region was enough to prompt one of the ringleaders of the rebellion, King Luli of Sidon, to abandon the cause and "flee afar into the midst of the sea." Later versions of the Annals reveal that Lulî found exile on Cyprus, where he seems to have died. He was replaced by a pro-Assyrian king by the name of Tu-Ba'lu, who was also given power over the mainland sectors of Tyre. The heavily fortified island city of Tyre remained unconquered but refrained from interfering with the Assyrian operations.

As a result of this initial success, Sennacherib claims, several former vassals came forward to resume the annual payments they owed the Assyrians. Among them were the leaders of the cities of Samsimuruna, Sidon, Arwad, and Byblos in Phoenicia; the city of Ashdod in Philistia (which had been a short-lived Assyrian province after 711); and the lands of Ammon, Moab, and Edom east of the Jordan River. Their tribute is described by Sennacherib as having been "fourfold," which must mean that the rulers who brought it provided reparations for the missing deliveries of the years that had passed since the beginning of the revolt in 705 BCE. Whether they all gathered in Phoenicia or made their payments locally remains unclear.

Such willingness to submit to Assyria was far from universal, however, and several pockets of resistance remained. Some were more easily dealt with than others. In Ashkelon, the Assyrians quickly gained the upper hand. They captured King Sidqâ—who was probably betrayed by his own people—and brought him together with his wife, sons, daughters, brothers, and family gods to Assyria. The new king Sennacherib installed in Ashkelon had an Assyrian name, Sharru-lu-dari (May the [Assyrian] king last forever), which suggests that he had been a hostage in Assyria and had gone through a thorough "reeducation program" before being sent back home.

Not everywhere, however, was the popular sentiment so much in favor of yielding to the pressure the Assyrians exerted. In the city of Ekron, some 35 kilometers (22 miles) west of Jerusalem, anti-Assyrian rebels were determined not to back down. According to Sennacherib's account, the revolt in Ekron had started with local officials and other citizens deposing their pro-Assyrian ruler, King Padî, and handing him over to Hezekiah of Judah—who must have been a major force in the rebellion from very early on. When Ekron's new leaders realized that an Assyrian army was on its way to them, they decided to carry on the fight. But they knew they needed outside help if they were to have any chance of victory in the impending showdown. They found it in Egypt.

AT THE TIME OF SENNACHERIB'S THIRD CAMPAIGN, EGYPT WAS ruled by the Twenty-fifth—or Kushite—Dynasty, whose origins lay in the region of Napata in northern Sudan. The Kushites seem to have established themselves in Egypt shortly after 730 BCE. Around 720 BCE, Pharaoh Shabaka moved northward and consolidated Kushite power over Lower Egypt and the Nile Delta. Many of the local dynasties—often of Libyan background—that had ruled there for some time formally stayed in place, but were deprived of sovereign power. The Kushites had thus reunited most of Egypt again, bringing a long period of political fragmentation to an end.

Today, the kings of the Kushite Dynasty are often called the "Black Pharaohs." This is to some extent in line with how they were perceived at the time of their rule. Esarhaddon writes about the wives, sons, and daughters of Taharqa, the Twenty-fifth Dynasty's penultimate ruler, that "their bodies, like his, have skins as black as pitch." Outsiders as they were—probably not so much because of their dark complexion as that they were a people from beyond the traditional borders of Egypt—the Kushites adopted Egyptian culture with particular zeal. The inscriptions of their kings abound in allusions to the great works of classical Egyptian literature. In this regard, the Kushites were actually quite similar to the Assyrians, who showed comparable enthusiasm in their endeavors to make Babylonian culture their own.[6]

The rulers of the Twenty-fifth Dynasty also shared some of Assyria's political goals. Both monarchies had similar geostrategic interests in the southern Levant, a region Egypt had always considered part of its own sphere of influence, but that was now increasingly under the sway of imperial Assyria. Undoubtedly, the intelligence services of the two "superpowers" kept a very close eye on the activities of the other side in the region, and open conflict between them was only a matter of time. Already early in the reign of Sargon II, an Egyptian general by the name of Raya was involved in skirmishes with Assyrian troops at Raphiah south of Gaza. Later, in 711 BCE, Pharaoh Shabaka granted asylum to an anti-Assyrian rebel from Ashdod by the name of Yamani. Shabaka's successor, Shebitku, who ascended the throne in 707 BCE, extradited Yamani to Sargon in a gesture of goodwill, but Kushite Egypt remained wary of Assyria consolidating its power in Philistia and neighboring regions.[7]

When the people of Ekron needed their assistance against the advancing Assyrian troops, the Kushites—and their client rulers in Lower Egypt—were therefore ready to spring into action. They arrived on the scene speedily and with considerable resources. As Sennacherib's Annals put it, "The kings of (Lower) Egypt and the archers, chariots, and horses of the king of Meluhha (that is, Kush), forces without number, came to their aid." Near the small city of Eltekeh—probably somewhere north of Ashdod—the Assyrian and Egyptian troops met in pitched battle.[8]

Sennacherib contended that he scored a great victory over the enemy and captured many charioteers as well as a number of Egyptian princes. But there have been doubts about this claim. Several modern scholars have argued that for the Assyrians the battle was a draw at best. Their critical assessment is partly based on a strange passage in the *Histories* of the Greek writer Herodotus, which reports that the army of Sennacherib, "king of the Arabians and the Assyrians," had pitched camp at Pelusium in the eastern Nile Delta when it was attacked at night by large numbers of field mice. The mice gnawed through the strings of the Assyrian bows and the handles of the Assyrian shields, so that on the next day the Egyptian king, whom Herodotus calls Sethos, scored an easy victory over the now unarmed Assyrians.[9]

Does Herodotus's report, surreal as it is, somehow reflect what happened at Eltekeh in 701? All in all, despite its awareness of a battle between Sennacherib and Egyptian troops, the account seems more a story than history; but the matter is difficult to decide. An argument in favor of the accuracy of Sennacherib's own version of the Eltekeh episode is what Assyrian sources, most likely accurately, claim occurred thereafter. The Assyrians "approached the city of Ekron, killed the leaders and noblemen who had committed crimes, and hung their corpses on towers around the city." Only those who had not joined the rebels were spared. None of this, it can be reasoned, would have been possible if the Assyrian army had not somehow managed to repel the Egyptian enemy troops at Eltekeh.

A third source that mentions the Assyro-Egyptian confrontation does not fully settle the matter either. The Bible reports that the Egyptian troops fighting against Sennacherib had been led by Taharqa, the later Kushite king and perhaps a general at the time. But it does not say anything specific about who really won the battle.[10]

EVENTUALLY, ACCORDING TO SENNACHERIB'S ANNALS, EKRON'S former king, Padî, was brought back from his captivity in Jerusalem and reinstated in his office—of course, in the expectation that he would henceforth pay the required tribute again. Padî's repatriation, though, cannot have happened right away. It must have been a result of Sennacherib's war with Hezekiah of Judah, which is the topic of the final—and best known—section of the king's report about his "third campaign."

Sennacherib describes his operation against Judah as a triumphant success. He begins by saying that he "surrounded and conquered forty-six of Hezekiah's fortified walled cities and smaller settlements in their environs" with the help of ramps and siege engines and through breaches made in the city walls. Corroborating evidence for this claim is found in the Bible, which reports that "in the fourteenth year of King Hezekiah, King Sennacherib of Assyria came up against all the fortified cities of Judah and conquered them"—a statement fully in line with the Assyrian account. The biblical passage goes on to observe that Hezekiah "sent to the king of Assyria at Lachish" to submit to him, suggesting that Lachish was one of the Judean cities seized by Sennacherib, and that the Assyrian king had set up his military headquarters nearby.[11]

Lachish, located some 40 kilometers (25 miles) southwest of Jerusalem, is not mentioned by name in Sennacherib's Annals. But the city makes a prominent appearance in a most impressive visual source from Assyria: a panoramic cycle of bas-reliefs, now on display in the British Museum in London, from Room XXXVI of Sennacherib's palace at Nineveh. All extant reliefs from this room are devoted to the single theme of Sennacherib's siege and conquest of Lachish, which is identified by a cuneiform epigraph.[12]

The Lachish relief cycle, originally some 27 meters (90 feet) long, shows, in consecutive order, on the left side Assyrian troops approaching the city; on the central panels, prominently positioned opposite the main entrance, the grim business of the siege itself; and on the right the results of the operation: the relocation of the city's inhabitants, the punishment of evildoers, and gestures of submission toward Sennacherib, who is depicted sitting on an elaborately carved throne set up on a nearby hill. Particularly memorable scenes include Assyrian bowmen, slingers, and spearmen slowly ascending upon a newly built ramp toward the upper portions of the city wall, with the defenders showering them from above with arrows and torches; men and women leaving the city, facing deportation; and some of the ringleaders of the rebellion being flayed or beheaded by Assyrian soldiers, while others are being impaled on wooden stakes, their wrists bound together, in a public spectacle that heralds the later practice of crucifixion. Other scenes show life in the Assyrian military camp, and a family from Lachish, which includes a man, two women with headscarves, three girls, and a small boy, on their way into exile, with a cart drawn by two malnourished oxen carrying their possessions (see Plate 10).

When intact, the Lachish relief cycle was some 67.5 square meters (726.5 square feet) in size. Especially when taking into account that the whole ensemble was originally painted, one must acknowledge it as one of the world's most imposing depictions of armed conflict from all times, on a par with famous monuments such as the Trajan Column in Rome, with its elaborate scenes from the Roman emperor's Dacian Wars. What makes the Lachish reliefs truly outstanding is that they reveal in so much detail what warfare meant for both soldiers and civilians.

Further evidence of the Assyrian siege and conquest of Lachish has also been found at Tell ed-Duweir, the actual site of the ancient city. Excavations there have established that nearly all the public and private buildings of Lachish Level III were destroyed in a massive conflagration that must have been brought about by marauding Assyrian soldiers. Remains of a large Assyrian siege ramp, built with stones weighing between 13,000 and 19,000 metric tons (14,330 to 21,000 US tons) in total, were discovered near the southwest corner of the city. Some 70 meters (230 feet) broad at its bottom, the ramp was faced at the top by a counter-ramp built by the defenders. The excavations in this area also produced almost one thousand arrowheads, most of them made of iron, as well as numerous stone balls weighing about 250 grams (9 ounces) each that had served as sling stones. All this evidence shows how bloody and brutal the fight for Lachish must have been. The reliefs from Sennacherib's "Lachish Room" seem to paint a fairly realistic picture of it.[13]

SENNACHERIB SEIZED NUMEROUS JUDEAN CITIES, MOST NOTABLY Lachish, but the Assyrian sources and the Bible agree that he failed to conquer the heavily fortified Judean capital of Jerusalem, the city where King Hezekiah resided. In Sennacherib's Annals, the Jerusalem episode is, nonetheless, an Assyrian success story. Sennacherib claims that he "confined Hezekiah inside Jerusalem, his royal city, like a bird in a cage," by setting up blockades that made it impossible for the king and his people to leave the city. Even though no actual siege seems to have taken place, and the Assyrian troops never entered Jerusalem, the Annals state that Sennacherib's "lordly brilliance" eventually "overwhelmed" Hezekiah and prompted him to submit to the Assyrian king. In recognition of his new status as an Assyrian vassal, the Judean ruler sent precious gifts and various groups of people to the Assyrian court at Nineveh. Outlined in considerable detail in Sennacherib's earliest account of his third campaign, the tribute included the auxiliary troops that had helped Hezekiah defend Jerusalem (possibly Arabs, but the matter is not quite clear); several of the king's daughters, harem women, and singers; and "30 talents of gold, 800 talents of silver, ivory beds, elephant hides, garments with multi-colored trim, blue-purple wool, chariots, shields, and lances," plus other luxury goods and weapons. According to the Assyrian account, Judah suffered, moreover, substantial territorial and demographic losses. Parts of its western domains were handed over to the Philistine cities of Ashdod, Ekron, and Gaza, and huge numbers of Judeans were relocated, even though the number of 200,150 deportees given in Sennacherib's Annals is unrealistically high.[14]

How does the Assyrian version of the Jerusalem episode compare to the way the Bible describes this event? As already mentioned, a short passage at the beginning of the biblical account in 2 Kings 18 (verses 13–15) paints a picture of Assyria's attack that is largely in line with the Assyrian sources and thus most likely historically accurate. This also applies to the tribute listed in this section, allegedly taken by Hezekiah from the temple in Jerusalem and from the treasuries of his own palace. It is said to have included "300 talents of silver and 30 talents of gold," numbers close to or identical with the "30 talents of gold and 800 talents of silver" the king paid the Assyrians according to Sennacherib's Annals.

But the biblical accounts of Sennacherib's Judean campaign are composite texts, stitched together from different elements. The episode in 2 Kings 18:13–15 seems to have been taken from a Hebrew chronicle that provides a largely factual account of the events. In the narrative segments following this passage, history, theology, and fiction are often inextricably intertwined.

In the first—and historically most plausible—of these segments, it is stated that "the king of Assyria sent the Tartan, the Rabsaris, and the Rabshakeh with a great army from Lachish to King Hezekiah at Jerusalem" to enforce his submission. The three officials mentioned here bear actual Assyrian titles—they can be identified as the Assyrian field marshal (*turtānu*), the chief eunuch (*rab-ša-rēši*), and the chief cupbearer (*rab-šāqê*), respectively, all known to have led Assyrian military campaigns.[15]

What allegedly happened next was the event that opened this chapter: the Rabshakeh conveyed a message from Sennacherib requesting Hezekiah's surrender. It is unlikely that an Assyrian general spoke to Hezekiah's officials and the people of Jerusalem in exactly the way 2 Kings 18 suggests. But a similar speech may well have been delivered at the gates of Jerusalem. An Assyrian letter from 731 or 730 BCE provides an illuminating parallel. In it, two Assyrian officials inform King Tiglath-pileser III about how they had tried to convince the citizens of Babylon to give up their support of (Nabû-)mukin-zeri, a new Babylonian king who had taken an anti-Assyrian stance. The two officials write that "on the 28th day (of the month), we went to Babylon, took our stand in front of the Marduk Gate, and spoke with the citizens of Babylon. (Z)asin(n)u, a servant of Mukin-zeri, and some Chaldaeans who were with him, came out too, standing with the citizens of Babylon in front of the gate. We spoke to the citizens of Babylon as follows: 'The king has sent us to you.'" The situation described here is remarkably similar to the Rabshakeh episode in the Bible, adding to the likelihood that the latter is not a complete fabrication.[16]

After having been reassured by his spiritual adviser, the prophet Isaiah, that he would eventually prevail, Hezekiah, according to 2 Kings 19:8–14, receives another communication from Sennacherib. It comes in the form of a letter, whose message is similar to that delivered earlier by the Rabshakeh. Again, trust in Egypt is discouraged, and emphasis is put on the failure of local gods to save the "nations" that had formerly found themselves under attack by Assyria. This time, however, the chances that the historical Hezekiah ever received such a message are fairly slim. The Rabshakeh's speech in 2 Kings 18 had mentioned Hamath and Arpad, and also Samaria, as places previously conquered by Assyrian troops. These cities—with their surrounding territories—had indeed been incorporated into the Assyrian Empire during the second half of the eighth century. But the places mentioned in Sennacherib's putative letter are different. They include Gozan (Guzanu), Harran, and Rezeph (Rasappa), which had been part of the Assyrian kingdom since much earlier times—and would therefore have been poor precedents for the danger in which Jerusalem found itself in 701. All three of them, however, are known to have been seized in the late seventh century by the Babylonian kings Nabopolassar and Nebuchadnezzar II—and it is tempting to assume that the message in the "letter to Hezekiah" reflects these later conquests. The composition of the letter episode in 2 Kings 19:8–14 must accordingly be dated to the sixth century, long after Sennacherib's campaign. It was probably grounded in the preoccupation of later biblical authors with Nebuchadnezzar, the Babylonian monarch responsible for finally bringing Judah's independence to an end and sending the Judeans, in 597 and 586 BCE, to the "rivers of Babylon."[17]

TOWARD THE END OF THE ACCOUNT FOUND IN 2 KINGS 18–19, A miracle occurs. After a series of grim prophecies that Isaiah hurls at Assyria ("I will put my hook in your nose and my bit in your mouth; I will turn you back on the way by which you came"), the text provides a spectacular—and certainly surprising—denouement for the story of Sennacherib's Judean campaign: "That very night the angel of the LORD set out and struck down one-hundred eighty-five thousand in the camp of the Assyrians; when morning dawned, they were all dead bodies. Then King Sennacherib left, went home, and lived at Nineveh."[18]

What is one to make of this ending, which is clearly at odds with Sennacherib's own account? And what was really the outcome of the Assyrian attack on Judah in 701? Who won and who lost? Could the Bible be wrong? These questions have preoccupied scholars for more than 150 years, prompting very different answers.

For the faithful, who believe in the Bible's inerrant nature, the matter is simple: God killed the Assyrian soldiers by means of a miraculous angelic intervention, and thus delivered Hezekiah—a particularly righteous king—from all his troubles. From a historical point of view, such a scenario is, of course, difficult to accept. But quite a few modern scholars have declined to dismiss the biblical account of the outcome of Sennacherib's campaign out of hand. Instead, they have tried to rationalize it by providing a "naturalistic" explanation for the story of the angel's lethal action—a mode of reasoning much in line with other attempts, often enthusiastically endorsed by popular media, to scientifically vindicate biblical miracle stories. The parting of the "Sea of Reeds" by Moses, for example, has been explained as the result of a "wind setdown" that pushed away the waters of Lake Tanis in the eastern Nile Delta.[19]

In the case of the story of the angel defeating the Assyrians, the proponents of a naturalistic solution have argued that it was the sudden outbreak of an epidemic in the military camp that actually decimated the Assyrian troops. Deadly plagues did occur in Iron Age Western Asia: Assyrian and Babylonian chronicles, as already seen, record epidemics affecting Assyria for the years 802, 765, 759, and 707.[20]

Herodotus's story of the field mice might support the epidemic scenario. According to Herodotus, these mice gnawed through the quivers, bows, and shield handles of Sennacherib's army at Pelusium, leading to the defeat of the Assyrians at the hands of Pharaoh Sethos—and to the latter setting up an image of himself in the temple of "Hephaestus" (the Egyptian god Ptah) with a mouse in his hand. To be sure, it is rats rather than mice that normally spread particularly dangerous infectious diseases, but mice can carry the plague pathogen as well. It is, moreover, noteworthy that the Greeks considered the god Apollo Smintheus, that is, "Apollo of the Mice"—a deity represented on coins with a mouse in his hands—as bringing about deadly plagues, most famously the one that affected the Achaeans at Troy. Also of interest is that the Bible, in Isaiah 38:21, mentions Hezekiah's recovery from a grave illness. Its symptoms included "boils," which Isaiah treated with a fig poultice. Neither the exact nature nor the date of Hezekiah's illness—nor its historicity—can be established with certainty, but it has been suggested—not least because figs are known to have been used against plague swellings—that Hezekiah might have suffered from bubonic plague or some other highly contagious disease. That his illness fell into the time period of Sennacherib's western campaign is at least possible.[21]

Especially in view of the Herodotean account, the idea that it was a plague that led to the Assyrian retreat from Jerusalem is certainly intriguing. But it must be admitted that the evidence for it, for the time being, is at best inconclusive. No text that can be reasonably considered a primary source talks explicitly about an epidemic having befallen the Assyrian troops in 701 BCE. Herodotus's story, set in Egypt rather than in Judah, was authored some 250 years after Sennacherib's death. And according to the biblical account, only Hezekiah and no one else in Jerusalem was sick.

Another explanation for the Assyrian withdrawal from Jerusalem, one grounded in what one might call a feminist perspective, argues that Sennacherib's mother played a major, albeit indirect, role in the events. Advanced by the Assyriologist Stephanie Dalley, this theory draws on the discovery, made in 1989 by Iraqi archaeologists at Calah, of the burial chambers of several Neo-Assyrian queens. One chamber held a stone sarcophagus that contained the bodies of two women, identified, based on inscriptional evidence, as Yabâ and Atalya, the main wives of Tiglath-pileser III and Sargon II, respectively. Dalley astutely observed that the name Atalya is otherwise known only from the Bible, where it was borne by a daughter of the ninth-century Israelite king Ahab and his Phoenician wife Jezebel. Atalya later married into the royal family of Judah and effectively ruled that country for some time. In Dalley's opinion, Sargon's wife Atalya was likewise a member of the Judean royal family and probably the mother of Sennacherib. If this really was the case, Dalley reasons, Sennacherib must have felt sympathy with Judah, which might have prevented him from conquering Jerusalem and from replacing the Judean king Hezekiah with another ruler.[22]

This stimulating hypothesis is fraught with difficulties too, however. Most importantly, it is now virtually certain that Atalya, while indeed at one point a wife of Sargon II, was actually not Sennacherib's mother. Sennacherib was instead in all likelihood the son of a woman by the name of Ra'imâ, and as such probably not particularly infatuated with Atalya, who seems to have been a later spouse of Sargon. It is also not certain that Atalya was indeed of Judean— or Israelite—extraction, even though the possibility cannot be ruled out. One could try to argue that the biblical story of the Assyrian Rabshakeh speaking Hebrew with the people of Jerusalem somehow backs up the idea of family connections between the Assyrian and Judean royal dynasties, but this would be a very speculative line of reasoning.

A third theory regarding the Assyrian retreat from Jerusalem holds that it was the Kushite intervention that forced Sennacherib's troops out of Judah. Proposed in 2002 by a Canadian journalist,

Henry Aubin, this thesis is grounded in an Afrocentric approach—the author states explicitly that his work on the Kushites had been inspired by his adopted son of African descent. Though he is not an academic, one would do Aubin an injustice to consider his ideas as uninformed or as an exercise in writing marginalized groups back into history at all costs. Aubin is familiar with the sources, and he is careful with his conclusions. Rather than claiming that the "Black Pharaohs" scored a major military victory over Assyrian troops in 701, he suggests that the encounter of the two sides at Eltekeh resulted in a "stalemate" and a "negotiated settlement" between them. Assyria would not lose all its influence in the region, but would refrain from annexing Judah, while Egypt would gain security and keep its commercial access to the southern Levant. Thanks to the Kushites, though, Jerusalem was saved, and the future emergence of Judaism and Christianity, otherwise inconceivable, thus secured.[23]

The debate about Aubin's thesis continues among modern scholars. In 2020, the peer-reviewed series *Perspectives on Hebrew Scriptures and Its Contexts* published a volume with essays by eight well-established academics who had been charged with reevaluating Aubin's theory. Most of them expressed support for it, albeit with certain reservations. But the only Assyriologist among the authors, K. Lawson Younger, abstained from a verdict.[24]

All things considered, Younger's polite skepticism seems apt: Aubin's thesis is not entirely convincing. It has already been pointed out that after the Battle of Eltekeh, Sennacherib was able to punish the Ekronite rebels who had apparently asked the Kushites for help, and to reinstate the loyal Padî as Ekron's king. There is no evidence for a "negotiated settlement" between Assyria and Kush. Philistia remained part of Assyria's imperial periphery in the following years, and nothing indicates that the Kushites had much of a say in the region. The absence of Egyptian sources related to the events of 701 is noteworthy as well. So far, archaeologists have failed to find a single more elaborate historical inscription from the reign of Pharaoh She-bitku, who ruled Egypt during the events of 701. This is in marked contrast to the many inscriptions left by his predecessors and successors, and thus perhaps not an accident of discovery. Shebitku may simply not have had much to brag about.[25]

"ALL TRUE HISTORY IS CONTEMPORARY HISTORY," THE ITALIAN philosopher and historian Benedetto Croce once famously quipped. The three aforementioned theories about the reasons for Sennacherib's retreat from Jerusalem, all advanced during the past few decades, exemplify this adage. With their naturalistic, feminist, and identitarian proclivities, they are clearly rooted in intellectual currents of recent times.

None of the theories can be proven wrong in every respect. Even though the Assyrians seem to have won the battle with the Kushites at Eltekeh, having to fight it in the first place stretched Assyrian resources, which may have been a factor in Sennacherib's decision not to put Jerusalem to a long siege. Sennacherib's mother was no Judean princess, but there are a few hints pointing to an unusual interest among members of the Assyrian elite in the Hebrew world of Israel and Judah. And while there is no unequivocal evidence for a plague among the Assyrian troops campaigning in 701, it is noteworthy that Sennacherib conducted very few military operations in the following years, which leaves open the possibility that his armies had in fact returned from the west with a contagious disease in tow. The year 698 was, moreover, a time of hunger in Assyria, with very high barley prices.[26]

But the theories outlined above remain, nonetheless, highly speculative. The best explanation for Sennacherib's retreat from Jerusalem seems to be a different one: the Assyrian king had probably made a simple cost-benefit analysis when weighing his options. The effort to conquer the heavily fortified city, and the possible losses among his soldiers, would have been so great that Sennacherib deemed it preferable to leave Hezekiah in office, under the condition that he send him tribute and become an Assyrian vassal. This would have been very much in line with the Grand Strategy Sennacherib pursued in general. The concept of "Grand Strategy" has been defined by the historian John Lewis Gaddis as "the alignment of unlimited aspirations with necessarily limited capabilities"—and Sennacherib seems to have believed that the capabilities of the Assyrian state were insufficient to take full control of too many additional polities within its sphere of influence. In contrast to his three predecessors, he showed a strong preference for indirect over direct rule, handing power to client kings rather than creating new provinces. This was Sennacherib's modus operandi not only in Judah, but also in Ekron, Ashdod, Ashkelon, and elsewhere. It is possible that Sennacherib's decision to return to the east was hastened by some kind of illness that had befallen some of his soldiers—and perhaps also by intelligence reports about the deteriorating political situation in Babylonia, where the Assyrian military was now needed more urgently—but this is not certain.[27]

Hezekiah, for his part, may have been forced to pay a heavy price for staying in power, but had good reasons to accept what Sennacherib required of him. After all, recognizing the Assyrian king as his overlord spared Jerusalem the dire fate that had befallen the city of Lachish, which had been left in ruins. The Kingdom of Judah suffered a loss in wealth in the wake of Sennacherib's campaign, and the number of settlements in its countryside shrank; but it remained a formally independent state and an important hub in the international overland trade for another full century. It seems that for the authors of the biblical account of Sennacherib's campaign, this was enough to describe its outcome as a vindication of Hezekiah's decision—and not as the humiliation that it actually was for the Judean king.

AS NOTED EARLIER, SENNACHERIB'S ATTACK ON JUDAH HAS BEEN called "the first world event"—and it is true that there are very few earlier events that implicated such a vast and international cast of characters. In geographic terms, what happened in 701 had global dimensions as well. The capitals of the two most powerful participants, Napata in Kush and Nineveh in Assyria, located on different continents, were some 2,300 kilometers (1,430 miles) away from each other, as the crow flies. But Sennacherib's Judean adventure can be considered even more a "world event" with regard to the place it came to hold in the cultural memory of later times. The stories about it in the Bible, and other early stories now lost, generated a whole "archipelago" of secondary and tertiary narratives, in Hebrew, Aramaic, Egyptian, Greek, Syriac, and Arabic, and from there spread out even further into the literatures of other nations. Some of these later narratives were closely linked to the ones from the Bible, while others were free adaptations. Many have a pronounced anti-imperialist bent. As time went by, Sennacherib—the evil "cosmocrator," as he was called in rabbinic traditions—became a cipher for oppressive tyrants and other thoroughly despised people all over the world. The eighth-century CE Byzantine emperor Leo III, notorious for his iconoclastic tendencies, was called a Nestorian, an Amalekite, a chameleon, and *Sennacherib* by his opponents. An etching by the sixteenth-century German draughtsman Hanns Lautensack presents the Ottoman siege of Vienna in 1529 as a reenactment of Sennacherib's siege of Jerusalem. And Lord Byron's poem "The Destruction of Sennacherib," with its famous and often parodied first two lines—"The Assyrian came down like the wolf on the fold, / And his cohorts were gleaming in purple and gold"—was published in the year of Napoleon's defeat at the Battle of Waterloo.[28]

Sennacherib himself would probably have been thoroughly surprised if he had known that his third campaign would be so fervently remembered by future generations. To be sure, as his inscriptions reveal, the Assyrian king considered his victory over the western rebels in 701 an important achievement. But he was much more committed to another political mission: the subjugation and pacification of Babylonia, and the adoption and adaptation of Babylonian culture for a far-reaching reform of Assyrian religion.

9

Sennacherib's Babylonian Problem

Assyria's relationship with Babylonia, its southern neighbor, was a special one. As in the case of Rome and Greece, it featured an emerging superpower, militarily strong yet culturally immature, that became infatuated with a neighboring civilization that was older and more sophisticated, but politically fragmented. The superpower adopted many of the intellectual, religious, and artistic traditions of its neighbor and granted it significant fiscal privileges and the right of local self-government—but expected in return that its overall political hegemony would be accepted.

Under ideal circumstances, such an arrangement might work. But being madly in love while, at the same time, desperately wishing to dominate one's partner can also be a recipe for disaster.

The "relationship drama" between Assyria and Babylonia had many disastrous moments, particularly during the reign of King Sennacherib. For the conqueror of Judah, Babylon became an obsession that drove him to actions unprecedented in the history of the ancient Near East. But Sennacherib's Babylonian problem had a prehistory. Already under his three predecessors, Assyro-Babylonian relations had often been tense.[1]

EXCEPT FOR A FEW YEARS UNDER TUKULTI-NINURTA I IN THE thirteenth century BCE, Assyria had never been in full control of Babylonia. But in 729 BCE, when Tiglath-pileser III conquered the city of Babylon, Babylonia finally became an integral part of Assyria's political identity. Right away, Tiglath-pileser began to call himself, in addition to his Assyrian titles, "King of Babylon" and "King of Sumer and Akkad" (the traditional names for Babylonia's southern and northern parts, respectively). He thus formed what one could call in constitutional terms a "personal union" between Assyria and Babylonia. Other places occupied by Assyrian armies—for example, Arpad or Damascus—were simply annexed, without the Assyrian monarch taking on the titles of their previous rulers. But Tiglath-pileser was eager to communicate that Babylon, with its age-old cuneiform culture and familiar religious institutions, was different. The king's newly acquired royal appellations were not the only indications of Tiglath-pileser's regard for Babylonian traditions. Prior to his death in 727, he also participated twice in the Babylonian Akitu Festival, which was celebrated at the beginning of the year to honor and renew the power of Babylon's patron deity, Marduk.

Of course, ruling Babylonia also brought tangible material benefits to Assyria. Despite the fact that the first centuries of the first millennium had been marked by a series of political and economic crises in the Mesopotamian south, the land continued to be more densely populated than the areas farther north, and thanks to its fertile alluvial soil, barley and date harvests remained bountiful. Babylonia's irrigation agriculture was, moreover, less affected by the vagaries of shifting precipitation patterns than Assyrian dry farming.

No direct evidence reveals what the Babylonians thought about the putatively benevolent Assyrian occupation of their country that started with Tiglath-pileser III; but it is clear that many of the citizens of Babylon, Borsippa, Sippar, or Uruk were not swayed by the relatively privileged treatment they received from their new masters—and were looking for ways to regain their freedom. When the opportunity came, after the death of Tiglath-pileser's successor, Shalmaneser V, in 722 BCE, Babylonia's political elites formed an alliance with the neighboring kingdom of Elam and threw off the Assyrian yoke. For the following twelve years, the land was ruled by Marduk-aplu-iddina II, a scion of the Chaldean "tribe" of Bit-Yakin, whose center lay close to the Persian Gulf.

Remarkably enough, none of this seems to have dampened the excitement with which Sargon II, Assyria's new king, continued to view all things Babylonian. Even during the years when Babylonia was independent, Sargon peppered his royal inscriptions with allusions to the Babylonian Epic of Creation (which the people knew by its first two words, *Enūma eliš*, or "When above"), a text that celebrated the victory of the god Marduk over the forces of chaos. He also never ceased to consider Marduk the ultimate source of authority for the Assyrian god Ashur. In a "Letter to Ashur" from 714 BCE, Sargon claims that he embarked on his brutal attack on the holy city of Musasir in the Zagros Mountains "with the great support of Ashur, father of the gods and lord of all the lands, to whom, since distant days, Marduk had granted (power over) all the other gods of the lowland and mountain regions of the four quarters."[2]

Small wonder, then, that when the Assyrians finally reconquered Babylon in 710 and put Marduk-aplu-iddina to flight, Sargon would again participate in the Babylonian Akitu Festival. In fact, he stayed in Babylon until 707, leaving the administration of Assyria in the hands of his crown prince, Sennacherib, while granting Babylonia's temple cities tax privileges and freedom from corvée duty.

Sargon tried to be as Babylonian as he could, even if this meant that he had to model some of his inscriptions on those of his Babylonian arch-enemy Marduk-aplu-iddina. Playing on a famous line about Greece and Rome by Horace, one could say that, under Sargon, "captive Babylonia took captive her savage conqueror." Sargon's son and successor Sennacherib, however, had very different ideas about how best to deal with his southern neighbor. He would try to free Assyria from its "Babylonian captivity."[3]

WHEN SENNACHERIB, IN THE WAKE OF HIS FATHER'S VIOLENT death in 705 BCE, ascended the Assyrian throne, history seemed initially to repeat itself. Just as earlier, during the beginning of Sargon's reign, a rebellion now broke out in Babylonia, with the indefatigable Marduk-aplu-iddina reappearing on the scene and renewing his old alliance with Elam. It took Sennacherib several months to react, but eventually he met Marduk-aplu-iddina in a pitched battle at Kish, near Babylon, and defeated him. The much-maligned Chaldean—Assyrian inscriptions compare him to a bat, a pig, a cat, and a mongoose—fled to his homeland in the southern marches, where Assyrian soldiers searched for him in vain. In the meantime, Sennacherib and his victorious troops entered Babylon.[4]

Sennacherib's earliest account of the aforementioned events uses several phrases that were culled directly from the inscriptions of his father; and, like Sargon, Sennacherib claims to have rushed to Babylon "with a radiant face." But this is where the similarities end. While Sargon writes that, upon his entrance to the city, he "grasped the hands of the great lord, Marduk," and gave more than 154 talents (4.6 metric tons, or 5 US tons) of gold and 1,604 talents (nearly 50 metric tons, or 55 US tons) of silver to him and other Babylonian deities as gifts, Sennacherib states that he plundered Marduk-aplu-iddina's royal palace and counted gold, silver, and other precious goods, along with the king's "wife, his palace women, eunuchs, singers, and servants," as booty. References to presents for the Babylonian gods are notably absent. It does not take too much imagination to picture the faces of the Babylonians witnessing this behavior: they were undoubtedly much less radiant than that of the king.[5]

Sennacherib's attitude toward Babylonia would indeed prove markedly different from his father's. Rather than assuming the kingship of Babylon himself, Sennacherib preferred a more indirect form of rule. After his victory over Marduk-aplu-iddina, he appointed a man of local stock to govern the city and its hinterland. His choice fell on a certain Bel-ibni, who came from an old Babylonian family but "had grown up in (the Assyrian) palace like a young puppy." Late in 703 BCE, Bel-ibni ascended the Babylonian throne.[6]

Sennacherib preferred a Babylonia that was compliant to his wishes but formally independent. He pointedly diverged from Sargon, who had claimed that not only Ashur, but also the Babylonian gods Marduk and Nabû, had "bestowed upon (him) an unrivalled kingship." In Sennacherib's inscriptions, which otherwise use exactly the same language, only Ashur is considered the divine originator of the king's royal status.[7]

As the years passed, it became apparent that Bel-ibni's rule was failing to produce the stability Sennacherib had hoped for. Especially in Babylonia's southern parts, resistance against the Assyrian puppet king never fully stopped. In 700 BCE—the year after Sennacherib's campaign against Judah—the situation had gotten so bad that Assyrian troops were dispatched back to Babylonia, with the mission of neutralizing two of the most dangerous troublemakers. The first was a certain Mushezib-Marduk, a member of the Chaldean Bit-Dakkuri "tribe," who had served for a few years as a high-ranking officer in the army of Sargon II, but had defected out of fear of some bodily punishment. He had fled to a swampy region on the Persian Gulf, where he and a group of Aramaean outlaws had embarked on anti-Assyrian guerrilla warfare. The second was the notorious Marduk-aplu-iddina, ever ready to bounce back. Both rebels managed to escape to Elam. Eight years later, Mushezib-Marduk would make an impressive comeback from there; but for the time being, the flight of the two insurgents meant that Sennacherib was able to restore a reasonable degree of control over southern Babylonia. To further consolidate his power, he appointed a new king in Babylon: Bel-ibni was moved out of the way, and Sennacherib's own eldest son, Ashur-nadin-shumi, replaced him.

Babylonia remained calm for the next six years, giving Sennacherib breathing room to focus on his ambitious building program at home. It was during this time that he transformed Nineveh into Jonah's "great city"—a metropolis of legendary size and splendor. The few military campaigns undertaken by Assyrian armies in this period, all directed against territories in the north and northwest, were of modest scale. The only one that Sennacherib participated in personally, an attack on settlements in the area of the modern Judi Dagh in eastern Turkey, was little more than an extended mountain hike.

But in the spring of 694, the king felt a renewed urge to prove his military mettle. He led his army back to the south to embark on an—entirely unprovoked—attack on Marduk-aplu-iddina and his fellow exiles from Bit-Yakin, who were living in Elam. Rather than traveling by land, the Assyrians crossed the Persian Gulf on ships manned with Phoenician and Greek sailors to catch the enemy off guard. According to Sennacherib's Annals, his naval forces succeeded in conquering the Elamite cities where the Yakinites had found refuge, and brought at least some of them (albeit not Marduk-aplu-iddina, who might have died in the meantime) back as captives. The sacrifices for the god Ea that Sennacherib—along with a small golden boat, a golden fish, and a golden crab—had cast into the sea prior to the maritime expedition seemed to have paid off.[8]

But after everything had apparently gone quite well—although without really shifting the strategic balance in the region in favor of Assyria—two unexpected and catastrophic incidents occurred, interrelated and with wide-ranging consequences. In the fall of 694, the Elamites, deeply angered by Sennacherib's assault on their territory, raided Babylonia and attacked the Babylonian city of Sippar. And shortly thereafter, the anti-Assyrian faction in Babylon, eager to regain full independence, seized the moment and handed Babylon's puppet king, Ashur-nadin-shumi, to the Elamite invaders. A cuneiform letter written some twenty years later to King Esarhaddon identifies a Babylonian diviner and haruspex by the name of Aplaya as the ringleader of the conspiracy, and reveals that its participants had been sworn to secrecy by reciting an oath in the name of the deified heavenly bodies Jupiter and Sirius.[9]

In consultation with his Babylonian allies, the Elamite king Hallushu-Inshushinak appointed a citizen of Babylon, Nergal-ushezib of the Gahul family, as the city's new king. Ashur-nadin-shumi paid a high price for his failure to win the hearts and minds of his Babylonian subjects during his tenure as king. He was brought to Elam, where he was in all likelihood tortured and then killed. His death was a major turning point. It brought about a dramatic showdown between Sennacherib and his Babylonian enemies.

OFTEN, STRUCTURAL FACTORS—BE THEY POLITICAL, ECONOMIC, or ecological in nature—can be identified as the driving forces of history. But the events that ensued after the shocking reversal of Assyria's fortunes in Babylonia in 694 seem to have been rooted primarily in the personal emotions of the historical protagonists, most notably Sennacherib himself. The Assyrian king must have been horrified by the terrible fate that, as a result of Babylonian treason and Elamite cruelty, had befallen Ashur-nadin-shumi, his firstborn son. Sennacherib's inability to openly acknowledge what had happened, since it was so much at odds with the image of strength he wished to project, can only have exacerbated the hatred he felt toward those whom he deemed responsible for the disaster. For the following five years, Sennacherib pursued, almost single-mindedly, a mission of revenge against his enemies in the south.[10]

The situation in Babylonia was initially highly volatile. Some cities chose to side with Nergal-ushezib, while others remained in the Assyrian camp. Early in 693, Sennacherib, worried that an enemy attack was imminent, evacuated the statue of the patron deity of the city of Der, strategically located near the Babylonian-Elamite border. In the fall, Assyrian soldiers seized additional divine statues in the southern city of Uruk, in an operation more reminiscent of a hostile takeover than a rescue mission. On their way back from Uruk, the Assyrian troops met with a combined Babylonian-Elamite army near Nippur, which had only recently been conquered by the new Babylonian king, Nergal-ushezib. The Assyrians prevailed and defeated the enemy troops. Retaliating for Ashur-nadin-shumi's murder, Sennacherib's soldiers killed one of the sons of the Elamite king Hallushu-Inshushinak. Nergal-ushezib—who had fallen from his horse in mid-battle—was captured and brought to Nineveh. The fate that awaited him there was grim: Sennacherib put him on display at the gate leading to the citadel, chained up together with a wild bear that would slowly devour him. It was one of those gruesome spectacles that were held on a regular basis to provide entertainment for the citizens of the Assyrian capital.[11]

Yet if Sennacherib believed all this would tip the balance decisively in his favor, he was sadly mistaken. Even though one of the king's main adversaries had been eliminated, the Assyrian victory at Nippur did not restore Assyrian hegemony over Babylonia. It led, however, to an internal revolt against Hallushu-Inshushinak. The ensuing chaos in Elam prompted Sennacherib to embark on a direct attack on that land. In the winter of 693/692—outside the usual season for military campaigns—the king directed his army southeast, toward Elamite territory. A great many small hamlets in the border region with Elam were conquered and looted. But when the Assyrian troops moved on toward Madaktu, where the Elamite king had his main residence, they encountered a major problem. As Sennacherib himself put it with remarkable openness, "In the month of Tebetu, bitter cold set in and continuous rain fell, and then wind, rain, and snow came in equal force. I was afraid of the gorges, the outflows of the mountains, so I turned around and took the road to Assyria." And thus, the expedition against Elam ended with a whimper rather than a bang.[12]

In the meantime, a new king had been installed in Babylon. It was Mushezib-Marduk, the recalcitrant Chaldean adventurer and anti-Assyrian warrior who had fled to Elam in 700 BCE. As someone who had close relations with Elamites, Aramaeans, and other Chaldeans—and inside knowledge about the Assyrian military from his short stint in the Assyrian army—he seemed the right man to bring together and lead a broad coalition of all those eager to fight Assyria's ever-growing imperial ambitions.

For the first time in ages, Assyria's enemies were suddenly back on the offensive. The Babylonian elites had paid the new Elamite king, Humban-menanu, significant amounts of gold, silver, and precious stones from the treasury of the temple of Marduk to secure his continued support. Humban-menanu, in turn, had found additional allies among his Iranian neighbors. In 691 BCE, a massive army that included Elamites, Babylonians, Persians, and military forces from many other lands and tribal groups moved northward along the Tigris, in what seems to have been an attempt to enter the Assyrian heartland and fight Sennacherib on his own turf. But the coalition troops never reached this destination. An Assyrian army led by Sennacherib himself was waiting for them at Halulê, near modern Samarra, to block their advance.

Sennacherib's account of the Battle of Halulê is a beautifully crafted celebration of extreme bloodthirstiness in war. Written with passion and in an elevated style, replete with allusions to the Babylonian Epic of Creation and other literary texts, it presents the fight as a reenactment of the cosmic battles waged in primordial times by the gods against the forces of evil. When the hostilities began, Sennacherib claims, he "raged like a lion, roared like a storm, and thundered like (the weather god) Adad." Later, Elamite magnates were "slaughtered like fattened bulls restrained with fetters," their throats "slit like those of sheep" and their blood flowing "like a flood in full spate after a rainstorm in spring." A son of Marduk-aplu-iddina was "captured alive in the thick of battle." The horses that had drawn the enemy chariots but had been freed when their drivers had been killed, "galloping about on their own," were caught and counted as booty. When their defeat became obvious, the two leaders of the allied enemy troops, Humban-menanu and Mushezib-Marduk, escaped under humiliating circumstances. With their hearts "throbbing like those of pursued young pigeons," as Sennacherib put it, they "trampled the corpses of their (fallen) soldiers as they pushed on," "releasing their excrements inside their chariots." The vulgar humor of this last episode stands in marked contrast to the lofty style in which it is told.[13]

To what extent Sennacherib's account of the Battle of Halulê is fiction rather than fact is not easy to determine. A terse entry in the Babylonian Chronicle claims that the melee resulted in an Assyrian retreat—a statement hard to reconcile with Sennacherib's panegyrical description of the events. It would be wrong, however, to dismiss Sennacherib's version out of hand as a counterfactual propaganda piece. An inscription from Nineveh reports that the Assyrians seized several enemy chariots, including those of the Elamite and Babylonian kings, after the battle and brought them to Sennacherib's new arsenal at Nineveh. It stands to reason that the royal excrements that Sennacherib's ghostwriters described with so much glee were not a product of their imagination—they had probably been found on the chariots' floorboards by Assyrian soldiers removing enemy equipment from the battlefield.[14]

In all likelihood, the actual outcome of the Battle of Halulê was a temporary stalemate. The Elamite and Babylonian troops had to abandon their offensive and march back home, but the Assyrians were unable to seize the moment and follow them in hot pursuit. Their return to the south, however, was only a matter of time. Sennacherib was regrouping his forces. In fact, his account of the Halulê episode, with its allusions to mythological battles of yore and its tendency to highlight the archetypal wickedness of the

Babylonians—those "evil demons"—was probably aimed at paving the way, ideologically, for the next step the king had in mind: Babylon's complete annihilation.[15]

SENNACHERIB WASTED NO TIME. BY THE SUMMER OF THE FOL-lowing year, 690, Assyrian troops had gathered at Babylon to lay siege to the city. Babylon's alliance with Elam had been shattered, and the Elamite king, Humban-menanu, would soon be seized by a stroke that would leave him unable to speak for the rest of his life. An Assyrian attack on Dumatu in the Wadi Sirhan in northern Arabia thwarted any possible attempts by Arab tribes to come to Mushezib-Marduk's assistance.

Aware that the fate Sennacherib had in store for them would be fearsome, the people of Babylon resisted for fifteen months, under conditions described in a legal document from nearby Dilbat as extremely dire. Barley was being sold for more than fifty times the average price: "In the reign of Mushezib-Marduk, there were siege, famine, hunger, starvation, and hard times in the land. Everything had become non-existent. For one shekel (8.5 grams, or 0.3 ounces) of silver (one could buy no more than) two liters (or 2 quarts) of barley. The city gates were locked and there was no exit in all four directions. The corpses of the people filled the squares of Babylon because there was no one to bury them."[16]

In the late fall of 689, the Assyrians finally took the city. Mushezib-Marduk and his family were carried off alive, apparently after having been betrayed by a local citizen eager to reap the generous reward—his own weight in silver—that was offered for the rebel king's capture. We know about this last detail from a letter from the reign of Ashurbanipal, in which Sennacherib's grandson announces an even more generous reward for the arrest of another Babylonian rebel: "Just as my grandfather (Sennacherib), on account of Shuzubu (i.e., Mushezib-Marduk), placed Adad-barakka on scales, and weighed out and gave him his weight in silver, so I will now place on scales whoever takes him (the new rebel) prisoner, even if he should kill him, and weigh out and give him his weight in gold."[17]

What happened next in Babylon was an unprecedented orgy of destruction. Sennacherib later boasted of the carnage:

> (Babylon's) people, young and old, I did not spare. I filled the city squares with their corpses. I handed the property of that city over to my people, and they kept it for themselves. My people seized and smashed the gods dwelling in its midst. I destroyed, devastated, and burned the city and its buildings. I removed bricks and earth from the inner and outer wall, the temples, and the ziggurat, and threw them into the Arahtu river. I dug canals into the center of the city, inflicting destruction worse than what the Deluge had wrought. So that in the future the site of that city and its temples will no longer be recognized, I dissolved it in water and annihilated it, making it like a meadow.[18]

Even if the acts of violence outlined in this passage had been inflicted on some faraway city in the Levant or the Zagros Mountains, they would have been deemed extraordinary in their severity. That they were directed against Babylon, navel of the Mesopotamian world, fountainhead of cuneiform learning, and religious center par excellence, must have made them utterly incomprehensible to many contemporary observers.

To be sure, Sennacherib's description exaggerates the damage suffered by the city. Babylon was not washed away by some artificially created deluge, with the debris, as Sennacherib claims, carried by the Euphrates as far as Dilmun (modern Bahrain) in the Persian Gulf. But the destruction archaeologists have observed in Babylon's Merkes quarter, the limited number of Babylonian economic documents from the years after 689, and references in the Babylonian Chronicle to the cessation of the Akitu Festival during Sennacherib's remaining years and into the reign of his successor, Esarhaddon, suggest that his account is also not completely misleading.[19]

AFTER A DECADE AND A HALF OF UNFORGIVABLE BETRAYALS, bloody battles, extended sieges, and painful population transfers, Babylonia was finally quiet. What it experienced, though, was not the kind of tranquility the *pax Assyriaca* had brought to other parts of the empire—it was the peace of the graveyard. Sennacherib's goal had been to eradicate Babylon from the political and mental map of the world—and he seemed to have achieved it at last.

But had he really? Physically, large parts of the city of Babylon, especially its temples and palaces, were indeed obliterated after the Assyrian attack of 689. But as an idea, a *lieu de mémoire*, Babylon lived on. The city continued to loom large in the imaginations of the Mesopotamian people—so large, in fact, that Sennacherib's "court intellectuals" had to find ways to cope with the widespread phantom pain caused by the loss of its renowned sanctuaries and much-attended festivals.[20]

One way for them to do so was to denigrate and mock Babylonia's age-old traditions, which until recently the Assyrian kings themselves had so enthusiastically endorsed. The best example of this approach—which also helped suppress any guilt the perpetrators of the destruction might have felt—is the "Marduk Ordeal Text," known from clay tablets found at Nineveh, Ashur, and Calah. The cuneiform text, written in Assyrian, has the format of a cultic commentary, a genre that provides learned explanations of the ceremonies performed during temple rituals, often by linking them to mythological stories about the gods for whom the rituals were carried out. The Marduk Ordeal Text seems to comment on several different Babylonian rituals, but its main focus is Babylon's famous Akitu Festival, which had traditionally been celebrated over the first eleven days of the month of Nisannu, at the beginning of the

New Year. Highlights of the festival included a blessing of Marduk's Esagil Temple and a recitation of the Babylonian Epic of Creation, or *Enūma eliš*, on day four; the arrival of Marduk's divine son Nabû from the city of Borsippa on day five; a divine assembly, reenacted with the help of statues, at the "Dais of Destinies," where Marduk decreed the fates for the new year, and the subsequent procession of the gods to the so-called Akitu House outside Babylon, all on day nine; feasting and gift-giving in the Akitu House on day ten; and yet another assembly to decree the fates, plus the return of the gods to their main temples, on day eleven.[21]

The objective of the Akitu Festival was to emphasize the greatness of Babylon's chief deity, Marduk, and his divine retinue. But the Marduk Ordeal Text presents a very different picture of the cultic acts and paraphernalia associated with the festival. It reinterprets them as symbolic correlates of a trial—an ordeal—of Marduk, held against him at the Akitu House on behalf of Ashur and leading to his criminal conviction. The text states, for example, "The cloth beneath him (i.e., Marduk), and the red wool with which he is clothed, are the blows with which he was struck. They are dyed with his blood." Red was the color of vigor and power in Mesopotamian religion, and this was why Marduk—represented by his statue—was wearing red garments when making public appearances. But the Marduk Ordeal Text undermines this conventional understanding, claiming that the color actually stood for the wounds the god had received when he was taken prisoner. Even more blatantly revisionist is the text's assertion that the *Enūma eliš*—the heroic epic recited during the Akitu Festival—rather than celebrating Marduk's rise to absolute power, "concerns his imprisonment."

Cultic commentaries were often considered "secret knowledge" in ancient Mesopotamia, not to be disseminated beyond the narrow circle of the religious cognoscenti. But the Marduk Ordeal Text ends with a curse against anyone "who reads this tablet and does not disclose its content to those who do not know it." In other words, the text was an anti-Babylonian propaganda treatise meant for wide distribution, especially in Assyria.

AT SOME POINT, IT MUST HAVE BECOME CLEAR THAT RIDICULING Babylon's festivals and cults would not be enough to overcome the profound psychological reverberations of Assyria's attack on the city. The void left by the events of 689 was simply too great.

Sennacherib must have felt it himself. As the many allusions to the *Enūma eliš* in his account of the Battle of Halulê demonstrate, the king was obsessed with Babylon's religious traditions. But how to preserve a legacy that extolled the power of one's arch-enemy? The solution that Sennacherib and his inner circle found was to engage in a brazen act of "cultural cannibalism." Key elements of Babylon's religious infrastructure were transferred to Assyria and repurposed for the greater glory of the Assyrian Empire.[22]

This happened quite literally with the lavishly adorned cultic bed of Marduk, on which the god used to spend quality time with his wife Zarpanitu, and with a throne of his. Both had originally stood in the cella (the inner chamber) of Marduk's Esagil Temple, or in the cella of the small temple of Marduk on top of Babylon's ziggurat, the famous "Tower of Babel." Assyrian troops removed them from Babylon and brought them to Ashur, where Sennacherib rededicated them to the god Ashur. Henceforth, it would be Ashur and his wife Mullissu who would find pleasure and rest on the divine furniture, rather than Marduk and his spouse.

In 655 BCE, Sennacherib's grandson Ashurbanipal returned the bed and the throne to Babylon, where they were again to serve Marduk. But before he did so, his scribes copied on a clay tablet the inscription that Sennacherib's scribes had written on the two objects after they had arrived in Ashur. This inscription is of considerable interest. Replacing Marduk as the dedicatee, it is directed to "Ashur, the king of the gods, the father of the gods, the one who decrees the fates, who brings devastation like the Deluge to the land that has been treacherous and evil, and who makes a destructive flood sweep over all those places in the four corners of the world that do not submit to his governor (i.e., Sennacherib)." Sennacherib, in other words, claims to have acted on behalf of Ashur when attacking Babylon, an event indirectly referenced by the remark about the devastating flood that had ravaged an "evil land." At the same time, by calling Ashur "the one who decrees the fates," the inscription ascribes to the god a prerogative previously held by Marduk—and makes him, somewhat paradoxically, more Babylonian than ever before.[23]

This "Babylonianization" of Assyrian religion also took place on a much larger scale. During the 680s, the whole cultic infrastructure of Ashur was transformed after the model of Babylon. The old entrance to the cella of the Ashur Temple was closed and replaced by a new one, which faced a new eastern courtyard apparently replicating the eastern court of Marduk's Esagil Temple. Inside this courtyard, workmen erected a Babylonian-style, altar-like "Dais of Destinies," which could be used for a divine ceremony in the course of which Ashur, rather than Marduk, would decree the fates. An inscription on that dais—or on a ceremonial "Tablet of Destinies" placed on it—asked that Ashur "look after the reign of Sennacherib, King of Assyria, determine a good destiny, a destiny of good health" for him, and grant him political preeminence. The clay tablet on which these lines were copied is written in Babylonian script, suggesting that the religious reforms that Sennacherib put in place relied in part on the know-how of Babylonian priests who had been brought to Assyria.[24]

But the most obvious example of Sennacherib's attempt to recreate Babylon's sacred landscape at Ashur was the new Akitu House that he built in the 680s outside the western wall of the city. Modeled after the Akitu House north of Babylon and erected on massive foundations, it had a sumptuous, well-irrigated orchard around it and must have looked quite stunning. Its construction had started after the gods had given their consent by means of divination—and after Sennacherib had abandoned an earlier plan to build an Akitu House at Nineveh. An inscription mentions that inside the new sanctuary, Sennacherib heaped up earth taken from the ruins of Babylon, a grim memento of the building's origins in a Babylonian idea.[25]

THE CEREMONIAL SUMERIAN NAME THAT SENNACHERIB GAVE the new Akitu House in Ashur was Eabbaugga, the "House where the Sea is put to death." The "Sea" to which this name alludes was the primeval proto-goddess Tiamat, who embodied the deep ocean—Babylonian *tâmtu*. Tiamat was the main opponent of Marduk in the Babylonian Epic of Creation, the *Enūma eliš*. The epic played an enormously important role in first-millennium Mesopotamia—not only in the cult, especially in the Akitu Festival, but also in school and as a cultural text. Kings such as Sargon II and Sennacherib quoted it in their royal inscriptions. It starts with Tiamat and her partner Apsû—a male deity associated with fresh water—bringing forth, at the beginning of time, several generations of younger gods. The noise these young gods make annoys their progenitors, and Apsû decides to kill them; but Ea, one of the younger gods, defeats him and founds his abode within the waters of the slain god, where he engenders a son, Marduk. Soon, it becomes clear that the conflict with Apsû has only been the prelude to a much greater fight. This time, it is Tiamat who becomes fed up with the disturbances of the younger gods and wants to get rid of them. In a cataclysmic battle, Marduk vanquishes her, splits her in two, and uses the two halves of her watery corpse to form heaven and earth. He fashions the celestial bodies and crowns his great work with the creation of mankind. As a reward for his heroic achievements—and for having brought an end to primeval chaos and matriarchal misrule—the other gods make Marduk their king and build a dwelling place for him, the Esagil Temple in Babylon. It becomes the navel of the world and the central gathering place of the gods.[26]

The doctrine of absolute power laid out in *Enūma eliš* mirrored perfectly the imperial ambitions of the Assyrian kings. Small wonder, then, that the text had such tremendous appeal for them. There was only one problem: the god celebrated in the epic was Marduk and not the Assyrian state god, Ashur; and the city whose greatness the text praised was Babylon.

The solution that Sennacherib's literati found to deal with this dilemma after Babylon's destruction in 689 was a simple one: they created a new edition of *Enūma eliš* that rectified the aforementioned deficiencies. This did not require too many changes—it was by and large enough to replace the name of Marduk with that of Ashur the god, and the name of Babylon with that of Ashur the city. Henceforth it was no longer Marduk who had killed Tiamat and been exalted as the king of the gods, but Ashur, whose city became the new center of the cosmos. Fragments of clay tablets inscribed with the Assyrian version of the epic have been found at Nineveh and Ashur, indicating that the text was widely distributed.[27]

As its name makes abundantly clear, Sennacherib's new Akitu House in Ashur was conceived to remember and celebrate Ashur's victory over Tiamat as it was recounted in the new *Enūma eliš*. This happened in the course of an elaborate spring festival at the beginning of the year, when—in an attempt to refashion in Assyrian style Marduk's Akitu procession in Babylon—Sennacherib had statues representing Ashur, his family, and his divine retinue paraded along a new procession street from the Ashur Temple in the east of the city to the Akitu House. Once there, Ashur's triumph over the forces of chaos was ritually reenacted, though how exactly the reenactment played out remains unknown.

The decoration of the Akitu House featured Sennacherib's new Ashur theology as well. Except for its foundations, little is preserved of the building, but a clay tablet describes scenes depicted on a bronze gate leading into the sanctuary. They showed "Ashur, with his bow as he carries it, in the chariot that he rides; the 'Deluge' (a type of weapon) that he has harnessed; the god Amurru as the driver who rides with him; all the gods who go in front of him and go behind him, those who ride in vehicles and those who go on foot; and (the sea monster) Tiamat, with (some terrifying primeval) creatures inside her, against whom Ashur, the king of the gods, goes to fight."[28]

The text goes on to proudly emphasize that Sennacherib had invented new bronze casting techniques to fashion the—undoubtedly monumental—gate of the new Akitu House. The king, in other words, presents himself as a kind of master engineer, as he also did in some other contexts—for example, when claiming that he developed new devices for lifting water.

As with his engineering projects, there is something mechanical about the "copy-and-paste" approach Sennacherib employed in replicating Babylon's cultic landscape in Ashur and transforming the Babylonian *Enūma eliš* into an Assyrian text. At the same time, Sennacherib's reform represents a truly remarkable milestone in the history of religion, similar to the more famous religious revolution brought about in the fourteenth century by Egypt's "heretic" pharaoh Akhenaten. Both ventures were bold and brutal, were aborted and repressed soon after they had been initiated, and were yet of great consequence. They both had important political repercussions.[29]

But there are also some significant differences between them. Up to 700 BCE, Ashur was a deity mostly defined by his civic and political dimensions. He represented the city of Ashur and the Assyrian state. Sennacherib's reform provided him with additional facets of a mythological and cosmological nature. As an inscription written in Sennacherib's name on a kettledrum puts it, Ashur was now "the one who formed the cover of the heavens and the netherworld; who dwells in the bright firmament; and who dwells in (his temple) Esharra, which is in Ashur." The objective of Akhenaten's reform was almost the opposite. The Egyptian pharaoh sought to deprive the sun god of the mythological and cultic dimensions he had previously possessed, and to reduce him to his cosmological function as the life-giving sun-disk—a far more "negative" theology than the one Sennacherib had in mind for Ashur.[30]

EVEN THOUGH CERTAIN FEATURES OF SENNACHERIB'S RELIGIOUS reform remained in place until the very end of Assyrian statehood, its main ideas were soon abandoned. Sennacherib's son and successor Esarhaddon decided to put Babylon back on the map by rebuilding it, and to endorse a political theology that was based on the idea of a balance of power between Ashur and Marduk. Sennacherib's end was a sad one. In 681 BCE, eight years after his assault on Babylon, he was brutally assassinated. That the king's murder was in some way related to his Babylonian politics is a distinct possibility. Sennacherib's unprecedented actions against Babylon, and disagreements about the future direction of Assyria's approach toward its southern neighbor, must have led to serious conflicts among the members of the king's inner circle, and some of them probably hated their royal master. But the main reason for Sennacherib's death was a different one: a violent dispute among his sons about who was to succeed the king.

For several years, Sennacherib's crown prince was a certain Urdu-Mullissu, who may have been selected by his father as early as 700 BCE. Since Assyrian crown princes had a large staff, including military personnel, Urdu-Mullissu must have been very powerful. He was also enormously affluent. A substantial dossier of economic documents indicates that his "third man" (the shield bearer on his chariot) owned large tracts of lands and numerous slaves, almost certainly by virtue of being a close associate of the crown prince.[31]

But sometime around 683, under circumstances that are not quite clear, Urdu-Mullissu was abruptly removed from his position as heir to the throne and replaced by one of Sennacherib's younger sons, a man by the name of Esarhaddon. Torn by jealousy and hatred, and unperturbed by the oaths they had been forced to swear on behalf of the new heir to the throne, Esarhaddon's elder (half) brothers, most notably Urdu-Mullissu, began to conspire against the new crown prince and forced him into exile in a western land. Yet despite the pressure he faced, Sennacherib refused to reinstate Urdu-Mullissu or nominate another crown prince. This sealed his fate. A variety of sources reveal that in the winter month of Tebetu, in 681, Urdu-Mullissu killed his father, or had him killed by a proxy, possibly while Sennacherib was visiting a shrine of the god Nusku in the temple of the moon god at Nineveh. The prince probably had accomplices. The Bible mentions that a second son of Sennacherib, Sharezer (Assyrian Sharru-usur), was likewise involved in the assassination.[32]

The plot had nearly been uncovered before it could be carried out. Three Babylonian goldsmiths residing in Nineveh, all brothers, had heard of Urdu-Mullissu's nefarious plans, and one of them tried to warn Sennacherib. But he never managed to get through to him. When requesting an audience with the king, two court officials asked him what he was calling about. The Babylonian informer answered that he wanted to talk about Urdu-Mullissu, whereupon the officials covered his face and pretended they would lead him before the king. Assuming he was speaking to Sennacherib, the informer divulged that Urdu-Mullissu was about to assassinate the monarch. Only when his face was uncovered did he realize that the officials had actually brought him, not to the king, but to the ringleader of the conspiracy, Urdu-Mullissu himself. Urdu-Mullissu interrogated the would-be informer, and then he probably had all three of the goldsmiths killed.[33]

After Sennacherib's murder, some of the regicides turned on each other. The exiled Esarhaddon, realizing that the chaos at home gave him a chance to regain power, decided to march back to Assyria. He assembled a small army and crossed, eagle-like and unafraid of the snow and cold brought by the month of Shabatu (XI), the western land of Hanigalbat. According to one of Esarhaddon's inscriptions, the crack troops sent by the rebel brothers to block his advance "became like crazed women" and changed sides. The brothers themselves, panicking in the face of Esarhaddon's imminent arrival, fled to the north, and on the eighth day of the month of Addaru (XII), Esarhaddon "joyfully entered Nineveh" and sat on his father's throne. "The south wind, the breeze of the god Ea, was blowing," and "favorable signs" were seen "all over heaven and earth."[34]

SENNACHERIB'S DECISION TO NOMINATE A YOUNGER SON AS crown prince—the root cause of all this family strife—had probably been prompted by his close relationship with a woman: his wife Naqia, Esarhaddon's mother. Urdu-Mullissu and the other elder (half) brothers of Esarhaddon had been children of a different royal wife, who had apparently fallen out of favor at some point. Having the ear of the king almost entirely to herself, Naqia cannot have failed to advance her son's interests. After Esarhaddon ascended the throne, she continued to help him navigate the political landscape.

While perhaps the most powerful at that time, Naqia was clearly not the only Assyrian royal woman to wield a great deal of authority. A few others influenced the fate of the Neo-Assyrian kingdom as well, including its relations with Babylonia. In fact, as time went by, royal women seem to have played an ever-increasing role in Assyrian imperial politics. To draw on a statement by Aristotle, women may not have ruled Assyria, but it seems as though more than one of Assyria's rulers "was ruled by women." It is worth taking a closer look at them.[35]

10

Mother Knows Best

The Assyrian succession crisis of the late 680s was a dramatic experience for Naqia—perhaps the most dramatic in her long and extraordinary life. After Urdu-Mullissu and his supporters had forced her son Esarhaddon into exile, her position at the Nineveh court had become highly precarious. Fearing for her safety, she must have been worried and anxious. In this defining moment, when everything seemed to be on the line, Naqia prayed to the goddess Ishtar—and received an answer. A prophetess from Arbela by the name of Ahat-abisha fell into a frenzy and spoke to Naqia in the name of the goddess: "Because you implored me, saying, 'You have placed the ones at the (king's) right and left side in your lap, but made my own offspring roam the steppe'—now, fear not, o king! The kingdom is yours, yours is the power!"[1]

The prophecy is known from a clay tablet that also records similar divine messages directed to Esarhaddon. In fact, the Naqia prophecy includes at the end encouraging words addressed to the son, rather than the mother. The two clearly had a very close relationship, and it is obvious that Naqia had been enormously eager to help her son ascend the Assyrian throne. Fortunately for her, Ishtar had not promised them too much. After his return to Nineveh, Esarhaddon assumed power, and Naqia saw herself elevated to the position of

235

queen mother. Soon, she began to play a central role in the affairs of the Assyrian state.[2]

It was a remarkable rise for Naqia. When she was young, she had few reasons to expect that she would one day become the most powerful woman—and perhaps for a while the most powerful individual—in the Assyrian Empire. Her origins are shrouded in darkness. Because Naqia, "the Pure One," is a West Semitic name, and because her son found refuge somewhere in the west during his time in exile, it has been suggested—even though there is no final proof—that Naqia hailed from the region west of Assyria's core area, perhaps from the city of Harran. Presumably, Naqia was betrothed to Sennacherib while the latter served as Sargon II's crown prince, and gave birth to Esarhaddon at some point between 715 and 710 BCE. But she was neither the only wife of Sennacherib at this time nor his first. Similar to Assyrian kings, Assyrian crown princes apparently had the right to have sexual relations with multiple women, and Naqia initially played second fiddle, at best.[3]

Sennacherib's first wife, and the mother of his older children, including Urdu-Mullissu, was in all likelihood a woman by the name of Tashmetu-sharrat. What is known for sure is that Tashmetu-sharrat served as Assyria's official queen a few years into Sennacherib's reign, and that the king was so fond of her that he supplied her with lavishly equipped lodgings in the royal palaces of Nineveh and Ashur. In an unusually intimate inscription found on a pair of stone sphinxes in the entryway to her private quarters in the Southwest Palace at Nineveh, Sennacherib romanticizes Tashmetu-sharrat as "my beloved spouse, whose features the (birth) goddess Belet-ili has made more perfect than that of all other women," and describes her residence as a place of "lovemaking, happiness, and exultation." The text, which dates to about 695 BCE, ends with the only instance in the large corpus of Assyrian royal inscriptions where the royal "I" becomes a "we": "May we both live long in these palatial halls, be satisfied with our prosperity, and be in good health and full of joy."[4]

But Sennacherib's hopes that the undiluted happiness he enjoyed with Tashmetu-sharrat would last forever would be dashed. Tashmetu-sharrat either died or—a more probable scenario—was increasingly sidelined by Naqia, without falling out of favor entirely. As a rule, Assyrian kings had only one official "queen" at a time, but it may be that for parts of the 680s Sennacherib allowed both Tashmetu-sharrat and Naqia to hold that position. During these years, the Assyrian state god Ashur became associated with two wives as well, the goddesses Mullissu and Sherua, a "bigamist" arrangement that may have reflected Sennacherib's relationship status at the time. Tellingly, there was apparently some competition between the two goddesses. A ritual text composed under Sennacherib describes in considerable detail exactly how some altars of Ashur, Mullissu, and Sherua were to be placed next to one another.[5]

Toward the end of his reign, Sennacherib may have been deeply involved with yet another woman. A letter sent from Ashur seems to indicate that the king had begun a relationship with the wife of the governor of Ashur and had ordered that she stay in the royal palace—an episode that brings to mind the biblical story of King David's infatuation with Bathsheba, the wife of the elite warrior Uriah. After Sennacherib's death, the governor took the woman back and celebrated the king's passing by dressing his staff in festive robes and listening to joyful music, which prompted the anonymous letter writer, who was appalled by this behavior, to inform on him.[6]

Sennacherib may not have been a "feminist," as one scholar half-jokingly once suggested. But he seems to have been an *homme à femmes* who attached great importance to his relationships with women. And while the majority of the female members of his royal court remained very much in the shadows, a few of them, most notably Naqia, got used to exerting more and more power.[7]

WHATEVER EXACTLY HAPPENED BETWEEN SENNACHERIB AND his wives and consorts, Naqia's beloved son Esarhaddon did eventually become crown prince, and after many trials and tribulations also Assyrian king. Overwhelmed by the responsibilities he now had to shoulder, and repeatedly stricken by sickness and depression, he began to rely extensively on the manifold skills of his mother.

The written documentation on Naqia's activities during Esarhaddon's reign presents quite an astounding picture. For starters, she is the only Assyrian queen of all times to have ever left a building inscription in royal style. It records, even more remarkably, how Naqia constructed a palace for her son, after the great gods of Assyria and Babylonia had "gladly placed him on the throne of his father." As Naqia writes, "Esarhaddon gave to me as my lordly share people from foreign lands, enemies conquered with the help of his bow, and I had them carry hoe and basket so they would make bricks." The new palace was located on the citadel of Nineveh, the very center of Assyrian royal power, and stood in close proximity to the temple of the moon and sun gods—conceivably the place where Sennacherib had been murdered a few years earlier. When the building work was completed, Naqia claims, she invited the gods, along with Esarhaddon himself, into the palace for a lavish inauguration party.[8]

Naqia was able to pay for this construction project because she was fabulously rich. In her capacity as queen mother, she received a share of the tribute regularly delivered to the Assyrian court and owned large agricultural estates in various corners of the empire. She had residences in all the major cities of Assyria and a large staff that included not only high-ranking administrators but also military personnel. Several inscriptions reveal that Naqia dedicated valuable objects, including a golden breastplate inlaid with precious stones, to the divine "Lady of Nineveh" (that is, Ashur's wife Mullissu) and the divine "Lady of Babylon." The gift to the Babylonian deity is, incidentally, a clear indication that Naqia fully endorsed Esarhaddon's decision to reverse Sennacherib's anti-Babylonian policy. There is other evidence that supports that fact—indeed, Naqia may have been the driving force behind the new approach.[9]

In various places, images of Naqia were put on display. A fragmentary bronze relief, probably from the facing of the base of a throne or altar, depicts her standing behind the king with a mirror in her hand, carrying out a religious ritual. And a cuneiform letter sent to Esarhaddon by a functionary of the temple of Nabû in Calah mentions "statues of the king and a statue of the queen mother," for which an administrator had failed to procure gold deposited in a royal storehouse. Fashioning monumental images depicting an Assyrian queen or queen mother was something entirely new. No such images are known from the time before Esarhaddon.[10]

The enormous respect that Naqia commanded can be gauged from a number of letters from the Assyrian "state archives" in Nineveh. One of them, sent to Esarhaddon in 670 by his chief exorcist, Marduk-shakin-shumi, assures the king that Naqia had recovered from a severe illness and then concludes, "The mother of the king is as capable as (the mythological sage) Adapa." The only other person ever compared to this antediluvian paragon of wisdom was the Assyrian king himself.[11]

Several letters written by priests and high officials were addressed to the queen mother herself. Most of them cover donations to various temples or religious festivals, or the performance of apotropaic rituals (that is, rituals meant to repel evil) after a lunar eclipse, all matters that may have been part of the traditional portfolio of high-ranking Assyrian royal women. But there are also letters that deal with political and military affairs. One was sent to Naqia in the early 670s by the governor of the Sealand, a region near the Persian Gulf. It informs her about an Elamite raid on southern Babylonia:

> To the mother of the king, my lord, your servant, Na'id-Marduk. Good health to the mother of the king, my lord!...After the

Elamites had marched against us and taken control of a bridge, I wrote, as soon as they came, to the mother of the king, my lord. Now they have dismantled the bridge.... We do not know if they will go on. If they do, I shall write to the mother of the king, my lord, again. The forces must reach us, my lord![12]

The letter demonstrates unequivocally the scale of Naqia's direct involvement in matters of major strategic significance. Revealingly, the sender addresses her at the end as "my lord" rather than "my lady": Naqia, it seems, did not just act on behalf of the king—she was very much like a king herself.

NAQIA WAS NOT THE ONLY ANCIENT NEAR EASTERN ROYAL woman who became extremely powerful during her life. The Egyptian queens Hatshepsut and Cleopatra (as sole rulers of their kingdom) and the Hittite queen Puduhepa did so, too, as did some other female members of the Assyrian royal family. In general, though, female agency in the political sphere was quite limited in the patriarchal societies of the ancient world, and the rise of women to positions of political authority exceptional. The Assyrian King List—which is called a "King List" for a reason—does not include any women among the more than one hundred Assyrian rulers it names.

While average Assyrian citizens usually lived in monogamous relationships, Neo-Assyrian kings often had hundreds, if not thousands, of female "companions." Most of them spent their time shut away from the world in the constrained quarters of the various "harems" kept by Assyrian monarchs. It has been estimated that royal palaces in no fewer than twenty-two Assyrian cities included such harem quarters.[13]

Many of the Assyrian harem women must have been royal concubines chosen for their beauty, but the harem populations also included members of the harems of the king's predecessor; female relatives of the monarch; the daughters, sisters, and nieces of vassal kings and political allies; and relocated harem women of defeated enemies. All of them were called *sekretu*, that is, "sequestered woman," a title semantically close to *ḥarīm*, the Arabic word for "harem woman."

Neo-Assyrian sources have little to say about how these women actually lived, but based on evidence from the second millennium BCE, it seems likely that many of them were singers or musicians, and that eunuch guards made sure they did not leave their lodgings without some very good reason. Female chief administrators with the title *šakintu* were responsible for the management of these sprawling communities of women. Legal documents reveal that the *šakintu*s bought slaves and land, made loans, and helped organize the production of textiles, an activity in which many harem women were engaged. The staff of the *šakintu*s included female scribes writing in Aramaic.[14]

Many Assyrian royal women came from outside the Assyrian core area. It seems the Assyrian kings often preferred women from the culturally more advanced regions in the Levant and southwestern Anatolia to women from the east and northeast. Ashurbanipal— the Assyrian king later charged by the Greeks with having spent far too much of his life among his women—claims in one of his inscriptions that the rulers of Tyre and Arwad in Phoenicia and of Tabal and Cilicia in Anatolia had all brought him "their daughters, their own offspring, together with large dowries, so they could serve as female stewards." While their presence at the Assyrian royal court must have helped improve diplomatic relations with their home countries, the fact that these high-ranking women were put to work in Assyria shows that those kingdoms were not considered equal partners but inferior vassal states.[15]

The accumulation and sequestration of women, and their sexual exploitation by the elites and other citizens, may have been an essential reason for ancient empires to exist in the first place. The Greek story of Zeus's abduction of the Phoenician princess Europa in the form of a bull is a mythologized expression of this underexplored aspect of premodern imperialism. Assyria makes for a good case study. Like the gold and silver, the textiles and the timber, and the foreign craftsmen and soldiers transferred to the Assyrian capitals, the countless women from all over the known world who were placed at the disposal of Assyrian men embodied Assyria's power, improved the empire's "fitness," and helped secure its future. This is particularly true for the hundreds of women sent over time to Assyria's imperial rulers. In a civilization where infant mortality was high, having a large harem raised the chances of reproductive success for the Assyrian kings, with important political implications, as a steady stream of royal sons guaranteed the continuation of the royal line. In this regard, Assyria was different from imperial Rome, where strict adherence to the legal rule of monogamy left quite a few emperors without a legitimate biological son, leading on more than one occasion to dynastic instability.[16]

Almost all of the many women who populated the Neo-Assyrian harems remain nameless to us. But two types of Assyrian royal women in particular played more prominent roles: the "mother of the king" (*ummi šarri*) and the king's chief consort, whose rather bland title "Palace Woman" (*issi ekalli* or *segallu*) obscures the fact that she effectively served as Assyria's queen. In most cases, the "Palace Woman" was probably also the mother of the crown prince. Given their unrestrained access to the king, both the queen mother and the ruler's chief consort could wield enormous influence, including in the political sphere.

ESARHADDON, IN FACT, APPARENTLY RELIED HEAVILY NOT ONLY on his mother, Naqia, but also on his wife, named Esharra-hammat. Esharra-hammat's death on the twelfth day of the month of Addaru, 672 BCE, is recorded in the Babylonian Chronicle, a source not generally inclined to indulge in idle gossip. She was buried with great pomp in a mausoleum in Ashur, and regular funerary offerings were established for her. Even dead, the royal spouse continued to make an impact. According to a letter written shortly after her passing, her ghost had appeared to her son, the crown prince Ashurbanipal, and had blessed him, saying, "May his descendants rule over Assyria." The letter writer, anxious that the dead queen be properly remembered, adds, "Honoring the gods brings forth good; honoring the gods of the underworld restores life."[17]

Another woman of consequence during Esarhaddon's reign was Naqia's sister Abi-ramu, who is mentioned in a legal document about a land lease from 674 BCE. While her economic activities are thus well documented, it is less certain, but possible, that she also held an important political position. An individual by the name of Abi-ramu (which was borne by men as well as women) is known to have served under Esarhaddon as grand vizier, governor of the western land of Hanigalbat, and eponym of the year 677 BCE—and even though this official is nowhere identified as female, it is tempting to think that Naqia's sister might have been the one to hold these positions. Royal women, after all, had a lot of authority during Esarhaddon's reign, and the position of grand vizier and governor (or king) of Hanigalbat was traditionally given to a member of the Assyrian royal family. The last prominent incumbent had been Sargon II's brother Sîn-ahu-usur. Since Esarhaddon could not trust his brothers, who had been involved in the plot to kill their father, after all, it would have made sense for him to choose his aunt instead, the sister of his beloved mother, to hold the age-old office.[18]

UNTIL A FEW DECADES AGO, VERY LITTLE WAS KNOWN ABOUT Assyrian royal women from the period prior to the reigns of Sennacherib and Esarhaddon. A few short references in royal inscriptions to Sammu-ramat, the wife of Shamshi-Adad V and mother of Adad-nirari III, was almost all scholars were able to work with. This changed dramatically in the late 1980s, when Iraqi archaeologists led by Muzahim Mahmood Hussein made a number of stunning discoveries in the southern, domestic wing of Ashurnasirpal II's Northwest Palace in Calah. In the spring of 1988, the excavators had observed an unevenness in the brick floor of a room labeled "MM." When they removed the flooring, they found a ninth-century BCE subterranean burial chamber, accessible by means of a shaft with a stairway. It held a terracotta sarcophagus containing the body of an unidentified female (or perhaps a eunuch), a silver bowl, some gold jewelry, a collection of cylinder seals, and other precious items. Also found, and very much in line with a harem setting, were three finely glazed terracotta sculptures depicting erotic scenes: a man penetrating a woman from behind, another man kneeling over a woman lying on her back, and an act of fellatio.[19]

The discoveries made below the floor of Room MM suggested that the southern wing of the Northwest Palace might house burial chambers of additional royal women, and in 1989, the Iraqi excavators set out to search for such structures. Their efforts were rewarded spectacularly. Under the floors of two rooms farther west of Room MM, they came across two more vaulted burial chambers with a number of sarcophagi. The harem women at Calah had apparently lived their lives with their dead predecessors directly below their feet.

Even though they had been disturbed in antiquity, the newly found tombs were still filled with enormous amounts of jewelry and other valuable artifacts, some imported from the west: crowns, earrings, necklaces, bracelets, anklets, beads, stamp and cylinder seals, amulets, mirrors, fibulae, textiles, and a variety of vessels. Many objects were made of gold, but there were also artifacts made of silver, bronze, ivory, and other materials. Several pieces of jewelry were inlaid with beautifully cut semiprecious stones. It was a once-in-a-lifetime discovery, on a par with the famous treasures from Tutankhamun's tomb from the Valley of Kings in Thebes. If the artifacts from the Calah tombs never received the same amount of attention, this is because they were soon stored away in Iraq's Central Bank in Baghdad, where they barely survived massive bombing campaigns conducted during the First and Second Gulf Wars in 1991 and 2003.

Unlike the first tomb, the two burial chambers found in 1989 produced texts that revealed a lot about the royal women who were interred in them. The older of them, "Tomb III," as it was soon called, held a large alabaster sarcophagus that had been robbed and was found empty. But based on the inscription on its lid, it could be ascribed to a woman with the elaborate Assyrian name Mullissu-mukannishat-Ninua, who was the "queen (literally, 'Palace Woman') of Ashurnasirpal (II), king of Assyria, and of Shalmaneser (III), king of Assyria." A curse, continued on a stone tablet found in the tomb's antechamber, warned that "no one later may place herein (anyone else), whether some harem woman or queen, nor remove this sarcophagus from its place. Whoever removes this sarcophagus from its place, his spirit will not receive funerary offerings along with (the other) spirits: it is a taboo of (the sun god) Shamash and (the netherworld goddess) Ereshkigal." The text then states, "(As for me), the daughter of Ashur-nirka-da"in, Chief Cupbearer of Ashurnasirpal (II), king of Assyria: anyone who later removes my seat from before the spirits of the dead, may his spirit receive no food. May someone later clothe me with a shroud, anoint me with oil, and sacrifice a sheep (for me)."[20]

Mullissu-mukannishat-Ninua's anxiety that her final resting place might one day be violated was well founded: her sarcophagus, after all, was already empty by the time it was found. But thanks to the funerary inscriptions she left, her memory was preserved, and we know a great deal about this eminent ninth-century royal woman. She was the main consort of Ashurnasirpal II and kept her title of an Assyrian "Queen" under his successor Shalmaneser III, who was most likely her son. She was, moreover, the daughter of a high-ranking Assyrian official, the chief cupbearer Ashur-nirka-da"in. Early in Ashurnasirpal's time, in other words, when the king still

resided in Ashur, at least some of the most powerful Assyrian officials
were not yet eunuchs but members of old Assyrian families with children of their own—and the king married into this very aristocracy.

Many of the Assyrian queens who followed Mullissu-
mukannishat-Ninua bore West Semitic rather than Assyrian names,
which suggests a shift in the marriage practices among Assyrian rulers in the wake of Ashurnasirpal II's move to Calah. From this time
forth, the Assyrian monarchs made a concerted effort to concentrate
power in their own hands, at the expense of the old elite families,
and apparently no longer married women from the highest echelons
of Assyrian society. This did not mean, however, that the women
now rising to the position of queen were any less influential. On the
contrary, some of them became extremely powerful. Sammu-ramat,
the wife of Shamshi-Adad V and model of the later Greek Semiramis legend, served as a sort of regent when her son Adad-nirari III
ascended the throne, and she clearly was involved in military campaigns and foreign affairs.[21]

Presumably, Sammu-ramat was buried at Calah as well, though
her final resting place has not yet been discovered. But in the antechamber of Mullissu-mukannishat-Ninua's tomb, in a bronze sarcophagus deposited there under circumstances that remain obscure,
the mortal remains of another Assyrian queen were found. A gold
stamp seal pendant, placed around her neck before she was buried, identifies her as "Hamâ, queen (literally, 'Palace Woman') of
Shalmaneser (IV), king of Assyria, and daughter-in-law of Adad-
nirari (III)." The imagery on the seal shows the queen praying to a
goddess, most likely Ishtar or Mullissu, who is sitting on a throne
supported by a recumbent lion. To the left of the throne, a super-
sized scorpion is depicted, a widely used symbol of Assyrian queens
and their households. Queens guaranteed the continuity of the royal
line, and female scorpions—which tend to ruthlessly defend their
offspring with their poisonous tails—were considered ideal models
of motherhood.[22]

As revealed by a scientific examination of her bones conducted in 1997 at the University of Göttingen, Hamâ was between eighteen and twenty years old when she died. As an infant, she had survived a severe illness, and she suffered from poor teeth and chronic sinusitis. Despite her young age at the time of her death and the relative insignificance of her husband, Shalmaneser IV (r. 782–773 BCE), Hamâ was buried with enormously rich grave goods, most importantly a spectacularly beautiful golden crown decorated with leaves, flowers, pomegranates, grape clusters, and winged female figures fashioned out of gold and semiprecious stones (see Plate 9). It was placed on her head at the time of her interment. Hamâ's family background is unclear. In 773 BCE, Shalmaneser IV's last year in power, the king's influential field marshal, Shamshi-ilu, had undertaken a campaign against Hadianu, the ruler of Damascus, and brought back rich tribute to Assyria, including a daughter of Hadianu and her dowry. It could be that Hamâ was this very daughter and that she died together with Shalmaneser, perhaps violently, when the latter passed away a few months later, but this is entirely speculative.[23]

THE FINDS MADE IN 1989 IN YET ANOTHER BURIAL CHAMBER IN the Northwest Palace, soon dubbed "Tomb II," were stunning as well. The chamber contained a stone sarcophagus with the skeletal remains of two slightly later Assyrian queens, along with a remarkable array of jewelry and other grave goods. Based on inscriptional evidence, the woman on the bottom of the sarcophagus can be identified with some confidence as Yabâ, the main consort of Tiglath-pileser III. An alabaster tablet discovered in a niche of the tomb is inscribed with a curse on her behalf:

Whoever, in the future, be it a queen who sits on the throne or some harem woman who is the love interest of the king, removes me from my tomb, or puts anybody else with me, and lays his (sic) hand upon my jewelry with evil intent or breaks open the seal of this tomb: above, under the rays of the sun, let his (*sic*) spirit roam outside in thirst; below in the underworld, when the water-libation ceremony is carried out, (s)he must not receive with the (infernal) Anunnaki gods any funerary offerings in the form of beer, wine, or food.[24]

Just as in the case of Mullissu-mukannishat-Ninua, the curse—which provides interesting insights into the Neo-Assyrian funerary cult—failed, in the end, to protect the queen's corpse from undue interference. At some point, her sarcophagus was opened and a second woman's mortal remains were placed on top of hers. The remains of this second woman have been identified as those of Atalya, chief consort of Sargon II. Her name and title are engraved on a beautiful golden bowl that was placed upon the dead queen's breast. As mentioned earlier, Atalya's name is identical with that of the daughter of a ninth-century Israelite king, which has led to speculation that she might have been of Israelite or Judean extraction. This suggestion remains highly conjectural, however.[25]

Even though she served for a while as Sargon II's queen, Atalya, as also mentioned earlier, was probably not the mother of Sennacherib, the king's crown prince and eventual successor. Sennacherib is instead now thought to have been the son of a woman by the West Semitic name of Ra'imâ (which means "the Beloved"), to whom a monumental stela in Ashur was dedicated. If the poorly preserved inscription on it has been read correctly, it calls Ra'imâ "mother of Sennacherib, king of the world, king of Assyria," but notably not "Palace Woman of Sargon (II)," presumably because of Sennacherib's reluctance to invoke the memory of his father after the latter's inauspicious death on the battlefield in 705 BCE. Given her West Semitic background, it is likely that Ra'imâ conversed with her son in Aramaic, whereas Sargon spoke Assyrian with Sennacherib. If one were to psychoanalyze Sennacherib, one could speculate that this form of "gendered communication" instilled in the young prince a long-lasting notion of an aggressive, conquering Assyria, represented by his father, and a more passive, yielding, and "feminine" western periphery, embodied by his mother.[26]

Ra'imâ seems to have lived longer than Yabâ and Atalya, who were both in their thirties when they died. She was still active in 692 BCE, when a debt note from Nineveh mentions "the mother of the king." At that time, she must have been about seventy years old.[27]

SIMILAR TO QUEENS AND QUEEN MOTHERS (AND, IN THE CASE OF Abi-ramu, a sister of the queen mother), the sisters and daughters of Assyrian kings occasionally gained considerable prominence. Some were married off to foreign rulers, when clearly it was hoped that they would keep an eye on their husbands and make sure they remained loyal political vassals. Not always did such schemes succeed. Sargon II's daughter Ahat-abisha, for example, who had become the wife of Ambaris, the powerful king of Bit-Purutash in central Anatolia, failed to prevent her spouse from rebelling against Sargon. The insurrection ended in 713 BCE with Ambaris's defeat, and he and his family were deported to Assyria, although Ahat-abisha's ultimate fate remains unknown. It is also not clear what became of a daughter of Esarhaddon who was apparently married off to Bartatua, a king of the Scythians mentioned by Herodotus under the name Protothyes. A cuneiform oracle query addressed to the sun god reveals that Esarhaddon considered the marriage an opportunity to end a period of conflict with the Scythians and win them as allies.[28]

One Assyrian princess, Sherua-etirat, rose to a position of considerable authority at the Assyrian court. The eldest daughter of King Esarhaddon and sister of his successor Ashurbanipal, Sherua-etirat never suffered from a lack of self-confidence. During the period when Ashurbanipal was still crown prince, she wrote a bullying letter to Ashurbanipal's wife Libbali-sharrat, making it quite clear that, as a blood relation of the Assyrian royal family, she—Sherua-etirat—held a far higher rank than her sister-in-law. Adding insult to injury, she even mocked Libbali-sharrat's attempts to follow the example of her intellectually inclined husband and dabble in the scribal arts: "Why don't you just write your tablets and recite your exercise?"[29]

But during the waning years of Esarhaddon's reign, the most influential member of the Assyrian royal family continued to be Naqia. In fact, the power of this formidable woman reached its peak in the weeks after Esarhaddon's death in the fall of 669, when she became the guardian of his succession arrangement. Esarhaddon, who had at least eighteen children, had made the unconventional decision to have a younger son of his, Ashurbanipal, replace him on the Assyrian throne, while an older one, Shamash-shumu-ukin, would become the next king of Babylon. Following the example of his father, Sennacherib, Esarhaddon had enforced a long series of loyalty oaths on his Assyrian subjects and foreign client kings to make sure they would respect this scheme. At some point during the twenty-two days between Esarhaddon's passing and Ashurbanipal's accession to the Assyrian throne, Naqia imposed her own loyalty oaths on the Assyrian citizens. The tablet from Nineveh that records these oaths calls her Zakutu rather than Naqia, giving the Assyrian translation of her West Semitic name:

The treaty that Zakutu, the "Palace Woman" of Sennacherib, king of Assyria, and mother of Esarhaddon, king of Assyria, (concluded) with Shamash-shumu-ukin, his (Ashurbanipal's) favorite brother, with Shamash-metu-uballit and the rest of his brothers, with the royal seed, with the magnates and governors, the bearded and the eunuchs, with Assyrians high and low: Anyone who is included in this treaty that Zakutu, the "Palace Woman," has concluded with all the people of the land concerning her cherished grandson Ashurbanipal—anyone (of you) who should fabricate and carry out an ugly and evil scheme or a revolt against your lord

Ashurbanipal, king of Assyria, may Ashur, Sîn, Shamash, Jupiter, Venus, Saturn, Mercury, Mars, and Sirius (punish him).[30]

When Ashurbanipal assumed power, apparently without facing any serious opposition, Naqia had fulfilled her final mission. A little later, she either retired from public life or passed away.

It seems that, for reasons that remain unclear, Naqia's role as Assyria's foremost female "politician" was not passed on to Ashurbanipal's wife Libbali-sharrat, but rather to his sister Sherua-etirat. A papyrus from Egypt written in Egypt's Demotic script but in the Aramaic language provides a fictionalized account of a peacekeeping mission undertaken by Sherua-etirat during a bloody civil war fought from 652 to 648 BCE between Ashurbanipal, the king of Assyria, and his brother Shamash-shumu-ukin, at the time king of Babylon. A fragmentary cuneiform letter from Nineveh mentions Sherua-etirat and the later Babylonian king Kandalanu in connection with the eastern land of Elam, which further strengthens the assumption that the princess—very much like Naqia a few decades earlier—helped shape Assyria's politics vis-à-vis its southern and southeastern neighbors.[31]

Libbali-sharrat, Ashurbanipal's wife, seems never to have carried out political tasks of comparable significance, even though she managed to overcome the disdain initially shown to her by some members of the royal family. A monumental stela from Ashur is decorated with an image of her on which she wears a magnificent "mural crown" (a crown in the shape of a city wall); and one of the most famous artworks from ancient Mesopotamia, a relief from Ashurbanipal's North Palace at Nineveh, depicts her banqueting with her husband beneath an arbor of vines while musicians play merry tunes (see Plate 12).

But even for Libbali-sharrat, a carefree life was not really in the cards. Showered with favors as she was, she was also confronted with the dark side of imperial politics. She witnessed vicious acts of violence and had to worry about possible conspiracies and other attacks on the royal family. On one occasion, making use of her unusual familiarity with the scribal arts, Libbali-sharrat seems to have asked a god if a political plot against Ashurbanipal would result in the assassination of herself and her royal husband: "I ask you, God Lahar, our creator(?): this rumor of an impending rebellion that has been reported to Ashurbanipal, king of Assyria, by people saying: 'They will instigate a rebellion against you'—is it decreed and confirmed? Will it happen? Is it true? Will they attack me? Will I die? Will they capture me in the course of it?" The query ends with the words, addressed to the god: "Disregard that a woman has written (this tablet) and placed it before you."[32]

ALTHOUGH ENORMOUSLY PRIVILEGED, ASSYRIAN ROYAL WOMEN clearly did not have the same opportunities and freedoms the men around them enjoyed—as Libbali-sharrat's query reveals, they could not even speak to their gods without apologizing. Still, as members of the king's inner circle, Assyrian queens and princesses played roles that had far greater political implications than the shenanigans of the minor royals who are the bread and butter of modern tabloid journalism.

As described above, women were particularly influential during Esarhaddon's reign, a time full of ups and downs. Assyrian armies scored some great victories, but inside Assyria, a number of rebellions occurred that shook the empire to its core. Even Naqia, her considerable political talents notwithstanding, could not prevent these crises. Perhaps the outsized role she had gotten used to playing actually contributed to them. It was in 671 BCE that the political drama of Esarhaddon's tumultuous last years reached its peak.

11

671 BCE

O n December 8, 671 BCE, in the midst of the darkest time of
the year, a man called Nabû-ushallim was passing through a
lonely area in the city of Ashur when he was approached by the city's
mayor, Abdâ. According to a cuneiform letter that Nabû-ushallim
later sent to the Assyrian king, Esarhaddon, the mayor took Nabû-
ushallim aside to tell him of two recent dreams. In the first dream,
Abdâ reported, a child had risen from a tomb and handed him a
staff, saying, "Under the protection of this staff, you will become
mighty and powerful." In the second, Abdâ had suddenly caught
sight of a star flaring up in the dead body of the "father of the king."[1]

Abdâ's strange dreams are reminiscent of a famous prophecy
in the Hebrew Bible, ascribed to the diviner Balaam: "A star shall
come out of Jacob, and a scepter shall rise out of Israel." Interpreted
as a reference to David or the Messiah, Balaam's prophetic vision
was later read by Christian theologians as an allusion to the Star
of Bethlehem. But, more generally, it announces the rise of a new
ruler—and this is, sure enough, also the hidden meaning behind
Abdâ's dreams.[2]

Nabû-ushallim was fully aware of the implied symbolism. Abdâ,
he wrote, had gathered 120 elite soldiers, who had sworn an oath
of allegiance to him, and was obviously eager to seize the Assyrian

throne from the reigning king. He wanted Nabû-ushallim to join his rebel group. But Nabû-ushallim had declined. Instead, he had warned Abdâ that someone would "pour lead" into his blasphemous mouth, and then wrote to Esarhaddon to inform him of the mayor's secret machinations (see Plate 11).

Abdâ's conspiracy was not the only coup initiated in 671. Simultaneously, insurgents in at least two other Assyrian cities were engaging in subversive activities against the king. This flurry of rebellions seems rather strange, for in the very same year that Abdâ and his partners in crime were seeking to remove Esarhaddon from power, Assyrian troops had scored one of the greatest triumphs in the kingdom's long history: a successful invasion of Egypt, the richest and most sophisticated state within Assyria's orbit.

Esarhaddon's reign often seems like a "tale of two kings": it is marked by a strong contrast between striking military breakthroughs in faraway places, on the one hand, and problems at home, on the other. The monarch participated in an impressive number of victorious campaigns and pursued ambitious political projects. But at the same time, his personal weaknesses led to a great deal of friction within the inner circle of Assyria's elite. In perhaps no other year in Assyria's long history were triumphs and tribulations, conquests and crises, so closely intertwined as in 671 BCE.

ESARHADDON'S TIME AS KING HAD BEGUN WITH GREAT PROMISE. Right after his victory over his faithless brothers, in 680, he had initiated a series of ambitious military campaigns against various lands outside the Assyrian borders. The first of them was directed against Nabû-zer-kitti-lishir (a son of Assyria's much-hated archenemy Marduk-aplu-iddina II), who had attacked the pro-Assyrian governor of Ur. As his father had done on more than one occasion, Nabû-zer-kitti-lishir fled to Elam, but rather than finding refuge there, he was executed by the Elamite king. One year later, Assyrian troops conquered Arza in the southern Levant, close to the Egyptian border—a first step in Esarhaddon's efforts to seize control of the land on the Nile. His armies also fought in Cilicia and engaged in battles against warriors from Tabal and nomadic Cimmerians, although without scoring a decisive victory. The altercations with the Cimmerians, and with the Scythians, both famous for their equestrian skills as they menaced the ancient states of Western Asia, had continued in 678. In 677, Assyrian troops seized the Phoenician city of Sidon and captured its king Abdi-Milkuti, "like a fish from the midst of the sea." Esarhaddon had Abdi-Milkuti beheaded and turned the territory of Sidon into an Assyrian province. A few months later, he concluded a treaty with the king of Tyre, Sidon's eternal competitor, to consolidate Assyria's commercial interests in the Eastern Mediterranean. In the meantime, an Assyrian expedition force ventured into unknown territories on the eastern edges of the Arabian Peninsula, a region called Bazu, where it defeated a number of Arab kings and queens and conquered, among others, the cities of Dihranu and Qataba (modern Dhahran and Qatif). The northern parts of the Arabian Peninsula were frequent targets of Assyrian military pressure as well, and in the east, a campaign against Median chieftains led Assyrian troops far into central Iran. In 675, an Elamite attack on Sippar required another Assyrian intervention in Babylonia. Esarhaddon had Shumu-iddina, the mayor of Nippur; Kudurru, a son of a Dakkurean chieftain; and a few other high-ranking Babylonians deported to Nineveh, where, among other tasks, they were set to work copying learned cuneiform texts.[3]

These were impressive military achievements. But Esarhaddon also experienced several serious setbacks. Campaigns against a certain Mugallu, king of Melid (modern Malatya in eastern Anatolia) and later of Tabal, and against the land of Mannaya, northeast of Assyria, proved unsuccessful. Assumptions that a lunar eclipse pointed to Mugallu's imminent death, and prophetic utterances made in the name of the goddess Ishtar about Melid's impending destruction, turned out to be wishful thinking.

Even worse, an ambitious military campaign undertaken by Assyrian troops late in 674 against Egypt ended in complete failure. Unsurprisingly, the episode does not feature in any of Esarhaddon's own inscriptions. But the Babylonian Chronicle is quite clear about the outcome of the operation: "On the fifth day of the month of Addaru (XII), the Assyrian army was crushed in Egypt." Among the repercussions of the defeat were a series of defections by Assyrian allies, including Ashkelon and Tyre, on the Eastern Mediterranean shore. The king had much to answer for, and members of the Assyrian elite began to have serious doubts about his fitness for office.[4]

WITH THE AFOREMENTIONED STRING OF MISADVENTURES SEverely compromising his reputation, Esarhaddon found it necessary to compose, a few months after the Egyptian debacle, an apologetic inscription justifying the circumstances under which he had become king. In addition to reinforcing his legitimacy, an important purpose of the text was to set the stage for the arrangement that he made at about the same time for his own succession. Its centerpiece was the nomination of a younger son of his, Ashurbanipal, as crown prince of Assyria—a step that meant, for better or worse, that Esarhaddon was about to repeat history. He himself, after all, had been a younger child as well and not the original heir apparent. Shamash-shumu-ukin, Ashurbanipal's older brother, did not end up entirely empty-handed—he was to become the next king of Babylon. But this was clearly a far less powerful position.[5]

Ashurbanipal's appointment, in the early spring of 672 BCE, was accompanied by an elaborate ceremony. Members of the Assyrian elite, Assyrian citizens, and foreign vassals had to swear a long series of oaths to demonstrate their loyalty to the king and his new crown prince. The oath takers were not only required to protect Ashurbanipal and be willing to "fall and die for him," but also had to vow that they would inform on anyone who had even the slightest reservations about the succession arrangement.[6]

Esarhaddon was clearly extremely anxious about people not being happy with his nomination of Ashurbanipal as the new heir apparent. And indeed, even within his inner circle, there was apparently considerable uneasiness about the decision. Esarhaddon's chief exorcist, Adad-shumu-usur, praised it with somewhat poisoned words: "What has not been done in heaven, my lord, the king, has done on earth and shown us. You have donned a (younger) son of yours with the diadem and have entrusted to him the kingship of Assyria. Your elder son, in the meantime, you have set to the kingship of Babylon. You have placed the first on your right and the second on your left side."[7]

THE NOMINATION OF THE KING'S ELDER SON, SHAMASH-SHUMU-ukin, as crown prince of Babylon was a result of Esarhaddon's decision to abandon the radical anti-Babylonian politics of his father and rebuild Babylon. Dealing with Babylon was always a political minefield for Assyrian kings, regardless of the specific approach they took, and it is likely that some of the internal opposition Esarhaddon faced resulted from the more conciliatory attitude he showed toward the famous city.

Esarhaddon had to walk a fine line here. In his inscriptions, he had to explain why it was necessary to rebuild Babylon, while at the same time making sure not to openly criticize his own father, Sennacherib, for the catastrophic attack that had devastated the city in the first place. The solution found by Esarhaddon's scribes was to place the blame squarely on the Babylonians themselves, and to picture the events through a theological lens:

> Before my time, in the reign of a previous king, bad omens occurred in Sumer and Akkad (i.e., Babylonia). The people living there were answering each other yes for no and were telling lies. They put their hands on the possessions of the Esagil Temple, the palace of the gods, and sold gold, silver, and precious stones (from

its treasury) to the land of Elam (to buy military assistance). The god Marduk thereupon became angry and plotted to level the land and destroy its people. The river Arahtu (i.e., the Euphrates) became a huge flood, like the deluge, and turned the city, its dwellings, and its shrines into ruins. The gods and goddesses dwelling there went up to the heavens; the people were distributed among the (foreign) riffraff and became slaves. The merciful god Marduk had initially written that the calculated time of its (i.e., Babylon's) abandonment should last seventy years, but his heart was soon soothed, and he reversed the numbers and thus ordered its reoccupation to take place after eleven years.[8]

This stands out as one of the most carefully crafted examples of "spin" found anywhere in the large corpus of Assyrian royal inscriptions. All Assyrian responsibility for Babylon's devastation has been struck from the record. Particularly elegant is the explanation of Marduk's change of mind at the end of the passage. In the numeral system of ancient Mesopotamia, which has sixty as its base, the number seventy is written with a vertical wedge representing sixty, followed by a small diagonal wedge called a *Winkelhaken*, representing ten. Eleven, in contrast, consists of a Winkelhaken followed by the same vertical wedge, now representing one. By reversing the two elements, Marduk reduces the sentence originally given to Babylon by nearly sixty years, and thus provides Esarhaddon with the opportunity to rebuild the city much earlier than initially planned.

In several inscriptions, Esarhaddon claims that he started the reconstruction process right at the beginning of his reign. In actual fact, serious work in the city seems not to have begun until a few years later, and it did not proceed without significant setbacks.

Conditions in Babylon continued to be grim. According to a letter sent to Esarhaddon by Mar-Issar, his personal agent in Babylonia, the people who were left in Babylon after Sennacherib's 689 attack on the city were "poor wretches who had nothing." When asked to pay taxes to help equip chariots for the Assyrian army, they wailed and protested, which prompted Babylon's Assyrian commander to imprison some of them under the allegation that, incited by a local judge, they had thrown lumps of clay at his messengers. In spite of the turmoil, the temples of Babylon were rebuilt, bit by bit. But it was only in 668, and thus after Esarhaddon's death, that a new statue of Marduk was set up in the Esagil Temple. An earlier attempt, in the spring of 669, to bring the statue from Ashur to Babylon had to be aborted when it became apparent that rebels or robbers might be lying in wait for it near the city of Dur-Kurigalzu.[9]

THE SITUATION IN THE SOUTH WAS COMPLEX. ON THE ONE HAND, Esarhaddon had to face an old guard of Assyrian officials who thought his attempts to help Babylon get back on its feet were misplaced. On the other, he had to cope with popular protest by Babylonians who felt the opposite was true: that he was not doing enough to restore Babylon's former glory. Even a ruler physically and mentally stronger than Esarhaddon would have found it taxing to balance such contradictory demands. But in addition to everything else, Esarhaddon seems to have been of a sickly disposition. He was frequently ill, requiring constant ministrations by a variety of personal physicians and spiritual advisers. All too often, the king's "body natural" interfered with his ability to fulfill the requirements of his "body politic."

Frustrated that his health was not improving, Esarhaddon posed a question to his chief physician, Urad-Nanaya: "Why can you not diagnose the nature of this illness of mine and bring about its cure?" Esarhaddon's symptoms, described in a series of letters, included fever, weakness, lack of appetite, stiffness, an infection of the eye, blisters, chills, and earache. Based on these indications, and drawing on medical knowledge not yet available to Urad-Nanaya, some modern scholars have suggested that the king suffered from lupus, an inflammatory disease caused by a compromised immune system.

The theory seems plausible, though retrospective diagnosis is not without problems.[10]

Esarhaddon also showed signs of depression. His habit of refusing to eat anything for days on end prompted two of his personal astrologers, Balasî and Nabû-ahhe-eriba, in a letter from the spring of 670, to admonish him that he was behaving more like a beggar than a king. In another letter from about the same time, his chief exorcist, Adad-shumu-usur, complained that the monarch was staying in a dark room in his palace for far too long. He reminded him that such behavior was not in line with his royal duties as a proper representative of the sun god: "The king, the lord of all the lands, is the very image of Shamash. He should keep in the dark for half the day only!" Like Balasî and Nabû-ahhe-eriba, Adad-shumu-usur recommended as a remedy that the king "eat food and drink wine."[11]

THERE WAS, HOWEVER, A BRIGHT SPOT: THE SUCCESSFUL EGYP-tian campaign of 671. Despite the failed operation three years earlier, Esarhaddon remained determined to conquer the land on the Nile. In the spring of 671, his army set out from Ashur for another attempt to do just that. In his inscriptions, Esarhaddon suggests that he participated in the whole campaign in person. In truth, he accompanied the troops only as far as Harran, where he stayed behind to pray to the moon god Sîn, a deity closely associated with the Assyrian royal family since the days of Sargon II.

The army continued its march westward and, after restoring Assyria's authority over Tyre, headed straight for the Egyptian border. Royal inscriptions reveal that the soldiers moved "from Apqu in the region of Samaria to the city of Rapihu," modern Rafah in the southern Gaza Strip. From here, the easiest road to Egypt would have been the Via Maris (the sea road) along the Mediterranean coast. This, presumably, was how the Assyrian army had tried to enter Egypt in 674, when it had been defeated near Sile in eastern Egypt. But the Assyrians knew now that the Egyptians were well prepared to block this road. The leader of the Assyrian troops, probably Esarhaddon's chief eunuch, Ashur-nasir, decided to surprise the enemy by taking an alternate route through the Sinai Desert, moving southward initially and then turning sharply to the west. Turkish forces used the same strategy in 1915, during World War I, when trying to reach Ismailia from Beer Sheva.[12]

Crossing an inhospitable desert with a large army poses enormous logistical challenges. The Assyrian troops had gained some experience with arid terrain during their earlier campaign against Bazu, but they would not have been able to travel the Sinai Desert without support from a number of Arab tribes, who likely supplied them with camels, waterskins, and guides. Even so, the obstacles were huge: Esarhaddon's inscriptions describe a journey of altogether 390 kilometers (242 miles) "over mighty sand dunes." Some areas, they state, were full of "two-headed snakes whose venom (or: touch) is deadly," and "yellow snakes spreading their wings." These were most likely not actual animals, though. The Greek historian Herodotus, writing some two hundred years later about the same general area, claimed to have seen large numbers of "bones" of "winged serpents" there, and both he and Esarhaddon may have been alluding to the fossilized amphibian remains found at sites such as Makhtesh Ramon in the southern Negev Desert. Yellowish in color, some of them look as though they might have wings. Passing such a site must have been both terrifying and exhilarating, and certainly surreal for the Assyrian soldiers.[13]

Eventually, the Assyrian caravan arrived at Magdalu, a fortress town located near the Isthmus of Suez. The biblical exodus story calls it Migdol. From here, the troops began the final leg of their expedition. On their way to the Nile, they met Egyptian armies on three occasions that tried, but failed, to stop their advance. After a journey of some 1,850 kilometers (1,150 miles) in all, they finally arrived at the royal city of Memphis. Its defenders, unprepared to engage in serious siege warfare, offered little resistance, and on the twenty-second

day of the summer month of Tammuz, more than three months after their departure from Ashur, the Assyrians took the city. Pharaoh
Taharqa, of Kushite ancestry, managed to flee southward despite the
arrow wounds he had suffered, but the Assyrians captured his chief
wife, his crown prince, and some of his other children, plus many of
his harem women, and brought them all to Nineveh.[14]

Esarhaddon presents the outcome of the Egyptian campaign of
671 as a liberation: according to one of his inscriptions, he had "torn
out the roots of Kush from Egypt." This claim was not entirely off the
mark. At least for the time being, the Assyrians had indeed chased
away the nonindigenous "Black Pharaohs" of Egypt's Twenty-fifth
Dynasty—and they reorganized the country by putting power over
Egypt's major cities back into the hands of members of the traditional Egyptian elites. Among others, they installed Necho, a local
strongman, as the new governor, or "king," of Memphis and Sais.
But even if some Egyptians had considered the Kushites as oppres-
sors, they cannot have liked their new Assyrian overlords any better.
For real independence was surely not what Esarhaddon had in mind
for Egypt. He gave the Egyptian cities, and even some of their "rulers," Assyrian names, assigned Assyrian agents to each of them, and
imposed taxes and tribute on his new Egyptian subjects. Unlike later
conquerors of Egypt, from the Persians to the Greeks and Romans,
Esarhaddon seems, moreover, to have made no effort to present himself to the Egyptian people in the traditional role of a pharaoh, or
to be depicted in the temples with a pharaoh's characteristic double
crown or customary dress.[15]

The Egyptians must also have resented the fact that Esarhaddon's troops took so much booty back to Assyria: royal tiaras,
statues, and precious stones; utensils made of silver, gold, bronze,
and ebony; horses, oxen, sheep; and much more. Three statues of
Pharaoh Taharqa and one of the Egyptian goddess Anuket were
found during excavations at Esarhaddon's palace on Nebi Yunus in
Nineveh. People were brought to Assyria as well. Some were from

Egypt's leading families—for example, Necho's son Psamtik—and served as hostages. But there were also significant numbers of Egyptian specialists, from charioteers, archers, and shield bearers to incantation priests and dream interpreters; from veterinarians, scribes, and snake charmers to singers, bakers, and brewers. The Assyrians had been aware of the great achievements of Egyptian civilization for some time. Now they were able to access them directly. The new Assyrian "Egyptomania" even had an impact on the style of some of the reliefs created during the reign of Esarhaddon's successor Ashurbanipal.[16]

FOR THE EGYPTIANS, THE ASSYRIAN CONQUEST OF THEIR LAND was a traumatizing blow. Initially repressed, and nowhere mentioned in the official historiography of the country, it was only much later, in several popular Egyptian stories, that the subject was taken up again. In the Assyrian Empire, in contrast, the campaign of 671 was an event celebrated in numerous royal inscriptions, some of a monumental character. Stelae from Zincirli (ancient Sam'al in Turkey's Gaziantep Province) and Tell Aḥmar (ancient Til-Barsip on the Middle Euphrates) display Esarhaddon holding the captured Kushite crown prince and another prisoner on lead ropes. The conquest of Egypt allowed Esarhaddon to proudly claim a number of additional titles. He was now no longer only the "king of Assyria, governor of Babylon, king of Sumer and Akkad, and king of Karduniash (i.e., Babylonia)," but also "the king of the kings of Lower Egypt, Paturisi (an Assyrian rendering of the Egyptian term for Upper Egypt), and Kush (Nubia)."[17]

But beyond the veneer of official proclamations of triumph, the king's uneasiness abided—and those around him shared it. While his troops were in the process of conquering the city of Memphis—and for quite some time thereafter—Esarhaddon sat in his palace and feared for his life. He was not only suffering from poor health but also scared by bad omens. His trusted agent Mar-Issar had informed him that a total lunar eclipse had occurred on the fourteenth day of the month of Tammuz (July 2, 671), and had advised him to perform the so-called substitute king ritual. Lunar eclipses, especially when the planet Jupiter was not visible, were believed to be signs that the king was about to die. The solution was to put someone else, usually a prisoner of war, a simpleton, or some other outsider without connections to the royal family, on the throne, to formally assume the role of king. He would be wined and dined and provided with a virgin, who would serve as his "queen." But after a hundred days at the most, he would "go to his fate"—a euphemism hiding the fact that the substitute king was killed to absorb the evil that would otherwise have befallen the actual monarch. The latter, the real king, was symbolically addressed by his courtiers as "the farmer" during the period of the ritual, even though he would remain effectively in charge of the empire's political affairs.[18]

THE SUBSTITUTE KING ENTHRONED IN ASSYRIA IN THE SUMMER of 671 kept his position for a full one hundred days before his liquidation, in the month of Tashritu, sealed his fate as a ritual scapegoat. All the while, Esarhaddon had withdrawn from public life, keeping a low profile.[19]

Under these circumstances, many high-ranking members of Assyria's military, political, and religious establishment must have found it difficult to give their king any credit for the successful campaign against Egypt that had just been completed. Indeed, there were increasing calls for his removal from power. As the year 671 progressed, several rebel groups, beholden to different leaders, began to conspire against Esarhaddon. Their activities were centered in three of Assyria's most important cities: Harran, Nineveh, and Ashur.[20]

Harran had been the place where, earlier in the year, Esarhaddon had prayed for an Assyrian victory over Egypt—and where the moon god Sîn and his son Nusku had promised him that he would "go forth and conquer all the lands." In a shocking reversal, the city now became the stage of a wide-ranging conspiracy against the king. Right at its outset, a divine utterance very different from the one previously made by Sîn and Nusku provided the would-be insurgents with crucial theological support. As reported in a letter, a slave girl from the household of a certain Bel-ahu-usur, who lived on the outskirts of Harran, had suddenly started to prophesy, saying, "It is the word of Nusku: The kingship is for Sasî. I will destroy the name and seed of Sennacherib." The "name and seed of Sennacherib" clearly identifies Esarhaddon and his sons as the targets of the evolving coup. The letter writer, a certain Nabû-rehtu-usur, claimed that several individuals were involved in it, among them at least one eunuch as well as the daughter of a deputy vizier who was important enough to have served as eponym in 676. Nabû-rehtu-usur was so concerned that in the letter he repeatedly implores the king to "let these people die, and quickly!" At the same time, feeling a need to assure Esarhaddon of his personal loyalty, he offers supplications to serve as a kind of counter-prophecy to the words of the slave girl: "May the name and seed of Sasî, Bel-ahu-usur, and their accomplices perish, and may Bel and Nabû establish the name and seed of the king, my lord, until far-off days." Nabû-rehtu-usur concludes his letter with a plea: "Rescue your life from the hands of the eunuchs!"[21]

A eunuch was also a central character in another attempted coup carried out in 671, one that took place in Nineveh. Information about it comes from an extraordinary letter sent to Esarhaddon by a certain Kudurru, most likely the son of a ruler of Bit-Dakkuri in southern Babylonia who had been deported to Assyria by Assyrian troops in 675.[22]

Apparently, Kudurru was not only a prince but also a scholar—while in captivity, he was forced to copy learned cuneiform texts. According to his letter, his learnedness was the very reason why he had become personally involved in the emerging plot. Kudurru writes that in the month of Arahsamna (VIII), an officer from the staff of the chief cupbearer had fetched him from his prison and had asked him, "Are you not an expert in scribal lore?" Kudurru was then brought to the temple of the "Lord of Harran," an epithet of the moon god Sîn, in Nineveh—the very place where Sennacherib might have been murdered in 681. In an upper room of the temple, he encountered the chamberlain, the chief cupbearer, and the overseer of the city—all officials of extremely high rank. They tossed him a seat and drank wine with him until the sun set. Then they got to the point. Reminding him that he was not only an accomplished scribe but also an expert diviner, they ordered Kudurru to ask the god Shamash whether "the chief eunuch will take over the kingship."

If he was not, in fact, initiated from the very beginning, this was the moment when Kudurru must have realized what was actually going on: he had become implicated—involuntarily, he claims—in an act of high treason whose aim was to depose Esarhaddon and replace him with the chief eunuch—probably the very Ashur-nasir who had just returned victoriously from the Assyrian campaign against Egypt. As a rule, eunuchs were considered unfit to hold the highest office in ancient Assyria, but Ashur-nasir's military accomplishments might have been deemed outstanding enough to make an exception.

Kudurru claims he had no choice but to comply with the demand made by the traitors: to find out the will of the gods by means of divination. Because it would have been too conspicuous to slaughter a lamb and inspect its entrails, which would have been the standard procedure, he resorted to the less eye-catching art of lecanomancy, that is, oil divination. He washed himself in an upper room of the temple, donned fresh garments, and, having been supplied with two skins filled with oil, poured it along with some water into a bowl. The patterns created by the two liquids provided clues that allowed Kudurru to answer the question that had been posed to him—and he delivered a resounding yes. The sun god had indicated that the chief eunuch would indeed take over the kingship.

The conspirators were happy to hear it. The next day, they expressed their gratitude to Kudurru by offering to release him, send him back to his homeland, and make him king of Babylonia. By now, however, Kudurru had begun to realize that Esarhaddon might have gotten word of the whole affair. Terrified that "the king might hear about it and kill me," he grabbed a stylus and some clay and wrote to Esarhaddon. He told him that he had been forced to participate in the plot, and that his divinatory pronouncements had been "nothing but wind and air." Whether the king believed his proclamations of innocence—and whether they were actually true—remain unclear. Neither seems very likely, though. Kudurru may well have been a co-conspirator from early on, and he might have been punished accordingly.

Yet another conspiracy against Esarhaddon took place in the fall of 671 in Assyria's ancient religious capital, Ashur. As mentioned, its instigator was a mayor of Ashur by the name of Abdâ, who sought to become king himself and justified his claim to the throne with messages conveyed to him in two dreams. Interestingly, the enig-matic Sasî, whom the slave girl from Harran had announced in her prophecy as the future king, also makes an appearance in the story of Abdâ. Nabû-ushallim, Esarhaddon's informer, suggests that Sasî was in some way involved in the conspiracy. He adds that an earlier letter that he had written about the events had gotten into Sasî's hands and disappeared.

HIGH TREASON HAD BECOME ALMOST ROUTINE IN ASSYRIA IN the fall of 671 BCE. Three conspiracies took place during this time, each hatched in a major Assyrian city and supported by some of the highest-ranking officials of the Assyrian Empire. Yet sick, weak, and weary as he was, Esarhaddon managed to survive these well-planned attempts to remove him from power.

The reason why may be found in the king's controversial rise to the throne. Esarhaddon had never forgotten his time as crown prince, when the machinations of his brothers had led to his temporary exile from the Nineveh court and the eventual murder of his father Sennacherib. Fully aware that he himself and his crown prince, Ashurbanipal, could fall prey to a similar plot, the king took measures to prevent a repetition of the events of 681. Among other things, he refashioned the heavily fortified armories of Nineveh and Calah into residential quarters for himself and parts of his family. Here he was better protected against possible assassination attempts than in the palaces where he had previously lived.[23]

Even more important, though, was Esarhaddon's transformation of Assyria into a new kind of surveillance state. Survival, the king may have realized (with John le Carré's Jim Prideaux), "is an infinite capacity for suspicion." Unlike in previous times, during Esarhaddon's reign the denunciation of unreliable political elements was now no longer only encouraged, but became a duty for every Assyrian citizen, whether male or female, high or low. When swearing loyalty to Esarhaddon and Ashurbanipal in 672, all Assyrians, and all vassal rulers, had to commit to a requirement that makes this abundantly clear:

> If you hear any evil, improper, ugly word which is not seemly nor good to Ashurbanipal, the great crown prince designate, either from the mouth of his enemy or from the mouth of his ally, or from the mouth of his brothers or from the mouth of his uncles, his cousins, his family, members of his father's line, or from the mouth of your brothers, your sons, your daughters, or from the mouth of a prophet, an ecstatic, a dream interpreter, or from the mouth of any human being at all, you shall not conceal it but come and report it to Ashurbanipal, the great crown prince designate, son of Esarhaddon, king of Assyria.[24]

Even though it would be anachronistic to compare Esarhaddon's Assyria to the totalitarian states of the twentieth and twenty-first centuries, it is hard not to sense a certain "Stalinist spirit" in this passage, with its open encouragement of spying on one's closest family members. Of particular interest, moreover, is the specific concern of the clause with disparaging political comments by prophets, ecstatics, and dream interpreters. With almost uncanny precision, it anticipated what actually happened just a year or so after the oath ceremonies of 672, when the conspirators in Harran relied on the utterances of a prophetess; those in Nineveh requested a Babylonian expert to perform oil divination; and in Ashur, Abdâ found encouragement for his dangerous ambitions in two dreams.

Despite their considerable military strength and the divine reassurances they received, Esarhaddon's enemies were unable to carry out their subversive plans. In the end, they were all betrayed. The loyalty oaths sworn by the king's Assyrian subjects in 672 actually worked. The conspiracies in Harran, Nineveh, and Ashur, and numerous other acts of insubordination, are known today because people from all over the empire and from all walks of life did inform the king about the political mood in their personal and professional spheres. They flooded him with letters—found some two and a half millennia later at Nineveh—about activities they deemed suspicious.

Some of these letters were anonymous, while others were written by people who tried to ingratiate themselves with the king by expressing their devotion to him in the most obsequious terms: "Why should I not embrace the ground where the tracks of the chariot of the king, my lord, pass by?" is how the astrologer Nabû-ahhe-eriba puts it when writing to Esarhaddon in the summer of 671. Occasionally, the accusations made by the letter writers veer into the hysterical. An anonymous informer from Guzana, for example, informs the king that Tarsi, a powerful official, and his wife Zazâ had taunted royal messengers, and that Zazâ and the unnamed wife of a local priest were engaged in "drawing down the moon from the sky," an act of witchcraft that had to be punished, in the view of the letter writer, by death. The same writer then accuses a chariot driver of having laid his hands on a ritual implement and having said, "(Someone) bring me an iron knife, so I can cut off (its pointed part) and stick it into the governor's ass." It is often quite difficult to establish whether denunciations like these were based on fact or fiction.[25]

MOST OF THE PEOPLE WHO FELT A NEED TO BLOW THE WHISTLE on their fellow citizens in 671 were probably ordinary Assyrians with axes to grind, but a few may have been professional informers. Nabû-ushallim, for instance, who wrote to Esarhaddon about Ab-dâ's conspiracy in Ashur, begins his message by stating, "Because of what I see and hear and betray to the king my lord, because of this, many people hate me and are plotting to kill me." The remark brings to mind the famous "eyes and ears of the king" who, according to Herodotus, Plutarch, and other Greek authors, spied on behalf of the rulers of the Persian Empire. It also reveals that being a professional snoop did not make one a particularly beloved member of the community in ancient Assyria.

Esarhaddon not only employed spies to observe what was going on. Apparently, he also infiltrated some of the leading circles of Assyria's main cities with agents provocateurs. The task of these men was to actively incite their targets to start a rebellion, or to entrap them into discussing the possibility of doing so, in order to establish whether they were loyal subjects of the king or traitors who had to be eliminated. The most notable of these agents was, in all likelihood, none other than Sasî, the man who played such a prominent role in the conspiracies at Harran and Ashur, and also in a few other episodes of political turmoil. Sasî's role as a "double agent" is nowhere explicitly acknowledged, but given that he was probably still alive and well during Ashurbanipal's early years, when he had close

1. The ruins of the city of Ashur in 2022: panorama view from the ziggurat. *Photo: Urike Bürger, Ashur Project, Heidelberg.*

2. Excavations in the center of Ashur, undertaken in 2001 under the direction of Peter Miglus. *Photo: Eckart Frahm.*

3. Nineveh in 2001: view from the citadel mound of Kuyunjik over to Nebi Yunus, with the mosque of Jonah on top. *Photo: Eckart Frahm.*

4. Stone figurine, 44.3 cm in height, of a praying woman from the archaic Ishtar Temple in Ashur, ca. 2400 BCE. *VA 8141. Photo: Staatliche Museen zu Berlin— Vorderasiatisches Museum / Olaf M. Teßmer.*

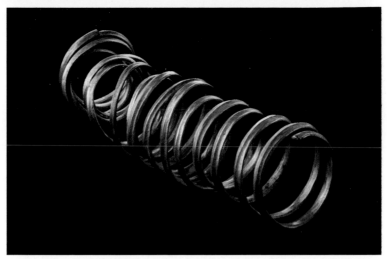

5. Silver coil from Khafajah in southern Iraq, first half of the second millennium BCE. Removing small pieces to make payments, Babylonian and Assyrian merchants used such coils as money. *OIM A9545. Courtesy of the Oriental Institute of the University of Chicago.*

6. Stone pedestal from the Ishtar Temple in Ashur with depiction of King Tukulti-Ninurta I (r. ca. 1243–1207 BCE), first standing and then kneeling in front of a similar pedestal with a clay tablet or writing board, a symbol of Nabû, patron god of scribes. *VA 8141. Photo: Staatliche Museen zu Berlin—Vorderasiatisches Museum / Olaf M. Teßmer.*

7. Ashurnasirpal II (r. 883–859 BCE) with an attendant on a bas-relief from the Northwest Palace in Calah. Across the relief runs a royal inscription. *32.143.4. The Metropolitan Museum, New York.*

8. A winged genie between two sacred trees. Bas-relief from Room I in Ashurnasirpal II's Northwest Palace in Calah, with original colors restored. *Artwork: Klaus Wagensonner, based on a relief in the Yale Art Gallery (1854.4, B-II-e-i-3).*

9. Golden crown of the Assyrian queen Hamâ, wife of Shalmaneser IV
(r. 782–773 BCE), from her tomb in Calah. *ND 1989-309. From Muzahim
M. Hussein,* Nimrud: The Queens' Tombs *(Chicago: Oriental Institute of the
University of Chicago; Baghdad: State Board of Antiquities and Heritage of Iraq),
Plate 129.*

10. The Assyrian assault on the Judean city of Lachish in 701 BCE. Detail from a bas-relief from Sennacherib's Southwest Palace at Nineveh, ca. 700 BCE. On the right, Assyrian soldiers carry away booty and lead Judean men, women, and children into exile. *From David Ussishkin,* The Conquest of Lachish by Sennacherib *(Tel Aviv: Tel Aviv University, Institute of Archaeology, 1982), Segment IV. Drawing by Judith Dekel.*

11. Cuneiform letter by Nabû-ushallim about a secret plot in Ashur against King Esarhaddon, ca. 671 BCE. *YBC 11382. Yale Babylonian Collection. Photo: Klaus Wagensonner.*

12. Ashurbanipal banqueting with his queen Libbali-sharrat, with an enemy head hanging in a nearby tree. Bas-relief from the North Palace at Nineveh, mid-seventh century BCE. *Cast of the original. Yale Babylonian Collection. Photo: Klaus Wagensonner.*

13. A crudely carved steatite amulet against the child-snatching demoness Lamashtu. Second half of the second or first half of the first millennium BCE, possibly from Uruk. *YBC 10196. Yale Babylonian Collection. Photo: Klaus Wagensonner.*

14. Bronze statue of Ashurbanipal, founder of the Nineveh libraries, designed by Fred Parhad and dedicated "by the Assyrian people" to the city of San Francisco. The statue stands near San Francisco's former main library. *Photo: Jacob Rosenberg-Wohl.*

relations with the new king's chariot driver Remanni-Adad, it can hardly be doubted that Sasî had always been on the side of the Assyrian royal family. Otherwise, one must assume, he would have been killed for his involvement in the political crimes of which several letters to Esarhaddon accuse him.[26]

For that was the fate of many of the rebels and agitators who had participated in the various plots carried out against Esarhaddon in 671—and probably also of some people who were incriminated unjustly. As the Babylonian Chronicle reports in a short entry for the year 670, "The king executed a large number of his nobles in Assyria." No other note of this type is found in the chronicle, which makes it likely that the purge, presumably implemented by Esarhaddon early in the year, was of massive proportions. Numerous members of the Assyrian elite must have died violent deaths. The massacre consolidated Esarhaddon's position as king and Ashurbanipal's as crown prince, but one cannot but wonder if the loss of so many capable and experienced officers and administrators did not have an adverse effect on the long-term prospects of the Assyrian state.[27]

Esarhaddon, at any rate, only became more misanthropic over the course of these events. In the fall of 671, when the insurgencies in Harran, Nineveh, and Ashur were about to be quelled, he ordered that another substitute king ritual be initiated and retired again from public view. The execution a few months later of the nobles accused of high treason did not do much to improve his mood. As Esarhaddon's chief physician, Urad-Nanaya, writes, while "the criminals who plotted against the king's goodness" had been "caught up" by this very goodness, their betrayal "had made all other people hateful in the eyes of the king, as if a tanner had smeared them with fish oil."[28]

The years 671 and 670 had been full of drama and contradictions. Despite his spectacular military triumph, Esarhaddon had been faced with serious attempts to remove him from power, and he emerged from the events worn out and deeply distrustful. In the fall of 669, he nonetheless embarked on another campaign, which turned out to be his last. It was again directed against Egypt, where Assyrian rule had crumbled within barely a year. On the way to the Nile, Esarhaddon fell ill. He passed away on the tenth day of the month of Arahsamnu (November 1). His body was brought back to Ashur, where the king, after a sumptuous state funeral, found the final rest he might have secretly hoped for for quite some time.[29]

Esarhaddon's son and successor Ashurbanipal tried very hard to be a very different type of king. Eager never to show his father's weakness, he strove for perfection. Yet, as it would turn out, Assyria's new ruler was a troubled man as well. Ashurbanipal would propel the quality of Assyrian literature and art to unprecedented heights, but his idiosyncratic political style contributed to an accelerating crisis that would eventually lead to the empire's fall.

12

Scholar, Sadist, Hunter, King

Most of the Assyrian rulers of the eighth and seventh centuries BCE were shrewd politicians and military men, interested in conquest and massive building projects. Esarhaddon's son and successor Ashurbanipal, who ruled from 669 to 631, clearly wanted to excel in these areas too. In a unique autobiographical text, composed early in his reign, the last "great" king of the Assyrian Empire describes his upbringing and his education in a variety of martial and political arts:

> I cantered on thoroughbreds, rode stallions that were raring to go. I made arrows fly as befits a warrior. I threw quivering lances as if they were javelins. I took the reins of a chariot like a charioteer and made the rims of its wheels spin. At the same time, I was learning proper lordly behavior, becoming familiar with the ways of kingship. I stood before the king who engendered me, giving orders to officials. No governor was appointed without me, no prefect installed without my consent.[1]

But having learned how to be tough and amass power was not enough for Ashurbanipal. In addition, he claims, he had received the training of a true scholar and literary man:

I learned the craft of the sage Adapa, the secret lore of all of the scribal arts. I have become well read in the signs of heaven and earth, and can discuss them in an assembly of scholars. I can argue with expert diviners about (the chapter) "If the Liver is a Mirror of Heaven." I can resolve complicated divisions and multiplications that do not have an easy solution. I have read cunningly written texts in obscure Sumerian and Akkadian that are difficult to interpret. I have carefully examined cuneiform signs on stones dating from before the Flood, whose meaning is sealed, inaccessible, and confusing.

Ashurbanipal wanted it all. He had the ambition to be a true "Renaissance man" or, to be less anachronistic, a new Gilgamesh. Like the famous hero of yore, first an explorer and warrior, then a sage, Ashurbanipal wished to combine the qualities of the conqueror with those of the philosopher king. The passage about his intellectual upbringing alludes, in fact, to a line from the beginning of the Babylonian Gilgamesh Epic: "He saw the secret and uncovered the hidden, / He brought back instruction from before the Flood."[2]

As king, Ashurbanipal left a record that asserted in no uncertain terms that his reign lived up to his lofty ambitions. In his "autobiography," he describes the effects of his rise to power as nothing short of miraculous: "The enemies' readied weapons eased to rest, they dissolved their well-organized battle array. Brazen men calmed down. Within city and household, no one took anything from his neighbor by force. A traveler on his own walked in safety on remote roads. Violent crimes did not occur." Even nature had to adapt to the new period of harmony and prosperity that had begun with Ashurbanipal's rule. In a long text from the 640s, the king claims that upon his accession, "the god Adad released his rains and Ea opened up his springs. Grain was five cubits high in its furrow and ears of corn were five-sixths of a cubit long (about 38 centimeters, or 15 inches). Orchards were lush with fruit, and cattle gave birth to their young. During my reign, there was plenitude and abundance."[3]

Several modern scholars have endorsed the idea that Ashurbanipal's rule brought knowledge, progress, and general welfare. The French Assyriologist René Labat, calling the king "enlightened," stresses his learnedness and his investment in creating the enormous tablet collections discovered at Nineveh. According to Labat, Ashurbanipal is the living proof that the archaeologist Jacques de Morgan had been utterly wrong when describing "the Assyrian" as "neither an artist nor a literary man nor a legal scholar." The Austrian historian Sebastian Fink argues that Ashurbanipal showed so keen an understanding of supply and demand and the development of prices that he should be considered a true economic expert. And the Japanese Assyriologist Sanae Ito goes so far as to call Ashurbanipal a "humanist," albeit with a question mark, because the king, she claims, treated his interlocutors on the diplomatic stage equally, showed pity to defeated enemies, was willing to communicate with people high and low, and allegedly believed in good intentions.[4]

To be sure, there are aspects of the king's reign that cannot fail to impress, among them, most notably, the royal libraries at Nineveh and the highly accomplished bas-reliefs that lined the walls of Ashurbanipal's palaces. Modern scholars seeking to reconstruct the intellectual world of ancient Mesopotamia continue to rely heavily on the former, while modern museum-goers derive considerable aesthetic pleasure from looking at the latter. For most people of the seventh century BCE, however, the sophisticated literary and visual culture of the Assyrian royal court was of little consequence—other factors that defined Ashurbanipal's reign were more important. When one reads between the lines of Ashurbanipal's own inscriptions and takes other sources, such as letters and economic texts, into account, a picture emerges that is quite different from the one the king himself sought to promote of his reign.

ASHURBANIPAL'S ARMIES WERE INVOLVED IN NUMEROUS WARS, some of them long and bloody. The king's fondness for reading and studying had clearly not turned him into a pacifist. During Ashurbanipal's early years on the throne, the main focus of Assyria's military operations was Egypt, where the Kushite pharaoh Taharqa, ousted in 671 BCE, had slowly but steadily staged a comeback. After Esarhaddon's last campaign in 669 had to be aborted, Taharqa had consolidated his position. In 667, Ashurbanipal dispatched his army to reconquer Egypt. The Assyrian vassals in the Levant and the Eastern Mediterranean, among them the Judean king Manasseh and the rulers of Edom, Moab, and Cyprus, supported the Assyrian war effort with auxiliary troops, boats, and other equipment, and after defeating enemy troops in northern Egypt, the Assyrians seized Memphis a second time. Pharaoh Taharqa was forced once more to flee southward, where he died shortly thereafter. Several petty rulers in northern Egypt who had conspired with him were taken prisoner and brought to Nineveh. One of them was Necho of Sais, who played a particularly crucial role in Egyptian politics during this period. Realizing that Assyria was unable to rule Egypt without his cooperation, Ashurbanipal made him swear a new loyalty oath and sent him back to Egypt.[5]

In the meantime, Taharqa had been replaced by his nephew Tanutamun, who was eager to take back control from the newly installed Assyrian officials. His attempts to reestablish Kushite rule prompted yet another Assyrian invasion of Egypt, carried out at some point between 666 and 664 BCE. Ashurbanipal's troops were again met with little resistance. This time, they marched as far south as Thebes, the famous capital of Upper Egypt and one of the wealthiest urban centers in the world. After conquering the city, the Assyrian soldiers went on a looting spree. In anticipation of later Roman practices, they took as their greatest prize "two tall obelisks, cast with shiny *zaḥalû*-metal, whose weight was 2,500 talents (72 metric tons, or 80 US tons) and which stood at a temple gate."[6]

But Ashurbanipal's efforts to secure control over Egypt on a permanent basis proved futile. The campaign against Tanutamun was the last time the Assyrians intervened in Egypt with a large military force. In the aftermath of the campaign, Ashurbanipal appointed Necho's son Psamtik I as the new ruler of Memphis and Sais. But shortly after his installation, Psamtik rose against the Assyrian garrison, defeated several internal rivals, and reunited Egypt as the founder of the new Twenty-sixth Dynasty. He ruled for more than fifty years, stationed mercenaries from Greece and Caria (in southwestern Anatolia) in northern Egypt to secure his borders— and at one point allegedly tried to find out what mankind's original language was. By the time he finally died, in 610 BCE, the Assyrian Empire had been relegated to the dustbin of history.[7]

Psamtik's rise had been facilitated by military aid provided by Gyges of Lydia, another former Assyrian ally who had gone rogue. Gyges ruled considerable portions of western Asia Minor and was not only a figure of history but also of memory: he was later summoned up by Plato as the owner of a ring that granted him the power to become invisible, and some scholars associate him with the Bible's apocalyptic Gog. Early in Ashurbanipal's reign, Gyges had caused great excitement at the Assyrian court with a mounted messenger whom he had dispatched there. Initially, no one had been able to grasp what the messenger was saying, but somehow—a break in the text hides by what means exactly—communication with him was established, and Ashurbanipal learned some happy news: Gyges had seen the god Ashur in a dream, and this had prompted him to solicit Ashurbanipal's friendship and Assyrian aid against the Cimmerians, who kept putting military pressure on the kingdoms of Anatolia and the Levant.[8]

It was another hopeful beginning—and another political episode that would end in bitter disappointment for Ashurbanipal. Perhaps disenchanted by a lack of support from his new friend in the east, Gyges did not stay an ally for long. Instead, he turned against Assyria and helped Ashurbanipal's enemy Psamtik gain his independence. For the Assyrian king, Gyges's defection was a grim setback. That the Lydian ruler was later swept away by the Cimmerians was of little consolation to him. Just like his attempts to consolidate his rule over Egypt, Ashurbanipal's efforts to wield indirect control over western Asia Minor had been all but wasted.

ANOTHER MAJOR THEATER OF WAR DURING ASHURBANIPAL'S reign was Elam in Western Iran, where Assyrian armies intervened on several occasions. Elam's political landscape was extremely fragmented, with numerous contestants vying for power. This facilitated short-term advances by Assyrian troops but made it hard for them to take full control of the country.

In 653, the Elamite king Teumman, "the very image of a demon," as he was described by Ashurbanipal, tried to turn the tables by launching his own surprise attack on the Assyrian heartland. But Assyrian spies had learned about his plans, and Ashurbanipal initiated a counteroffensive. The Elamites were forced to retreat, with Assyrian troops in hot pursuit. Eventually, the two sides met at Til Tuba on the Ulay River (the modern Karun in Western Iran), where a pitched battle ensued, later depicted in Nineveh on bas-reliefs possibly influenced by Egyptian models. The Assyrians prevailed, and a common soldier cut off Teumman's head, which was sent to Assyria and put on display in a series of victory parades. Ummanigash, an Elamite prince who had earlier, together with sixty family members, fled to Assyria, was installed as king of Elam, and his younger brother Tammaritu became ruler of the city of Hidalu.[9]

In inscriptions from later in his reign, Ashurbanipal suggests that he had personally participated in the campaign that led to Teumman's disastrous defeat. He even claims to have been the one who cut off Teumman's head. But the king's earliest account of the operation tells a very different story. It begins with Ashurbanipal asking the warrior goddess Ishtar to grant him victory over the evil Elamite king, which the goddess, swayed by his tearful entreaties, promises to do. Then, during the night, a professional seer "lay down and saw a dream":

> The goddess Ishtar who resides in Arbela came towards me. She had quivers hanging on her right and left, was holding a bow at her side, and was unsheathing a sharp sword, ready to do battle. You (Ashurbanipal) stood before her, and she was speaking to you like a mother, saying: "You are looking forward to waging war. But I myself am about to set out towards my destination (the battlefield)." You then said to her: "Wherever you go, O Lady of Ladies, let me go with you." She replied to you: "You shall stay in the place where you currently are. Eat food, drink wine, make merry, and revere my divinity. In the meantime, I will go and accomplish this task. Your face shall not become pale, your feet shall not tremble, you shall not wipe off your sweat in the thick of battle." She took you into her sweet embrace and protected your entire body. Fire flared up in front of her, and furiously she went off and advanced towards Teumman, the king of Elam.[10]

It was a remarkable divine epiphany—and a convenient one for the king, to whom it was immediately reported. In fact, it seems almost too convenient, so much so that one suspects the supposed revelation was nothing of the sort, but an excuse manufactured by Ashurbanipal. Whatever the case, Ashurbanipal must have been delighted by the prospect of being relieved of the duty of going to war. Earlier Assyrian kings had not fought on the front lines either but had at least often been present at some distance when their troops met the enemy in battle. Ashurbanipal, in contrast, simply stayed home, recited some prayers—and enjoyed himself. Given the belligerent rhetoric of his royal inscriptions, which emphasize the king's prowess and his expertise with various types of weapons, many of his subjects must have been irritated by this failure to show up in a moment of actual crisis, interpreting it as a lack of courage; and the whole incident, including the dream episode, may have shaped Ashurbanipal's later image as a lazy pleasure-seeker.[11]

Not only did the events of 653 put a stain on Ashurbanipal's reputation, but the outcome of the battle at Til Tuba proved to be a Pyrrhic victory, for Elam was far from being defeated. When only a year later Ashurbanipal's brother Shamash-shumu-ukin started a rebellion, the newly appointed Elamite king Ummanigash immediately sided with the rebels.

THE CONFLICT BETWEEN ASHURBANIPAL AND SHAMASH-SHUMU-ukin, the king of Babylon, was emotionally charged like no other war in Assyrian history. The two royal antagonists were siblings, and the two polities involved, Assyria and Babylonia, were sister civilizations that shared many cultural and religious traditions. As Ashurbanipal's father Esarhaddon had discovered, sibling rivalry can lead to particular viciousness. Brothers can resemble each other not only in terms of their physical and mental characteristics but also with regard to the objects they wish to possess—whether it is a woman, a throne, or a father's estate. Such mimetic desire may easily lead to bloody strife.[12]

When Esarhaddon decided to nominate a younger son of his, Ashurbanipal, as the next king of Assyria, he had actually anticipated this possibility. Eager to placate his elder son, Shamash-shumu-ukin, and give him something of his own to satisfy his ambitions, he installed him as king of Babylon. The arrangement was a clever compromise and might have worked if only Ashurbanipal had respected his brother's limited autonomy. But deeply fascinated as he was with Babylonian culture, scribal and otherwise, the temptation for him to interfere in the political and religious affairs of his brother was simply too great. As indicated by numerous inscriptions, it was Ashurbanipal who carried out (or took credit for) much of the building work that went on in Babylonia between 668 and 652. Thus, even within the small domain that was supposed to be his, Shamash-shumu-ukin had to play second fiddle.

Officially, the two kings were on good terms during the first fifteen years of Shamash-shumu-ukin's reign. They addressed each other endearingly as "favorite brother." Ashurbanipal expected Shamash-shumu-ukin to perform Babylonian religious rites and to engage with traditional culture, but to refrain from carrying out transregional politics of his own, and Shamash-shumu-ukin lived up to these expectations. He played the part allotted to him—to serve as a kind of Babylonian pope—quite faithfully. He composed learned, albeit grammatically flawed, inscriptions in the ancient Sumerian language and promoted the cult of Marduk and other Babylonian gods. Except for Ishtar of Nineveh, whose temple in Babylon he patronized, Shamash-shumu-ukin abstained from engaging with Assyrian deities, most notably Ashur. He largely shed his Assyrian identity, replacing it with a Babylonian one. But at some point, he became fed up with Ashurbanipal's endless meddling—and started, secretly, to assemble a coalition of anti-Assyrian forces, including Elamites, Aramaeans, Chaldeans, Arabs, and others, to cast off his brother's yoke.[13]

Ashurbanipal became aware of the emerging rebellion in the spring of 652. In a letter to the people of Babylon sent on the twenty-third day of the month of Ayyaru (II), he made a last-ditch effort to avert war: "I have heard the lying words that this non-brother of me has spoken to you. They are indeed nothing but lies. Do not trust him. I swear by Ashur and Marduk, my gods, that I have never pondered in my heart nor spoken with my mouth any of the detestable things he has charged me with. If you do not want to sully yourself with him in this affair, let me see an answer to my letter immediately." But it was too late. Shamash-shumu-ukin, his "non-brother," as Ashurbanipal would from now on call him, commanded the support of his Babylonian subjects, and military action became inevitable. On the nineteenth day of the month of Tebetu (X), hostilities began.[14]

Civil wars are often more "total" than conventional conflicts between nations. The private becomes political in them and the political private. The conflict between Ashurbanipal and Shamash-shumu-ukin, fought from 652 to 648 BCE, provides a good example. During its first two years, there were numerous clashes between Assyrian and Babylonian armies throughout Babylonia. Key cities repeatedly changed hands. Nippur, for example, initially in Shamash-shumu-ukin's camp, fell late in 651 to the Assyrians. Cutha, in contrast, at the outset an Assyrian ally, was captured in the same year by Babylonian troops. On all of these occasions, the civilian populations, divided by conflicting allegiances, suffered considerable hardships. Several succeeding kings of Elam and a number of Arab tribal leaders sent Shamash-shumu-ukin reinforcements. Onetime allies of Ashurbanipal, most notably the governor of the Sealand in the Babylonian south, a man by the name of Nabû-bel-shumate, changed sides and fled to Elam, an act of treason that enraged Ashurbanipal more than almost anything else.

Despite several serious setbacks, by the summer of 650 the tide had turned decisively in favor of the Assyrians. On the eleventh day of the month of Du'uzu (IV), they laid siege to Babylon. The cities of Borsippa, Cutha, and Sippar were besieged as well. It may have been around this time that Sherua-etirat, the sister of the two warring brothers, tried to talk Shamash-shumu-ukin into submitting. Her involvement in the conflict is described in a dramatized narrative known from a fourth-century BCE papyrus from Egypt. Ashurbanipal, called Sarbanabal, is very much the hero, and Shamash-shumu-ukin, called Sarmugi, the villain of the story. Sarbanabal shows initially laudable restraint when he hears about Sarmugi's rebellion. Rather than retaliating right away, he is willing to give his brother a last chance. This is the point where Sherua-etirat—whose name is rendered as Saritra—makes her appearance. Sarbanabal sends her to Babylon as his envoy to negotiate a peaceful solution with their faithless brother. Saritra mounts a chariot and sets out for her mission. Upon her arrival in Babylon, Sarmugi mocks and even physically abuses her, but Saritra stays on message, reminding her brother of her status and pointing out that even a maidservant deserves some respect. When her appeals to Sarmugi to surrender and repent turn out to be futile, she advises him to take refuge in the temple of Marduk. Saritra then returns to report to Sarbanabal, who orders his field marshal and the Assyrian army to attack Babylon. Saritra is sent back to Babylon on yet another peace mission, but it is too late. The temple of Marduk is set on fire, and Sarmugi perishes in the flames.[15]

Of course, this "Tale of Two Brothers" is a literary text and not a historical account. But what happened at Babylon toward the end of the conflict was actually not so different from the story on the papyrus. The Assyrian siege of Babylon went on for more than two years and brought enormous suffering. Ashurbanipal describes the situation of the people in the city in graphic terms:

They ate dogs and mongooses. Their sin was great. They gnawed on animal hides, leather straps, shoes, and sandals. Instead of bread, they ate the flesh of their sons; instead of beer, they drank the blood of their daughters. They became like corpses. The faces of the people darkened as if by smoke with depression and mourning. In the city squares, the young man saw the young woman naked, and the young woman the young man. Plague and illness reduced the people. Their corpses were obstructing the streets and alleys. A deadly hush had been poured out. The people's storerooms were laid waste, their fields wept and mourned, and their watercourses, which had once gushed with an abundance of water, were now filled with silt.[16]

What is outlined here, with gleeful triumph, is a depressing picture of humanitarian catastrophe and social breakdown, eerily similar to "total wars" of more recent date. In the end, all the sacrifices of the Babylonian people were in vain. In mid-648, Babylon fell to the Assyrian troops. In line with the story of Saritra's unsuccessful intervention, Shamash-shumu-ukin perished in the flames of his palace, either by accident, by suicide, or by murder.

Ashurbanipal replaced his brother with a new puppet king by the name of Kandalanu, who left no inscriptions and had so little occasion to distinguish himself that some modern historians have suggested—most likely erroneously—that he was nothing but a metal standard representing Ashurbanipal. For the next twenty years, Babylonia remained calm. But the hatred that Ashurbanipal's brutal treatment of their land had planted in the hearts of the Babylonians would germinate and eventually produce yet another anti-Assyrian rebellion—one finally more successful than all the others that preceded it.

Throughout the civil war between Ashurbanipal and Shamash-shumu-ukin, the Elamites had supported the Babylonian side. Now, with his brother out of the way, Ashurbanipal finally got his chance to take revenge for their constant interference. It proved even more devastating than the king's siege of Babylon. In 646, after much previous fighting, Assyrian troops entered the Elamite capital of Susa and engaged in an orgy of destruction. They demolished the ziggurat after stripping it of the copper "horns" installed on its top, sacked the palace treasuries, tore down the city's temples, and "counted its gods and goddesses as ghosts," apparently an allusion to the smashing of some of the statues of the city's deities. Susa would join the other deserted Elamite cities as a home for gazelles and onagers.

In the wake of the attack on the Elamite capital, statues of nineteen Elamite deities and thirty-two Elamite kings were removed and taken to Assyria, along with the bones of the kings, which had been removed from their desecrated tombs. A statue of the goddess

Nanaya, seized more than a thousand years earlier by the Elamite ruler Kudur-Nahhunte, was returned to her home city, Uruk. Nabû-bel-shumate, finally cornered, committed suicide-by-proxy: his personal attendant killed him with a sword while being simultaneously stabbed to death by his master. The Elamite king Ummanaldashu preserved the corpse of the Sealand governor in salt and sent it to Ashurbanipal, before being himself stripped of his power and ending his days as a captive at Nineveh, where he had to serve the Assyrian king food and, during religious festivals, pull his chariot like a horse.[17]

By 645, Ashurbanipal could claim that his troops had defeated two particularly dangerous enemies: Babylonia and Elam. But these victories would prove a very mixed blessing. Babylonia was biding its time, getting ready for a new war. And the destruction of Elam had broken up a state that had kept another power in check, one that was ready to rise against the Assyrian Empire: the Medes.

During the late 640s, Assyrian troops fought against various Arab tribes, but without gaining any lasting control over them. In some of the latest inscriptions known from his reign, dating to 639 or 638, Ashurbanipal reports that the rulers of faraway countries such as Persia, Dilmun (modern Bahrain), and Qadê (modern Oman) had sent messengers with precious gifts to the Assyrian court—diplomatic encounters that were largely symbolic in nature. Then, for Ashurbanipal's last eight years in power, the sources fall completely silent. Of course, it cannot be ruled out that this is due to the accidents of discovery. But it seems more likely that the absence of royal inscriptions from Ashurbanipal's final years is the result of a growing political and economic crisis gripping the empire.

ASHURBANIPAL'S ATTEMPTS TO PRESENT HIMSELF AS AN ARDENT warrior and a successful statesman were in many ways at odds with a far less impressive reality, and it can reasonably be asked whether the king's self-image as a fearless hunter was just as compromised.

Hunting was an activity that Mesopotamian rulers and members of the elite had pursued for millennia, a "blood sport" that prepared its participants for the fight against dangerous human enemies, while also echoing it. Ashurbanipal left extensive written accounts of the hunting expeditions in which he allegedly participated, and his artists depicted him in pursuit of wild animals on numerous bas-reliefs lining the walls of his newly built North Palace at Nineveh. These images are among the most accomplished works of art known from the ancient Near East. They are especially notable for the naturalistic rendering of the majestic beasts hunted down by the king, many of them in their death throes.[18]

While Ashurbanipal probably never slew anyone with his own hands in the midst of battle, it is virtually certain that he hunted down hundreds of wild animals in the course of his life. The game Ashurbanipal preyed on included wild asses, deer, and gazelles, but his most formidable kills were the lions that then roamed the Mesopotamian steppes, woods, and reed thickets. Even though smaller than those known from Africa and India, Mesopotamian lions were dangerous animals. They threatened travelers and rural communities, embodying the chaos that Assyrian kings, by virtue of their strength, were expected to overcome on their subjects' behalf. The Assyrian royal seal, in use from the mid-ninth century onward and impressed countless times on clay bullae and clay tablets, featured the king standing in front of a rampant lion, and stabbing it with his sword.

It is unlikely that any Assyrian king fought with lions in the highly risky fashion depicted on the royal seal. But Ashurbanipal was committed to conveying the message that he, in his unprecedented prowess, actually accomplished such feats. Several of his bas-reliefs show the king putting upright lions to death while standing face-to-face with them. Others depict him on horseback, killing one lion approaching from ahead with a spear while another attacks his spare horse from behind. On one relief, Ashurbanipal even grabs a rampant lion by its tail before clubbing it to death with a mace.

Many such scenes were probably highly embellished representations of lion hunts undertaken by the king somewhere in the countryside. But Ashurbanipal was not satisfied with hunting expeditions that took place far away from the urban world of Nineveh. He wished to reenact the image of the Assyrian royal seal before a large audience of admiring spectators. To help him realize this ambition, royal servants created a confined space within the city limits where he would be able to hunt lions in public. Reminiscent of a Roman arena, the space was protected, during lion hunts, by two solid rows of soldiers armed with long spears and bows, and in addition guarded on the inside by a number of large dogs. The area was consecrated to the goddess Ishtar, on whose behalf the king would pour libations of wine over the slain lions once the hunt was over.

A relief cycle from Room C of Ashurbanipal's North Palace illustrates how the lion hunt in the Nineveh arena was actually carried out. First, a child or a small adult released the lions from a cage. The king then killed them one by one, shooting his arrows from the royal chariot while racing around the arena. Citizens watched this spectacle from a nearby hill, while men carrying waterskins sold them drinks. One relief shows a royal monument atop a hill with an image of the king hunting a lion from his chariot—an early example of what art historians call *mise en abyme*: the playful technique of placing a copy of an image within itself. It is likely that this monument really existed—and that it was inscribed with a text known from a fragmentary clay tablet found at Nineveh. In the text, Ashurbanipal claims that "(no later than) forty minutes after daybreak, with a single team harnessed to my royal vehicle, I had already quelled the tumult of eighteen lions," a statement that corresponds perfectly with the eighteen lions depicted in various states of agony on the relief cycle from Room C.

Why this emphasis on eighteen, a number otherwise not considered particularly meaningful in ancient Mesopotamia? Perhaps it had something to do with the fact that during Ashurbanipal's reign, the city of Nineveh had eighteen gates. As Ashurbanipal noted in his inscriptions, lions had multiplied throughout the empire and were blocking the roads. "By killing eighteen lions in the Nineveh arena," it has been suggested, "Ashurbanipal symbolically secured each exit from the capital city, every gate and road leading out of it being secured by the killing of one lion." Read this way, the whole scene can be regarded as an emblematic display of the king's triumph over the forces of chaos.[19]

Ashurbanipal's royal hunts once again highlight the complexity of the king's personality. On the one hand, Ashurbanipal was evidently eager to help his people get rid of a dangerous nuisance: an ever-growing number of lions roaming the land. But at the same time, he could not resist turning his hunting activities, allegedly pursued for altruistic reasons, into a gigantic show, a circus-like performance to be watched by admiring crowds.

One suspects, moreover, that the personal risk the king took when he went hunting was actually much smaller than his texts and images suggest. The lions released into the Nineveh arena were probably well fed—and perhaps even sedated—when they were unleashed to face the merciless weapons of the Assyrian king. Presumably, Ashurbanipal's lion hunts were no more dangerous than the rather pathetic hunting expeditions undertaken between the 1960s and 1989 by Romania's bloodthirsty dictator Nicolae Ceauşescu. This self-proclaimed "greatest hunter of all time," who won dozens of hunting trophies, killed over the years some four hundred bears in the Carpathian Mountains—on one occasion no fewer than twenty-four in a single day. But he was only able to do this because the pitiable animals were lured to feeding troughs set up next to his high seat or pushed there by dozens of beaters in organized drives. Those witnessing the dictator's hunting exploits considered them ridiculous rather than heroic—a sentiment that some of Ashurbanipal's hunting companions may secretly have harbored as well.[20]

THE ASSYRIAN ECONOMIC SPHERE REVEALS A SIMILARLY PRO-nounced discrepancy between Ashurbanipal's claims and the reality of his reign. As outlined earlier, the king proudly declared in his inscriptions that his rule brought "plenitude and abundance" to his people. The corn, he maintained, grew high, and the amounts of booty brought home by Assyrian armies were so large that on some occasions, periods of short-term inflation ensued: after one of the king's Arab campaigns, "the female tavern keeper for a serving, the beer brewer for a jug of beer, and the gardener for his bag of vegetables were all receiving camels and slaves."[21]

At the same time, and somewhat at odds with this statement, Ashurbanipal boasted that during his reign, prices for staple goods were exceedingly low. Drawing on an age-old tradition of Mesopotamian kings guaranteeing ideal prices, Ashurbanipal writes that "throughout my entire land, on account of abundant trade(?), one could purchase for one shekel (8.5 grams, or 0.3 ounces) of silver ten donkey-loads (1,000 liters, or about 1,060 quarts) of grain, one donkey-load (100 liters, or 106 quarts) of wine, two seahs (20 liters, or 21 quarts) of oil, and one talent (30 kilograms, or 66 pounds) of wool." A flattering literary letter to Ashurbanipal from one of his own sons mentions advantageous prices as well.[22]

Although it is not easy to assess the actual state of the Assyrian economy during Ashurbanipal's reign, it is plainly evident that the king's ideal prices had little to do with the real ones, and that there were not only good years but also some very bad ones. Initially, during Ashurbanipal's first decade on the throne, Assyria's economic situation seems to have been quite satisfactory, although perhaps not quite as good as the king claimed. Economic documents show that the prices for grain and slaves were by and large stable. Over the course of the 650s, however, signs of a crisis begin to appear. In a letter to Ashurbanipal from the beginning of the third month of the year 657, Akkulanu, one of the king's personal astrologers, mentions "the rains that were so scanty this year that no harvest was reaped." Even though Akkulanu, true to form, interprets this lack of precipitation and the concomitant crop failure as a "good omen pertaining to the life and vigor of the king," it is quite clear that it was actually a matter of grave concern to everyone in the empire who was not entirely deluded.[23]

During the last dozen years of Ashurbanipal's reign, things seem to have gotten even worse. A legal document from Calah from 643 or 641 BCE records the sale of a slave woman, Urkittu-hamat, not for silver, but rather, quite unusually, for twenty minas (10 kilograms, or 22 pounds) of the less valuable copper, and adds that the transaction had taken place "in a year of dearth, when 1 liter or quart of grain went for 1.5 minas (0.7 kilograms, or 1.6 pounds) of copper." Assuming an exchange rate of roughly 1 shekel of silver for 1 mina of copper, the price for grain in this year was 1,500 times higher than the ideal grain price mentioned in Ashurbanipal's inscriptions. Several economic documents from the eponymate of Ashur-gimillu-tere (638 or 636 BCE) record, moreover, that people in Assyria had been forced to sell their own children or give them as a pledge to their creditors—another sign of economic hardship. In other words, Ashurbanipal's proud promises of economic prosperity must have rung more and more hollow as his reign progressed.[24]

IF THERE IS ONE ACHIEVEMENT FROM THE REIGN OF ASHURBANIpal whose significance cannot be put into question, it is the library the king assembled at Nineveh. Strictly speaking, Ashurbanipal created several libraries, set up in his own new North Palace, in Sennacherib's Southwest Palace, and in the temples of Nabû and Ishtar, which were located between the two royal residences. When Austen Henry Layard and his workmen, in 1850, discovered the first of these collections in the Southwest Palace, they were astonished by the large number of clay tablets they had stumbled upon:

> To the height of one foot or more from the floor, [the chambers] were entirely filled with [tablets]; some entire, but the greater part broken into many fragments, probably by the falling in of the upper part of the building. They were of different sizes; the largest tablets were flat, and measured about 9 inches by 6½ inches… and some were not more than an inch long, with but one or two lines of writing. The cuneiform characters on most of them were singularly sharp and well defined, but… minute.[25]

Almost all the tablets from Nineveh, those from Layard's excavations as well as others that were found later, were brought to the British Museum in London. Its "Kuyunjik Collection" comprises today some thirty thousand tablets and fragments. Their decipherment, and the rejoining of the broken pieces of this gigantic jigsaw puzzle, have been main preoccupations of Assyriologists since the mid-nineteenth century. Even though this process is still not complete, a lot is now known about the contents of Ashurbanipal's libraries.

It seems that the king sought to assemble at Nineveh all the written knowledge ever produced in ancient Mesopotamia. Two groups of texts were particularly essential to him: omen treatises and rituals and incantations. The former included, most importantly, a compendium of some seventy tablets related to astrology and another one, of one hundred tablets, dealing with extispicy, the art of reading the entrails of a sacrificial lamb. Astrology and extispicy were the two most prestigious techniques of prognostication in first-millennium Mesopotamia, and the king used them whenever he had to decide whether his army should go to war or whether to appoint some specific individual to high office.[26]

As his "autobiography" reveals, Ashurbanipal had become acquainted with "the signs of heaven and earth" in his youth, when he had proved to be such a quick learner—or so he claimed—that his teachers assigned to him the extremely demanding penultimate tablet of the extispicy compendium, an esoteric commentary titled "If the Liver Is a Mirror of Heaven." Today, more than five hundred commentaries and commentary fragments from Ashurbanipal's libraries are known. Along with cuneiform sign lists and dictionaries, these commentaries helped Mesopotamian scholars—and of course also the king—in their endeavors to fully understand the meaning of the texts they studied. Since these texts were often quite ancient, with roots in the second or even the third millennium BCE, and were sometimes written not in Babylonian or Assyrian but in the venerable Sumerian language, an idiom as archaic in the seventh century BCE as Latin is to us, such study aids were of great importance. Some commentaries provide, moreover, completely new layers of meaning for specific text passages, which facilitated, among other things, the reinterpretation of omens that made little sense when read literally. The astronomically impossible omen protasis "If stars stand in front of a solar disk," for example, is redefined in a commentary as actually meaning that "Mars was standing in front of another planet."[27]

Tablets inscribed with rituals and incantations were found in large numbers at Nineveh as well. They include anti-witchcraft rituals, such as the Maqlû series; a compendium called Šurpu, which provides instructions for a ritual exfoliation (the removal of dead skin cells from the outer layer of the skin), aimed at cleansing a person polluted by moral or religious failings; and a long compilation of incantations against ghosts, Udug-ḫul. Ashurbanipal's libraries also produced, long before Hippocrates and Galen, one of the largest sets of medical texts from the ancient world. Many of them formed part of a massive compendium that covered afflictions of individual body parts—with sections on the cranium, the eyes, ears, neck, bronchia, kidney, and hamstrings—as well as skin diseases and wounds, mental illness, sexual dysfunction, gynecology, obstetrics, and veterinary care. Letters from exorcists and physicians to the kings Esarhaddon and Ashurbanipal show how the magical and medical knowledge recorded in such texts was applied in attempts to restore the physical and mental health of the king and his family in moments of crisis.

Of particular interest to modern audiences are the historical and literary texts found among the tablets from Ashurbanipal's libraries. Among the latter, the famous Epic of Gilgamesh takes pride of place. Its protagonist, the tragic hero Gilgamesh, who finds fame but strives in vain for physical immortality, was a role model for Ashurbanipal. Other mythological epics from the libraries include the Babylonian Epic of Creation, the Erra Epic, and the Epic of Anzû, which recounts the warrior god Ninurta's defeat of a primeval bird that has stolen the tablet of destinies from Enlil, the king of the gods. If Ashurbanipal wished to enjoy some light reading, his library provided options as well—for example, a large collection of proverbs, riddles, and jokes, or an amusing prose narrative about a poverty-stricken resident of the city of Nippur, who takes a threefold revenge on the mayor of the city after the latter has wronged him. The story has recently been turned into the first film in Babylonian.[28]

The creation of a royal tablet collection at Nineveh had already begun under Ashurbanipal's predecessor, Esarhaddon, who had employed Babylonian hostages and prisoners of war to copy cuneiform texts for him. Babylonia had been considered the fountainhead of cuneiform culture for centuries, and it remained the main source for scholarly, religious, and literary texts when Ashurbanipal began to look for additional materials to stock his royal libraries. Letters from the correspondence between Ashurbanipal and the scholars of Babylon and Borsippa, all known from later copies, reveal the king's keen desire for learned texts from their collections. When writing to the scholars of Babylon on one occasion, Ashurbanipal asked that they send him "the entire corpus of scribal learning, the craft of the gods Ea and Asalluhi, (the terrestrial omen treatise) 'If a city,' the corpus of exorcistic texts, the corpus of liturgical lamentations, and the song corpus."[29]

The texts the king requested were to be taken "from the possession of the great lord Marduk, my lord," that is, the library of Marduk's Esagil Temple in Babylon. The Babylonian scholars were shrewd enough, however, to provide the king with newly made copies rather than sending him their irreplaceable originals. Since the Babylonian script in which the tablets from Babylon and other southern cities were written was less readily legible than the more regular Assyrian script, Ashurbanipal's staff copied many of them on beautifully shaped new tablets written in a particularly neat Assyrian style and ruled into regular columns with a string. All these tablets were supplied with so-called Ashurbanipal colophons, subscripts indicating that they belonged to the king and praising his erudition. The subscripts also specify which compilation a tablet belongs to and the number or title of the chapter it represents within it.

In a subscript of a botanical handbook, Ashurbanipal proudly proclaims that he himself had reorganized the plant names he had found collected in earlier treatises, and had thus single-handedly compiled a new reference work, which was much superior to its forerunner:

> First (var.: tenth, twelfth) chapter of (the handbook) "Uruanna means 'soapwort.'" Regarding the plant names that had formerly been explained in bilingual and monolingual dictionaries but from old times had not received an authoritative new edition (*zarâ lā ṣabtū*) and were not organized in sections, Ashurbanipal, king of the world, king of Assyria, newly arranged them.[30]

The phrase *zarâ lā ṣabātu*, otherwise rare, is also found in the context of editorial work undertaken by a Babylonian master-scholar by

the name of Esagil-kin-apli, who had lived in the mid-eleventh century BCE and had created new compilations of numerous exorcistic
and divinatory handbooks. His work had never been forgotten, and
it is clear that Ashurbanipal, in the subscript just quoted, wished to
present himself as an Esagil-kin-apli *redivivus*, a new incarnation of
the renowned scholar of yore.

During the first decade and a half of his reign, Ashurbanipal had
offered generous monetary rewards to the Babylonian scholars who
supplied him with reading material. On one occasion, he wrote to
them, "You will own one talent (about 30 kilograms, or 66 pounds)
of silver. As soon as I come to Babylon, I shall establish special privileges for you. I shall please your hearts and set your minds at ease."
But after the civil war with his brother, a disillusioned Ashurbanipal
was no longer willing to shower the faithless Babylonians with such
favors. The tablets that were brought from Babylonia to Nineveh in
the wake of the conflict in 647 were probably taken by force as war
reparations, an act of "booknapping" similar to Tukulti-Ninurta I's
pillaging of Babylonian libraries more than five and a half centuries earlier. Many of the tablets came from the libraries of private
individuals—for example, an exorcist from Nippur by the name
of Arrabu, who had to provide 185 tablets, among them liturgical
lamentations and dream omens. As Assyrian library records show,
Assyrian officials requisitioned not only clay tablets but also numerous writing boards, wooden tablets covered with a layer of wax that
were occasionally combined to form "books" of two or more hinged
leaves. Writing boards played a significant role in Mesopotamian administration and scholarship, as they later did in the classical world.
A few specimens have been recovered at Ashur and Calah, but none
at Nineveh.[31]

Ashurbanipal collected not only tablets but also scholars. Causing significant "brain drain," he recruited in Babylonia numerous
diviners, priests, exorcists, and physicians to advise him on matters of religion, health, and sometimes also politics. Like his father,

Esarhaddon, he received, moreover, hundreds of letters from astrologers spread all over Assyria and Babylonia. Their task was to inform the king on a regular basis on celestial observations they had made, from lunar eclipses to the appearance and disappearance of specific planets and stars. By sponsoring the systematic study of such phenomena, Ashurbanipal may have contributed to a paradigmatic shift toward a new, mathematically informed "science" of astronomical prediction that would define Mesopotamian scholarship until the very end of cuneiform culture.[32]

Ashurbanipal created what many consider to have been the first universal library in history, a gigantic repository of written knowledge that existed long before Hellenistic scholars founded the similarly ambitious libraries of Pergamon and Alexandria. His promotion of astrology and astronomy may have triggered, moreover, nothing less than a scientific revolution. But was the king a great scholar himself? Taking into account that he had many other things to do, holding Ashurbanipal to the standards of professional literati may, of course, not really be fair. But since he does it himself, the question must be asked.

The seriousness of Ashurbanipal's commitment to the scribal arts can hardly be doubted: even when hunting lions, he is depicted on many of his palace reliefs with a stylus tucked into his belt (see cover image). But letters the king received from his scholars make one wonder about his actual proficiency in cuneiform culture. All too often, letter writers found it necessary to explain to him some actually rather simple terms and concepts. When discussing a series of bird omens, for example, Ashurbanipal's personal teacher Balasî had to point out the meaning of the common word *išdiḫu*, "profit"; and in a letter he wrote together with the astrologer Nabû-ahhe-eriba, the same scholar gave a pronunciation gloss, *ur-ḫu*, for the widely used logogram ITI, which means "month." Finally, there is the one letter that has been identified as having been written by Ashurbanipal himself, during his time as crown prince. Addressed to Esarhaddon, it is unusually short, and its script appears "large, ungainly, and un-even." This was not the work of a truly accomplished scribe.[33]

ALAS, EVEN IF ONE WERE TO APPLY THE WORD IN THE BROADEST possible sense, Ashurbanipal was also no humanist. He was, instead, a spiteful, brutal man who lived in constant need of affirmation. The king's descriptions of the fates of defeated enemies are unusually gruesome and seem driven by a deep-felt hatred. Ashurbanipal claims, for example, that after the Assyrian conquest of Babylon in 648, he rounded up the people who had opposed him and "destroyed their faces, flayed them, and chopped up their flesh." Too frightened to join his troops on military campaigns, he demonstrated particular inventiveness when it came to humiliating captured enemies at home. The king, along with his people, would watch the elaborate choreographies of terror that he had devised to punish his opponents at the principal gate of the royal citadel at Nineveh. About the Arab ruler Uaite' (Yauta'), Ashurbanipal notes, with a good dose of callous humor aimed at removing all moral inhibitions, "I placed him in a neck-stock, bound him up with a bear and a dog, and made him guard the Citadel Gate of Nineveh." The gate also served as the place where the severed head of the Elamite king Teumman was displayed to the public, after it had been hung around the neck of the Gambulean leader Dunanu, who had to parade it around the city. Dunanu himself was later "cast on a slaughtering bench and slaughtered like a lamb." And it was at the Citadel Gate that the two sons of Nabû-shumu-eresh, a governor of Nippur who had sided with the Elamites, were forced to grind the bones of their father. Some of these episodes are not only known from Ashurbanipal's texts but were also depicted in all their bloody horror on his palace reliefs.[34]

Ashurbanipal's inscriptions also recount, often in graphic detail, how royal clients and foreign rulers cringed and crawled at his feet to demonstrate their submission. *Proskynesis*, the act of prostrating oneself in a solemn gesture of respect, was a widespread practice in the ancient Near East and nothing Ashurbanipal had invented. But no other Assyrian king uses equally humiliating language to describe it. The fugitive Elamite prince Tammaritu, for example, is said to have come to Nineveh to "kiss the feet of my royal majesty and sweep the ground with his beard," and in a short text meant to accompany a palace relief, Ashurbanipal talks about a delegation of Elamite notables that "came to me with massive gifts and licked the doorsill with their tongues." These are not the recollections of a humanist, but the ruminations of a sadist.[35]

ASHURBANIPAL IS ONE OF THOSE HISTORICAL CHARACTERS WHO seem both fascinating and deeply flawed. The literary and artistic culture he promoted was highly sophisticated. The lion hunt reliefs in his North Palace are strikingly beautiful, and some of his inscriptions can be considered poetic masterpieces. But at the same time, the king showed a disquieting tendency to indulge in vicious acts of cruelty.

The most renowned relief from Ashurbanipal's reign, a banquet scene that shows the king drinking wine with his queen (see Plate 12), illustrates his two sides well. At first glance, the viewer seems to gaze at an idyll—a peaceful rendezvous between the king and his wife in a beautiful garden, with musicians playing their instruments and birds flying through the sky and nesting on trees. But things are not quite as harmless and harmonious as they appear, for upon closer inspection, one can see something else in one of those tree-tops: the severed head of a defeated enemy, possibly Teumman. The scene is reminiscent of the "snow dream" in Thomas Mann's novel *The Magic Mountain*, in which the protagonist finds himself in the beginning in a paradise-like coastal landscape with beautiful people, before he is lured into a nearby temple with archaic columns where two disheveled, half-naked old women tear apart and eat a young boy. The twentieth-century German-Jewish philosopher Walter Benjamin's famous adage that "there is no document of civilization that is not at the same time a document of barbarism" comes to mind as well.[36]

Ashurbanipal was an extremely ambitious ruler, but one with a tendency toward self-delusion. Earlier Assyrian kings had declared as well that they were strong, powerful, and, like the famous antediluvian sage Adapa, full of wisdom. But realizing that such claims applied to their "body politic," while their "body natural" remained that of an imperfect mortal man, they refrained from putting their protestations of personal greatness to a series of public tests. Ashurbanipal did just that. A populist *avant la lettre*, eager to be loved rather than just respected, he seems to have labored under the misapprehension that he could really become another Adapa, another Esagil-kin-apli, or, even better, a new Gilgamesh. He constantly playacted, as if on a stage, to fill those roles, instead of actually ruling his country.

Unfortunately, if Gilgamesh was a tragedy, the drama enacted by Ashurbanipal was increasingly a farce. He was a poor military leader, an overrated hunter, and a mediocre scholar. With his sadistic propensities, he resembled more a Nero than a philosopher-emperor like Marcus Aurelius or Akbar. When, later in his reign, Assyria's political and economic situation deteriorated, Ashurbanipal must have realized that many members of the Assyrian elite had begun to see his rule as a failure. He withdrew more and more from public life, relied increasingly on eunuchs, and neglected, it would seem, his governing duties. Among the eponyms whom he nominated was a chief tailor and a chief singer, Bullutu—a clear violation of the age-old rule to assign this office only to respectable military officers and administrators.[37]

In the legendary tradition later handed down by the Greeks, Ashurbanipal morphed into Sardanapallus, the decadent last king of Assyria. In reality, three short-lived additional rulers followed him on the Assyrian throne before the kingdom collapsed. But the legend gets something right when it puts Sardanapallus at the end of Assyrian history. There are many indications that the reign of Ashurbanipal, despite the king's lofty ambitions, precipitated the fall of the Assyrian Empire in decisive ways.[38]

For the time being, though, life in the empire went on. The farmers and herdsmen, traders, artisans, and slaves who formed the backbone of Assyrian society were probably little affected by Ashurbanipal's eccentricities and what happened at the Assyrian court.

13

Everyday Life in the Empire

The sources that have come down from the Neo-Assyrian period have a "regicentric" bias: they talk a lot about kings, and less about anyone else. This may allow for detailed psychological profiles of Ashurbanipal and some other Assyrian rulers. But focusing so much on "great men" and writing history primarily from their perspective comes with a price: it tends to silence the experiences of average citizens, farmers, and slaves, of women, children, and the elderly. These were the people who made up the largest section of the population of all ancient societies, and the lives they led were the rule—Ashurbanipal's was the exception. Fortunately, when properly investigated, Assyrian sources also reveal a great deal about how commoners lived and died in the empire, both during its heyday and after.

Starting with farmers and animal herders in the countryside before zooming in on life in Assyrian cities, this chapter will take a closer look at Assyria's "normal people." The poor and the affluent, women and men, slaves and free citizens, they were all "Assyrians," but each group had its own identity, which was shaped by a variety of social, economic, and cultural forces.

IN MOST STATES OF THE ANCIENT AND PREMODERN WORLD, A large majority of the population resided in nonurban areas, growing crops and practicing animal husbandry. This makes Assyria's origins somewhat atypical: the early Assyrians—those living at the time of the city-state of Ashur in the first half of the second millennium—were almost exclusively townspeople. But with the transformation of Ashur into a territorial kingdom, rural communities became an integral part of the state's makeup. In the eighth and seventh centuries BCE, Assyrians lived in small settlements, villages, and hamlets throughout the empire.

While farming in the alluvial plain of Babylonia was based on artificial irrigation and produced extremely high yields, the more extensive rain-fed agriculture practiced in the Assyrian territories could be a rather precarious affair. The minimum of 200 millimeters (about 8 inches) of rain per year needed to sustain a community was barely reached in the area around Ashur, even though precipitation in the plains farther north, and in the foothills of the Zagros range, was more abundant. During Neo-Assyrian times, aqueducts and artificial canals along the Tigris and the Upper and Lower Zab, and in the area of the Khabur River, improved the situation to some extent, but without creating the paradise-like fertility of Babylonia's green plains. To what degree Assyrian agriculture continued to depend on rain is indicated by an eighth-century BCE letter from Ishtar-duri, the governor of Arrapha, to Sargon II: "It has rained a lot, so the crops are fine. The king, my lord can be glad."[1]

The most common crop in Assyria was barley, which was harvested in the spring, threshed and winnowed, and then processed into flour and beer. Orchards yielded a variety of fruit and vegetables. The imperial period brought an increase in the production of wine, especially in the area around the city of Harran, but elsewhere too. In 2021, Italian archaeologists found several stone-cut pits near Khinis in Iraq's Dohuk Governorate that were used in around 700 BCE to press grapes, whose juice was subsequently processed into wine. Date palms, in contrast, were not cultivated in Assyria on a large scale. While ubiquitous in southern Iraq, where they allow a second harvest in the fall, they are unsuited to survive the occasional night frosts of the regions farther north. Several Assyrian kings reported, however, that they brought other plants and trees from foreign lands and planted them in palace gardens and on agrarian estates in Assyria. Sennacherib imported "trees that bear wool," that is, cotton, from some unnamed place, presumably India, but seems to have ultimately failed in his attempt to establish a viable cotton industry.[2]

Large swaths of agricultural land in Assyria were owned by the king, who assigned them to temples, military officers and soldiers, high-ranking administrators, and deportees. While crown land could normally not be sold without royal permission, there were other rural estates that were not subjected to such restrictions. Unless they were exempt, landowners had to pay taxes on corn and straw to the state.[3]

The actual work in the annual agricultural cycle, from plowing and seeding to harvesting, was normally performed by semifree or unfree farmers. They tended to reside with their small families, and a number of pigs, cows, oxen, and goats, near the fields they tended. We know very little about their daily lives, but it is clear that they had their own traditions and religious customs, which included specific rituals to keep away field pests such as locusts, grasshoppers, insect larvae, and weevils. Collected in a cuneiform handbook called Zu-burudabbeda, that is, "To Paralyze the Locust-Tooth," the rituals included food offerings and libations of wine to Ninurta, patron god of agriculture and war, during dark winter nights. To secure his support in the upcoming barley harvest, the god was addressed on such occasions with an incantation: "Accept it, O Ninurta, foremost one of the Ekur Temple! Eat the tasty food, drink the sweet drink! Show goodwill towards this plot of farmland and expel them, the great dogs of Ninkilim (that is, 'Lord-Rodent,' the supernatural leader of vermin), locust (and) 'devourer'-pest, whose mouths are the Deluge!"[4]

Of course, people also took practical measures against field pests. When a plague of locusts struck vast stretches of the Assyrian Empire around 710 BCE, the governor of Ashur, following royal orders, made sure the people within his jurisdiction fumigated the spots where the locusts had laid eggs with juniper powder, in order to kill them at the moment they hatched.[5]

Farther out in the steppe, where no crops could be grown, shepherds tended their sheep and goats, which provided the Assyrian kingdom with milk, meat, wool, and leather. Controlling these seminomadic communities was not always easy for the central authorities. On one occasion, as revealed by a letter to Esarhaddon, shepherds refused to deliver the sheep they owed the Ashur Temple for as long as seven years. Instead, they armed themselves, saying, "Whoever comes against us we will cut down with our bows." Dadî, a representative of the temple, warns the king that anarchy of this kind might have dangerous consequences for his authority: "If these people, who are Assyrians, refuse to respect the king, my lord, how will foreigners behave towards the king, my lord?" The episode is a reminder that Assyrian royal power, while extensive, did have its limits.[6]

LIFE IN ASSYRIAN CITIES IS MUCH BETTER DOCUMENTED THAN life in the countryside. Urban society in imperial times was highly stratified, even among citizens who were formally free. House sizes in Ashur varied only moderately, usually between 50 and 150 square meters (538 and 1,615 square feet), thus accommodating only relatively small households. But the so-called Red House in Dur-Katlimmu, owned by a certain Shulmu-sharri, measured some 5,200 square meters (56,000 square feet), with eighty-two rooms grouped around five large courtyards. Over three decades, Shulmu-sharri, a powerful military officer under Ashurbanipal, and a confidant of the king, bought some fifty slaves, two-thirds of whom were female.[7]

Many free citizens in Assyrian towns seem to have been literate. One out of every three private houses excavated in Ashur has yielded a cuneiform archive with business documents, and quite a few also contained libraries with literary, religious, and scholarly texts. Elsewhere, a significant portion of Assyria's urban population could likewise read and write. So far, some thirty sites across Western Asia have produced private archives with legal and economic texts from the Neo-Assyrian period. Although the texts are often quite formulaic, they reveal a lot about the ways people in Assyrian cities made a living.[8]

Neo-Assyrian society, as it turns out, was characterized by a great deal of functional differentiation—a division of labor that seems almost modern. In addition to various priestly, administrative, and army ranks, there were architects, augurs, bailiffs, bakers, barbers, boatmen, bow-makers, brewers, builders, butchers, carpenters, confectioners, cooks, diviners, dyers, exorcists, fowlers, gardeners, gatekeepers, gem and stone cutters, hatters, horse trainers, interpreters, leatherworkers, masons, measurers, merchants, messengers, musicians and singers, oilpressers, perfume makers, potters, prophets, scouts, scribes, smiths, tailors, tanners, tutors, victualers, washermen, weavers, and winemakers, and within these professions, people could further specialize and hold various ranks.[9]

The legal documents from Neo-Assyrian archives can be divided into two main groups. So-called strong tablets (*dannutu*) record the acquisition of real estate or slaves. Because they served as title deeds, they remained in a family's archive for many years, sometimes over several generations. Debt notes, in contrast, about silver or barley loans—which were normally made at an annual interest rate of 25 percent—could be discarded by the creditors once the debt had been paid back.

Many Neo-Assyrian debt notes are known in the form of "dockets," inscribed clay lumps once attached to leather scrolls, which do

not survive but must have been inscribed with an Aramaic version
of the note. Quite a few dockets, and even some clay tablets, are
written in Aramaic as well, or, in addition to cuneiform, have Aramaic epigraphs scratched on them or written on them with ink.
Along with cuneiform and Assyrian, the alphabetic Aramaic script
and the Aramaic language were evidently widely used in imperial
Assyria.[10]

Following in the footsteps of their Old and Middle Assyrian
forebears, many citizens pursued lucrative careers as merchants. The
empire had removed borders and trade restrictions, facilitating commercial exchange. The biblical prophet Nahum, while emphasizing
the importance of the Assyrian traders, paints a rather negative picture of them, perhaps because he felt that their closeness to the center of power gave them some unfair advantages:

> *You have increased the number of your merchants*
> *till they are more numerous than the stars in the sky,*
> *but like locusts they strip the land*
> *and then fly away.*[11]

A well-off resident of Ashur by the name of Duri-Ashur is a typical
representative of the Neo-Assyrian merchant class. During the last
decades of the Assyrian Empire, he organized donkey caravans that
traded a variety of goods, including hats and textiles, in the area of
the modern Jebel Sinjar. When everything was sold, including the
donkeys, Duri-Ashur's representatives would buy large quantities
of wine and pour them into animal skins. The skins were bound
together with beams to form rafts and shipped on the Tigris back
to Ashur, where both the wine—kept cool during its journey by
the river—and the beams could be sold for a considerable profit.
To finance his trading ventures, Duri-Ashur raised money from
small investors—among them several Egyptian women who lived in
Ashur. They would later receive a share of the earnings.[12]

Assyrian merchants tended to be affluent. Although much smaller than the "Red House" in Dur-Katlimmu, Duri-Ashur's house covered an area of some 150 square meters (1,615 square feet), which made it one of the largest in Ashur. Assyrian scribes and scholars, in contrast, their considerable prestige notwithstanding, were usually fairly poor. As a letter from Nineveh reveals, the residence of the Assyrian chief scribe, one of the leading "intellectuals" in the empire, was "tiny," and apparently so dingy that "even a donkey would not want to enter it."[13]

Scholars and religious experts who had fallen out of favor with their royal patrons faced particular distress. When Ashurbanipal became king, for example, the exorcist and physician Urad-Gula, a grandson of the famous Nabû-zuqup-kenu, found himself all of a sudden unemployed. In a letter to the new ruler, he complains bitterly about his fate: "In the days of the king's father, I got to receive gifts from him; he used to give me a mule or an ox, and yearly I earned a mina or two of silver. But now I cannot even afford a pair of sandals. I have not got a spare suit of clothes, and I have incurred a debt of almost six minas (3 kilograms, or 6.6 pounds) of silver. People say: 'Once you have reached old age, who will support you?'" To be sure, Urad-Gula's extensive list of grievances, wrapped in beautiful language, belongs in a long tradition of Mesopotamian literati displaying all their rhetorical skills to prompt their royal employers to treat them more favorably. But even when one acknowledges that the disgruntled scholar may have exaggerated his plight, it is clear that academic pursuits were far less lucrative in ancient Assyria than commercial ones—a situation not so different from that of today.[14]

AS IN EARLIER TIMES, ASSYRIAN FAMILIES OF THE IMPERIAL PEriod tended to be small. A husband would normally live with his wife and children, sometimes a few slaves, and occasionally also his parents, in his private residence. Women from well-off families would bring a dowry into the marriage, consisting of jewelry, textiles, containers, toiletry articles, tools, furniture, and silver. In the case of divorce, it would remain in the woman's possession, providing her with some material security.[15]

The primary purpose of marriage in Assyria was to produce offspring. Children, apart from bringing joy, were expected to take care of their parents when the latter grew old, to bury them—normally in vaults located below the family home—and to keep their memory alive by performing monthly rituals in honor of the dead. But as in all premodern societies, in Assyria, too, being pregnant and giving birth were fraught with danger. Due to poor hygiene and an inability to cope competently with obstructed labor, postpartum hemorrhage, and childbed fever, maternal mortality was high. A short elegy known from a clay tablet from Nineveh—one of the few literary texts written in Assyrian rather than Babylonian—provides a moving, deeply poetic reminiscence of an anonymous Assyrian woman who died in childbirth. The text begins with the woman's husband bemoaning her fate and asking why she had to cross the river of the underworld:

> "Abandoned like a boat adrift midstream,
> "Your thwarts all broken, painters severed:
> "Why cross the City's river, veiled in a shroud?"

The woman, or rather her ghost, responds by telling her husband what happened to her:

> "How not to drift abandoned, my painters
>   severed?
> "During the days I was with child, how happy I
>   was!
> "Happy I was, and happy my husband!

"The day my pains began, a shadow fell across my
    face,
"The day my labor started, brightness faded from
    my eyes.
"I besought the mother goddess, fists unclenched:
"'O mother, you that bore me, spare my life!'
"The mother goddess heard, then veiled her face:
"'[Who are] you, and why beseech me so?'"
"[My spouse, who] loved me, cried aloud:
"'[Who(?) has robbed] me of my wife and
    comfort?
"'[. . .] through all eternity,
"'[. . .for] ever in the place of ruin.'"

The text ends with the woman's ghost crying out in desperation about her untimely death:

Passing through the City's [streets, the woman's
    shade] gave wail:
"[Alas for all] that time my husband was my
    company!
"With him I dwelt, the property of him that loved
    me,
"Then to our bedroom stealthy Death did creep.
"From my house he drove me forth,
"From my husband cut me off;
"My footfall here he planted, in a place of no
    return."[16]

Not only the mothers but also their babies were at grave risk when something went wrong, whether at birth or in the weeks and months thereafter. How miserable the loss of children could make their parents is indicated by a letter from Adad-shumu-usur, a leading exorcist, to King Esarhaddon: "As to what the king, my lord, wrote to me: 'I am feeling very sad; how did we act that I became so depressed for this little one of mine?'—well, had it been curable, you would have given away half of your kingdom to have it cured. But what can we do? O king, my lord, it is a matter where nothing can be done."[17]

In the absence of effective medical treatments, young couples would resort to apotropaic rituals and incantations to ward off the dangers associated with giving birth and raising young children. Because the fundamentally benevolent gods could not be deemed responsible for the loss of pregnant women and little babies, people projected their fears onto a malevolent, baby-snatching demoness named Lamashtu, a kind of anti-mother who was depicted with a lion's head, the talons of a bird, and the upper body of a female (see Plate 13). At her sagging breasts, a piglet and a dog could nurse, and her clawed fingers sometimes grasped snakes. In the incantations that were used to battle her, Lamashtu is said to "count the months" of the mothers about to give birth, and "mark their days on the wall," before "slithering into a locked house" to "strangle the young children."[18]

One way to get rid of this terrifying demoness—and secure a safe delivery and life for the children—was to produce a figurine of her, recite incantations over it, and then dispose of it in the steppe or set it on a little boat that was placed on the Tigris and sent away downstream. Another way to counter Lamashtu was to solicit the help of a second supernatural being, Pazuzu, "the king of the evil wind demons." Sporting taloned feet and hands, a leonine face with protruding eyes, and an erect penis (all of which gives him an appearance similar to that of the Egyptian god Bes), Pazuzu looked almost as scary as Lamashtu, but served as an agent of "white magic": his powers were used to drive the evil child-eater away. Small Pazuzu heads could be worn on clothes or around the neck, while larger amulets depicting the demon were set up in domestic spaces to protect pregnant women and small children. Pazuzu had a spectacular comeback in the 1971 novel *The Exorcist* and the subsequent film adaptation—but these immensely popular specimens of the horror genre associate him with the devil, rather than casting him in the benevolent role he actually played in Assyria and Babylonia.[19]

While normally greeted with great happiness, the arrival of a healthy new child also brought challenges, as parents up to the present day know only too well. At night babies were often crying, which would wake up the parents and, much worse, disturb the house ghosts, among them the easily irascible *kusarriku*, a kind of semidivine bull-man. To hush their little ones and keep the domestic spirits at ease, parents would sing lullabies, some of which are known from cuneiform handbooks. The Assyro-Babylonian cradle-songs ask why the baby had not cried while still in the womb and entreat it in poetic language to be as calm as well water, "to be given sleep like a sleepy gazelle buck," and to doze like a shepherd nodding mid-watch.[20]

AS EVERYWHERE ELSE, RELATIONS BETWEEN HUSBANDS AND wives in Assyria were sometimes cordial, sometimes contentious. The sources of marital disharmony were manifold. One was male sexual dysfunction, which was treated with the help of rituals and magic spells. A typical potency incantation, from the cuneiform handbook Shaziga, reads, "Wild ass, wild ass, wild bull, wild bull. Who has made you limp like loose ropes, who has poured cold water on your heart (i.e., penis)? Who has caused depression in your mind, and sleepiness?" The ritual acts accompanying spells like this one projected the problem onto figurines of outside agents such as evil spirits or witches. Magical procedures of this type were hardly capable of curing physiological issues, but they might have helped against "performance anxiety."[21]

Every so often, wives would suspect their husbands of erotic indiscretions. A liver omen known from several clay tablets from Nineveh reads, "If the Presence (a feature of the liver) is like the sting of a scorpion, the wife of a man, with her crotch burning, will set the man's house on fire." A commentary note added to this entry explains, "If you have the word 'crotch' before you: 'crotch' refers to jealousy: she is jealous and therefore sets the man's house on fire." Wives, too, of course, could fancy a partner outside of marriage—and were thought to sometimes become so fed up with their husbands that they were capable of taking rather drastic steps to escape their marital bonds. As another liver omen states, "If lines are drawn three times between the Presence and the Path (two features of the liver), the wife of a man will keep on sending messages (to another man) with instructions to kill her husband, saying: 'Kill my husband and marry me!'"[22]

Most Neo-Assyrian texts dealing with women were composed and written by men and reflect specifically male perspectives. A satirical literary dialogue between a weak-minded master and his savvy slave is a case in point. In the text, the master, unsure what could give his life meaning, proposes a series of activities, only to immediately change his mind and give up his plan. Each time, the slave, eager to humor his master, provides a good reason for action or inaction. One stanza outlines the benefits and—in the most literal sense—the pitfalls of becoming attached to a woman:

> Slave, listen to me!—Here I am, my lord, here
>   I am.
> I am going to love a woman.—So love, my lord,
>   love!
> The man who makes love to a woman forgets
>   sorrow and fear.
> No, slave, I shall not make love to a woman.

Then do not make love, my lord, do not make
love.
A woman is a pitfall, a real pitfall, a hole, a
ditch!
A woman is a sharp iron dagger that cuts a young
man's throat.[23]

In the patriarchal world of eighth- and seventh-century Assyria, women were normally expected to behave as in the Roman adage "She served her household, she made wool." But there were exceptions. Neo-Assyrian women whose husbands or sons had died or had become incapacitated would often take over the family business. Temple priestesses, too, were more independent than was typical of women.[24]

There were also a certain number of women who lived completely outside the domestic sphere, whether as prophetesses, tavern-keepers, or prostitutes. But they were often social outcasts and occasionally suspected to be witches. The image of womanhood as a threat to order and cosmic harmony is also found in religious contexts, whether in the figure of Lamashtu or that of Tiamat, the primeval originator of the gods in the Babylonian Epic of Creation, who later sought to annihilate her own offspring.

Many powerful goddesses of earlier times, for example Nisaba, a deity associated with writing and bringing in the harvest, had been demoted by the first millennium BCE and no longer played a prominent role. On the other hand, the people of Neo-Assyrian times worshipped with all the fervor they could muster the goddess Ishtar, patroness of love and war, defender of transvestism and gender fluidity, and the only deity who had ever descended to the netherworld and ascended to heaven. It seems as if all the repressed urges to escape from the patriarchal restrictions of everyday life were projected onto this one goddess, the embodiment of contrariness and transgression.

AT THE BOTTOM OF SOCIETY IN NEO-ASSYRIAN TIMES WERE THE slaves. They were deemed the property of others, and as such sometimes valued—like the slave in the satirical dialogue—but otherwise considered dispensable. An example of this dismissive attitude toward them is found in a note to Esarhaddon from the exorcist Adad-shumu-usur—the same man who had praised the king for his concern for the life of one of his own children. Here he was writing about finding guinea pigs to try out an untested drug, to determine whether it should be administered to Esarhaddon's son Ashurbanipal, and he is far less philanthropic: "Let us make those slaves drink first, and let the crown prince drink only afterwards."[25]

Men as well as women could enter the state of slavery as prisoners of war or through debt bondage. The children of slaves inherited the status from their parents and were considered house-born slaves. What could happen to enslaved prisoners of war is shown by a contract from Ashur about the sale of two women, a mother and her daughter, who were "captives from Elam whom the king had given to (people from) the city of Ashur." The sellers are ten men with different professional backgrounds who had, in all likelihood, participated as members of the same military unit in the sack of Susa in 646 BCE, receiving the two women as a reward for their service. Since joint ownership of the women would have been of little practical use for them, they sold them for one mina of silver to a certain Mannu-ki-Ashur, who was henceforth their sole master. Slave women were particularly vulnerable, of course, since their bodies could be exploited both for work and for sex.[26]

Debt slavery was a practice no less widespread than the enslavement of prisoners of war, and one that could bring equally great hardship on those subjected to it. The case of a woman sold by her father, presumably because he was in debt, is discussed in a letter from Nineveh. The father, who lived in Karalla in Western Iran—and was apparently deeply distressed by his daughter's predicament—sent her a secret message in which he implored her, "Run away and come to me."[27]

Attempted escape from the harsh conditions under which slaves lived was a regular occurrence across the Assyrian Empire, all the more so as cases of manumission seem to have been rare. Sometimes, attempts by slaves to regain their freedom led to violent confrontations with their masters and state authorities. In a letter from the reign of Esarhaddon, an official reports that a merchant from Carchemish had been killed by his slaves, and then remarks, "But not even one of them escaped; we have arrested them all."[28]

To make it as difficult as possible for slaves to abscond, it was not unusual to burn the names of their owners, or a message about their status, into their skin, a treatment originally applied to cattle. A handbook on legal practices known from Middle Assyrian and Neo-Assyrian copies instructs the owners of undependable slaves to engrave on their faces the phrase *ḫalaq ṣabat*, "He is a runaway— seize him!" Before this is taken as another sign of a specifically Assyrian—or Mesopotamian—penchant for inhumanity, it must be stressed that later civilizations had very similar procedures in place. In ancient Greece, the foreheads of runaway slaves were marked with the words *kátekhé me pheúgo*, "Seize me, I am a fugitive," while the Romans forced slaves to wear metal rings around their necks that were inscribed with the Latin phrase *fugi tene me*, which means the same. Later, in the American South, fugitive slaves, if they were caught, had the letter R (for "runaway") branded on their cheeks.[29]

The Assyrian government was eager to help recapture slaves who had fled; but it was also concerned that powerful businessmen and officials might abuse their positions to unjustly enslave defenseless women and children. A document from Ashur accuses two tax collectors of having forged debt notes to force the widows of seven deceased oil-pressers into debt bondage, and in a letter from the reign of Sargon II, an official is asked to investigate the situation of the families of fallen soldiers, and whether anyone had "forced a widow (of a soldier) to be his slave girl, or a son or a daughter into servitude."[30]

LIFE IN MESOPOTAMIAN CITIES WAS PUNCTUATED BY RELIGIOUS holidays, with divine processions and public sacrifices, and by the celebration of family events such as weddings and funerary rites. Birthdays played no major role, even though people seem to have had a fairly clear idea of their age. How the Assyrians thought about getting old is shown by a text from Huzirina near Harran. Being forty years of age is considered in the text the "prime of life," fifty means "short days," sixty "manhood," seventy "long days," eighty "old age," and ninety "extremely old age." Given the generally fairly low life expectancy in the ancient world, these numbers may seem rather astonishing, but it is known that at least some people in first-millennium Assyria and Babylonia reached a remarkably old age: Adda-guppi, the mother of the Babylonian king Nabonidus (r. 555–539 BCE), who was born in the city of Harran during the reign of Ashurbanipal, was more than a hundred years old when she died. Urad-Nabû, a priest from Calah, wished in a letter that Esarhaddon would "live one hundred years."[31]

The cuneiform omen handbook "If a City" deals with a wide variety of features of Mesopotamian urban life. A well-balanced population was considered important for a city to thrive. Too many fools were a problem, but so was the opposite: "If wise men are too numerous in a city, that city will be abandoned." We learn that houses located on a height were bad and houses nested in a depression good, what it meant when the appearance of a house was flashy (bad) or unprepossessing (good), in which direction doorways opened, and much more. Domestic animals and pets are covered as well. There are, for example, a number of cat omens, such as "If a cat cries in a man's house, that house will experience grief," "If a cat vomits in the window of a man's house, losses will be in store for that house," or "If a cat discharges its urine onto a man, he will become rich."

Even sexual mores receive some attention. The relevant omens reveal, among other things, that being in a homosexual relationship with another man was socially acceptable, as long as one was the active partner rather than the passive one. Students had to study such sexually explicit omens as part of their schoolwork, but proved, unsurprisingly, not always up to the task. With reference to the omen protasis "If a man 'comes' between her thighs," for example, one scribal apprentice noted in an omen commentary from Nineveh, "I do not know what that means."[32]

Assyrian culture also had its lighter side. When, in 1950, the French Assyriologist George Contenau declared that he felt unable to imagine the people of Mesopotamia ever laughing or enjoying themselves, he could not have been more wrong. Satires and other humorous texts from Assyrian libraries reveal how Assyrians could be funny and irreverent. Of particular interest is a collection of proverbs, jokes, and short stories that was named, after an Old Babylonian scholar from Nippur, the "Series of Sidu." Its ninth tablet includes a number of preposterous speeches made by a fox, the self-obsessed archetypal trickster, including the following: "The fox, having urinated in the sea, said: 'The entire sea is my urine.' The fox, having urinated in the Tigris, said: 'The flood has risen thanks to my urine.'" Narcissists today are of course no different. Another text describes how a jester, the so-called *aluzinnu* (who reappears in Greek tradition under the term *alazôn*), impersonated various respectable professionals, poking fun at their pompousness and questioning the efficacy of their crafts. An exorcist, for example, succeeds in driving out an evil spirit—but only by burning down the house where the demon had taken up residence. Another section of the text, sometimes dubbed "The Infernal Kitchen," provides a series of short culinary recipes, one for each month:

Month of Kislimu (IX), what will be your food? You shall eat donkey dung on bitter garlic and chaff in spoiled milk.

Month of Shabatu (II), what will be your food? You shall eat
bread that is still hot and the buttock of a donkey stallion stuffed
with dog poop and the excrement of dust flies.[33]

This was, evidently, not the way the Assyrians actually prepared their
dishes. For those, a broad selection of very different ingredients was
used: vegetables included onions, garlic, shallots, leek, cress, arugula,
lettuce, mustard, chickpeas, lentils, peas, beans, radishes, turnips,
and mushrooms; and fruit included apples, pears, plums, pomegranates, apricots, dates, grapes, and figs as well as berries. Aromatics,
such as cedar and licorice, and nuts, such as pistachios, enhanced
Assyrian dishes. On special occasions, people would eat fish or various types of meat, such as goat, beef, pork, and mutton. They also
consumed ducks, geese, pigeons, quails, and partridges, along with
their eggs, and different kinds of game, including deer, gazelle, boar,
turtle, and rabbit. More exotic foodstuffs ranged from small rodents,
such as bandicoot rats, to grasshoppers and locusts. For fat, people
used sesame oil and the fat from the tails of sheep; and for condi-
ments, mint, vinegar, and fish brine, which, although costly, was
also extremely important in later Roman cuisine. Honey and date
syrup served as sweeteners. Various types of bread and porridges
were daily staples. Drinks included water, fruit juice, beer, and grape
wine. Wine consumption became more and more fashionable among
Assyria's elites during the imperial period.[34]

Beer was often consumed in taverns, where Assyrian citizens,
especially men, would find release from their daily cares and worries. Some taverns also served as brothels. Assyro-Babylonian rituals
prescribed a visit to the tavern as a means to undo the evil that
loomed over a man due to some negative portent, and at the same
time reintegrate him into society. Many tavern-keepers were female,
like the legendary Siduri, who ran the "tavern at the end of the world"
where Gilgamesh found rest before his journey across the waters of
death to the flood hero Utanapishti. The witticisms and wisecracks

recorded in the "Series of Sidu" and the "Aluzinnu Text" most likely also circulated orally in the bawdy atmosphere of the taverns, where alcohol loosened tongues, which on occasion led to bloody bar brawls. In a letter to Esarhaddon about three recently promoted military officers, an official warns the king that "these three men are drunkards. When they get drunk, none of them can turn his iron sword away from his colleague." Another letter talks about drunken soldiers on horses who are making the streets of Calah unsafe. Small wonder, then, that the biblical Books of Isaiah (28:7–8) and Proverbs (31:4–9) strongly discourage alcohol consumption among people of authority, such as kings, priests, and prophets.[35]

The tone in the tavern was probably often rough. How people in the Assyrian Empire cursed and swore can be gauged from a small tablet from Nineveh inscribed with invectives against a certain Bel-etir. The words used in this text were better to be avoided in polite conversation: "Bel-etir, you fucked hostage, doubly so, with runny eyes, doubly so, with bulging eyes, doubly so, son of Ibâ, that missed period, that shit bucket of a fart factory, of a vile family, lackey of a dead god, of a house whose star has vanished from the heavens, a slave girl, a chattel, he, the slave of a Syrian country girl, the only bearded one among a crowd of over-fornicated women."[36]

BEL-ETIR WAS PROBABLY A FOREIGNER—HE MAY HAVE BEEN AN opponent of Ashurbanipal from the time of the civil war with Shamash-shumu-ukin in the mid-seventh century BCE. Tensions existed, of course, also among the residents of Assyrian cities. People quarreled mostly over money, disputing over wills and ownership claims; but occasionally, homicides, robbery, theft, and damage to property occurred as well. To restore the peace, such cases required conflict management and legally binding rulings.

Remarkably enough, there was no written Neo-Assyrian code of law. Scribes and scholars continued to copy the famous Code of Hammurapi, which had been composed some one thousand years before Tiglath-pileser III had established the Assyrian Empire—but the text was read as a classical work describing an ideal state of justice, rather than as a source for laws to be applied in actual court proceedings. There were also no courthouses and no professional judges. In fact, the Akkadian word for "judge," *dayyānu*, is largely absent from Neo-Assyrian documents. Instead, administrative and temple officials served as judicial authorities: on the state level, the vizier and the *sartennu*-official; on the provincial level, the governor; on the municipal level, the mayor; and within temple contexts, high-ranking priests. Cases were decided based on depositions made by the plaintiff and the defendant, statements by witnesses, and documentary evidence. If the truth was hard to establish, the official in charge could ask one of the parties to swear an oath, or send the litigants to the "river ordeal," where those unable to withstand the rushing waters were considered guilty. In most cases, the losing party was sentenced to pay a fine to the other side, rather than having to face prison time or corporal punishment.[37]

The ultimate judicial arbiter in Neo-Assyrian times was the king, but he intervened only in cases involving capital crimes of public interest, such as high treason or temple theft. Examples of the latter are documented in a number of letters. In one of them, Sîn-na'di, the mayor of Ashur, reports to the king that a sheet of gold taken by temple thieves had been recovered, that the thieves were in custody, and that the goldsmith Basali had made a repair, perhaps remounting the sheet. The culprits in such cases may have received more severe punishments than was usual for most crimes, perhaps even the death penalty, but the sources do not clearly spell this out.[38]

To be called before a royal official, whether in the context of legal proceedings or for some other reason, such as conscription for military service or forced labor, often caused great anxiety among those who were summoned. Serving in the army, in particular, must have been a great burden for many Assyrians, and often a traumatizing experience as well, despite the substantial rewards, mostly in the form of booty, that the service provided. While professional or semiprofessional soldiers were used for the Assyrian chariotry, cavalry, and heavy infantry, as well as to man multiethnic elite units of auxiliary archers and spearmen, the regular infantry was composed mainly of Assyrian peasants, who were recruited during the summer months, when they had little work to do in the fields.[39]

Many Assyrian commoners seem to have felt an almost Kafkaesque uneasiness when summoned by the authorities. To calm nerves and increase their chances of not having to suffer too much abuse, they resorted on such occasions to a set of rituals and incantations that were known as Egalkura, that is, "(Rituals to successfully) enter the palace." The incantations to be recited before an encounter with an official provide interesting insights into the views the ruled held of their rulers and the bureaucrats employed by them. The following passage is from an Egalkura incantation on a tablet from Ashur:

> The palace, whose tasks are harsh, arduous to the point of being unbearable, and whose punishments are severe—labor for it is fraught with protests. Behind its doors(?) terror reigns, its resident is a merciless lion. He who enters it will pray to (the sun god) Shamash: "O Shamash, watch over my speech in there, make my entreaties (before the authorities) successful, so that I go in safely and come back well-pleased. My lord Shamash, may I see your grace."[40]

The king and his representatives as merciless lions and the palace as a place of terror: descriptions like this belie the claim made by so many Assyrian monarchs that they exercised their authority first and foremost for the benefit of their subjects. The truth was that the ruler and the state were more often feared than loved, and encounters with them better avoided.

As the seventh century BCE advanced, though, the time for the Assyrian kings to pursue their rapacious—and sometimes murderous—agenda was quickly drawing to a close. The end of the Assyrian Empire was nigh. It would be violent, and it would sweep away the powerful and the weak alike.

14

Imperial Twilight

The defenders posted in the outer entrance of the Shamash Gate, in the southeastern corner of Nineveh, were fighting desperately, while Babylonian and Median soldiers showered them with arrows. They knew full well that if their efforts to repel their opponents failed, they would not survive.

During the previous months, work crews had frantically tried to narrow the gates of Nineveh by haphazardly extending their side walls with poorly dressed stone blocks. The Assyrian kings—most notably Sennacherib, who not that long ago had turned Nineveh into the greatest city of its time—had wanted the city gates to be monumental and beautiful. Even in their wildest dreams, they would never have imagined that the generous proportions of the entranceways might one day prove a strategic liability. But now, in the heat of the summer of 612 BCE, it turned out that this was exactly the problem. The size of the gates, and the enormous length of the city wall, made it impossible to defend Nineveh effectively.

And then, on a fateful day in August, after a three-month-long siege, the enemy finally broke through. The Babylonian and Median troops and their allies swarmed into the city to do what the Assyrians had done so many times to others: they engaged in an orgy of slaughter, pillage, and destruction. Nineveh's palaces, temples, and private residences went up in flames.

The Assyrian soldiers stationed in the Shamash Gate—along with a number of citizens who had tried to escape through the gate at the very last minute—were dead at this point, victims of the enemy attack that had resulted in Nineveh's conquest. Hit by arrows or killed by other means, their bodies were strewn on the ground in outflung or contorted positions, some face downward, others looking as if they had expired in a running pose. And no one was left to pick them up and bury them.

The skeletons of the fallen remained where they lay for some 2,600 years. Along with the arrowheads that had pierced their bodies and the stone blocks hastily moved into the outer entrance as a last barrier against the advancing enemy, they were still in situ when a team from the University of California at Berkeley excavated the Shamash Gate in 1989 and 1990, removed the rubble that covered the scene—and began to reconstruct the story behind it.[1]

The conquest of Nineveh, which led to the death of the soldiers and civilians struck down in the Shamash Gate, and of tens of thousands of other people, is a key episode in the dramatic narrative of the Assyrian Empire's collapse. Assyria's fall was a sudden one, playing out over just a few years. It was an event rather than a process, and thus very different from the slow decline of the Roman Empire, a state that otherwise had so much in common with Assyria. The French Assyriologist Paul Garelli has called it a "historical scandal," and modern historians are indeed hard pressed to explain how it was possible that a state as large, wealthy, and powerful as ancient Assyria, with a dynasty that had been in place for more than one thousand years, could disappear so suddenly and completely. But what happened did not come entirely out of the blue—several long-term trends had contributed to it.[2]

THE SOURCES AVAILABLE FOR THE LAST TWENTY YEARS OF THE Assyrian Empire are somewhat different from those extant from other periods of Assyrian history. Assyrian royal inscriptions, while not entirely absent, are of little help, as Assyrian kings did not write about setbacks and humiliations. The inscriptions of the Babylonian kings are not particularly informative either, albeit for a different reason: in keeping with an age-old tradition of Babylonian rulers focusing on their relationship with the gods, on sacrifices and temple building, rather than their military activities, Nabopolassar and Nebuchadnezzar II—who played decisive roles in the defeat of Assyria—said little about their great triumph over their northern neighbor. Nabopolassar claimed that he "overthrew the Subarean (that is, Assyria) and turned his lands into tells and desolate places," using "the weapon of the awe-inspiring (warrior god) Erra, who strikes my enemies with lightning," but he added no further details.[3]

Other texts are more revealing. Legal and economic documents from Babylonia (and to a lesser extent from Assyria) have helped scholars reconstruct the chronology of events and clarify when some of the different cities of Babylonia changed sides as the conflict progressed. A key source is the Babylonian Chronicle series. After a lacuna for the years 622 to 617, it picks up in 616 BCE and provides detailed information on the havoc the Babylonian and Median troops wrought in the Assyrian heartland from then on, as well as the last tragic convulsions of the Assyrian state and the role the Egyptians played during those fateful years. Two recently published letters from the Assyrian northwest cast new light on the situation shortly after the conquest of Nineveh. Some historical-literary texts known from cuneiform tablets from the Seleucid period, including the so-called Nabopolassar Epic, are likewise of interest, even though it remains uncertain to what extent they accurately reflect what had happened in the late seventh century, some three hundred years before they were written. The same applies to the Hebrew Bible, most notably the Book of Nahum, and to Greek sources such as the accounts of Berossus and Ctesias. These sources contain many inaccuracies but also include some intriguing details that seem to be taken from firsthand accounts. Finally, there is considerable archaeological evidence, not only at Nineveh but also at Ashur, Calah, Dur-Katlimmu, and elsewhere. Together, these sources paint a portrait of an empire in its death throes, unable to withstand the onslaught of a series of major challenges.[4]

AS POINTED OUT EARLIER, ALMOST NOTHING IS KNOWN ABOUT the last years of Ashurbanipal's reign. From the early 630s onward, his royal inscriptions no longer talk about military exploits. At first glance, the political situation seems to have been calm during this period. Elam was substantially weakened, Babylonia was quiet, and Tabal and Urartu, Assyria's old enemies in eastern Anatolia, were in dire straits. But there are also signs that Assyria was in considerable trouble. Archaeological evidence, and the testimony of the Greek historian Herodotus, suggest that the empire's hegemony over the Eastern Mediterranean and parts of the Levant had come to an end shortly after 640, perhaps as a consequence of Scythian raids. Egyptian troops eventually filled the void. At the same time, Assyria seems to have experienced some internal economic hardship caused by poor harvests.[5]

In 631, after a reign of nearly forty years, Ashurbanipal passed away. He may have died from old age, although there is no definitive evidence to shed light on the circumstances of his end. He was succeeded by his young son Ashur-etel-ilani, who ruled from about 630 to 627. But Ashur-etel-ilani turned out to be little more than a figurehead, the puppet of a powerful eunuch by the name of Sîn-shumu-lishir. The preamble of a grant made in Ashur-etel-ilani's name leaves no doubt about his dependent status:

> After my father and begetter (Ashurbanipal) had departed, no father brought me up or taught me to spread my wings, no mother cared for me or saw to my education. Sîn-shumu-lishir, however, the chief eunuch, one who had deserved well of my father and

begetter and had constantly guided me like a father, installed me safely on the throne and made the people of Assyria keep watch over my kingship while I was a minor.[6]

These are the words of a king who was clearly not in charge. And his weakness did not go unobserved. As the same preamble reveals, Ashur-etel-ilani's accession to the throne was soon followed by an inner-Assyrian rebellion, led by a certain Nabû-rehtu-usur. It was eventually quelled, but only through the good services of Sîn-shumu-lishir.

Then, in 627, Ashur-etel-ilani disappeared from the scene. Since he was still very young at this point, he was quite possibly murdered. At about the same time, Kandalanu, the Assyrian puppet installed as king of Babylonia, also passed away.

The implications of these two royal deaths were enormous. They led to political chaos, both in Assyria and Babylonia, and then to the protracted war that would end with the fall of Assyria. The Babylonian "Akitu Chronicle" puts it well: "After (the death of) Kandalanu...troubles took place in Assyria and Akkad (i.e., Babylonia); a permanent state of hostility ensued, and there was a long succession of battles."[7]

EVEN BEFORE ASHUR-ETEL-ILANI'S DEMISE, ANOTHER SON OF Ashurbanipal, Sîn-sharru-ishkun, had sought to win the Assyrian throne for himself. Now, with his brother out of the way, he found his position substantially strengthened. But he was not the only contender. In a highly unusual move, Sîn-shumu-lishir, the chief eunuch, claimed kingship over Assyria as well. Eunuchs, biologically unable to sustain a dynastic line, had never served as king in Assyria before. They were supposed to support the king, not to hold his office. There can be little doubt, therefore, that Sîn-shumu-lishir's machinations triggered a major crisis of legitimacy for the Assyrian crown.[8]

The man who was to take advantage of the infighting between the two competing Assyrian leaders—and in the process change the course of history—was a Babylonian official by the name of Nabopolassar. Possibly a member of the Chaldean Bit-Dakkuri "tribe," he was in all likelihood the scion of a family of high-ranking administrators who served on behalf of several Assyrian kings in the city of Uruk in southern Babylonia. Kudurru, Nabopolassar's father, was the governor of Uruk, and Nabopolassar himself must have held some office in the city as well. Both father and son were, in other words, local "collaborators" with the Assyrian occupation forces, part of the Assyrian intelligence network, and deeply familiar with Assyrian military and administrative practices.[9]

After the death of Ashur-etel-ilani, Kudurru rebelled against his Assyrian overlords, but pro-Assyrian forces defeated him and "dragged his corpse through the streets" of Uruk. His son, however, having escaped the punitive measures the Assyrians implemented, soon proved a more formidable leader of the liberation movement that had emerged to end Assyria's rule over Babylonia once and for all.

By the second month of 626 BCE, with the Assyrians unable to intervene, Nabopolassar was recognized as king in Uruk. At about the same time, he made a first attempt to also establish his rule in the city of Babylon. He initially failed to hold the city: within a few months, his troops were pushed back by an Assyrian counteroffensive. But the Assyrian forces, engaged both at Uruk and at Babylon, soon found themselves stretched dangerously thin. Attacked on two fronts, they suffered a series of humiliating defeats. Nabopolassar returned to Babylon, and, as the Babylonian Chronicle reports, on the twenty-sixth day of the month of Arahsamna (VIII), ascended the throne there. His coronation is described in some detail in the Nabopolassar Epic. He received the crown, a royal seal, and other symbols of power in a ceremony that included a group of Babylonian noblemen joyfully addressing their new ruler with the words, "O lord, o king, may you live forever. May you conquer(?) the land of your enemies, to avenge Babylonia."[10]

"AVENGING BABYLONIA" WAS INDEED WHAT NABOPOLASSAR, over the next years, strove for with all his heart. He meant for Assyria to pay the ultimate price for the many humiliating defeats it had inflicted on its southern neighbor over the previous decades and centuries.

One of the first victims of Nabopolassar's wrath, it seems, would be Sîn-shumu-lishir. The Nabopolassar Epic reports that the king encountered the "almighty chief eunuch"—presumably Sîn-shumu-lishir himself—on the roof of a palace in the city of Cutha near Babylon, where the eunuch, at some point late in 626 BCE, had attempted to find refuge. The cornered leader beseeched him, "Do not kill me, mighty king." But Nabopolassar was unmoved by his enemy's desperate appeal for mercy. He sounded the order, "Let the Assyrian be killed."[11]

With the death of Sîn-shumu-lishir, Ashurbanipal's son Sîn-sharru-ishkun became the sole holder of the Assyrian throne. He would rule Assyria until 612 BCE. Almost instantly, he tried to win back control over the south. The years between 625 and 620 were punctuated by a series of brutal battles in Babylonia, with Babylonian cities, especially Uruk, repeatedly changing sides and sieges getting underway in different places. In a repeat of former conflicts twenty-five years earlier, during the war between Ashurbanipal and Shamash-shumu-ukin, the statues of important gods were removed from their home sanctuaries—by the Babylonians to Babylon and by the Assyrians to Arrapha—and civilians suffered enormous hardship. The disruptions must have led repeatedly to breakdowns of the social order. Many legal and economic texts from this period include notes that "the city gate was closed," or that "there were hostilities in the land." The situation within Assyria itself was not consistently stable, either. Even though the details are murky, it seems that Sîn-sharru-ishkun had to beat back another internal rebellion in 623.

After six years, Nabopolassar managed to drive the Assyrians out of Babylonia. Again, details about what happened, or how, are not available, but the date formulas of Babylonian documents suggest that both Nippur and Uruk were under Nabopolassar's permanent control by 620. A stalemate between the two sides followed, with the Babylonians slowly taking charge of contested territories in the Eastern Tigris region.

During the year 616 BCE, the hostilities between Sîn-sharru-ishkun and Nabopolassar were concentrated on the Middle Euphrates region, where the Babylonian king scored another victory over Assyrian troops, now reinforced by Iranian allies from the land of Mannaya. But his westward move stirred up the Egyptians, who had taken control of vast areas west of the Euphrates during the waning years of Ashurbanipal's reign. Egypt was ruled at this time by Pharaoh Psamtik I, whom Ashurbanipal had appointed decades ago. Perhaps Psamtik still harbored some sympathy for the empire on the Tigris, his onetime benefactor; or maybe he just thought that Nabopolassar posed a greater threat to Egypt's new territorial ambitions in the Levant than the Assyrians under Sîn-sharru-ishkun. At any rate, he interfered on behalf of the Assyrian king and drove Nabopolassar back to Babylonia. It was a move that turned the Assyro-Babylonian war, irrevocably, into an "international" conflict.[12]

Nabopolassar, sensing that a major confrontation with Egyptian forces would be unwise at this point, decided to refocus his attention on the Eastern Tigris region. Toward the end of 616, he defeated an Assyrian battalion near the city of Arrapha. The next year, emboldened by this success, Babylonian troops marched along the Tigris up to Ashur, Assyria's old religious capital. But they were pushed back and had to retreat as far south as Takritain, modern Tikrit in central Iraq. The Assyrian counteroffensive, however, did not get very far either: attempts by Sîn-sharru-ishkun's troops to dislodge the Babylonians from their stronghold at Takritain proved unsuccessful, and the Assyrians had to return home again.

BY MID-615, ASSYRIA'S POLITICAL AND MILITARY SITUATION WAS challenging but not yet desperate. There had been earlier occasions when Assyrian troops had been ousted from Babylonia, and unsuccessful Babylonian and Elamite attacks on the Assyrian heartland had taken place even in the not-so-distant past. In none of these instances had the integrity of the Assyrian Empire been in serious peril. Even better, Sîn-sharru-ishkun could count on support from the powerful kingdom of Egypt. But in the fall of 615, a new outside force joined the fray: the Medes. And with their arrival on the battlefield, Assyria's very existence was suddenly at stake.

First attested in inscriptions from the reign of Shalmaneser III from the ninth century BCE, the Medes were a group of initially half-nomadic but increasingly sedentary Iranian tribes inhabiting the central regions of the Zagros Mountains around Ecbatana, modern Hamadan in Western Iran. The Greek historian Herodotus suggests that by as early as 700 BCE the Medes had established a large empire, but there is no evidence for this in the archaeological record or in cuneiform texts. It was, on the contrary, the political fragmentation of the Medes that made it so hard for the Assyrian kings from Shalmaneser III to Ashurbanipal to gain full control over them. At the same time, their disunity guaranteed that for more than two hundred years the Medes did not pose a serious military threat to Assyria.[13]

But a major change during the last quarter of the seventh century upended Assyria's strategic calculus. A Median chieftain, whom the Babylonian Chronicle calls Umakishtar and the Greeks referred to as Cyaxares, managed to bring the different Median tribes together in a kind of confederacy, if not a truly unified state. Although the circumstances that enabled him to do so are murky, it is likely that (along with encounters with other states, such as Elam and Ellipi) repeated Assyrian attempts to create provinces in the Median territories and enhance trade in the region, especially along the eastbound "Great Khorasan Road," contributed to the eventual emergence of a more cohesive Median polity. By facilitating this classic case of "secondary state formation," the Assyrians had actually created a monster—and dug their own grave.[14]

In the Babylonian Chronicle, the Medes are first mentioned toward the end of the entry for the year 615, when they "went down to Arrapha," an Assyrian city and province east of Ashur. Despite a gap in the text, one can confidently assume that they brought death and destruction to the region. A few months later, in the summer of 614, the Medes returned, this time with a greater prize in mind. After passing Nineveh and ravaging the nearby city of Tarbisu, they encamped against the city of Ashur, which had been haphazardly reinforced after the failed Babylonian attack the year before. The residents of the city seem not to have expected the worst: legal and economic documents from the last years and months before Ashur's fall show no signs of the impending crisis. But within weeks, the Medes conquered the city, plundered and devastated it, and—as the Babylonian Chronicle expressively puts it—"inflicted a terrible defeat upon a great people." Archaeological evidence confirms the textual record: traces of destruction, and of a series of massive fires, were found all over the city. Roasted emmer wheat, burned by the flames, was discovered in the Old Palace, the "Eastern Palace," and the Anu-Adad Temple. It must have been hoarded in these buildings in great quantities in anticipation of a prolonged Median siege. The skeletons of some of the fallen, including a woman whose head had been severed, were found, more cast away than buried, near the street leading from the western Tabira Gate into the city.[15]

The loss of Ashur was a disaster for Assyria—not so much because of its military and strategic implications, even though those were significant as well—but for ideological reasons. Since time immemorial, Ashur had been the religious heart of the kingdom, the seat of the Assyrian state god Ashur, and the place where the Assyrian kings were crowned and buried. Now, both the Ashur Temple and the royal tombs lay in ruins, and the bones of Assyria's great kings were scattered throughout the city. It must have been a fatal blow for the morale of Assyria's elites and military forces, who had lost their main source of spiritual energy.

The Babylonians had arrived too late to participate in the assault on Ashur. The Babylonian king Nabonidus (r. 555–539 BCE) would later characterize the Medes as barbarians who, much to the dismay of the more civilized Nabopolassar, had no qualms about destroying sanctuaries that should have been spared and disrupting cults that should have been left unmolested. But if Nabopolassar ever actually had such scruples, they did not prevent him from happily collaborating with the warriors from the east. As the Babylonian Chronicle reports, he and Cyaxares "met each other near the city (of Ashur) and came to an agreement." The goal of this fateful alliance is not spelled out, but seems obvious: together, the two kings wanted to seize the Assyrian capital, Nineveh, and sound the death knell on the Assyrian Empire.

The final attack on Nineveh took place in 612 BCE. In the preceding year, when he had sent his troops back to the Middle Euphrates region, Sîn-sharru-ishkun had shown for a last time that he had not yet completely lost the ability to take the initiative. But he had failed to achieve any lasting success with this operation. And so he found himself in 612, from the month of Simanu (III) onward, cooped up in his palace on the citadel mound of Nineveh. From there he could watch, undoubtedly with ever-increasing alarm and despair, the combined forces of the Babylonians and the Medes, probably strengthened by troops from Elam and the Arabian Peninsula, encamped against the city.[16]

Hundreds of years later, Babylonian scribes studied a number of cuneiform letters that Nabopolassar and Sîn-sharru-ishkun had allegedly exchanged during the last days of Nineveh. The authenticity of this correspondence is in dispute, but that similar or nearly identical letters were sent back and forth during the time of the siege of Nineveh is quite possible. Nabopolassar writes scornfully to his Assyrian counterpart:

> You have been hostile to Babylon; you filled the lands with disorder; you inflicted defeat on the people of Babylon; you introduced crime, guilt, and sin; you fostered evil; you fomented rebellion in the land; you failed to create peace. I shall avenge Babylon. I shall pile up (the debris of) the wall of Nineveh, which is made of strong stone, like a mound of sand; I shall uproot (the seed of) Sennacherib, son of Sargon, the offspring of a house-slave, conqueror of Babylon, plunderer of the land of Babylonia. Because of the evil deeds that you committed against the land of Babylonia, Marduk, the great lord, and the other great gods shall call you to account.[17]

Sîn-sharru-ishkun, whose situation was desperate, could only plead for mercy. He addresses Nabopolassar as a "mighty king who achieves everything he desires," identifies himself as his servant, and admits his own faults: "I did not perform my duties to the king, my lord." But if he had hoped that his submissiveness would give him a last chance to find a diplomatic way out of his predicament, he was fooling himself. The time for negotiations was long past. Late in the summer of 612, the enemy troops finally broke through the Assyrian defenses. They entered Nineveh, plundered it, killed thousands of its residents, and deported most of the others. Sîn-sharru-ishkun perished in the course of the attack, though a gap in the Babylonian Chronicle leaves us in the dark about the exact circumstances of his death.[18]

The devastation of Nineveh followed a carefully devised plan. Before the temples and palaces of the city were burned down, they were not only stripped of valuable objects, but the victorious enemies also systematically disfigured many of the ubiquitous images of Assyrian kings, destroying, in particular, their eyes, mouths, ears, and noses. This was all very similar to what had happened thirty-four years earlier during Ashurbanipal's sack of Susa. When the Assyrian troops, in the course of their rampage, chanced upon an image of Hallushu-Inshushinak, the Elamite king responsible for the death of Sennacherib's son Ashur-nadin-shumi in 693, Ashurbanipal claimed to have "cut off its nose, which had sneered, sliced off its lips, which had spoken insolence, and broken off its hands, which held a bow to fight against Assyria." Now, the images of Sennacherib and Ashurbanipal were subjected to comparable symbolic acts of posthumous killing—and there is indirect evidence that Elamite soldiers participated in the desecration as well.[19]

The old Assyrian capital Calah likewise fell prey to a brutal attack. Since written sources do not mention the fall of the city, it remains unknown whether it occurred in 614 or in 612, and who exactly was responsible for it. But the archaeological evidence is again unmistakable: traces of intense fire and ash deposits in many public buildings testify to the extent of the destruction. Copies of the Succession Treaty that Esarhaddon had concluded with Median chieftains in 672 BCE were found broken in hundreds of pieces on the floor of the temple of Nabû on the citadel of Calah, where the Median conquerors of Calah had probably deliberately smashed them, in order to avenge their ancestors' humiliating submission. A particularly grim find was made when Iraqi archaeologists excavated a well located in a courtyard in the southeastern part of Ashurnasirpal II's Northwest Palace. It was filled with at least 180 skeletons of mostly able-bodied young men aged eighteen to thirty, many with iron fetters around their feet and hands. The conquerors must have thrown them into the well while they were still alive.[20]

After the conquest of Nineveh, Nabopolassar sent some of his troops westward, where they plundered Nasibina (Nisibis) and deported parts of the population of the Assyrian province of Rusapu (Rasappa). In regions farther north, the war continued as well. Assyrian resistance in the provincial capital of Tushhan (modern Ziyarat Tepe in Turkey's Diyarbakır Province) seems to have lasted until 611. Recent excavations there have produced a cuneiform letter most likely written during this very year. It paints a vivid picture of the hopeless situation in which the city found itself. The sender, a certain Mannu-ki-Libbali, probably the governor of Tushhan, addresses the treasurer of Assyria, a high-ranking official in charge of the Assyrian border march on the eastern bank of the Tigris in the Turkish-Iraqi border region, writing, "Concerning the horses, Assyrian and Aramean scribes, cohort commanders, officials, coppersmiths, blacksmiths, those who clean the tools and equipment, carpenters, bow-makers, arrow-makers, weavers, tailors, and repairers, to whom should I turn? Not one of them is there. How can I command? Death will come out of it. No one will escape(?). I am done!"[21]

The letter, probably never dispatched, is a cry of despair. Mannu-ki-Libbali lacked the means to continue the fight against the Babylonian and Median troops. And so, death did come out of it. Archaeological evidence indicates that Tushhan was captured and destroyed—most likely just days after the governor had drafted his last letter—and then largely abandoned. As in other Assyrian cities, its residents, and the unfortunate Mannu-ki-Libbali, must have been either killed or carried away as prisoners of war.[22]

EVEN AFTER THE FALL OF TUSHHAN, THE FIGHT FOR ASSYRIA'S survival was not entirely over. In a shadowy historical coda, an Assyrian prince who called himself Ashur-uballit (II) made a last attempt to restore the Assyrian state and the royal dynasty. As the Babylonian Chronicle reports, he had "ascended the throne in Harran to rule as king of Assyria" in an unknown month late in 612. Harran, the city of the moon god, was located on the Balikh River and lay so far out in the west that the Babylonians and Medes had not yet attacked it.

The throne name adopted by the new ruler, Ashur-uballit, conveyed two messages. On the one hand, its meaning, "The god Ashur has kept alive," expressed hope for an eventual Assyrian revival. On the other, the name harked back to Ashur-uballit I (r. 1363–1328 BCE), the first Assyrian ruler to assume the title "king" (šarru), and the one who had been instrumental in transforming Ashur into a territorial state. When Ashur-uballit II chose this founder figure as his role model, he must have been fully aware that the challenges ahead of him were just as great as or possibly greater than those his eponymous ancestor had once successfully faced.

For a couple of years, people in the territories along the Khabur and Balikh Rivers and in the Taurus foothills—the only Assyrian areas not yet conquered—seem to have acknowledged Ashur-uballit II as their ruler, although without assigning to him the title "king." Because he could not be properly crowned in Ashur, as tradition required, Ashur-uballit seems instead to have been called "crown prince," literally, "son of the king"—which suggests, incidentally, that Sîn-sharru-ishkun was his father.[23]

In 610, an army of Babylonian and Median soldiers under the leadership of Nabopolassar marched westward to deal with the remaining Assyrian resistance once and for all. In the meantime, Ashur-uballit had managed to again secure the support of the Egyptians, who had already helped Sîn-sharru-ishkun. But when the news of Nabopolassar's impending attack reached Harran, "Ashur-uballit and the Egyptian army were overcome by fear," as the Babylonian Chronicle reports. They abandoned the city and crossed the Euphrates, leaving the territories east of the river to the mercy of the Babylonians and Medes. Nabopolassar captured Harran "and took a great amount of plunder in the city and the temple."

In the following year, the chronicle tells us, Ashur-uballit returned once more to the Harran region. At his side were Egyptian troops led by a new pharaoh, Necho II. On their way they had defeated and killed the Judean king, Josiah, in a battle fought at Megiddo. Ashur-uballit seems to have scored an initial victory at Harran, but then his advance stalled. This is the last time we hear from him. What exactly happened to him remains unknown, but after 609, he disappeared from the scene.

Babylonian troops, no longer constrained by the threat of Assyrian counterattacks, were now able to march as far as Urartu. Egyptian army units continued to fight against them for a few more years, but in 605, Nabopolassar's son and crown prince Nebuchadnezzar II, most famous as the conqueror of Jerusalem, inflicted two crushing defeats on the Egyptians, one at Carchemish on the Euphrates and one at Hamath in Syria. With Ashur-uballit's disappearance and Egypt's exit from the Levant, a new imperial power had been established in Western Asia: the torch had been passed from Assyria to Babylonia.

Assyrian cities on the Khabur River seem to have been spared the massive destruction suffered by the urban centers in the Assyrian heartland, and Assyrian scribal traditions continued a little longer in this area. The latest documents in the Assyrian language and script from Dur-Katlimmu are from 603 and 600 BCE. They are dated with reference to the Babylonian king Nebuchadnezzar II, which shows that Dur-Katlimmu's residents fully acknowledged Babylonian rule by the turn of the seventh to the sixth century.

Another recently discovered text in Assyrian style, a document about the sale of several fields and orchards in the vicinity of the city of Ilhina, probably came from about the same time. It was found farther north, in a field near Hasankeyf in the Tur Abdin region in southeastern Turkey. The text is, quite fascinatingly, dated to "the ninth year of Lâbasi, the chief cupbearer," while "Ubakisteri was the Median king." Ubakisteri can only be the Median ruler Cyaxares, called Umakishtar by the Babylonians. It seems as if in the wake of the Assyrian breakdown, the chief cupbearer, Lâbasi, one of the highest officials of the Assyrian state, had carved out for himself a little fiefdom in a remote and hilly area not easy to conquer. He formally recognized the Medes as his overlords but probably didn't have to cope with too much interference from them. The scribe of the Hasankeyf document, named in its penultimate line, was a certain Kisir-Ashur "from the city of Ashur." He could be identical with a well-known exorcist of the Ashur Temple who wrote many of the more than one thousand medical, magical, and other texts that were excavated in 1908 in his family home in Ashur. Either shortly before or after the Median attack on the city in 614, he may have managed to flee and join Lâbasi and his supporters in their lair.[24]

Lâbasi's little mountain realm remained a relatively inconsequential breakaway fiefdom—albeit one that would deserve to be covered one day in a historical novel. When and how exactly it ended we do not know. Through which means the Medes ruled over the northern and eastern parts of Assyria that became part of their sphere of influence—if they ever actually implemented some form of organized government at all—remains obscure as well. Most likely, the Median confederacy slowly disintegrated. Despite protestations to the contrary in later Greek sources, a Median "empire" seems never to have come into being.

THE EVENTS OF THE YEARS BETWEEN 627 AND 605 BCE CAN BE described as nothing less than a first "World War." They were marked by a series of major revolts, battles, and sieges; led to massive casualties among the civilian populations of several Babylonian, Assyrian, and Levantine cities; and caused the death of large numbers of soldiers. They brought about the deportation of tens if not hundreds of thousands of people and the complete destruction of Assyria's major urban centers. Initially limited to two powers, Assyria and Babylonia, the confrontation morphed over time into an international conflict on a scale never seen before. The Iranian Manneans went into battle on the side of the Assyrians and the Iranian Medes on the side of the Babylonians. Elamites, and possibly also Arabs, took part in some of the fighting as well, helping Nabopolassar, while with Egypt another great power joined the fray in support of Sîn-sharru-ishkun and Ashur-uballit II. Judah became involved when it sought to stop the Egyptians from reestablishing their hegemony in the Levant. From Suhu and Carchemish on the Euphrates to Urartu in eastern Anatolia, there were numerous additional theaters of war.[25]

After the hostilities had drawn to a close, stories of the conflict entered the cultural memory of several ancient civilizations. Assyria's fall was vividly remembered in Babylonia, not only through chronicles, letters, and historical epics, but also in the Hebrew Bible and in the historical writings of ancient Greece and Rome. Everywhere, the war was perceived as a paradigmatic event, a morality tale on the perils of political hubris. Within barely two decades, Assyria, an imperial state of unprecedented influence and wealth, had suffered a collapse that was, in its scope, unprecedented as well.

Even though a few features of Assyrian civilization survived, what was lost in the catastrophe was enormous. The Assyrian state ceased to exist. The Assyrian royal line, which had endured for more than a millennium, was abruptly cut off. Assyrian urban life continued only on a most rudimentary scale, and cuneiform writing in the Assyrian heartland came to a complete stop. Assyria's rural hinterland suffered massive depopulation, brought about by killings, deportations, flight, and a breakdown in the maintenance of the elaborate canal system that Sennacherib and other kings had created. Archaeological surveys point to a sharp reduction in the number and size of small settlements in the Assyrian countryside in the period after 612.[26]

THE SUDDENNESS AND MAGNITUDE OF THE DISASTER THAT BE-fell Assyria at the end of the seventh century BCE has befuddled modern historians—prompting them to look for causes deeper than the vagaries of political decision-making to explain what happened.

Some scholars have gone so far as to declare politics a mere epiphenomenon in the unfolding events. Greater forces, they claim, were at work. Two recent theories about Assyria's fall stand out.

The first looks to environmental changes as the driver of the empire's collapse. In 2014, the American paleoclimatologist Adam W. Schneider and the Turkish Assyriologist Selim Adalı suggested that Assyria's fall was triggered by a severe drought that set in during the mid-seventh century. The drought, the authors argued, caused a series of famines in the Assyrian heartland, where population numbers had swelled in the previous decades as a consequence of the mass deportations undertaken by Assyria's imperial kings. This crisis, in turn, allowed the Babylonians and Medes to overrun Assyria and conquer its main cities.[27]

A detailed 2019 study by the American geologist Ashish Sinha and other scholars has tried to substantiate this theory by using a more elaborate set of paleoclimatic data. The data was retrieved by tracking the ratios of oxygen and uranium isotopes in two limestone stalagmites—so-called speleothems—from the Kuna Ba cave, located near the city of Sulaymaniyah in Iraqi Kurdistan, some 300 kilometers (186 miles) southeast of Nineveh. Similar to ice cores or tree rings, speleothems provide information on a year-to-year basis about the amount of rainfall during the time of their formation.[28]

The Kuna Ba data revealed that the period between 850 and 740 BCE, termed by the authors the "Assyrian megapluvial," was one of the wettest times in the history of ancient Assyria. "Pluvial conditions" had started even earlier, around 925, and lasted until 725 BCE. The authors correlate the environmental circumstances of this time, a blessing for Assyria's agrarian productivity, with "one of the most prominent phases of the Assyrian imperial expansion." The Assyrian megapluvial was followed by a long phase of diminishing precipitation, which culminated in a 125-year period of peak aridity between 675 and 550 BCE, dubbed by the authors the "Assyrian megadrought." During this time, Assyria's agrarian economy contracted, with eventually catastrophic consequences for the empire's ability to withstand attacks by foreign powers. The loss of Babylonia in 620 BCE was a particularly disastrous blow. Because the irrigation-based farming practices of the south were less affected by the drought than the rain-fed agriculture of Assyria and other regions of Western Asia, Nabopolassar was able to rely on harvests that continued to be bountiful—an enormous strategic advantage in his fight against the Assyrians. The continuing drought conditions in the north, the authors claim, would also explain why most Assyrian cities and many rural settlements were not resettled in the decades after 612.

The second theory focuses on a different crisis to explain the fall of Assyria: an alleged invasion of mounted warriors of Scythian extraction. The German Egyptologist Karl Jansen-Winkeln has claimed that this event had a major impact on the fate of Assyria. His suggestion is based on a passage in Herodotus's *Histories* in which the Greek historian describes the Scythians raiding Syro-Palestine. Herodotus says they had an encounter with the Egyptian pharaoh Psamtik I, who kept them away from Egypt by paying a large ransom, and that they ruled the region for twenty-eight years. Because Herodotus is the only source for this Scythian intermezzo, many scholars have considered the report unreliable. Jansen-Winkeln argues that such doubts are unfounded, and compares the Scythian raid, a real event, in his view, to other, similar ones—such as when hosts of horsemen, seemingly coming out of nowhere, under the Turco-Mongol leader Timur, conquered vast stretches of territory during the fourteenth century CE in practically no time. Jansen-Winkeln postulates that the Scythian invasion of the Levant took place around 640 BCE, which would mean that the Scythians cut right through the Assyrian provinces in Syria and on the Eastern Mediterranean. Later, after they withdrew again, Egyptian troops would have filled the void. Such a course of events would have stripped Assyria of its western possessions and severely weakened the empire, so much so, according to Jansen-Winkeln, that the kingdom was to become easy prey for the Babylonians and Medes. In Jansen-Winkeln's view, the territorial losses Assyria experienced during the last years of Ashurbanipal's reign might also have triggered the internal conflicts between different contenders for the Assyrian throne.[29]

IN WEIGHING WHETHER ENVIRONMENTAL FACTORS OR RAIDS BY foreign invaders led to Assyria's collapse, the cuneiform sources provide little help. It should also be noted that the two explanations are not mutually exclusive. On the contrary, climate change leading to greater aridity in Western Asia could have prompted the Scythian migrations. Still, it is difficult to gauge the plausibility of the climate hypothesis and the idea of a "barbarian invasion" by mounted warriors.

Right at the outset, it might be wise to recall that monocausal explanations of Assyria's fall are somewhat suspicious: a theory that explains everything explains nothing, as Karl Popper quipped. That said, the idea that climate change can impact history is of course intrinsically plausible. And while Sinha's 2019 climate study may suffer to some extent from the fact that its data comes from the Mesopotamian periphery rather than the Assyrian heartland, and from margins of error generally contained in isotope data, the information culled from the Kuna Ba cave seems to be corroborated by proxy data from other locations.

Sinha and his coauthors claim that Assyria's agriculture profited from "pluvial conditions" for some two hundred years, from 925 to 725 BCE. During this period, especially its beginnings, Assyria experienced an impressive political and economic rise, and it is indeed tempting to posit a causal nexus between these two phenomena.

But correlating the drier phase that apparently began in around 740, when the Assyrian "megapluvial" came to an end, with Assyria's downfall is more problematic. After all, an Assyrian Empire in the true sense only came into existence with the reign of Tiglath-pileser III

(r. 744–727 BCE). In other words, Assyria entered the phase of its greatest power at exactly the time when climate conditions became not more favorable, but less so. The one hundred years from 740 to 640, when rainfall was increasingly sparse, were the time of Assyria's greatest geographic extent. One could therefore argue that the Assyrians adapted to the drier conditions starting around 740 by expanding their borders to acquire grain and other goods from elsewhere. The epidemics that ravaged Assyria in the mid-eighth century may have contributed to this somewhat paradoxical development as well.[30]

With the loss of its westernmost territories, perhaps as early as 640, and of Babylonia in around 620, Assyria might still have suffered substantially from the decline in precipitation that the new studies postulate for the empire's final decades. But the degree to which Assyria's heartland was affected by more arid conditions is actually hard to gauge. Legal documents from Assyrian cities suggest that Assyria experienced considerable economic hardship during the years 643 (or 641) and 638 (or 636) BCE. The same applies to 624, 623, and 612 (in Guzana). But for many other years of the final decades of the Assyrian Empire, the written evidence indicates that the economic situation was actually quite normal. In 622, for example, grain prices were down again, and one could hypothesize that the higher prices of the two preceding years were a consequence of internal and external strife rather than drought. Besides, as already mentioned, the citizens of Ashur seem to have done "business as usual" during the city's last years, and the authorities were able to store huge amounts of grain in various buildings in Ashur prior to its conquest by the Medes. In various locations in the city, the roasted remains of these cereal supplies were found piled up about one meter (3 feet) high. The latest excavator of Ashur, Peter Miglus, has argued that they would have sufficed to feed the whole population of Ashur, estimated by him at eleven thousand, plus some eight thousand soldiers, for at least a month, and probably much longer. None of this points to a situation in which changes in precipitation would have caused a major agrarian crisis in Assyria.[31]

As for the scenario of a Scythian invasion, the main problem is that only Herodotus speaks of it. It is true, as emphasized by Jansen-Winkeln, that the cuneiform documentation for the history of the years from 640 to 627 is very limited, but the complete lack of references to a Scythian raid of massive proportions is nonetheless hard to explain. A mid-first-millennium BCE pseudo-historical Babylonian text mentioning a campaign against "Ashur, the Suteans, and the Scythians" by Shulgi of Ur, a Babylonian ruler of the twenty-first century BCE, could be interpreted as an encrypted allusion to Nabopolassar's war of liberation and a hint that the Scythians played a certain role in it, but this is speculation. That Assyria lost its western territories to the Scythians is not impossible but remains highly conjectural.[32]

THE MORE CONVENTIONAL EXPLANATIONS FOR ASSYRIA'S FALL look to political factors. One argument that has been made is that the Assyrian Empire could not be maintained without constant expansion. Therefore, when during Ashurbanipal's reign the military and administrative costs for further conquests became too great, the kingdom was doomed. But this idea of "diminishing returns" is not completely persuasive either. Empires that cease to grow are not inexorably bound to implode. One only needs to remember how long Rome lasted after it had reached its greatest extent under Trajan in the early second century CE.[33]

This brings us back from structural and systemic considerations to more contingent factors. Even though it has become somewhat unfashionable among serious historians to emphasize the impact that specific individuals and their decisions can have on the course of history, it cannot be denied that in a state like Assyria, where the king was the linchpin of the whole political machine, failures of particular rulers can sometimes have drastic consequences. And some of the Assyrian rulers of the seventh century BCE, it seems, made major mistakes. There are, for example, the purges that Esarhaddon, worried about possible conspiracies, inflicted on the military and civilian apparatus of his kingdom. Ashurbanipal further sidelined this highly competent elite when he showered his courtiers and palace eunuchs with favors while giving state officials the cold shoulder. In the 630s, recall that he appointed his chief singer, Bullutu, as eponym, an act that brings to mind the apocryphal story of Caligula making a horse a consul in the Roman Senate. Ashurbanipal's successors seem to have put their trust in a similar cadre of palace staff, individuals without much experience in foreign policy and military leadership. Among the eponyms of the time after 631 are several chief eunuchs, two palace scribes, a palace overseer, a chamberlain, and even the king's chief cook, a certain Sa'ilu, who served as eponym of the year 620. As reflected in the Greek Sardanapallus tradition of later times, the Assyrian kings from Ashurbanipal onward seem to have spent their time mostly in their palaces rather than on campaigns, where they would have met army officers and administrators and received a more realistic impression of the affairs of the state. Especially Ashurbanipal's transformation from "populist" to recluse must have hampered decision-making processes in the empire, damaged the reputation Assyrian kings enjoyed among their leading officials and their subjects, and reduced the fear enemies felt toward Assyrian rulers.[34]

It was unfortunate from an Assyrian point of view that this leadership crisis—which reached its peak with the short-lived rule of the eunuch Sîn-shumu-lishir—occurred at exactly the time when a number of major challenges affected the empire in short succession: the loss of the western territories in the Levant, whether prompted by a Scythian invasion or some other cause; the Babylonian rebellion under Nabopolassar; and finally, the sudden rise of a formidable new military power: the Medes. Both Nabopolassar, a onetime Assyrian official in Uruk, and the Medes, united through Assyrian attempts to turn the central Zagros region into a governable political entity, were, in a somewhat paradoxical way, Assyrian creations. Supplied with a good sense of how the Assyrians thought and operated, they were particularly dangerous adversaries.

Even though hardly the main reason for Assyria's sudden collapse, it is possible that a climate-induced drought exacerbated Assyria's woes. A lack of cohesion among the people who lived all over the Assyrian state might have weakened Assyria's political immune system even further. An "empire without mission," except for the accumulation of power and wealth, Assyria had never been particularly good at creating something akin to an Assyrian "identity" beyond its core territories. Apart from order and stability—and an artistic language that extolled Assyria's unlimited authority—it had little symbolic capital to offer to the citizens it ruled. Those citizens, in turn, had little reason to support their Assyrian overlords when the latter suddenly found themselves under fatal military pressure.[35]

All in all, Assyria between the 630s and 609 was ravaged by a perfect storm. It was the combination of several factors, both internal and external, that brought about Assyria's collapse. That afterward no attempt was made to resurrect the Assyrian state probably had a lot to do with the central role played by Assyria's royal dynasty. Assyrian kings were, on the one hand, political leaders; but in contrast to their Babylonian counterparts, who had no sacerdotal functions, they were, on the other, also high priests of the god Ashur. Without its kings, Assyria ceased to exist, not only as a secular polity, but also as a religious idea, a symbolic order.

Not everything, however, was gone. Figuratively speaking, Assyria might have been blown into thousands of pieces, but many of the pieces were still there. Certain aspects of Assyrian culture endured, especially in the city of Ashur, where Assyrian statehood had once originated. The political apparatus of the Assyrian Empire had vanished after the catastrophe of 612. But although shaken, bruised, and fragmented, an Assyrian identity lived on.

AFTERLIFE

15

Assyria's Legacy on the Ground

In the late summer of 401 BCE, the Greek general Xenophon and his army of ten thousand men found themselves stranded deep in central Mesopotamia. They had come on a mission to support the Persian prince Cyrus the Younger in his fight for the throne, but after Cyrus died in battle at Cunaxa near Babylon, that mission came to an abrupt end. With the victorious Persian king, Artaxerxes II, close on their heels, the Greek mercenaries had to get out of danger and back home as quickly as possible.

They were ultimately successful. Their trek ended at the Black Sea, where the troops, relishing their escape, famously exclaimed "Thalatta, thalatta!" (The Sea, the Sea!). What is most interesting, though, is what the soldiers from the Far West experienced along the way. As they moved upstream along the eastern bank of the Tigris, they crossed the lands that only 250 years earlier had been the bustling heart of the Assyrian Empire.

Xenophon mentions three settlements that he and his men passed in this region. First, they saw, across the river, on its western bank, "a large and prosperous city named Kainai, from which the barbarians brought over loaves, cheeses, and wine, crossing upon rafts made of skins." Then, a little farther northward, "there was a large deserted city." "Its name was Larisa," reports Xenophon, "and

351

it was inhabited in ancient times by the Medes. Its wall was twenty-five feet in breadth and a hundred in height, and the whole circuit of the wall was two parasangs (11–12 kilometers, or about 7 miles). Near by this city was a pyramid of stone; and upon this pyramid were many barbarians who had fled away from the neighboring villages." From Larisa, Xenophon continues, they "marched one stage, six parasangs, to a great stronghold, deserted and lying in ruins. The name of this city was Mespila, and it was once inhabited by the Medes. The foundation of the wall was made of polished stone full of shells, and it was fifty feet in breadth and fifty in height. Upon this foundation was built a wall of brick, fifty feet in breadth and a hundred in height; and the circuit of the wall was six parasangs (33–36 kilometers, or 20–22 miles)."[1]

The settlements Xenophon and his soldiers glimpsed on their northbound journey were, in all likelihood, Ashur, Calah, and Nineveh. Ashur, which Xenophon called "Kainai," was full of citizens and supplies, and had apparently recovered from the Median attack of 614. Calah, in contrast, referred to as "Larisa," is described as deserted, even though Xenophon saw many people on top of a "pyramid"—most likely the ziggurat dedicated to Calah's patron god, Ninurta, where local residents took refuge when they saw the Greeks approaching from the south. Nineveh, called "Mespila," too, is said to have been "in ruins" and uninhabited. Xenophon is unaware that the three cities had once been famous centers of the Assyrian Empire and, most remarkably, he uses names for them that have nothing to do with the ancient ones local citizens had proudly used during Assyrian times.

Xenophon's march through the Assyrian heartland some two hundred years after the empire's fall reveals the sheer scale of the region's dramatic decline and transformation. All traces of an Assyrian identity, whether in terms of political structures or with regard to the names of cities, appear to have been wiped out.

Yet at the same time Xenophon's account should not be taken as definitive. After all, he did not visit the region out of an ethnographic interest—he had to pass it as fast as he could to lead his troops out of harm's way. Xenophon did not cross the Tigris to explore "Kainai," that is, Ashur, in person; and he did not stop to inspect what was going on behind the long, high walls of "Larisa" and "Mespila," the names he uses for Calah and Nineveh.

To be sure, if Xenophon had toured these cities more extensively, he would indeed have found a lot of debris. But he would also have seen signs of life within the ruins—and he would have come across elements of a continuing Assyrian culture. Nineveh's ancient name was, actually, never forgotten. It survived and remained attached to the site down to modern times. As for Calah, even centuries after its fall the area around the city was still called "Calachene." There are archaeological traces of some resettlement at both places from the decades after their destruction, although on a scale so modest that modern scholars refer to it as "squatter occupation." At Nineveh, repairs were made in particular to the Nabû and Ishtar Temples and the Southwest Palace, at Calah to the Nabû Temple and the Northwest Palace. The Assyrian heartland continued to have names such as "Athura," "Assyria," or "Asorestan" for centuries, all harkening back to the ancient name "Ashur." And the Greek term "Syria," applied to the formerly Assyrian territories farther west, in the Levant, ultimately derives from "Ashur" as well. "Tho' much is taken, much abides," one could say with Lord Tennyson.[2]

Given such signs of continuity, "post-imperial" is a more apt term than "post-Assyrian" for the period that followed the collapse of the Assyrian Empire. This was no "empty land," and the fall of the empire was no "end of history."[3]

Still, our knowledge of the region during the period in question—especially up to the Parthian conquests in the second century BCE—is woefully sketchy. This is to a significant extent due to changes in local writing practices. Cuneiform clay tablets are almost indestructible, which explains why tens of thousands of them are available from the last 150 years of the Assyrian kingdom. Leather and papyrus, in contrast, which after 600 BCE must have replaced clay tablets as the main writing materials in the Middle Tigris region, are perishable, and do not survive in the climate of northern Iraq. As a consequence, we have very few written sources from this area from the six centuries following the fall of Assyria. And since the excavators of many Assyrian sites focused on the exploration of the imperial layers, while often discarding the post-imperial ones, the available archaeological evidence is likewise limited. For all these reasons, much of Assyria's post-imperial history has to be pieced together with the help of references in texts from Babylonia, Persia, and the Mediterranean world, which are often biased or for other reasons unreliable. And yet, some glimpses into the shattered world of what had previously been the mighty Assyrian Empire are possible through this glass darkly.

THE MOST TELLING EVIDENCE FOR A CONTINUATION OF ASSYR-ian life—not only in the economic, but also in the cultural sphere—has been found in Ashur. As hinted at by Xenophon, Assyria's religious center was not abandoned after the Median attack of 614. A clay tablet from the Babylonian city of Sippar, most likely dated to 559 BCE, mentions a Babylonian governor of Ashur who had dedicated a slave as a gift to the temple of the sun god of Sippar. Clearly, Ashur and the region around it had become a well-administered part of the newly formed Babylonian Empire.[4]

The massive Ashur Temple, Assyria's former spiritual center, continued to lie in ruins during this time. But at some point, immediately above the debris of its southern enclosure wall, a new sanctuary was erected. Known today as "Temple A," a designation assigned to it by its excavators, it was much smaller than the old Ashur Temple; but with its thick walls, 18 × 19 meters (60 × 62 feet) long, and a new enclosure wall separating it from its surroundings, the building was nonetheless imposing.[5]

The most remarkable feature of Temple A is that it was, quite literally, built out of and upon the historical records of the fallen Assyrian kingdom. More than one hundred Assyrian royal inscriptions, ranging from the reign of Erishum I in the early second millennium down to Assyria's last king, Sîn-sharru-ishkun, were found inserted into the pavement, placed inside the walls, or reused as door sockets within the temple. They might have been retrieved from the ruins of a nearby old temple library that had served as a repository of Assyrian historical texts. Within their new context as part of the fabric of Temple A, the often fragmentary texts were no longer meant to be carefully studied and read. But everyone who entered the temple would have known that he or she was standing on and surrounded by the written legacy of the world's first empire.

Without knowing the date of Temple A's erection, or the god to whom it was dedicated, it is hard to interpret this strange and exceptional setting. One possibility is that Temple A was built within a generation or so of the destruction of the Ashur Temple by remnants of the local population. They might have wished to provide the god Ashur with a new home and tried to draw new confidence from physical encounters with the written records of their glorious past.[6]

A slightly different scenario holds that Temple A was erected by members of an Assyrian community that had survived the time of the Babylonian Empire in exile in the southern Mesopotamian city of Uruk (where cuneiform documents attest to their presence). Munich Assyriologist Karen Radner has contended that when the Persian ruler Cyrus II seized power in Babylon in 539 BCE and founded the Persian Empire, these Assyrians had been allowed to return to Ashur. Indeed, Cyrus claims in an inscription on a clay cylinder from Babylon that he had "brought (the images of) the gods back to their sanctuaries, from [...] to Ashur, Susa, Akkad, Eshnunna, Zamban, Me-Turan, Der, as far as the border of Gutium," and that the people who had been deported from these cities, as well as their descendants, were allowed to go home as well.[7]

As the Hebrew Bible famously reports, Cyrus's generosity had also included the Jews, who received permission from him to return to Judah from their exile in Babylonia and rebuild the temple in Jerusalem, which previously had been ravaged by Nebuchadnezzar II. Radner posits that something quite similar happened at Ashur: upon their return from Babylonia in the late sixth century, the Assyrians built a "Second Temple" in their old religious capital, from which they had been driven away some seventy years earlier. This temple, Radner believes, Temple A, can be seen as the missing link between some of Ashur's ancient religious traditions and their continuation well into Parthian times.

Not every scholar agrees with the idea of Temple A as a post-imperial sanctuary of the god Ashur. During the later Parthian period, between the first and third centuries CE, Temple A was replaced by a new temple that was apparently dedicated to Heracles, the Greek equivalent of the Babylonian warrior god Erra-Nergal. Based on this history of the site, it has been argued that the earlier Temple A might actually have been a temple of Erra-Nergal, too, built not by local residents but by Ashur's new Babylonian overlords who had taken control of the city shortly after 614 BCE. The purpose of this temple would have been to marginalize the god Ashur and give another deity center stage in the cultic topography of the city. The integration of Assyrian royal inscriptions into the fabric of the building would have been an act of humiliation: rather than drawing strength from them, people entering the temple would have trampled on these texts to symbolically reenact Assyria's devastating defeat.[8]

Without further evidence or new archaeological findings, it is impossible to decide which of these theories is correct. But the similarities between the religious practices of the Parthian period and those of Neo-Assyrian times can only be explained if one assumes that the cult of Ashur was not interrupted for too long. It therefore seems more likely that Temple A served as a post-imperial sanctuary in honor of the god Ashur, rather than as a monument of anti-Assyrian hatred put up by the Babylonian conquerors.

FARTHER TO THE WEST OF ASHUR SEVERAL OTHER IMPORTANT Assyrian urban centers continued to be settled after the fall of the empire as well. Among them was the city of Dur-Katlimmu on the Lower Khabur, which was now under Babylonian jurisdiction. Dur-Katlimmu's rural hinterland was not entirely abandoned either. According to archaeological surveys, some 36 percent of the Assyrian sites in the Lower Khabur area were still inhabited in the post-imperial period, even though on a reduced scale. Especially sites close to the river survived, while those farther away in the steppe were often given up, probably because their agrarian yields were so modest that they were no longer competitive once they had lost their consumer base with the fall of Assyria's great cities.[9]

During the early years of Nebuchadnezzar II, the formerly Assyrian town of Guzana in northeastern Syria became the seat of another Babylonian governor. Harran, the last Assyrian stronghold, was apparently not completely destroyed either, even though it must have suffered major damage during the battles of 610 BCE: the Babylonian king Nabonidus (r. 555–539 BCE), whose mother hailed from Harran, restored the city's famous temple of the moon god Sîn. In nearby Edessa, later capital of the kingdom of Osroëne, Assyrian religious traditions survived deep into the common era. Even in some places beyond the Euphrates, the legacy of Assyria lived on. A prominent example is the city of Nappigi, where Shalmaneser III had settled substantial numbers of Assyrians. Later renamed Hierapolis (the "Holy City"), the town is described in Lucian's Greek treatise on the "Syrian Goddess" from the second century CE as a place where the deeds of the legendary Assyrian rulers Semiramis and Sardanapallus were faithfully remembered.[10]

In the Assyrian east, the city of Arbela—less devastated by the wars of the late seventh century than Assyria's urban centers on the Tigris—remained yet another important bastion of Assyrian culture. Because Arbela, modern Erbil in Iraqi Kurdistan, has always been inhabited and is a bustling modern city today, extensive archaeological excavations at the site are virtually impossible to carry out. But written evidence from elsewhere demonstrates the city's continued prominence after the fall of the Assyrian Empire. For a while, it seems to have served as a regional stronghold under Median control, and it kept this function after the creation of the Persian Empire. In his famous inscription from Bisitun, the Persian king Darius I claims that in the summer of 521 BCE he impaled his Sagartian opponent Tritantaichmes, a member of the Median royal family, in Arbela.[11]

Officials from Arbela, and from a few other towns in the Eastern Tigris region, are mentioned in an Aramaic letter from Egypt from the late fifth century BCE. The letter talks about the travels of an Egyptian estate manager by the name of Nakhthor in the area on behalf of his Persian master. He visited the region at about the time when Xenophon and his ten thousand men passed the ruins of Calah and Nineveh. During this period, Arbela must have been an important regional center in the Persian satrapy of Athura, a province mentioned in Persian inscriptions from Bisitun, Naqsh-i Rustam, and Susa. Persian reliefs show people from Athura delivering cattle and textiles at the Persian court.[12]

Of course, the political and economic significance of the formerly Assyrian territories under Persian rule should not be overstated. In 331 BCE, Arbela served as a base for the Persian king Darius III, who set out from there to meet the army of Alexander the Great and hinder its advance. Pitching East against West, the Battle of Gaugamela (probably Tell Gomel in eastern Assyria) took place on October 1 and ended with a decisive victory for Alexander.

It ushered in a period of Hellenistic rule over large parts of Asia and was a turning point in world history. But while on earlier occasions Assyrians had been the driving force behind such decisive moments, all that Assyria now had to contribute was the setting for the event. The people on the Middle Tigris were no longer actors on the stage of history—they had become mere spectators.

IT IS LIKELY THAT THE TERRITORIES IN THE TRIANGLE BETWEEN Ashur, Nineveh, and Arbela, sparsely populated during the time of the Babylonian and Persian Empires, experienced some revitalization when the Greek Seleucids established themselves as the new rulers in Mesopotamia in the wake of Alexander's conquests. The most significant evidence for the presence of Greeks in the region comes, however, from the post-Seleucid period, when a new dynasty, the Iranian Parthians, had assumed power.

The Parthians had conquered Mesopotamia in the second half of the second century BCE and ruled it for nearly four hundred years, but with government structures less centralized than under the preceding empires. At Nineveh the Parthians granted a colony of mostly Greek-speaking residents, probably established in Seleucid times, the right to govern itself more or less autonomously. A Greek inscription on a column from Nineveh, most likely from 32 or 31 BCE, mentions a certain Apollophanes and reveals that he served as military commander (*strategos*) and superintendent (*epistates*) of the city. A first- or second-century CE limestone statue of Heracles, found at the site of Sennacherib's Southwest Palace, bears another Greek inscription that identifies someone named Diogenes as its sculptor. The statue is of high quality and fashioned in classical style. A Greek graffito referring to the same or another Diogenes was found on a beautiful Neo-Assyrian relief showing a huntsman from Ashurbanipal's North Palace at Nineveh. Since it is hard to imagine that palace reliefs created more than half a millennium earlier were still freely accessible during Greco-Parthian times, it has been suggested that the undoubtedly intrigued Diogenes had come across the slab when driving a drain into the tell during construction work.[13]

Assyria's former core territory was split up into several semi-independent vassal kingdoms in Parthian times. Osroëne, the kingdom of Edessa near Harran, which became Roman in 165/166 CE, lay in the west. The kingdom of Adiabene, centered on Arbela and stretching westward as far as Nineveh, was in control of Assyria's former heartland in the east. In fact, according to Pliny the Elder, "Adiabene" was nothing but a new name for "Assyria." The caravan city of Hatra, located some 50 kilometers (30 miles) west of Ashur, served as an important trading hub and the center of a newly emerging "Kingdom of the Arabs." It included several substantial temple buildings in Parthian style, such as a massive sanctuary dedicated to the old sun god Shamash, Hatra's patron deity. Finally, there was the city of Ashur itself. During the first three centuries of the common era, it reemerged as a semiautonomous regional center of considerable prosperity and importance.[14]

Parthian Ashur—which might have been called Labbana (from Assyrian Libbi-āli, "Inner City")—was in certain respects quite different from the Neo-Assyrian town of the seventh century BCE. The new Parthian-style palace, for instance, probably the residence of a series of local governors, was erected in the southern area of the city, rather than on the site of the Old Palace on the city's northern edge. But especially in the cultural and religious spheres, there were also some remarkable continuities. Quite a few key deities from Assyria's imperial period, most notably Ashur and his wife Sherua, but also Ishtar, Nanaya, Bel, Nabû, and Nergal, were worshipped in Parthian times as well. A new temple of Ashur—now called Assor—was built on a grand scale on top of the rubble of the god's old temple, which had been torn down in 614 BCE. And several Parthian-period stone stelae of local governors—who bore the Aramaic title *Marya*, "Lord"—are highly reminiscent of similar monuments from the time of the Assyrian kingdom. A particularly well-preserved example is a stela from perhaps 112 or 113 CE inscribed in the name of a certain R'uth-Assor (Aramaic for "Pleasure of Ashur"). It has the same rounded top that characterizes the stelae of Neo-Assyrian rulers and depicts its patron in an act of worshipping symbols of the sun and the moon in an image that looks as though it could have been copied directly from a Neo-Assyrian model. The only difference is that R'uth-Assor wears a Parthian-style trouser-suit rather than the traditional dress of a Neo-Assyrian king.[15]

The personal names of many of the residents of Parthian Ashur represent another area of continuity. To be sure, the number of Aramaic, Iranian, Greek, and Arabic names had significantly increased in the meantime. But a lot of people still bore Assyro-Akkadian names virtually identical with those that had been used in the seventh century BCE. We find a governor of Ashur by the name of Nbudayyan, which means "Nabû is judge"; a Qib-Ashur ("Command of Ashur"); and even an Ashur-heden, that is, Ashur-ahu-iddina, the name of the great Assyrian king Esarhaddon. Not only names survived the fall of Assyria in the seventh century BCE: other elements of the Neo-Assyrian language did so as well, as indicated by a noticeable lexical heritage in dialects of Aramaic that were in use in northern Mesopotamia.[16]

The most astonishing Neo-Assyrian legacy in Parthian Ashur, however, is the continued observance of certain religious holidays. Inscriptions scratched into pavement slabs within the precinct of the new Parthian Ashur Temple provide, besides the names of the worshippers who had come to pay homage to Ashur and Sherua, the dates when they visited the temple. These dates overlap in striking ways with the time frames of two important religious festivals from Assyria's imperial period: the New Year (or Akitu) Festival, which was celebrated during the first twelve days of the month of Nisannu (I), and a series of rituals related to the "Dais of Destinies" that were performed between the twentieth and the twenty-sixth day of the month of Shabatu (XI). The lasting importance of Ashur's Akitu Festival is also indicated by the fact that during Parthian times a new sanctuary was built on top of the ruins of Sennacherib's old Akitu House located northwest of the city wall.[17]

These continuities notwithstanding, there is also an important difference between the religious celebrations of the imperial period and those of Parthian times. The former were state events—they involved the Assyrian king, the clergy, and members of the Assyrian elite. During the Parthian period, in contrast, it was ordinary citizens who came to the temple of Ashur to pray to the god and receive divine support from him for their daily lives. The steep hierarchies built into Assyria's imperial religion had apparently been replaced by more "democratic" forms of worship.[18]

Ashur's renaissance as an important religious center in northern Mesopotamia was not to last. In 224 CE, an Iranian warrior by the name of Ardashir defeated the last Parthian king, Artabanus IV. In 226, he was crowned in the Parthian capital Ctesiphon as the first ruler of the new Sasanian Empire, named after his ancestor Sasan. Two years later, Ardashir attacked Hatra, one of the last Parthian strongholds; conquered Ashur; and demolished the temple of its main god. A second attack on Ashur under Ardashir's successor, Shapur I, in 257 CE was the final blow. Some 850 years after its first destruction by the Medes, the city of Ashur ceased to exist—and the cult of Ashur's eponymous god was finally relegated to the dustbin of history.[19]

DURING THE EARLY CENTURIES OF THE COMMON ERA, NORTHern Mesopotamia had seen the newly emerging monotheistic creeds of Judaism, Christianity, and (during Sasanian times) Zoroastrianism slowly sideline the old "pagan" cults. In the first century CE, the rulers of Adiabene, the "new Assyria," had converted to Judaism. As reported by the Jewish historian Josephus, Queen Helena of Adiabene moved to Jerusalem, where she supplied residents suffering from a famine with food and generously supported the Jewish Temple. Soon thereafter, Christianity took hold in Adiabene. According to the so-called Teachings of the Twelve Apostles, a text from the late first or the second century CE, the region received its earliest instruction in Christian doctrine from Aggai, a disciple of Addai the Apostle. Arbela became an important early center of eastern Christianity and served from the second century CE onward as a bishopric.[20]

Strikingly, the rise of Christianity in the region did not mean that the old Assyrian religion was entirely wiped out. The Syriac *Acts of Persian Martyrs* report that a certain Aitilaha, who was allegedly killed by Zoroastrian zealots in the mid-fourth century CE, had been a priest of "Sharbel, the lady of Arbela," prior to his conversion to Christianity. This Sharbel can only be the old Assyrian goddess Ishtar of Arbela, the divine patroness of the city and a deity once worshipped with particular zeal by the great Assyrian king Ashurbanipal.[21]

With the church slowly taking root in Adiabene, priests and clerics deliberately suppressed some of the customs persisting from Assyria's imperial period. But at the same time, church authorities integrated memories of Assyrian kings and their deeds into the newly emerging stories and legends they were promoting—undoubtedly with the goal of creating a Christian identity in the region that was compatible with its local traditions. The aforementioned *Acts of Persian Martyrs* claim, for example, that one of the most popular saints of the eastern church, Mar Behnam, and his sister, Sarah, had been children of the Assyrian king Sennacherib. After a Christian ascetic and refugee by the name of Mattai (i.e., "Matthew") healed Sarah from leprosy, according to the story, both she and her brother converted to Christianity. Sennacherib, appalled that his children would no longer sacrifice to the pagan gods, had them both killed, but when he, too, fell ill, shortly thereafter, and required the ministrations of Mattai himself, he had to acknowledge the power of

Christ and asked the ascetic to baptize him. The story is a rather daring attempt to merge historical figures and events that, by conventional chronological calculations, were separated from one another by more than a millennium. But it did not fail to make a deep impression on the people of the region.[22]

Another Christian legend with a decidedly Assyrian bent is found in the Syriac *History of Mar Qardagh*, probably written in the early seventh century CE but set some three hundred years earlier, at a time when the Sasanian ruler Shapur II (309–379 CE) was persecuting and killing many Christians in his realm. Qardagh, the protagonist of the story, is said to have been "from a great people and from the stock of the kingdom of the Assyrians": "His father was descended from the illustrious lineage of the house of Nimrod, and his mother from the illustrious lineage of the house of Sennacherib." Initially, Qardagh is the powerful viceroy of all the lands from the Diyala River in eastern Iraq to the city of Nisibis in the west—Shapur had appointed him to the position in recognition of his enthusiasm for Zoroastrian doctrine and because of the physical prowess he had displayed when playing polo. At Melqi, a site in the vicinity of Arbela, Qardagh builds a fortress and a fire temple and celebrates a great pagan festival. But when a saint named Abdisho convinces him of the truth of the gospel, Qardagh converts to Christianity and burns down all the fire temples in his territory. He dies as a martyr at the hands of Persian troops, stoned to death at the gate of his fortress at Melqi, which over time becomes a place dedicated to keeping his memory alive.[23]

What makes this story particularly fascinating is the fact that Melqi, Qardagh's stronghold, is in all likelihood identical with Milqia, a small Neo-Assyrian town near Arbela where an Akitu House dedicated to the goddess Ishtar of Arbela was located. Both Esarhaddon and Ashurbanipal had restored this sanctuary during their reigns and had shown great interest in it. Just like at Ashur, the Akitu House in Milqia/Melqi seems to have remained a site for religious festivities long after the fall of the Assyrian Empire, perhaps in connection with an annual New Year's celebration. The story is thus an illuminating example of how the Christian community of Adiabene sometimes fused scriptural lore with local history and the legacy of ancient Assyrian religious sites.

OVER THE NEARLY TWO MILLENNIA OF THEIR PRESENCE IN THE territories once inhabited by the ancient Assyrians, Christians experienced some dramatic changes. For a long time, they fared quite well. Under the Sasanians, the emerging Church of the East enjoyed a considerable degree of autonomy—the new rulers, who were often at war with Rome and the emperors of Byzantium, appreciated the church's opposition to Christian denominations associated with the Western powers. Persecutions and attempts to silence local clerics were relatively rare. With the advent of Islam in the seventh century, this advantageous state of affairs initially did not change. East Syriac Christians, fluent in Greek, Syriac, and soon also in Arabic, played leading roles as translators and scholars in the cultural "Golden Age" of early Abbasid Baghdad. But, over time, the Christians of northern Iraq, who as *dhimmis* had fewer rights than Muslims, were increasingly marginalized. As the centuries went by and army after army of foreign conquerors marched through the region, their communities dwindled. During Ottoman times, many local Christians took refuge in remote districts such as the Tur Abdin—the "Mountain of the Worshippers." In exactly the same area, the Assyrian chief cupbearer Lâbasi had once established a last Assyrian stronghold after the fall of the empire in 612 BCE.[24]

Up to the nineteenth century, the Syriac Christians of northern Mesopotamia refrained from using the term "Assyrian" as a self-designation. But when Western travelers, archaeologists, and missionaries began to emphasize that the Christians they encountered in the region were "the descendants of the ancient Assyrians," as Austen Henry Layard put it in his 1849 book *Nineveh and Its Remains,* more and more local Christians began to endorse the label. Undoubtedly, one reason for this reorientation was the hope that an association with the powerful Assyrian Empire would improve their standing.[25]

Such expectations, however, turned out to be sadly illusory. Caught up between the emerging nationalisms of Turks and Kurds and the imperial interests of the European powers, the Assyrian Christians, as they now called themselves, experienced a period of dreadful pogroms and displacements, rapes and abductions. In the course of the upheavals that brought the Ottoman Empire to its knees, especially during World War I, more than 250,000 Assyrian Christians were killed, and many others forcefully resettled. After the war, attempts to create an independent homeland for the Assyrian Christians were soon aborted, and the nation-states carved out of the carcass of the Ottoman Empire became the arena for new massacres targeting Christian communities. One of them, committed by local tribesmen and Iraqi military troops, took place in 1933 in the Iraqi village of Simele and the surrounding area and led to the deaths of between 600 and 3,000 Assyrian Christians.[26]

Today, the dechristianization of the Middle East has reached dramatic proportions. During the numerous political crises of the past four decades, many of the remaining Christians have fled the region. Assyrian Christians are now found in greater numbers in Sweden, Germany, Australia, and the United States than in northern Iraq, southeastern Turkey, or northwestern Iran. Most of the people who consider themselves the last descendants of Sargon and Sennacherib—and continue to give their children the names of these and other Assyrian kings—no longer live in their homeland.

In their various exiles, however, they seek to preserve their religious and cultural traditions, emphasize their links with imperial Assyria, and share their heritage with their new environments. A notable example of Assyrian Christians showcasing their history and culture in the West is a large bronze statue of the bookish Assyrian king Ashurbanipal designed by the Iraqi-born Assyrian Christian

Fred Parhad. Dedicated "by the Assyrian people" to the city of San Francisco, it was erected in front of San Francisco's Main Library (see Plate 14).[27]

All that is now left "on the ground" of ancient Assyria are the massive ruins of the empire's great cities. Sadly, those, too, just like the Assyrian Christians, are in danger of eradication, as the events during the rule of ISIS in the Assyrian heartland have shown. But ancient Assyria left yet another legacy, one less prone to the ravages of time: the idea of empire.

16

A Model Empire

While some components of Assyria's culture lived on after the devastating Babylonian and Median attacks of the late seventh century BCE, and some Assyrian cities continued to be inhabited, the Assyrian Empire, it would seem, had come to an irrevocable end by 609 BCE. Mario Liverani, a leading historian of the ancient Near East, argues that the Assyrian Empire "vanished into thin air." According to Liverani, the "elements of the Assyrian imperial structure that survived the collapse of the empire" were "few and ephemeral."[1]

Or were they? Peter Bedford, a scholar of comparative history and religion, takes a diametrically opposed view: "The empire did not end," he writes. "Rather, its center shifted from the upper Tigris south to Babylon, arguably continuing under the Persians with its center shifting again further east."[2]

The truth is surely less categorical when it comes to something as mercurial as empire. When the Assyrians founded their empire, they created a form of government that endured beyond the fall of Nineveh—and in this sense, the Neo-Babylonian and Persian Empires that followed the Assyrian one were indeed extensions of Assyrian practices. Yet empire is a shape-shifting phenomenon. When an earlier empire is replaced by a later one, what ensues is usually not only a change of place, but also a qualitative transformation. Adoption of established political structures goes hand in hand with adaptation and with the creation of new components of governance and political ideology.[3]

Accordingly, there were both continuities and changes when first the Babylonian and then the Persian Empire became established as successor states of Assyria. In some respects, the two polities followed the precedents set by the Assyrians, while in others, they deviated from them. Subsequent empires did the same with the imperial legacies of their predecessors. But they were all links in a chain that runs from the Assyrians to the modern age.

THE STATE FOUNDED BY NABOPOLASSAR (R. 626–605 BCE) AND consolidated during a long reign by his son and successor Nebuchadnezzar (r. 604–562 BCE) lasted for some seventy years and covered a region, at least eventually, that was more or less equal in size to Assyria's dominions around 648 BCE. Known as the "Neo-Babylonian" or "Chaldean" Empire, it was centered on Babylon, Mesopotamia's most renowned city. It came to an end in 539 BCE, when the Persian king Cyrus II seized power from the last Babylonian king, Nabonidus. Because of the crucial role it plays in the Bible, the most famous episode in the history of the Neo-Babylonian Empire is its conflict with the Kingdom of Judah. Twice, first in 597 and then again eleven years later, Nebuchadnezzar II achieved what Sennacherib had failed to do: he conquered Jerusalem. When he took the city in 586, he destroyed Jerusalem's temple and deported a large portion of the Judean population to the rivers of Babylon.

For all the anti-Assyrian resentment that Assyria's brutal wars had instilled in the hearts and minds of the Babylonian people, the Neo-Babylonian Empire was in many respects deeply indebted to its Assyrian predecessor. It borrowed important elements of the Assyrian "imperial toolkit," from forms of imperial control and

administrative organization to ideological concepts and their artic-
ulation in art.[4]

Given the military and political entanglements that had existed
during the previous 120 years between Assyria and Babylonia, it
is not so surprising that the former provided the blueprint for the
newly emerging Neo-Babylonian Empire. Ever since the days when,
in 729 BCE, Tiglath-pileser III had conquered Babylon, members of
Assyria's military and civilian elite had held important positions in
Babylon and other southern cities. To be sure, unlike elsewhere in
their empire, the Assyrians never completely replaced Babylonia's
traditional system of governance. Many Babylonian cities retained
a significant degree of municipal autonomy. But Assyria's influence
was nonetheless strong. What was more, the first ruler of the Neo-
Babylonian Empire, Nabopolassar, came from a family of Babylonian officials who had represented the Assyrian crown and were in
regular contact with it. At the beginning of his career, Nabopolassar
had been an Assyrian appointee himself, which must have given him
deep insights into the ways in which the Assyrian Empire operated.[5]

Particularly noteworthy is the degree to which the central bureaucracy of Nabopolassar's new empire was rooted in Assyrian
models. Though no Babylonian "state archives" have been found like
those discovered at Nineveh, a building inscription on a fragmentary
clay prism from the early years of the reign of Nebuchadnezzar II
provides some important clues to how the Neo-Babylonian state
apparatus actually worked. At its end, the text lists all the palace
officials, governors, and municipal administrators who had in some
way contributed to the construction of Nebuchadnezzar's new palace in Babylon. Remarkably, fourteen out of the seventeen state officials mentioned in the preserved portions of the text bear titles with
Assyrian roots. Some of these titles—for example, *mašennu* ("chief
administrator" or "treasurer")—are genuinely Assyrian words, unat-
tested in Babylonia prior to the time of the Neo-Babylonian Empire.

The rules that governed communication between the Babylonian king and his subjects, emblematized by an institution known as the "royal word" (*amat šarri*), and the recurring administration of loyalty oaths (*adê*) by the monarch, had Assyrian origins as well.[6]

Babylonian monumental art is, in general, quite different from the art on display in the Assyrian palaces and temples at Calah, Dur-Sharrukin, and Nineveh. Neither bas-reliefs with scenes of warfare nor sculptures similar to the bull and lion colossi found in the entrances of royal suites in the Assyrian capitals have been discovered at Babylon or other Babylonian sites. In the western parts of the Neo-Babylonian Empire, however—which took a great deal of effort for the Babylonian armies under Nebuchadnezzar to reconquer—the iconographic language of some rock reliefs is clearly based on earlier Assyrian models. A relief from the reign of Nebuchadnezzar found at Wadi Brisa in northern Lebanon shows the Babylonian king fighting a rampant lion, a motif of central importance in Assyrian imperial art. Such borrowings represent a deliberate attempt on the part of the Neo-Babylonian kings to showcase themselves in faraway places as the legitimate heirs of their Assyrian predecessors.[7]

An example of Babylonian rulers mimicking Assyrian models at home, in the center of their power, is the architectural setting of Nebuchadnezzar's North Palace in Babylon. Raised across the city wall like a fortress, the palace recalls similarly positioned royal residences on Assyrian citadel mounds, such as Sargon II's palace at Dur-Sharrukin. The rectilinear plan that characterizes Babylon's inner city in the sixth century BCE seems likewise more grounded in Assyrian than Babylonian traditions. Again, Dur-Sharrukin offers a close parallel.[8]

DURING THE YEARS THAT THE ASSYRIAN EMPIRE FELL, MOST OF the Assyrians residing in Babylonia were stripped of the authority they had previously exercised, or else simply killed. Assyrians who arrived in the south afterward, whether as prisoners of war or as refugees, were often assigned menial tasks, such as working on temple estates. But at least some of the Assyrians who made their home in Babylonia after 612 BCE seem to have held more prestigious positions. Among them was a group of Assyrian scribes in the city of Babylon. As indicated by archival documents written in Assyrian script from Nebuchadnezzar's South Palace, the latest dated to 599 or 596 BCE, they served as bureaucrats within Babylon's central administration. The texts they wrote belong to a set of tablets that record, inter alia, expenditures of barley, dates, and oil to political hostages, including members of the Judean royal family.[9]

A few Assyrian "intellectuals" seem to have found a new life in Babylonia as well. An undated astrological tablet from Babylon is designated in its subscript as "property of Kundu-ilaya-ukin(?)," which could be a distorted reference to the Bel-kundi-ilaya family from Ashur. Members of this family might have escaped to Babylonia shortly before or after the destruction of Ashur in 614 BCE.[10]

In the city of Uruk, Nabopolassar's hometown, an Assyrian community that had established itself during the mid-seventh century was still around in the second half of the sixth century, well into Persian times. Members of this community are mentioned in administrative texts from Uruk's Eanna Temple. They are identifiable by genuinely Assyrian personal names, many of which, such as Remanni-Ashur or Pani-Ashur-lamur, include the name of Ashur. The Assyrians in Uruk continued to worship their traditional god and to serve him as priests, temple brewers, and butchers in a sanctuary specifically dedicated to him.

The Eanna texts render the god's name as AN.ŠÁR, a common spelling of "Ashur" since the early seventh century, but also the name of an ancestor of the sky god Anu. The latter played an increasingly important role in Uruk during the first millennium BCE. In all likelihood, the Assyrian exiles sought to gain approval for their veneration of Ashur by assimilating him to a local deity of some consequence. The leaders and priests of Uruk, in turn, might have found inspiration in the newly imported Assyrian god when they made Anu the primary deity of their city—a religious reform with beginnings in the fifth century BCE that is in several respects reminiscent of the conception of a new Yahweh theology at about the same time in Jerusalem.[11]

Uruk's Assyrian residents had apparently brought some heirlooms from their native land when they moved to their new home. Among them was a beautiful Middle Assyrian seal depicting a royal hunting scene. An administrative document from 520 BCE found in Uruk's Eanna precinct bears an impression of it. Also discovered at Uruk, among the tablets of a learned exorcist active in the late fourth century BCE, was an Assyrian commentary on liver divination. As a note on the tablet reveals, it had once belonged to Ashurbanipal's famous library at Nineveh. Unless the commentary came to Uruk as war booty, it must have found its way to the city through channels similar to those that had brought the seal there. Many learned treatises from Hellenistic Uruk show notable similarities with earlier Assyrian texts, suggesting that in Uruk, Assyrian scholarly traditions discarded everywhere else may have survived the fall of the empire for a few centuries.[12]

DESPITE THEIR RELIANCE ON ASSYRIAN PRECEDENTS, MOST NEO-Babylonian kings had little to say about the Assyrian Empire, other than castigating it for its mistreatment of Babylon. But even such criticisms are usually vague, and no Assyrian kings are mentioned by name in the royal inscriptions of Nabopolassar, Nebuchadnezzar, or the three rather negligible rulers who succeeded them until 556 BCE. Following earlier Babylonian rather than Assyrian models, the inscriptions of these monarchs are largely silent about political history in general, focusing instead on building projects, temple sacrifice, and the relationship between the kings and the gods.

All of this changes, at least to some extent, with the rule of Nabonidus, the last Neo-Babylonian king. To be sure, Nabonidus, too, has harsh words for Assyria, disparaging Sennacherib for his attack on Babylon in 689. But in the context of temple rebuilding, his inscriptions mention the achievements of several other Assyrian kings with approval. Nabonidus refers to Ashurnasirpal II, Shalmaneser III, Esarhaddon, Ashurbanipal, and Ashur-etel-ilani by their official title, "King of Assyria," and even calls them in two cases "my ancestors."[13]

Nabonidus showed a particularly keen interest in Ashurbanipal. When he commissioned a new statue for the moon god Sîn of Harran—a deity he promoted far beyond the call of duty— Nabonidus needed a model for it, because the old statue had been destroyed by the Medes. As described by the king in an inscription from Babylon, he found such a model on "a cylinder seal made of valuable jasper, the stone of kingship, upon which Ashurbanipal, the king of Assyria, had an image of Sîn conceived, and which he had firmly placed around the neck of the god Sîn." This seal, Nabonidus tells his readers, had somehow survived Harran's destruction and had been brought to Marduk's Esagil Temple in Babylon, where he had stumbled on it.[14]

Crediting Ashurbanipal with the creation of the "correct" image of the god whom he worshipped more than any other deity is a remarkable show of respect on the part of Nabonidus. Other aspects of Nabonidus's self-representation were rooted in Assyrian models as well. On two stelae from Harran, the king is depicted wearing a cloak that resembles the richly decorated ceremonial garment worn on many Assyrian monuments by Neo-Assyrian monarchs. The stelae themselves, with their rounded tops, are shaped just like royal stelae from Assyrian times.

The main reason for Nabonidus's infatuation with Assyrian culture and religion, and with Harran, in particular, is that the king hailed from this very city himself. His mother, Adda-guppi, who was born in the twentieth year of Ashurbanipal's reign and apparently reached the mature age of 102, lived in Harran for decades and might have experienced its partial destruction. She remained throughout her life a devoted worshipper of the moon god, the patron deity of the city. It has even been claimed, although without proof, that she was a member of the Assyrian royal family. Nabonidus—who commissioned a long inscription in the name of his mother upon her death—probably spent his childhood in Harran before moving to Babylon. It is a somewhat ironic twist that the last ruler of the Neo-Babylonian Empire, which had been founded on the ruins of its Assyrian predecessor, was more "Assyrian" than any of the other kings who had held the Babylonian throne before him.[15]

IN MANY REGARDS, THE RULERS OF THE NEO-BABYLONIAN KING-dom followed the example set by the Assyrian Empire. But certain aspects of the way they governed were actually quite different. Beginning with the reign of Tiglath-pileser III in the eighth century BCE, Assyrian kings had created numerous new provinces to rule their imperial periphery. These provinces, administered on behalf of the crown by local governors and their staff, generated a steady flow of taxes. The specifics of how the Neo-Babylonian Empire ran the regions outside Babylonia proper are still poorly understood, but it is clear that in the years prior to the 580s, the kingdom's periphery, especially in the west, was not as neatly subdivided into provinces as Assyria's outer territories had been in the empire's heyday. During these years, the Babylonian kings mostly limited themselves to the collection of tribute, which they extorted by means of annual military campaigns from largely independent local strongmen, among them the kings of Sidon, Tyre, and Ashdod.[16]

About halfway through Nebuchadnezzar's long reign, the Babylonians managed to establish, if not full-fledged provinces, then at least pockets of local presence in the west, which allowed for tighter control. Something akin to provincial structures seems to have been implemented in upper and northwest Syria, while elsewhere in the periphery Babylonian temples were granted land that they had to exploit for their own benefit and for the benefit of the crown with the help of local authorities and laborers. All in all, though, the system seems never to have achieved the same level of control that existed under the Assyrian Empire—and at no point were the Babylonians able to extend their rule to Egypt and the territories of the Medes.

Closer to home, in Babylonia and the "near periphery," introducing streamlined structures of governance proved not much easier for the Neo-Babylonian kings. In the cities in central Babylonia, the power of mayors and high priests remained largely uncurbed, while the Eastern Tigris region and the south, including the important city of Uruk, stayed under the control of influential "magnates" and tribal leaders only loosely linked to the central government in Babylon. This fragmentation of power led on two occasions during the relatively short history of the empire to internal unrest that resulted in dynastic changes: first after the reign of Nebuchadnezzar's son Amel-Marduk in 560, and then again after Labashi-Marduk's reign in 556 BCE.[17]

Despite the enormous efforts the Neo-Babylonian kings put into their building projects, Babylonia's great urban centers never became "royal cities" the way the term applies to Calah, Dur-Sharrukin, or Nineveh. Even the urban landscape of Babylon, the greatly expanded capital of the empire, remained dominated by the gigantic complex of the Esagil Temple of Marduk and the adjoining ziggurat, the "Tower of Babel," in the center of the city. The royal palaces were tucked away farther to the north. And while the Assyrian kings, having a finger in every pie, were also high priests of Ashur, the Neo-Babylonian rulers, for all the pious chatter of their inscriptions, were never able to assume leading religious ranks. The high priests of Marduk of Babylon continued to be recruited from long-established local families.[18]

What this suggests is that the Neo-Babylonian kings were less powerful than their Neo-Assyrian predecessors, and that their empire was, in a sense, less formidable and cohesive. Still, this relative weakness of the central authority had an important upside: it facilitated the endurance of Babylonian municipalities and religious and cultural institutions in the period after the empire's collapse. In contrast to Assyria, where the fall of the monarchy led to an extensive, all-encompassing breakdown, the Babylonian cities and temples survived Nabonidus's surrender to the Persians for more than half a millennium.

THE PERSIAN EMPIRE, FOUNDED BY CYRUS II AFTER HIS VICTORY over Babylonia in 539 BCE, transcended its predecessors in several respects. At the time of its greatest extent, it was about four times as large as the Assyrian Empire, covering an area of some 5.5 million square kilometers (about 2.1 million square miles). Holding territory on three continents, it stretched into Central Asia and to the borders of India while at the same time ruling parts of southeastern Europe and northeastern Africa. And with a life span of more than two hundred years, from 539 to 331 BCE, it lasted longer than the Assyrian and Neo-Babylonian Empires combined.[19]

Earlier conquerors of Mesopotamia—for example, the Amorites and the Kassites in the second millennium BCE—had swiftly adopted the customs and political structures of the old civilizations on the Tigris and the Euphrates and established their royal courts in the traditional cities of Babylonia. The Persians pursued a different path. With their rise, power shifted eastward, to places such as Susa in the Lower Zagros Mountains and Persepolis in Fars—even though Babylonia, and to some extent also Assyria, remained areas of great economic significance.

The Persian rulers drew on features of both the Neo-Babylonian and Assyrian Empires when forming their own. But they also absorbed some traditions inherited from the kingdom of the Medes—conquered by Cyrus in 550 BCE—and especially from the old Elamite kingdom, located much closer to the Persian "homeland" in southwestern Iran than the Mesopotamian states. Tellingly, of the more than fifteen thousand administrative texts on clay tablets from the reign of Darius I found at Persepolis, only about one thousand are written in Aramaic, and only one is composed in Babylonian cuneiform. The vast majority are written in the Elamite language and script, and the Elamite influence on other aspects of Persian culture was similarly significant.

As time went by, most of the military and civilian posts of some consequence were assigned by the new rulers to ethnic Persians. But initially, especially in the first years after Cyrus's conquest of Babylon, members of the traditional Babylonian elite held important positions as well—and the Persians adopted a number of features of Babylonia's political, economic, and ideological makeup for their new empire.[20]

Even during this early phase, though, the Persian attitude toward the Neo-Babylonian Empire seems to have been an ambivalent one, as is most clearly shown by the so-called Cyrus Cylinder. Composed shortly after 539 BCE, with a Babylonian audience in mind, this well-known text reveals a lot about the image Cyrus wished to project of himself and of the empire he had founded. On the one hand, the text emphasizes Cyrus's merits as a traditional Babylonian king: it is written in the Babylonian language and script; it is inscribed on a large barrel-shaped clay cylinder, an age-old medium for texts of this type; and it ends with an account of building work done on Babylon's walls. What is more, the text presents Cyrus as a ruler about to restore Babylon's traditional historical role after Nabonidus, an alien and wicked king, had violated the cultic rules of the city of Marduk through his "lunatic" preference for the moon god.[21]

On the other hand, the Cyrus Cylinder—undoubtedly upon the king's request—also includes elements far less centered on Babylon. It stresses, for example, Cyrus's origin from an Iranian "Dynasty of Anshan," highlighting his foreignness—and it alludes in various ways to Assyria. Not only does it talk about the king letting the people and the gods of Ashur return to their home city, it also mentions that a foundation deposit of the Assyrian king Ashurbanipal—who had once sacked the city of Babylon—had been found in Babylon's walls. Here we get a first glimpse of the Persians seeking to portray their empire as a successor state to Assyria rather than Babylonia. The fact that Babylonian scribes were ordered right from the beginning of Persian rule to date documents after "Cyrus king of the lands," using a royal title previously assigned to Babylonia's Assyrian rulers, rather than a traditional Babylonian one, points in the same direction.[22]

A CLOSER LOOK AT THE NEWLY BUILT PERSIAN CAPITALS IN IRAN reveals in even more striking ways how the Persians struggled when having to choose between Babylonian and Assyrian models for their new empire. One of the most spectacular archaeological finds made there in recent years, by an Italian-Iranian team, is a monumental gateway located not far from the main terrace of the royal palace at Persepolis. Probably erected during the earliest phase of the Persian Empire, prior to the rule of Darius I (521–486 BCE), the structure resembles in remarkable detail, both in terms of its architecture and its decoration, Nebuchadnezzar's famous Ishtar Gate in Babylon. Its glazed bricks, displaying dragons, strident bulls, and cuneiform inscriptions, seem to have been made from the same brick molds that were used for the Ishtar Gate, which suggests that the gate in Persepolis was built by workmen from Babylon. The gate is, without question, an architectural homage to Babylon and its religious and cosmological significance.[23]

But the Persians soon abandoned the Babylonian traditions they had adopted when they erected the Persepolis gate. Within a few years, the architects of the great Persian capitals began finding models in other artistic languages—including those of ancient Assyria. In fact, already during the reign of Cyrus, reliefs decorating a stone gateway in Palace S in Pasargadae show a lion-demon, a figure wearing a fish-cloak, and a bull-man, for which the closest parallels are to be found in reliefs from Sennacherib's Southwest Palace at Nineveh.[24]

The artistic style of later buildings at Persepolis and other urban centers of the Persian Empire displays a mix of different elements reflecting Egyptian, Elamite, and Greek styles, but the Assyrian influence remains persistently strong. The monumental bull colossi in the "Gate of All Nations" at Persepolis, the image of the Persian king killing a rampant lion-demon from the same site, and the way many Persian reliefs render the king's hairstyle and beard are very similar to Assyrian models. Persepolis's stone landscape of endless rows of reliefs depicting tribute bearers breathes an Assyrian spirit too. Clearly identifiable examples of Babylonian influence are far less evident.

Another famous Persian monument more in line with Assyrian than Babylonian models is Darius I's trilingual inscription on the Bisitun rock. Although one of its three versions (the other two are written in Elamite and Old Persian) is in the Babylonian language and script, the content of the text, with its emphasis on military action and the physical punishment of traitors, is far more reminiscent of Assyrian royal annals than of Babylonian royal inscriptions.[25]

The relief that accompanies the Bisitun inscription is one of many Persian artifacts to depict a winged sun-disk containing a human torso—probably a representation of the king. This enigmatic symbol of cosmic order has a close Assyrian antecedent as well. It is still unclear whether the Assyrian solar disk represents the god Ashur, the sun god Shamash, or some combination of the two; and the same uncertainty applies to the identification of the disk in Persian imperial art, where it may or may not stand for the Persian state god Ahura Mazda. But the close association of the symbol in both traditions with the figure of the king makes it very likely that one of its main functions was to convey the idea of the ruler as a representative of the main god, and to highlight that the ruler's chief task was to carry out the universal mission of imposing order on the world on behalf of the deity. The Assyrians and Persians, in other words, shared not only the artistic motif of the solar disk, but also elements of the royal ideology behind it.[26]

In the course of the nearly two hundred years that followed its completion, no Persian ruler apparently ever commissioned another inscription like the one on the Bisitun monument. Cyrus's account of his deeds on the cylinder from Babylon remained the only text of this type as well. The royal messages of later Persian kings focus instead, in rather anodyne, deindividualized, and abstract fashion, on general statements, especially about how the crown helped maintain the cosmic order. Here Persian imperial ideology markedly deviated from earlier Babylonian and Assyrian models.

Still, in other respects, Assyria, in particular, remained a central reference point for the Persian Empire—not only in the arts, but also in terms of the empire's structure and mode of operation. The well-maintained provincial system of the Assyrian Empire was reborn in Persian times in the form of the roughly two dozen "satrapies" into which the new state was divided by the time of Darius I, each administered by a governor who had to report directly to the great king. Persian land tenure systems and the empire's "Royal Road" had Assyrian antecedents as well.[27]

Assyria, it seems, became the Persians' model empire. The fifth-century BCE Greek historian Ctesias of Cnidus, who wrote a long history of the Near East after serving for nearly two decades as chief physician to the Persian king Artaxerxes II (and healing him from a wound he had suffered in the Battle of Cunaxa), collected numerous stories about Assyria during his time at the Persian court—stories that became part of the historical memory of the West after Ctesias's account had been integrated into later works, such as Diodorus Siculus's universal history. About the Neo-Babylonian state, in contrast, Ctesias had comparatively little to report—his Persian sources were apparently not very interested in it. The Babylonian priest Berossus, who wrote another history of the Near East during the early Hellenistic period, sought to rectify Ctesias's account by putting greater emphasis on the role Babylon had played, but his work, although more accurate, was later less extensively studied. And thus the Babylonian Empire was often glossed over in later accounts of "global history," whereas Assyria appeared center stage.

TWO QUESTIONS REMAIN TO BE ANSWERED: FIRST, WHY THE Persian rulers, after an initial period marked by a certain degree of respect and appreciation, suddenly became so disillusioned with Babylonia, turning instead to Assyria; and second, how the Persians actually received their knowledge of the history, politics, and art of the Assyrian Empire. After all, the Assyrian state had ceased to exist some seventy years before Cyrus conquered Babylon.

Persia's increasing disenchantment with Babylonia had several causes. Lacking a truly universal imperial ideology, the Neo-Babylonian kingdom had probably been a less attractive model for the ambitious Persian rulers from the start. But a series of anti-Persian revolts in Babylonia also played an important role in causing Persia to turn away from Babylonian models. The first of these took place during the politically chaotic phase after the death of Cyrus's son Cambyses in 522 BCE, the second a few decades later, in 484, when Babylonians rebelled against the newly appointed Persian king, Xerxes. Xerxes reacted with massive reprisals that ushered in a period of crisis in Babylonia. After these experiences, it does not come as a surprise that the Persian rulers considered the Assyrian kingdom of yore a more attractive paradigm for their new empire than unruly Babylonia.

It is still difficult to account for the distinctively Assyrian elements characterizing the Persian Empire, most notably in the realm of the arts. Assyria's great royal cities—Calah, Dur-Sharrukin, and especially Nineveh—all lay in ruins at the time of Cyrus II's rise to power. That Persian artists and craftsmen visited them during the early decades of the Persian Empire to study what was left of the great palaces of Ashurnasirpal II or Sennacherib seems a rather dubious proposition.

More likely is that elements of Assyrian art and civilization were transmitted to the Persians by intermediaries such as the Babylonians, Urartians, Medes, or Elamites. Especially the Median and Elamite kingdoms might have been "vectors for Assyrian inputs," as they were close to the Persian homeland. Another place where Persians might have encountered Assyrian art and culture is the Assyrian city of Arbela, which was less affected by the destructions of the late seventh century BCE than other Assyrian cities and remained an important regional center.[28]

It also bears remembering that around 640 BCE, when the Assyrian Empire was still flourishing, a certain Arukku, a son of Cyrus II's ancestor and namesake Kurash I, had spent some time at Ashurbanipal's court at Nineveh. A member of the dynasty that would eventually produce Cyrus II thus had a "front-row seat" to observe the workings of Assyria's imperial machine. That his experiences at Nineveh had a formative impact on the nascent Persian kingdom is not an unreasonable assumption.[29]

Finally, archaeologists have unearthed significant numbers of Assyrian art objects in the so-called Treasury at Persepolis. The most impressive example is a beautiful stone bowl with handles in the shape of lions that is inscribed in the name of Ashurbanipal. Along with other objects, it might have been looted in 614 or 612 BCE by the Medes. If the Medes brought it to their capital, Ecbatana, the Persians might have taken it from there. The Persepolis Treasury was ransacked in 330 BCE by the soldiers of Alexander the Great, and it is likely that many even more precious Assyrian artifacts had once been stored there. The images on some of these objects (and on others kept elsewhere) might have served Persian artists as models for the Assyrian-style images and monuments they created, thus bringing about a kind of Assyrian renaissance.[30]

AFTER THE COLLAPSE OF THE PERSIAN EMPIRE IN 331 BCE IN THE wake of Alexander's epoch-making campaign to the east, the Hellenistic Seleucids founded a new empire, which was subsequently replaced by the Iranian empires of the Parthians and Sasanians, and then, after the Islamic conquests, by empires dominated by Arabs. As time went by, the imperial idea also traveled to other parts of the world: to the east, climaxing in the Mauryan and Moghul Empires centered in India; to the north, with the Seljuk and Ottoman Empires as prime examples of imperial states in the Turkish world; and to the west as well. Here it was Rome, the greatest empire of the ancient world, that outshone everyone else.[31]

The conspicuous similarities between Rome and Assyria—whether in terms of their respective provincial systems or with regard to their emphasis on military matters and their cultural indebtedness to earlier, more sophisticated civilizations—are in general not the result of deliberate "borrowing." Rather, the two states produced similar answers to comparable political challenges. But there is no question that the Romans observed closely how the Seleucid Empire—Assyria's great-grandchild—operated, and how the Seleucids established an imperial Eurasian system of global proportions. This was a model the Romans were quite keen to emulate. To be sure, Pompey and Caesar, and later Augustus and the emperors after him, normally took great care to distance themselves from the kings of the East, whether they belonged to the Seleucid Empire or to the subsequent Parthian and Sasanian Dynasties, and to hide their own autocratic ambitions behind a smokescreen of republican play-acting. But the political structures they created, and eventually, in Late Antiquity, how the Roman emperors increasingly defined their own role, often followed eastern examples.

Rome served as a model for the Byzantine, Frankish, and Germanic Empires that succeeded it. Many more recent empires, including the British, the largest of all, can be considered links in the chain of imperial transmission as well. Even today, the idea of empire remains deeply embedded in political discourses, although modern states with imperial ambitions, eager to avoid the negative connotations the term has assumed, normally no longer advertise themselves as empires.

As the imperial torch was passed from one state to the next, Assyria receded more and more into the background. Whatever direct influence the Assyrian Empire might have had on its immediate successor states became a mediated effect, less and less detectable, as both the practice and the idea of empire changed over time. But within the discourse of empire, at least in the West, Assyria never ceased to play a crucial role. Proponents of the medieval doctrine of *translatio imperii* (the transfer of imperial rule) and their classical forerunners, from the fifth-century BCE Greek historian Herodotus to the fourth-century CE Roman theologian Orosius, regularly credited the Assyrians with having founded the first empire in world history. The ultimate root of this notion is to be found in the many stories that circulated in the ancient world about the Assyrian Empire and some of its most important kings and queens. And the main repositories preserving these stories, to which we now turn, are the Bible and the works of classical historians. In these texts, the Assyrians lived on, even if a self-contained Assyrian cultural tradition did not.[32]

17

Distorted Reflections

The last cuneiform texts in the Assyrian language and script were written around 600 BCE. Some seven hundred years later, Babylonian cuneiform writing came to an end as well. The latest clearly datable Babylonian tablet, an astronomical almanac from Babylon, is from 75 CE. From this moment onward, all that was known about the ancient civilizations of Mesopotamia, including the Assyrian Empire, came from secondary and tertiary outside sources—most notably the Hebrew Bible and the accounts of Greek and Roman historians. In many of these writings, Assyria and Babylonia appeared as models of alterity. Alternatively presented as oppressive or decadent, the two lands embodied the opposite of the truth, wisdom, and political efficacy associated with the worlds of Jerusalem, Athens, and Rome—a perception that lasted for some 1,800 years.[1]

The rediscovery of the cities and original writings of the ancient Near East in the nineteenth century changed everything. All of a sudden, Babylonia and Assyria spoke again in their own voices, prompting a major reassessment of Mesopotamian history and culture. But as it turned out, the new findings also did something else, something perhaps even more important: they brought about a reevaluation of the biblical and classical texts that had until then provided the West with the religious and historical models on which its identity was based.

As new evidence accumulated, the Hebrew Bible came to be interrogated more and more as a historical rather than a holy text. Initially, Assyrian and Babylonian records were used to confirm the reliability of the sacred history outlined in the biblical books as well as to illustrate it. The discovery of the names of biblical kings such as Jehu or Hezekiah in Assyrian royal inscriptions, and of bas-reliefs showing Sennacherib's siege of Lachish and other scenes set in the Levant, appeared to vindicate the Bible's faithful readers in their belief that the biblical writings were true. Soon, however, the texts and images found at Nineveh, Calah, and elsewhere also began to show the opposite: that, often enough, the Hebrew Bible had gotten it wrong. In other cases, newly deciphered cuneiform tablets seemed to suggest that biblical narratives of central importance, such as the story of the great flood, derived from much earlier Mesopotamian texts, many pieced together from fragments from Ashurbanipal's libraries at Nineveh. All this cast additional doubt on the authority of scripture, already greatly weakened by the intellectual revolutions ushered in by Copernicus and Darwin in the fields of cosmology and biology, respectively.

Unsurprisingly, members of the Christian establishment responded to the proliferation of new archaeological finds with considerable unease. As early as 1847, an Anglican cleric and fellow of Oxford's Exeter College protested "most vehemently" against the further prosecution of excavations at Assyrian sites, because their results might "test the credibility" of scripture.[2]

In stark contrast, critics of traditional religious views, some armed with anti-Semitic agendas, seized upon the new discoveries to completely reject the Hebrew Bible. The German Assyriologist Friedrich Delitzsch, son of an eminent Lutheran theologian and Hebraist, claimed in the early 1920s, in a book tellingly titled *The Great Deception*, that, since "the so-called 'Old Testament'" had proven derivative and unreliable, it was "entirely superfluous for the Christian church and also for the Christian family." Rather than in the Hebrew Bible, Delitzsch argued, truth and moral values were to be found, on the one hand, in earlier Mesopotamian traditions, and, on the other, in the Greek New Testament. In fact, according to Delitzsch, Jesus had promoted what were essentially "Babylonian ideals." Such triumphalist pan-Babylonian—and pan-Assyrian— revisionism often neglected to take into account the fact that the inscriptions of Mesopotamian kings were not exactly models of "objective" history writing either, and that the "ethical lessons" offered by Assyrian and Babylonian texts were often not all that edifying.[3]

In more recent decades, the debate about the entanglements between biblical traditions and Mesopotamian lore has somewhat receded from the front lines. But studying the Bible in its ancient Near Eastern setting remains instructive. One thing it can help with is to underscore the truly revolutionary character of the Bible. Only by focusing on how biblical narratives and legal texts draw on but then modify their Mesopotamian models is it possible to gain an idea of how radically new many religious and political ideas developed in the Hebrew Bible actually are. At the same time, by virtue of being "opposition literature," the Bible provides crucial information on how disenfranchised subjects, especially in the beleaguered or conquered imperial periphery, perceived the Assyrian, Babylonian, and Persian Empires. This view from the margins is a perspective rarely encountered in the cuneiform record. The works of classical authors provide similar insights: they, too, facilitate a better understanding of how the Assyrian Empire looked to others, including those who were not immediately affected by its aggressive politics. The images of Assyria found in the Bible and the classical sources are of course often heavily distorted, but they allow us to see the empire not as simply the purveyor of order and security it pretended to be, but also as the harbinger of disruption and suppression it was for so many.

LOCATED ON THE LAND BRIDGE BETWEEN THE GREAT CIVILIZA-
tions of Mesopotamia and Egypt, the cities and states of the southern Levant were hardly ever fully independent. Throughout history,
their identities were molded by the political and cultural pressures
exerted on them by the two power blocks looming on their horizons. The northern Kingdom of Israel and the southern Kingdom
of Judah, both founded in the early first millennium BCE, were no
exceptions. They had come into existence during a period when
Egypt, Assyria, and Babylonia were all comparatively weak. In time,
Assyria's inexorable rise presented them with a brutal dilemma:
Should they yield to or repudiate the demands made by the newly
emerging superpower?

When Tiglath-pileser III (r. 744–727 BCE) began to annex large
swaths of land in the west, the rulers of the Kingdom of Israel decided to fight the Assyrian conquerors, with catastrophic results. In
just a few years Israel was reduced to a rump state, which ceased to
exist altogether after Shalmaneser V conquered its capital, Samaria,
in 722 BCE. Many Israelites were deported to central Assyria and
other regions of the Assyrian Empire, while others found refuge in
the Kingdom of Judah. Before long, though, Judah was under Assyrian pressure as well. It barely survived Sennacherib's attack on
Jerusalem in 701 BCE and remained an Assyrian client state until
about 640 BCE.[4]

The Hebrew Bible describes these events in considerable detail.
The Book of 2 Kings presents them in the form of a historical narrative, while several biblical prophets, starting with Amos, engage
with them in more emotional and poetic ways. The Bible mentions
"Ashur"—which usually stands for "Assyria"—some 150 times;
names the imperial Assyrian kings Tiglath-pileser III, Shalmaneser
V, Sargon II, Sennacherib, Esarhaddon, and possibly also Ashurbanipal (Osnappar); identifies Sennacherib's son Urdu-Mullissu
(Adrammelech) as his father's murderer; and shows considerable

interest in the city of Nineveh, Assyria's last capital—its name appears seventeen times in the Bible.[5]

Despite their generally anti-Assyrian stance, the biblical texts are remarkably ambivalent in their judgment of how the kings of Israel and Judah should face the threat posed by Assyria. There are not only tales of heroic resistance but also pleas by prophets for a "realpolitik" aimed at self-preservation, even though this required accommodation and compromise with the imperial aggressor. The sheer complexity of the political reasoning hints that much of what the Bible has to say about Assyria does indeed reflect Israelite and Judahite discourses regarding the imperial Assyrian threat. At the same time, stories like the one about the Angel of the Lord "striking down" in a single night "185,000 Assyrian troops in their camp" show that the biblical accounts also include a good deal of historical fiction, most likely produced at a later stage in their editorial history and often informed by specific theological agendas.[6]

Regarding Assyria's final collapse, though, there is no ambivalence. The Book of Nahum portrays this momentous historical moment as a triumph of divine justice, particularly for the city of Nineveh:

> *Ah! City of bloodshed*
> *utterly deceitful, full of booty—*
> *no end to the plunder!...*
> *Piles of dead,*
> *heaps of corpses,*
> *dead bodies without end—*
> *they stumble over the bodies!*
> *Because of the countless debaucheries of the prostitute,*
> *gracefully alluring, mistress of sorcery,*
> *who enslaves nations through her debaucheries,*
> *and peoples through her sorcery,*

I am against you,
*   says the LORD of hosts,*
*   and will lift up your skirts over your face;*
and I will let nations look on your nakedness
*   and kingdoms on your shame.*[7]

Although the Book of Nahum is styled as an oracle, professing to refer to events in the future, scholars almost unanimously agree that it was written after Nineveh's destruction in 612 BCE. Even so, it describes what at least some people in Judah may have thought about Assyria prior to the empire's collapse. In the quoted passage, Nahum uses a whole range of sexual metaphors to denigrate the Assyrian capital. This strategy may be an attempt to polemically allude to Nineveh's main deity, Ishtar, a notoriously sex-craved goddess. Apparently, the author of the Book of Nahum was acquainted with Nineveh's sacred rites and religious lore, considered them an abomination, and rejoiced in their defilement. For the book's author, an empire that corrupt, both politically and religiously, deserved to be wiped out.

THE TIME WHEN THE KINGDOMS OF ISRAEL AND JUDAH WERE shaken up by the rise of Assyria happens to be the earliest period for which biblical authors provide a significant amount of accurate historical information. Though the Bible includes stories that reach back into the Late Bronze Age and the subsequent era of collapse, when Israel emerged as an ethnic—and eventually also a political—entity, it is evident that the biblical memories of these periods were vague. Hebrew historiography in a serious sense does not begin before the eighth century BCE, and the earliest Hebrew prophets whose pronouncements were handed down in writing were active during this time as well. The era of the Assyrian Empire, in other words, coincides with the first period in the formation of the Bible.

This observation raises the question of Assyrian influence not only in the political but also in the religious sphere. The Bible leaves no doubt that the Assyrian Empire drastically reshaped the way Israel and Judah were governed. What is less clear is whether Assyria also had a formative impact on how the Israelites and Judahites viewed their god and his relationship with them and the world.

There is no evidence to indicate that the Assyrians ever engaged in an active program of forcing subjugated people to worship Assyrian deities. To be sure, on special occasions the newly conquered had to swear loyalty oaths by these gods, and they had to send largely symbolic amounts of foodstuffs to the Ashur Temple in Ashur. But no temples exclusively dedicated to Assyrian deities, least of all Ashur, were ever built in the imperial periphery. It therefore comes as no surprise that the god Ashur is not mentioned a single time in the Bible. Genesis 10 talks about a figure called Ashur who, after leaving Babylonia, built Nineveh and Calah. This character, however, is not a god but a fictitious human founder named after the land.[8]

The effects of the trauma of Assyrian imperial oppression on the religion of the Hebrews can rather be seen in more indirect ways. While the political and intellectual elites of Israel and Judah never found themselves confronted with the demands of some Assyrian god, they had to cope with the enormous and highly visible power of the Assyrian king. Resisting this power by means of military or political action was futile, and so the Hebrew priests and prophets did something else: they projected it onto their own god.

This political-theological "transfer" was a revolutionary move that inaugurated a new type of religion. We can see it at work in the pronouncements of the prophet Isaiah, who criticizes the Assyrian king's claims for universal rule and deplores his wish to "gather all the earth as one gathers eggs that have been forsaken"—while at the same time saying about Yahweh, "Holy, holy, holy is the Lord of hosts; the whole earth is full of his glory." Here the god of the Hebrews seems to take on specific qualities of Assyrian authority.[9]

The clearest example of how God adopted features of the Assyrian monarch can be found in the biblical Book of Deuteronomy, portions of which seem to be modeled on the loyalty oaths contained in Esarhaddon's Succession Treaty, which the Assyrian king imposed on his subjects when he nominated his son Ashurbanipal as his heir in 672 BCE. Copies of the oaths, and of the curses accompanying them, were written on large clay tablets that bore the seals of several gods and were put on display in major temples around the empire. One such tablet was discovered in 2009 by archaeologists from the University of Toronto at the site of the ancient city of Kullania on the Orontes River in the Levant.[10]

In all likelihood, Esarhaddon also sent a copy of his Succession Treaty to Jerusalem, capital of the Assyrian vassal state of Judah, where it was almost certainly translated into Aramaic or Hebrew and carefully studied. But then something happened that the Assyrians had not anticipated: Hebrew priests reapplied the stipulations of the treaty to their own god and claimed that he—and not the Assyrian king—deserved unconditional loyalty and obedience.

The text the priests produced for this purpose was an early version of the so-called Deuteronomic Code, a collection of laws found in the Bible's Book of Deuteronomy in chapters 12 to 28. Its dependence on the Assyrian treaty text is suggested, among other things, by a series of curses against lawbreakers. In exchange for disobedience, the biblical text predicts, a man will experience first ulcers, then blindness, and finally the ruin of his marriage, when an enemy takes possession of his wife. Esarhaddon's Succession Treaty includes a section with very similar curses, listed in exactly the same sequence and presented as punishments meted out by the gods Sîn, Shamash, and Ishtar.[11]

In his Succession Treaty, Esarhaddon requires his subjects "to love Ashurbanipal, the great crown prince, son of Esarhaddon, king of Assyria, your lord, like yourself." The Deuteronomic Code asks that the people of Israel "love the Lord your God with all your heart and with all your soul." Whereas Esarhaddon promotes a vision of the king wielding unlimited power, Deuteronomy claims that such power was only legitimately held by God. No earthly king, it states, "must ever acquire many horses," or "many wives," or "silver and gold"—a strong indictment of activities no monarchs pursued with greater zeal than the Assyrian kings.[12]

What constitutes treachery, whether on the part of family members or religious specialists, is treated very differently in the two traditions as well, but the language is once again strangely similar. Esarhaddon demands of his subjects that "any evil, improper, ugly word against Ashurbanipal from the mouth of your brothers, your sons, or your daughters" or "from the mouth of a prophet, an ecstatic, or a dream interpreter" must be immediately reported to the crown prince, who will then punish the perpetrator. Deuteronomy, in contrast, states that "if prophets or those who divine by dreams" or "your brother..., your son, your daughter, or your wife" appear and say, "Let us follow other gods...and let us serve them," one must not heed their word and instead ruthlessly put them to death. Once more, loyalty to the king is replaced in Deuteronomy by loyalty to God.[13]

The Bible presents the Deuteronomic Code as a proclamation of divine laws conveyed by Moses to the people of Israel shortly before they entered the Holy Land. But ever since the early nineteenth century, scholars have questioned this narrative and the notion that the text stretches back to such early times. A historical account in 2 Kings 22–23 provides clues about the actual background of Deuteronomy. It describes how in the 620s, during the reign of the Judean king, Josiah, the high priest, Hilkiah, found in the temple of Jerusalem a "Book of Law" that required everyone to worship Yahweh alone, and to abandon all sanctuaries outside Jerusalem. Since the very same demands are made in Deuteronomy, it is likely that the writings reportedly "found" by Hilkiah were nothing but an early version of Deuteronomy itself—and that this version, rather than being an age-old text, had actually been composed not that long before its alleged discovery. When in the 1950s manuscripts of Esarhaddon's Succession Treaty were excavated—written only a few decades prior to Josiah's reign—and the parallels of the treaty with Deuteronomy were observed, this theory became even more plausible.[14]

The parallels with Esarhaddon's Succession Treaty not only help us better understand the origins of biblical views of the divine, but make us see Deuteronomy and other central parts of the Bible in a completely new light. Deuteronomic laws like the one about the need to kill one's own brothers, sisters, and wives if they worshipped other gods can seem at first glance oppressive and inhumane—and they were, in fact, eventually put to nefarious uses, especially after Christianity and Islam, with their more universal ambitions, adopted central tenets of ancient Judaism. Once it becomes clear, though, that such stipulations were originally meant to counter the repressive claims of Assyrian kings, they can also be read as the anti-imperial musings of a group of revolutionary thinkers bent on liberating their minds and, in the long term, their homeland, from mental and political slavery. The empire strikes, the imperial periphery writes back.[15]

Echoes of encounters with Assyria emerge elsewhere in the Bible as well—for instance, in the mocking dirge in Isaiah 14, which was probably originally aimed at the Assyrian king Sargon II, and perhaps even in the famous tale of Joseph and his brothers, where one can trace elements of the story of Esarhaddon's rise to power. Biblical narratives like the two creation stories, the story of the great flood, and the birth story of Moses seem to have a background in ancient Mesopotamia as well, and the idea that they, too, go back to Assyrian times cannot be ruled out. As there is no evidence for the presence of cuneiform libraries in the southern Levant during Neo-Assyrian times, it may be more likely, however, that the biblical authors of these stories came across their Mesopotamian models during the Babylonian exile in the sixth century BCE, when members of the Judean elite, including King Jehoiachin, lived in Nebuchadnezzar's palace in Babylon.[16]

A special case is the Book of Jonah, whose final chapter is set in Nineveh. But to properly understand how this famous story of a biblical prophet and the large fish that swallowed him might relate to Assyrian history, it will be necessary to take into account a second group of texts covering the Assyrian Empire: the classical tradition.

ASSYRIA LOOMS LARGE IN THE WRITINGS OF THE GREEK AND Roman historians. Two moments of Assyrian history were of particular interest to them: the founding of the Assyrian Empire, and its eventual fall. The most detailed accounts of these crucial episodes of formation and dissolution are found in the work of the first-century BCE Greek historian Diodorus Siculus, who drew heavily on an earlier history by Ctesias of Cnidus, the physician of the Persian king Artaxerxes II.[17]

According to Ctesias and Diodorus, Assyria's rise—and world history in general—began with a certain Ninus, who was reportedly Assyria's first ruler. Today, Ninus is probably best known from comedic references to his tomb in Shakespeare's *Midsummer Night's Dream*, where Bottom and his lowly friends misrepresent his name as "Ninny." Just as in the case of Ashur in Genesis 10, the true origin of Ninus's name was a toponym: the name of the city of Nineveh (Assyrian Ninua). Reversing cause and effect, the Greek historians present Ninus as the founder of Nineveh, the world's first metropolis, but this is clearly incorrect: Ninus has to be regarded as another largely mythical character, a figure of memory rather than history.

Diodorus writes that within seventeen years Ninus conquered all the lands between the Nile in Egypt and the Don River in what is now Russia, but initially failed to seize the city of Bactra, the capital of Bactriana in Afghanistan. It was during his siege of Bactra that he met his future wife, Semiramis—and with her entrance into the story things become much more intriguing.

The figure of Semiramis is based on an actual Assyrian queen: the powerful Sammu-ramat, wife of Shamshi-Adad V (r. 823–811 BCE) and mother of Adad-nirari III (r. 810–783 BCE), who went on campaigns with her son and held the reins of power during the early years of his reign. The Semiramis saga as recorded by Ctesias and Diodorus adds a lot of curious and even bizarre features to the image of this powerful royal woman. In some respects, it turns her into an "orientalist" fantasy, aimed at reinforcing Greco-Roman stereotypes about an effeminate, despotic, and violent East.[18]

The story begins with Semiramis's birth in the city of Ashkelon on the Eastern Mediterranean coast. Her mother, Derceto, is a Syrian goddess who has indulged in an affair with a good-looking youth. Deeply ashamed of her carnal union with a mortal man, Derceto exposes her baby daughter in the wilderness and then throws herself into a nearby lake, assuming the body of a fish with a human head. The situation of the motherless and abandoned little girl seems hopeless, but, against all odds, Derceto's daughter survives: she is nurtured by doves and then recovered by a group of shepherds, whose headman calls her Semiramis "after the word that, in the language of the Syrians, means 'dove,'" Diodorus explains. Semiramis is raised by the shepherds and becomes a great beauty. When an Assyrian officer, Onnes, on business in the Levant, sees her, he immediately falls in love with her and takes her as his wife. But his marital felicity is short-lived: Semiramis, brought by her husband to Bactra, proves herself a cunning military strategist when she devises a way to conquer the besieged enemy city, and thus catches the eye of the Assyrian king Ninus, who prompts Onnes to commit suicide so he can marry Semiramis himself. For a while, Ninus and Semiramis rule together. Following Ninus's death, Semiramis assumes the leadership of the Assyrian Empire alone. She continues to wage war in faraway regions while at the same time pursuing an intense love life: the thousands of artificial mounds found throughout the Near East are allegedly the tombs of her paramours, all killed after spending a night with the queen—a "Scheherazade-in-reverse" motif. When Semiramis finally dies, leaving the empire in the hands of her son Ninyas, she rises to heaven in the shape of a dove.[19]

The story of Semiramis, "the most renowned of all women," was told in the ancient world in many variations. A Greek novel—the earliest extant example of the genre—portrays her relationship with King Ninus in the form of a kitschy romance. In one of his epigrams, the Roman poet Martial turns her into a highly accomplished fashion designer. And the first-century CE Latin writer Valerius Maximus is particularly intrigued by her hairstyle. In an episode later often depicted in Western art, he reports, "Semiramis...was busy doing her hair when news came that Babylon had revolted. Leaving one half of it loose, she immediately ran to storm the city, and did not restore her coiffure to a seemly order before she brought it back into her power."[20]

Semiramis gained some eminence in the East as well. Early evidence for her fame is found in a cuneiform document written between 189 and 187 BCE in Hellenistic Uruk. It records a donation of three slaves by a woman of Greek descent who was called Shamê-rammata—which most likely stands for "Semiramis." Her seal shows the head of a female figure with the hair worn in a bun at the back—which is slightly disappointing, given Valerius Maximus's obsession with Semiramis's free-flowing tresses.[21]

In fact, even though it is better known from classical sources, the Semiramis legend must have originated in Mesopotamia and the Levant. Long before the Uruk reference to "Shamê-rammata," Ctesias, after all, had heard about Semiramis at the Persian court. The link between Semiramis's name and the Assyro-Babylonian word for "dove," *summu*, and the close connection of the name of Onnes, Semiramis's first husband, with that of Uanna, an antediluvian fish-man, primeval sage, and protégé of the god Ea, clearly demonstrate the legend's Mesopotamian roots as well. The earliest versions of the Semiramis saga probably circulated in Aramaic but are lost because they were written on perishable materials such as leather and papyrus.

THE LIKELY EXISTENCE OF AN ARAMAIC SEMIRAMIS TRADITION brings us back to the Book of Jonah, which tells the story of the prophet Jonah, son of Amittai. In very broad strokes, the narrative runs as follows: Deeply distressed by God's command to go to Nineveh and preach to its people, Jonah decides to set out in the opposite direction. He travels to Jaffa on the Eastern Mediterranean coast and boards a ship leaving for Tarshish on the Iberian Peninsula in the Far West. He never gets there, though: the ship is caught in a violent storm and the sailors throw Jonah into the sea. It is a moment of deadly peril. But Jonah is swallowed by a large fish and thus miraculously saved. After three days in the fish's belly—an episode later read as a prefiguration of Jesus's three days in the grave—Jonah is spewed out upon the dry land. A changed man, he decides to accept his divine mission and travels to Nineveh, where he starts preaching to the residents of the city. To his surprise and dismay, they repent, and are thereupon spared by God.

It is a strange story, one that has fascinated but also baffled its readers for more than two thousand years. This is especially true for the fish episode. The explanations so far offered for it, none really persuasive, have ranged from the assumption, made by an eighteenth-century German abbot, that Jonah spent some time in an alehouse called "The Whale" on an island in the middle of the sea, to claims that the motif is rooted in Indian mythology.[22]

Comparison with the Semiramis legend may actually help us understand the story of Jonah a little better. The two tales have several points in common: Jonah's name means "dove," the bird so closely associated with Semiramis. He departs from Jaffa, a harbor city not far from Ashkelon, Semiramis's birthplace. Jonah's mysterious three-day-long sojourn in the belly of the fish is reminiscent of what happens to Semiramis's mermaid-like mother, Derceto. The life journeys of both Jonah and Semiramis end at Nineveh. And both stories share a "global" setting and an imperial worldview that is quite different from the more inward-looking perspective of other prophetic books of the Bible. In other words, the Book of Jonah seems like a weirdly distorted version of the story of Semiramis.

To be sure, Jonah's name also has another reference point: according to 2 Kings 14:25, a "Jonah son of Amittai" had served as an eighth-century war prophet. But the parallels with the Semiramis legend are so close that it is hard not to arrive at the conclusion that the unknown author of the Book of Jonah—which was composed at some point between the sixth and third centuries BCE—drew on it when composing his story. What prompted him to transform a semidivine queen into a male prophet remains unclear, but the transformation itself is very much in line with the many metamorphoses that are found in the story of the Assyrian empress. Jonah, then, may well be another biblical figure modeled on an Assyrian prototype, albeit one from legend rather than history.

A FEW CLASSICAL AUTHORS—AND ALSO THE BABYLONIAN PRIEST Berossus in his Greek account of Mesopotamian civilization—briefly mention Assyrian kings such as Tiglath-pileser III, Sennacherib, and Esarhaddon. Most Greek and Roman historians, however, very much in contrast to the biblical tradition, have nothing to say about the period bracketed by the beginning of the Assyrian Empire—the era of Ninus, Semiramis, and Ninyas—and the time of its final collapse. Between these two poles, they claim, some thirty or forty kings had ruled Assyria, for a period of about a millennium and a half in total, but without ever accomplishing anything worth recording. It is an image of complete stagnation—an orientalist trope conveniently in line with Greek and Roman ideas about a largely unchanging barbarian East. But at the end of this eternal recurrence of the same, the Assyrian Empire suddenly finds itself in the grip of a major crisis—and history begins again.

For the classical historians, the central figure in the unfolding drama was Sardanapallus, Assyria's alleged last king. Herodotus, the first Greek writer to mention this ruler, characterizes him as rich and powerful. But Diodorus and other later historians describe Sardanapallus as an effeminate weakling, confined to his palace in Nineveh and unwilling to deal with the outside world. With skin "even whiter than milk, and painted eyelids," he is said to have "lived the life of a woman, spending his days in the company of his concubines and spinning purple garments." Worse still, "he pursued the delights of love with men as well as with women; for he practiced sexual indulgence of all kinds with no restraints." His sluggishness is so pronounced that the Median Arbaces and the Babylonian Belesys eventually launch a rebellion against him. Sardanapallus is forced into action, and the two sides become embroiled in a series of deadly battles. In the end, when the Tigris overflows and Nineveh's defensive walls collapse, Sardanapallus has to acknowledge that the game is over. He builds a large funeral pyre, with all his treasures piled upon it and his concubines and eunuchs boxed in, and commits suicide with them in a massive conflagration. His death marks the end of the Assyrian Empire.[23]

Sardanapallus's pleasure-seeking character also surfaces in an alternative classical tradition, one that deals with the king's tomb. This tomb was allegedly located in Cilicia, near the city of Anchiale, and had been seen in 333 BCE by soldiers and officers of the army of Alexander the Great. According to the Greek historian Aristobulus, a friend of Alexander who accompanied him on his campaign to the East, the tomb was decorated with a figure "with the fingers of the right hand brought closely together, as if snapping them," and inscribed, "in Assyrian letters," with the words "'Sardanapallus, the son of Anacyndaraxes, built Anchiale and Tarsus in a single day. Eat, drink, and love; the rest's not worth even this'—by 'this' meaning the snap of a finger."[24]

What is described here actually resonates with some genuinely Assyrian motifs. The "snapping" of the fingers could be an allusion to a characteristic gesture found on many Assyrian royal stelae: the Assyrian king extends the forefinger of his right hand in an act of worship. And the reference to food, drink, and merrymaking is strikingly similar to the prophecy in the name of the goddess Ishtar that saved the Assyrian king Ashurbanipal, in 653 BCE, from having to go to war against Teumman of Elam. The key passage of the prophecy, already quoted earlier, reads, "You shall stay in the place where you currently are. Eat food, drink wine, make merry, and revere my divinity. In the meantime, I will go and accomplish this task."[25]

As a matter of fact, the name Sardanapallus is a distorted form of "Ashurbanipal"—and the two kings have a lot in common in other respects as well. To be sure, the Greeks supplied their Sardanapallus with a number of features that can yet again be considered the result of an orientalizing "othering." And they got certain things badly wrong: Ashurbanipal was not the last king of Assyria; he did not die in a conflagration (even though his brother Shamash-shumu-ukin did); and he had no tomb in Cilicia. But Ashurbanipal was indeed reluctant to go to war, nominated his chief singer as eponym, and relied heavily on eunuchs, and he is the only Assyrian king who had himself depicted reclining on a bed and banqueting with his queen. That beds were important to him is also indicated by a letter in which he asked scholars from Borsippa to send him "(tablets describing?) four stone amulets for the head of the king's bed and the foot of the king's bed." Ashurbanipal, it seems, was an aesthete and bon vivant rather than a battle-hardened leader, even though he sought to portray himself in some inscriptions as the latter as well.[26]

Ashurbanipal was no longer in office when the Assyrian Empire collapsed; but his rule—which dragged on for far too long—contributed in decisive ways to Assyria's political decline. Regardless of their sensationalism, then, the accounts of the Greek historians do not completely misrepresent the reign of this remarkable ruler.

THE MASCULINE QUEEN SEMIRAMIS, COFOUNDER OF THE ASSYR-ian Empire, and the effeminate king Sardanapallus, its gravedigger, became "models of exceptionality" in the West. The topsy-turvy world they represented served as a warning never to do away with the patriarchal values and binary gender identities that undergirded the Occident's political and social order. But as representatives of something radically different, the two characters also had the potential to fascinate and open up new horizons. The stories that circulated about Assyria's first queen and last king were reminders that alternative modes of life, sexual relations, and gender identities existed, and that politics did not have to remain forever the domain of men alone. The way later writers, painters, and even composers engaged with Semiramis and Sardanapallus—and to a lesser extent with other figures of Mesopotamian history—illustrates this pronounced ambivalence.[27]

Sardanapallus's lifestyle was usually disparaged rather than praised. Among his ancient critics was the Roman poet Juvenal, who was active in the late first and early second centuries CE. In one of his satires, Juvenal asks his readers to "pray for a bold spirit, free from all dread of death, that deems the gnawing cares of Hercules, and all his cruel toils, far preferable to the joys of Venus, rich banquets, and the downy couch of Sardanapallus." The *pluma Sardanapalli* became a trope so popular that the Middle Ages credited Sardanapallus with the invention of the featherbed—a compelling idea if one takes the historical Ashurbanipal's actual obsession with the divan into account. The most famous pictorial elaboration of the motif is Eugène Delacroix's 1827 painting *The Death of Sardanapallus*, which shows the king, with his slain concubines, horse, and treasures around him, reclining on a huge bed that seems to slide menacingly toward the spectator. But unlike Juvenal, Delacroix portrays the king with a certain degree of sympathy. By so carefully arranging the tableau of his own final departure, Sardanapallus becomes in the picture a kind of model artist in his own right.[28]

Already in antiquity, Sardanapallus was occasionally presented in a more positive light. A notable example is a Roman statue of the god Dionysus as an older man with an ivy wreath and a long beard. At some point, someone supplied the statue with an inscription that identified it as an image of Sardanapallus, suggesting that at least some Roman citizens considered the Assyrian king a role model for a good life, spent with drink and pleasure, in line with the example set by a prominent deity.[29]

Unsurprisingly, the rise of Christianity put an end to such endorsements, and for several centuries, both Sardanapallus and Semiramis became unalloyed villains. The Late Antique Christian writer Orosius describes Sardanapallus as "a man more corrupt than a woman," which says it all. A section in Dante's *Divine Comedy* on twelfth-century Florence and its not-yet-corrupted ways obliquely alludes to the king's sexual perversions: "And Sardanapallus had not arrived / To show what may be done in private rooms." Semiramis fares even worse. Dante places her in the Second Circle of Hell and presents her as the first of several lustful souls who are punished by an infernal gale: "That empress / Who ruled over so many lands and languages," he writes, "She was so at the mercy of sensuality, / That she made laws allowing what she liked / So that her own conduct could not be blamed." Dante also talks about Sennacherib, whose fate was known to him from the Bible. Carved into the floor of the first terrace of Purgatory, he claims, among many other *exempla* of pride and how it was punished, was a scene that "showed how the sons of Sennacherib / Threw themselves on him in the temple / And how, when he was dead, they left him there."[30]

With the Renaissance and the onset of the early modern period, more sympathetic representations of Assyria's most famous characters began to complement the condemnations and indictments. Semiramis in particular received a lot of attention—not only as a *femme fatale*, but also a *femme forte*. Leading painters, from Guido Reni to Edgar Degas, depicted her power and beauty. Even more remarkable is Semiramis's popularity in the *opera seria* of the Baroque age. A recent study lists no fewer than nineteen operas from this period that feature Semiramis as their main protagonist. Some were composed to celebrate powerful women of the time. When, for example, the Habsburg empress Maria Theresa was crowned Queen of Bohemia on May 12, 1743, in St. Vitus Cathedral in Prague, the occasion was marked with a performance of a Semiramis opera.[31]

Sardanapallus was rediscovered as well. His role as a political and military leader offered few incentives to rehabilitate him, but those who hoped for the dawn of a more libertine age were intrigued by his erotic pursuits. The seventeenth-century English satirist and translator John Oldham dedicated a poem to Sardanapallus that is so obviously pornographic that one could not quote from it were it not for its old-fashioned language:

> *Methinks I see thee now in full Seraglio stand,*
> *With Love's great Scepter in thy hand,*
> *And over all its Spacious Realm thy Power extend:*
> *Ten Thousand Maids lye prostrate at thy Feet*
> *Ready thy Pintle's high Commands to meet.*
> *All C—ts of Honor, some of Queenly Breed*
> *That come to be Anointed with thy Royal Seed.*
>
> . . .
>
> *For as wide Nature spreads her Thighs*
> *Thy Tarse's vast Dominion lyes.*
> *All Womankind acknowledge its great Sway*
> *And to its large Treasury their Tribute pay.*
>
> . . .
>
> *And through all Ages, all Posterity,*
> *This my sole Glory shall Recorded be:*
> *No Monarch ever FUCK'd or Dy'd like Me!*[32]

The poem ends in style by portraying the immolation of the king and his women on the funeral pyre as a gigantic orgy.

DURING THE FIRST HALF OF THE NINETEENTH CENTURY, SEMIRA-mis and Sardanapallus experienced their last great moments in Western high art. Rossini's *Semiramide* from 1823 marked the climax of the genre of the "Semiramis opera." Two years earlier, Lord Byron had written a tragedy, "Sardanapalus," in which the protagonist served as a kind of alter ego of the author. "If then they hate me, 'tis because I hate not," Sardanapallus is quoted as saying, a statement highly uncharacteristic of the historical Ashurbanipal. Byron's drama inspired Delacroix's famous painting as well as an 1830 cantata on Sardanapallus by Hector Berlioz, but it failed to impress the man to whom it was dedicated: Johann Wolfgang von Goethe. In Goethe's *Faust II*, when the devil Mephistopheles offers to enable Faust to live the luxurious life of a lazy ruler, Faust responds with the words "Schlecht und modern! Sardanapal!" (Base and modern! Sardanapalus!).

Lord Byron is also associated with one of the last great artistic works based on the portrayal of an Assyrian king in the Bible. Written in a "galloping" anapestic meter, his 1815 poem "The Destruction of Sennacherib," which begins with the much-quoted line "The Assyrian came down like the wolf on the fold," draws on 2 Kings 19:35–36 when it ascribes the Assyrian defeat at Jerusalem to a direct divine intervention:

> *For the Angel of Death spread his wings on the*
> *   blast,*
> *And breathed in the face of the foe as he passed;*
> *And the eyes of the sleepers waxed deadly and*
> *   chill,*
> *And their hearts but once heaved, and for ever*
> *   grew still!*

In the wake of the rediscovery in the mid-nineteenth century of Assyria's "authentic" history, the biblical and classical accounts of the Assyrian Empire lost much of their authority. Assyria's semi-legendary rulers suddenly had to compete with the empire's "real" monarchs. Since these monarchs lacked the magnetism of the former, Semiramis, Sardanapallus, and the biblical Sennacherib, however, were never entirely sidelined. Paintings, poems, novels, musical compositions, and eventually even movies continued to feature them. But most of the works in question, whether Lytton Strachey's 1915 antiwar essay "Sennacherib and Rupert Brooke," Arthur Honegger and Paul Valéry's musical melodrama *Sémiramis* from 1934, or the Italian sword-and-sandal film *Io Semiramide* from 1962, failed to gain broad acclaim. As time went by, Semiramis's important role as the oriental *femme fatale* par excellence was more and more taken over by the Egyptian queen Cleopatra. Sennacherib and Sardanapallus fell into even greater obscurity.

One central event in the history of the twentieth century looks, however, as if it might have been inspired by the Sardanapallus saga. Adolf Hitler's suicide, with wife and dog, on April 30, 1945, in the Führerbunker of the Reich Chancellery in Berlin, seems like a farce-like reenactment of the Assyrian king's self-immolation, especially in view of the subsequent burning of the bodies. That it was really modeled on it, deliberately or in some subconscious way, cannot, of course, be proven.[33]

18

The Second Destruction

On February 25, 2015, the militant Islamic State group, also known as the Islamic State of Iraq and Syria (ISIS), posted a video on its social media channels.[1] Its first scene shows the Nergal Gate on the north side of the ancient city of Nineveh. Inside the gate can be seen a beautifully carved monumental bull colossus made of hard stone. The footage proceeds to document, in painful detail, the work of a man in black clothing, standing on a platform and armed with an electric drill, as he systematically destroys the head of the sculpture, cutting deeply into its fine facial features and its carefully crafted beard. Another man, standing next to the colossus and wearing traditional Islamic garb, explains, in an Arabic dialect that marks him as coming somewhere from the Arabian Gulf, "The Prophet Muhammad commanded us to shatter and destroy statues. This is what his companions did when they conquered lands. Since God commanded us to shatter and destroy these statues, idols, and remains, it is easy for us to obey. We do not care what other people think or if this costs us billions of dollars." The scene is followed by a second one, filmed inside the Mosul Museum, a few kilometers across the Tigris River. Men in strange attire are shown toppling Assyrian and Parthian statues and smashing them with sledgehammers, while verses from the Quran are recited and a voice offscreen sings in the style of a traditional *nashid*: "Hell is filled with idols and wooden images. Demolish the statues of America and its clan."[2]

Thus began the second destruction of Assyria's great capitals, more than two and a half millennia after the first. Just like in 612 BCE, the winged bulls in the gate buildings of Nineveh's city wall succumbed to an enemy whose deadly force they could not withstand. Rage against the global modern world had been converted into an attack on the ancient remains of the first "global" empire, with catastrophic results. The perpetrators put into practice what the loathsome Père Ubu had only fantasized about in Alfred Jarry's satirical play *Ubu in Chains*: "We shall not have succeeded in demolishing everything unless we demolish the ruins as well."[3]

THE CONDITIONS FOR THE DISASTER HAD BEEN CREATED WHEN, on June 10, 2014, to the surprise and horror of much of the world and many Iraqis, ISIS seized the city of Mosul. On June 29, ISIS's leader, Abu Bakr al-Baghdadi, used Mosul's Great Mosque to announce the establishment of a new Islamic caliphate. All of a sudden, what had once been the heartland of the Assyrian Empire was under the control of an extremely violent military group dead set on a mission of ethnic and cultural cleansing.

The movement that would later develop into the Islamic State had been founded in 1999 by the Jordanian jihadist Abu Musab al-Zarqawi. It gained momentum and many new recruits after the US-led invasion of Iraq in 2003, was involved in numerous terrorist attacks inside Iraq, and became even more influential after it expanded its activities into neighboring Syria in the wake of the outbreak of the Syrian Civil War in 2011. In 2013, after the movement rebranded itself as ISIS, it took control of the Syrian city of Raqqa, which became its de facto capital for more than three years.

It was in Raqqa that ISIS initiated its radical program of cultural mass destruction. During the previous ten years, many religious shrines, archaeological sites, museums, and monuments in Iraq and

Syria had been damaged or destroyed as the result of looting, shelling, and the implementation of military installations, with all sides engaged in the ongoing conflicts sharing part of the blame. But what ISIS started shortly after having seized Raqqa was something fundamentally new: the group began to deliberately tear down cultural heritage sites that it deemed incompatible with its Salafist ideology.

On March 26, 2014, ISIS militants demolished one of its first targets, the Shiite shrine of Uwais al-Qarni in Raqqa. Numerous other Shiite shrines and tombs were to follow. ISIS militants likewise attacked Christian churches and monasteries, Sufi shrines, and places holy to the religious community of Yazidis.

Although Syria has no Assyrian archaeological sites on the scale of Nineveh or Calah, some Assyrian-period artifacts were destroyed as well during the early phase of ISIS's assault on history. In April 2014, the Syrian Directorate-General of Antiquities and Museums posted an online notice about bas-reliefs and statues that local residents had illicitly excavated at Tell Ajaja, the ancient city of Shadikanni on the Khabur River. As revealed by a number of photos, they included an Assyrian statue from the 820s BCE with an inscription that threatened anyone "who would destroy this image" with the extermination of his offspring. Syrian members of ISIS, unable to read cuneiform, were undeterred: photos released online on May 5, 2014, show ISIS supporters with sledgehammers in hand smashing one of the statues from Tell Ajaja in front of a building the group had repurposed as an Islamic court.[4]

After the conquest of Mosul, ISIS intensified its campaign of cultural vandalism. Many religious buildings in and around the city were razed to the ground. On July 24, 2014, ISIS affiliates armed with explosives blew up the mosque of Jonas on the eastern side of the Tigris, reducing it to rubble. Considering that the mosque was not a Shiite but a Sunni holy place, this was a stunningly radical action, one that indicated that nothing would henceforth be safe from the group's lust for destruction.

Somewhat surprisingly, the Assyrian sites that had come under ISIS's control after its expansion into the Mosul region were initially left untouched. For a few months, nothing happened at Nineveh and Calah/Nimrud. But this was only the calm before the storm. Any hopes local residents and international observers might have entertained that the ancient Assyrian capitals would be spared were shattered when ISIS posted its February 2015 video of the devastation at Nineveh's Nergal Gate and in the Mosul Museum. It was a catastrophic turning point for the archaeology of ancient Assyria.

UP UNTIL THEN, ARCHAEOLOGICAL SITES IN NORTHERN IRAQ had suffered relatively little damage throughout the various political crises that had gripped Iraq since the beginning of the Iran-Iraq War in 1980. The situation in the south of the country was far different, as the economic sanctions imposed by the UN Security Council after the end of the Gulf War in 1991 had led to complete anarchy and to massive looting sprees at many sites. In the wake of the US-led invasion of 2003, the looting in the south had become even worse. The ruins of ancient cities such as Isin or Umma began to resemble lunar landscapes, with hole after hole dotting the mounds.

During the same period, Nineveh and some of the other sites in northern Iraq suffered from neglect and minor looting, but they largely remained intact. In the 1990s, the structure meant to protect the remains of Sennacherib's throne room on Nineveh's main mound of Kuyunjik had been stripped of its tin roof, exposing the bas-reliefs of the room to the elements; and a few reliefs had been broken into pieces and sold on the antiquities market. But little else happened. In fact, in 2010 archaeologists of the University of Mosul resumed excavations at Nineveh, hoping to inaugurate a new phase in the scientific exploration of the site.[5]

Promising developments like this were brutally cut short when the leadership of ISIS decided, early in 2015, to launch its concerted attack on the archaeological landscape of the Mosul region. The widely broadcast disfiguration of the bull colossus in Nineveh's Nergal Gate was only the beginning. On April 11, 2015, the terrorist group released a carefully choreographed new video showing how militants had arranged barrel bombs in front of the walls of Ashurnasirpal II's throne room in Calah's Northwest Palace, and then blew up the whole room and adjoining parts of the palace in a gigantic explosion. It was a major disaster: the only building well enough preserved to provide visitors on the ground with an impression of Assyrian palatial architecture had been reduced to rubble, and dozens of irreplaceable relief slabs were irretrievably lost. Later, the massive ziggurat of the god Ninurta, Calah's patron deity, was bulldozed away, and the temple of Nabû, with its remarkable "Fish Gate" (thus called because the gate was flanked by sculptures of mermen or mermaids), demolished. The tombs of the Assyrian queens in the southern area of the Northwest Palace were destroyed as well.

Other northern Iraqi sites also suffered substantial damage. At Hatra, the Parthian-period commercial center located some 50 kilometers (30 miles) west of Ashur, militants armed with assault rifles and sledgehammers wrecked statues and wall decorations of temples. Dur-Sharrukin and the old Assyrian capital of Ashur saw some deliberate destruction, too, with a focus, in the case of Ashur, on the elaborately restored Tabira Gate in the west of the city. At Nineveh, two additional city gates, the so-called Adad and Mashqi Gates, were leveled by bulldozers. Since they were for the most part modern reconstructions, this was a loss not quite as catastrophic as others. But the dismantling of the remaining bas-reliefs from Sennacherib's throne-room suite on Kuyunjik at some point in April or early May in 2016 was another devastating blow.[6]

Along with acts of deliberate destruction, ISIS engaged in the extraction of Assyrian artifacts for commercial purposes. After the mosque of the prophet Jonah on Nebi Yunus in the southwestern part of Nineveh had been blown up, workmen operating on behalf of the group dug tunnels into the mound underneath the rubble. Following

413

the walls of an old palace of the Assyrian king Esarhaddon—a method similar to that used at Nineveh by Austen Henry Layard and other mid-nineteenth-century British excavators—they were hunting for archaeological treasures that could be put up for sale. A document in Arabic found after the liberation of Mosul reports that, "thanks to a favor granted by Allah, on Sunday, the 28th of Raǧab, 1436 (May 17, 2015), in the course of excavation work in two spots on Tell Nebi Yunus, pieces of an Assyrian brick inscribed in ancient cuneiform were discovered in the first spot, and a massive winged bull came to light in the second spot; and we ask Allah for guidance and success." The document was addressed to the "Ministry of Natural Resources," which the Islamic State had established to sell oil, minerals, precious metals, and antiquities. Even terrorists have their bureaucracy.[7]

For a while, the head of this ministry was a senior ISIS leader best known under his nom de guerre, Abu Sayyaf al-Tunisi. In May 2015, while ISIS workmen were excavating at Nebi Yunus, US Special Forces conducted a raid on Abu Sayyaf's headquarters near the town of Der ez-Zor in eastern Syria. Among the items seized in the operation were multiple antiquities as well as computer files with photos of additional archaeological artifacts. One of the objects depicted on the photos was an Assyrian stela from Tell Ajaja (Shadikanni) inscribed in cuneiform in the name of a ninth-century BCE Assyrian governor, Shamash-abuya. In a landmark cultural heritage case, the stela and three other objects, all probably put up for sale by ISIS, were forfeited in December 2016 under the USA Patriot Act, but they still have not been recovered.[8]

THE DELIBERATE DESTRUCTION OF ASSYRIAN AND OTHER CUL-tural sites in Iraq by the Islamic State has received international condemnation in the strongest terms. A resolution adopted by the United Nations General Assembly on May 28, 2015, called it a war crime, and the director-general of UNESCO at the time, Irina Bokova, spoke of "cultural cleansing." Such assessments are certainly appropriate, but they do not answer a crucial question: Given that it would have been much more lucrative for the group to just stick to looting and selling antiquities (which it did as well), what was it that prompted ISIS to commit these acts in the first place and then widely broadcast them?[9]

While the February 25, 2015, ISIS video described at the beginning of this chapter provides some clues, a more extensive explanation is found in an article published in 2015 in the eighth issue of *Dabiq*, a professionally made English-language propaganda magazine freely distributed by ISIS on the Internet. The article attempted to justify the attacks on Nineveh, Hatra, and the Mosul Museum:

> Last month, the soldiers of the Khilāfah, with sledgehammers in hand, revived the Sunnah of their father Ibrāhīm (*'alayhis-salām*) when they laid waste to the *shirkī* legacy of a nation that had long passed from the face of the Earth. They entered the ruins of the ancient Assyrians in Wilāyat Nīnawā and demolished their statues, sculptures, and engravings of idols and kings. This caused an outcry from the enemies of the Islamic State, who were furious at losing a "treasured heritage." The *mujāhidīn*, however, were not the least bit concerned about the feelings and sentiments of the *kuffār*.... The *kuffār* had unearthed these statues and ruins in recent generations and attempted to portray them as part of a cultural heritage and identity that the Muslims of Iraq should embrace and be proud of. Yet this opposes the guidance of Allah and His Messenger and only serves a nationalist agenda.[10]

The passage gives a whole range of reasons for the destruction inflicted by ISIS on Assyrian sites and objects. The first is religious. When Islamic State militants assaulted the ancient sculptures with sledgehammers, the article claims, they essentially reenacted what "Ibrahim," that is, Abraham—and later also the prophet Muhammad—supposedly did in their own time: smashing idols and other images set up by "infidels" misled by their *shirkī*, that is, polytheistic beliefs. The archaic—and for outside viewers slightly ridiculous—clothes worn by the perpetrators in the videos and in the photos of the attacks were chosen for a reason: they were meant to convey that the demolition crews were following a precedent from Islam's formative period—or rather, ISIS's conception of it—even in small details such as attire.[11]

Of course, no one worships Assyrian- and Parthian-period sculptures anymore; and most of the statues that ISIS destroyed were actually not representations of gods. But it is nonetheless easy to understand why ISIS operatives would consider a monumental sculpture such as the winged bull in Nineveh's Nergal Gate an abomination. The human-headed Assyrian bull and lion colossi were composite creatures—they combined the features of different species, from animals to deities. For ISIS and its monochromatic cult of undiluted religious simplicity and purity, this complexity must have been particularly vexing and provocative.[12]

When ISIS militants, a few weeks after the events at Nineveh, embarked on the logistically far more challenging project of obliterating the archaeological remains of the ancient Assyrian city of Calah, it may have been the modern name of the site, Nimrud, that caused them to be particularly thorough. In Islamic tradition (which draws on earlier Jewish precedents), Nimrud—the biblical Nimrod—was the villain who built the Tower of Babel, an arch-polytheist, proto-imperialist tyrant, and the chief opponent of Abraham. In Islamic legend, God was said to have punished him in the most gruesome way possible: a mosquito entered his head through his nostril, pecked at his brain, and eventually killed him. Clearly, a city named after a figure that evil did not deserve to be treated any better.[13]

ALL THINGS CONSIDERED, THEN, IT WOULD BE A MISTAKE TO downplay *Dabiq*'s claim that ISIS destroyed ancient sites because the sites embodied the perils of worshipping false gods. The movement's radical religious ideology did matter. But regarding ISIS's cultural politics as nothing but an attempt to reenact life in Muhammad's seventh-century world is not enough to explain the group's actions— too many contradictions remain. ISIS claimed, for example, that images were a religious abomination—but the group constantly produced images of its own, living and still, that were then widely disseminated through social media: videos and photos of beheadings, of prisoners held in cages, of military attacks—and also of the destruction of ancient sites. In other words, ISIS broadcast its own acts of iconoclasm in an orgy of iconophilia that seems very much at odds with Muslim orthodoxy. And ironically, as many others have observed, the images that ISIS produced were heavily influenced by the aesthetics of Western video games—for example, *Call of Duty*— as well as movies and television series from *The Terminator* to *Game of Thrones*. ISIS quite successfully adopted the cultural codes of its greatest enemies. What is more, a few passages in the Quran seem to regard ancient ruins as visible warnings for those who question God's power to interfere in history, implying that they should be preserved rather than destroyed.[14]

There were, in fact, important additional reasons for ISIS's deliberate attacks on ancient Assyrian sites. The passage from *Dabiq* spells them out quite explicitly: the assaults were meant, on one hand, to devastate the unbelieving *kuffār* from the West and, on the other, to reshape the cultural identity of the Muslims of Iraq.

Regarding the former group, some of ISIS's claims were quite accurate. It was indeed the Western "unbelievers" who "had unearthed these statues and ruins in recent generations." Scholar-adventurers from Britain and France had initiated the archaeological exploration of the Middle East, a project inseparable from colonial motivations (even though it was also rooted in genuine intellectual interests). A medal cast in Paris in 1853 says it all. It shows on one side the head of the French emperor Napoleon III and on the other a figure representing France lifting a veil from a sitting female figure flanked by a bull colossus—a personification of the ancient city of Nineveh. The scene is accompanied by a Latin inscription: "Niniven latentem Gallia aperuit" (France has opened up long-buried Nineveh).[15]

Not only were the excavations of the Assyrian sites for a long time a largely Western endeavor, in which local residents would normally participate only as humble workmen, but the history uncovered in the process was considered an essentially Western one as well. To be sure, Assyria's reputation was far from unblemished in the eyes of many. But since the Assyrian Empire had played such an important role in the Bible and in the works of Greek and Roman writers, it was part of the history, sacred and profane, of the Western world, to which it first and foremost belonged. What happened later in the region, especially during the Islamic period, was perceived by many as a decadent and corrupt historical coda detached from the heroic history of the ancient Near East. It was, hence, only fair, in the eyes of Western audiences, that Assyrian and Babylonian art was put on display in Paris and London rather than in Istanbul and Baghdad—even though these cities would eventually likewise sport museums dedicated to the ancient Near East.

The leaders of ISIS were well aware of the West's infatuation with the civilizations of ancient Mesopotamia. And since provoking the West and breaking Western taboos wherever possible was one of their key strategies—not least in order to garner as much public attention as possible and gain new recruits—it made a lot of sense for them to order attacks on Iraq's archaeological sites. The twisted plan proved to some extent successful. Whereas the humanitarian crimes that ISIS committed, from enslaving Yazidi women to forcing children to shoot political enemies, although not entirely ignored, were often not extensively covered by Western media, the deliberate attacks on Nineveh and Calah led to an enormous public outcry and an endless flow of news reports.

WESTERNERS, HOWEVER, WERE NOT THE ONLY PEOPLE WHOM ISIS sought to reach by vandalizing Assyrian and other ancient sites and then broadcasting these acts. As the *Dabiq* article explains, there were also the "Muslims of Iraq" who, swayed by a "nationalist agenda," were in danger of considering such sites part of their own "cultural heritage and identity"—rather than being Muslims alone.

Indeed, modern attempts at nation building in the post-Ottoman Middle East, in Iraq and Syria as well as in Iran, Lebanon, and Israel, have often tapped into the ancient history of the region. In the case of Iraq, with its randomly drawn modern borders, it proved particularly challenging to turn its people into a nation that transcended deep-rooted sectarian and ethnic divisions. From early on, the country's rulers found it therefore useful to celebrate the ancient civilizations that had once flourished in the land as a potentially unifying element and to promote their study.[16]

The state of Iraq had been founded in 1921 out of the merger of the Ottoman provinces of Basra, Baghdad, and Mosul. Five years later, in 1926, the Baghdad Archaeological Museum (later renamed the Iraq Museum) was established, with the British traveler and political officer Gertrude Bell serving as its first director. The museum displayed both Babylonian and Assyrian artifacts but initially remained a fairly low-key institution. During the years between 1932 and 1958, when Iraq was an independent monarchy, Pan-Arabism dominated attempts to form a national identity in the country. After the revolution of 1958 had turned Iraq into a republic, though, Iraqi political leaders began to put more and more emphasis on the country's glorious pre-Islamic past.[17]

In 1959, General Abd al-Karim Qasim introduced a new Iraqi flag, in which the star of the Mesopotamian goddess Ishtar was merged with the sun-disk of the god Shamash—a symbol also used as a watermark on Iraqi banknotes. When the Ba'ath Party regained power in 1968 after a five-year hiatus, officials stressed Iraq's Mesopotamian roots with even greater vigor. New excavations were sponsored, new museums built, and some of the ancient temples, palaces, and gates at Babylon and Nineveh reconstructed. The annual "Babylon Festival," held at the ancient site itself, featured musical and theatrical performances celebrating Iraq's ancient past and brought together state and party members, diplomats, scholars, and artists from different countries. The political nature of the festival found expression in its mottos, which ranged from "Nebuchadnezzar yesterday, Saddam Hussein today," to "From Nebuchadnezzar to Saddam Hussein: Babylon is rising again." In 2001, an international conference held in Baghdad, with great pomp, celebrated five thousand years of writing in Iraq. It was opened by Iraq's deputy prime minister and acting minister for foreign affairs, Tariq Aziz, an Assyrian Christian.[18]

Saddam Hussein, Iraq's brutal dictator from 1979 to 2003, was particularly fond of the Babylonian kings Hammurapi—the great lawgiver who turned Babylon into a major political player—and Nebuchadnezzar II, the conqueror of Jerusalem. But Assyria loomed large in his imagination as well. Billboards put up near Nineveh displayed Saddam as a new Ashurbanipal, hunting lions from an Assyrian-style chariot. And in 2000, Saddam of all people anonymously launched a kitschy romance novel, *Zabībah wal-malik* (Zabibah and the King), that celebrates, not without political undertones, the love relationship between a powerful Assyrian king and a Semiramis-like married woman of great beauty and intelligence.[19]

Assyria featured prominently on Iraqi banknotes and stamps. Between 1958 and 1979, the back of the ten-dinar note depicted an Assyrian winged bull and an Assyrian priest. After 1990, ten-dinar notes displayed an engraving of the Assyrian king Ashurbanipal riding a horse. And a one-thousand-dinar stamp issued in 2011, eight years after the US-led invasion of Iraq, showed the reconstructed entrance to Ashurnasirpal II's palace in Calah—the very building that ISIS would blow up with so much dedication only four years later.[20]

THE LEADERS OF ISIS WERE FULLY AWARE OF THE CENTRAL ROLE that Mesopotamian civilization played in the nation-building efforts of Iraq's secularist Ba'ath Party, and also—although less passionately—by the governments that ruled the country after 2003. And they resented this emphasis on the remote past. The caliphate that ISIS wished to create was bound to transcend the artificially drawn borders of the Middle Eastern nation-states and was supposed to be rooted in Islam alone. Archaeological sites and museums that summoned up thriving pre-Islamic civilizations, and that served as physical reminders of a history that challenged this narrow-minded ideology, had to be obliterated at all costs. This was what ISIS sought to achieve with its attacks on Assyrian sites in 2015 and 2016.

Yet even though the group succeeded in doing an enormous amount of physical damage, it failed, in the end, in its endeavor to wipe ancient Mesopotamia from the mental map of the Iraqi people. The "Unite for Heritage" campaign that Director-General Irina Bokova of UNESCO launched during a visit to Baghdad in March 2015 received significant support from many Iraqis. And in November 2015, the Iraqi postal service issued yet another set of stamps with Assyrian themes, created by the Iraqi artist Saad Ghazi. This time, they showed the severed head of an Assyrian winged bull plus a depiction of the Assyrian kings Sargon II and Sennacherib with a hammer in the foreground; in an adjacent text, in Arabic and English, they recalled "(the crime of) the destruction of Iraqi antiquities."[21]

Outside Iraq as well, a variety of events sought to keep the memory of Iraq's cultural heritage alive and to decry the actions that had been taken in the attempts to eradicate it. In London, in a particularly evocative example, the Iraqi American artist Michael Rakowitz created a sculpture of a massive winged bull that was based on the lost Assyrian bull colossus from the Nergal Gate. Made of more than ten thousand empty cans of Iraqi date syrup in various colors, it was set on the fourth plinth in Trafalgar Square in March 2018, to great public acclaim.[22]

On the ground in northern Iraq, the situation has changed too. No longer do ISIS militants roam freely across ancient Assyrian sites such as Nineveh, Calah, or Ashur. In July 2017, Iraqi government troops, allied with Kurdish and international forces, retook the city of Mosul, successfully completing an arduous and bloody operation that had, tellingly, been dubbed "We Are Coming, O Nineveh" (*qādimūn yā Naynawā*). The archaeological sites in the region have been secured, experts are studying the damage, and attempts are being made to start the process of restoring structures that have not been irretrievably lost. Initiatives such as the Nahrein Network, founded by University College London professor Eleanor Robson, are trying to empower local stakeholders—Iraqi archaeologists, curators, and educators—and to help them safeguard the cultural heritage of their homeland.[23]

Even excavations have resumed in northern Iraq. One of the paradoxes of archaeological fieldwork is that the knowledge gained through it results inevitably from destruction. In order to dig down into the past, one must first remove the upper layers. In that sense, the demolition of the mosque of Jonas on top of the mound of Nebi Yunus at Nineveh, and the creation of a network of tunnels underneath the rubble by ISIS workmen searching for ancient treasures, was not only a disaster but also an opportunity. What ISIS had done enabled a team of German and Iraqi archaeologists, under the direction of Peter Miglus and Stefan Maul from Heidelberg University, to conduct systematic excavations at the site for the first time ever. Since 2018, these excavations have produced new insights into the architecture and function of one of Assyria's most important monumental buildings: a palace with an adjoining arsenal constructed and used by the Assyrian kings Sennacherib, Esarhaddon, and Ashurbanipal. The finds made in various rooms of the building included the upper part of a scepter with Egyptian motifs—another testament to Assyria's fascination with the land on the Nile—and cuneiform documents from the archive of the wife of Sîn-sharru-ishkun, Assyria's last king.[24]

Despite all the setbacks, then, and even though fundamentalists and iconoclasts may continue to resist it, the quest to better understand ancient Assyria continues. Future excavations—whether on the ground in Iraq or in museum and university collections all over the world—will confirm some of the arguments made in this book, disprove others, and reveal some completely new and unexpected aspects of Assyrian history. Much is still to be learned about the world's first empire, its political organization, the ways in which it helped create a more "global" economy and new communication networks—and how it coped with, and was eventually overwhelmed by, a whole set of challenges. Many of these, from epidemics to climate change to the rise of populist leaders, remain pressing issues today—issues that can be better understood through the study of earlier instances in which they occurred.

Epilogue

A fairy tale from the collection of the Brothers Grimm tells of a poor fisherman who lives with his wife in a modest hut on the sea. One day, the fisherman catches a flounder that turns out to be an enchanted prince. The flounder asks to be set free, and the fisherman obliges, but when he returns home, his wife scolds him for not having asked the magical fish for a nice house in return for his release. The fisherman goes back to the sea and his wish is granted. But the fisherman's wife is still not content: she asks, next, to live in a palace, and then to become king, emperor, and pope. Every time, the fisherman returns to the sea, which grows more and more fierce, and every time, the flounder gives him what he asks for. But when, at the end, at his wife's request, the fisherman tells the flounder that she wants to be like God, the flounder responds, with a terrible storm churning the sea, "Just go home, she is sitting in the old hut again."

Assyrian history followed a similar trajectory. It began in the third millennium BCE with the small city-state of Ashur. As time passed, "Ashur" became, first, a powerful territorial state, on a par with Babylonia and Egypt, and then, in the middle of the eighth century BCE, a massive empire that ruled large parts of Western Asia. But in the late seventh century, within no more than just a few years, it totally collapsed, never to be restored—except for the city where everything had started, where elements of Assyrian culture and religion survived for another eight hundred years. After that, the world's first empire lived on only in the memory of later civilizations and the legends of the Church of the East.

BASED ON TENS OF THOUSANDS OF CUNEIFORM TEXTS AND other artifacts excavated at Assyrian and other sites, this book has tried to give an up-to-date account of what is now known about Assyria, and the Assyrian Empire in particular. Toward its end, one last question remains: What really was the Assyrian state? Was it an oppressive machine that exploited the riches of its neighbors, or, at least in some respects, was it also a force for good? Scholars and other students of Assyrian history have so far given very different answers. The Assyriologist Jo Ann Scurlock, while acknowledging that "imperialists" may not always do the right thing, emphasized that, at least "in the judgment of the Biblical prophets"—who she claims knew what they were talking about—"the Assyrians represented the best that empires (and indeed human governance) had to offer."[1]

But other voices—following in the footsteps of Jacques de Morgan's pithy 1909 statement, "Ashur was its god, plunder its morals, material pleasure its goal, and cruelty and terror its means"—have repeatedly stressed the empire's dark sides. In 2016, the archaeologist Susan Pollock, criticizing what she considered a pro-Assyrian bias in modern scholarship, decried a lack of interest in the suffering of the victims of Assyrian wars. Jonathan Jones, an art critic at *The Guardian*, said that, when "passing from the British Museum's Assyrian Galleries to the graceful grandeur of ancient Egypt or the Greek gods exhibited nearby," he sensed "a greater human richness." He felt that "Egypt and Greece were civilizations; Assyria was not." Finally, to quote an example from popular culture, in Larry R. Gonick's *Cartoon History of the Universe* the reader encounters an Assyrian king who asks himself, in despair, "O dear! Wot shall it be today? Flay, flog, mutilate, impale, or put them on leashes in doghouses?"[2]

Such negative verdicts, however, especially when paired with much more generous assessments of other civilizations, do not seem entirely fair. To be sure, the Assyrians could be brutal, and proud of it. Yet, one could say to Jones that behind the beauty of the Parthenon Marbles, and the exquisite elegance of Pharaonic art in the Egyptian galleries of the British Museum, lie histories often no less bloody than that of Assyria. The Romans, likewise, were hardly more humane than the world's first empire. The Roman philosopher and statesman Seneca, in his *Epistolae morales*, is very clear about this: "We check manslaughter and isolated murders; but what of war and the much-vaunted crime of slaughtering whole peoples? There are no limits to our greed, none to our cruelty." Much the same applies to the modern colonial empires, which claimed to "civilize" the millions they oppressed, and to better the lives of those they all too often robbed, terrorized, and slaughtered. Compared to these empires of hypocrisy, the Assyrians' open celebration of plunder, torture, and military conquest was at least honest. It also does not help to equate the Assyrians with the Nazis, as Jones did in another article. The Assyrians never launched a program aimed at the mass murder of specific ethnic groups.[3]

"Essentializing" the ancient Assyrians is, in general, better avoided. After all, just like the status of the fisherman and his wife in the tale of the Brothers Grimm, Assyria's system of government underwent dramatic changes over time. Initially remarkably "democratic," it became progressively more and more focused on an all-powerful single ruler. Many features of Assyrian culture and religion changed as well.

There is one thing that can be said with confidence, though: that the Assyrian Empire was, for better or worse, an extremely modern and dynamic state—whether in terms of the multiethnic units of its armies, its highly efficient road system, or the political surveillance on which its rulers relied. Assyria can be described as an engine of history that thoroughly transformed Western Asia, the Eastern

Mediterranean—and, mediated through others—to some extent the world.

If anything, it is perhaps yet another mini-parable, complementing the one of the fisherman and his wife, that can best convey what Assyria truly was. Assyria's core territory was located along the Tigris River, and from there, the kingdom expanded its influence into regions farther and farther away. The Tigris is also one of the four rivers mentioned in the Bible's description of the location of the Garden of Eden, the terrestrial Paradise. In his "Theses on the Philosophy of History," the German critic and philosopher Walter Benjamin describes how the "Angel of History"—a figure based on a painting by Paul Klee—is confronting a terrible storm emerging from the biblical garden:

> [The Angel's] face is turned towards the past. Where we perceive a chain of events, he sees one single catastrophe which keeps piling up wreckage upon wreckage and hurls it in front of his feet. The angel would like to stay, awaken the dead, and make whole what has been smashed. But a storm is blowing from Paradise; it has got caught in his wings with such violence that the angel can no longer close them. The storm irresistibly propels him into the future to which his back is turned, while the pile of debris before him grows skyward. This storm is what we call progress.[4]

Is that storm not also, though, a most fitting metaphor for the ancient Assyrians? In many ways, the Assyrian Empire did bring "progress." But, in its wake, it also piled up a vast mountain of debris—cities devastated, lives destroyed, and cultures derailed.[5]

Acknowledgments

This book would never have been started, let alone finished, without the encouragement and support I received from people both near and far. I am particularly indebted to Adam Gauntlett of Peters Fraser and Dunlop, London, who came up with the idea that I write the book in the first place and who worked tirelessly to find me superb publishers, the seemingly remote subject notwithstanding. Richard Yanowitz (New Haven) kindly helped improve my original book proposal. During the writing process, several colleagues sent me manuscripts of their unpublished work and gave me useful advice. I am especially grateful to Gojko Barjamovic (Harvard) for sharing with me his unpublished essay on "Assur Before Assyria," which has been more important for my conception of Chapter 1 than my endnotes convey. Rocío Da Riva (Barcelona) and Stephanie Dalley (Oxford) sent me drafts of forthcoming articles; Mary Frazer (Munich), Stefan Jakob (Heidelberg), Julian Reade (London), and Tracy Spurrier (Toronto) answered questions; and Ann Guinan (Philadelphia) and Ambros Waibel (Berlin) helped with quotations. I am much indebted to Alessio Palmisano (Turin) for drawing the maps. Yale graduate students Jonathan Beltz, Evelyne Koubková, Pavla Rosenstein, Eli Tadmor, and Parker Zane listened patiently to my thoughts, coherent and incoherent, on various aspects of

Assyrian history and culture, providing valuable criticism and feedback. In addition, Pavla and Eli read portions of the final draft of the book. My Yale colleagues Benjamin R. Foster, Elizabeth Knott, Agnete W. Lassen, and Klaus Wagensonner helped with specific questions and illustrations, besides making my daily work easier. Kathryn E. Slanski found a better title for the book and supported me in numerous additional ways.

A broad-ranging book like this by nature draws heavily on the work of others, too many to list them all here. But I would be remiss not to single out my teachers Rykle Borger and Karlheinz Deller, both eminent experts in Assyrian civilization, as well as a number of colleagues and friends with whom on numerous occasions I have had fruitful conversations about Assyria and the empires that succeeded it: Rocío Da Riva, Frederick Mario Fales, Grant Frame, Andreas Fuchs, Michael Jursa, Stefan M. Maul, Peter Miglus, Jamie Novotny, Simo Parpola, Karen Radner, Hayim Tadmor, and Elnathan Weissert.

I wrote the bulk of this book in the fall of 2021, when a sabbatical granted by Yale gave me much-needed time, and finished it in the summer of 2022 in Munich, where I was generously hosted by Enrique Jiménez at the Ludwig Maximilian University's Institut für Assyriologie und Hethitologie. After I submitted a first version of the manuscript, Brian Distelberg, editor in chief at Basic Books, sent me an extensive and penetrating critique, pointing to mannerisms and structural deficiencies alike. In a second round of corrections, Brandon Proia heroically improved the flow of the text and helped expunge many of my Germanisms. Kathy Streckfus copy-edited the book with great care and attention to detail. That the errors and misconceptions that remain after all the help and feedback I received are mine and mine alone is a truism—but must be acknowledged all the same.

Abbreviations of Important Text Editions

RIMA. *The Royal Inscriptions of Mesopotamia: Assyrian Periods*

RIMA 1. A. Kirk Grayson, *Assyrian Rulers of the Third and Second Millennia BC (to 1115 BC)* (Toronto: University of Toronto Press, 1987).

RIMA 2. A. Kirk Grayson, *Assyrian Rulers of the Early First Millennium BC I (1114–859 BC)* (Toronto: University of Toronto Press, 1991).

RIMA 3. A. Kirk Grayson, *Assyrian Rulers of the Early First Millennium BC II (858–745 BC)* (Toronto: University of Toronto Press, 1996).

RINAP. *The Royal Inscriptions of the Neo-Assyrian Period*

RINAP 1. Hayim Tadmor and Shigeo Yamada, *The Royal Inscriptions of Tiglath-pileser III (744–727 BC) and Shalmaneser V (726–722 BC), Kings of Assyria* (Winona Lake, IN: Eisenbrauns, 2011).

RINAP 2. Grant Frame, *The Royal Inscriptions of Sargon II, King of Assyria (721–705 BC)* (University Park, PA: Eisenbrauns, 2021).

RINAP 3/1. A. Kirk Grayson and Jamie Novotny, *The Royal Inscriptions of Sennacherib, King of Assyria (704–681 BC)*, Part 1 (Winona Lake, IN: Eisenbrauns, 2012).

RINAP 3/2. A. Kirk Grayson and Jamie Novotny, *The Royal Inscriptions of Sennacherib, King of Assyria (704–681 BC)*, Part 2 (Winona Lake, IN: Eisenbrauns, 2014).

RINAP 4. Erle V. Leichty, *The Royal Inscriptions of Esarhaddon, King of Assyria (680–669 BC)* (Winona Lake, IN: Eisenbrauns, 2011).

RINAP 5/1. Jamie Novotny and Joshua Jeffers, *The Royal Inscriptions of Ashurbanipal (668–631 BC), Aššur-etel-ilāni (630–627 BC), and Sîn-šarra-iškun (626–612 BC), Kings of Assyria*, Part 1 (University Park, PA: Eisenbrauns, 2018).

RINBE. *The Royal Inscriptions of the Neo-Babylonian Empire*

RINBE 2. Frauke Weiershäuser and Jamie Novotny, *The Royal Inscriptions of Amēl-Marduk (561–560 BC), Neriglissar (559–556 BC), and Nabonidus (555–539 BC), Kings of Babylon* (University Park, PA: Eisenbrauns, 2020).

SAA. *State Archives of Assyria*

SAA 1. Simo Parpola, *The Correspondence of Sargon II, Part I. Letters from Assyria and the West* (Helsinki: Helsinki University Press, 1987).

SAA 2. Simo Parpola and Kazuko Watanabe, *Neo-Assyrian Treaties and Loyalty Oaths* (Helsinki: University of Helsinki Press, 1988).

SAA 3. Alasdair Livingstone, *Court Poetry and Literary Miscellanea* (Helsinki: University of Helsinki Press, 1989).

SAA 4. Ivan Starr, *Queries to the Sungod: Divination and Politics in Sargonid Assyria* (Helsinki: University of Helsinki Press, 1990).

SAA 6. Theodore Kwasman and Simo Parpola, *Legal Transactions of the Royal Court of Nineveh, Part I. Tiglath-Pileser III Through Esarhaddon* (Helsinki: University of Helsinki Press, 1991).

SAA 9. Simo Parpola, *Assyrian Prophecies* (Helsinki: University of Helsinki Press, 1997).

SAA 10. Simo Parpola, *Letters from Assyrian and Babylonian Scholars* (Helsinki: University of Helsinki Press, 1993).

SAA 12. Laura Kataja and Robert M. Whiting, *Grants, Decrees and Gifts of the Neo-Assyrian Period* (Helsinki: University of Helsinki Press, 1995).

SAA 13. Steven W. Cole and Peter Machinist, *Letters from Assyrian and Babylonian Priests to the Kings Esarhaddon and Assurbanipal* (Helsinki: University of Helsinki Press, 1998).

SAA 15. Andreas Fuchs and Simo Parpola, *The Correspondence of Sargon II, Part III. Letters from Babylonia and the Eastern Provinces* (Helsinki: University of Helsinki Press, 2002).

SAA 16. Mikko Luukko and Greta Van Buylaere, *The Political Correspondence of Esarhaddon* (Helsinki: University of Helsinki Press, 2002).

SAA 18. Frances Reynolds, *The Babylonian Correspondence of Esarhaddon and Letters to Assurbanipal and Sîn-šarru-iškun from Northern and Central Babylonia* (Helsinki: University of Helsinki Press, 2003).

SAA 19. Mikko Luukko, *The Correspondence of Tiglath-pileser III and Sargon II from Calah/Nimrud* (Helsinki: Neo-Assyrian Text Corpus Project, 2012).

SAA 20. Simo Parpola, *Assyrian Royal Rituals and Cultic Texts* (Helsinki: Neo-Assyrian Text Corpus Project, 2017).

SAA 21. Simo Parpola, *The Correspondence of Assurbanipal, Part II. Letters from the King and from Northern and Central Babylonia* (Helsinki: Neo-Assyrian Text Corpus Project, 2018).

Electronic Resources

Many Assyrian royal inscriptions, letters, and legal and administrative documents are also available online, in updated editions, at the web pages Official Inscriptions of the Middle East in Antiquity (OIMEA), http://oracc.museum.upenn.edu/oimea/index.html, and Archival Texts of the Assyrian Empire (ATAE), http://oracc.museum.upenn.edu/atae/index.html. Both sites are hosted on the Open Richly Annotated Cuneiform Corpus (Oracc) platform and were created by numerous scholars within the framework of the Munich Open-access Cuneiform Corpus Initiative (MOCCI) directed by Karen Radner.

Notes

This book cannot document every source on which the story it tells is based. The following notes reference quotations from primary texts, mention studies that are of special importance, and—with a focus on recent years—credit authors for particular insights and ideas. Baseline knowledge is not backed up by bibliographical references. Readers interested in finding additional resources can consult the *Companion to Assyria* (Malden, MA: Wiley, 2017), edited by the present author, and the *Oxford History of the Ancient Near East*, 5 vols. (Oxford: Oxford University Press, 2020–2022), edited by Karen Radner, Nadine Moeller, and Daniel Potts.

Introduction

1. For the Esarhaddon quotes, see RINAP 4, 21: iv 80–v 1; 135: 9'–12'.

2. RINAP 4, 184, rev. 13. The original quote is in the third-person singular.

3. Eckart Frahm, "Images of Assyria in Nineteenth- and Twentieth-Century Western Scholarship," in *Orientalism, Assyriology and the Bible*, ed. Steven W. Holloway (Sheffield, UK: Sheffield Phoenix Press, 2006), 74–94. The Nahum quote is from Chapter 3:1.

4. Quoted after Mogens Trolle Larsen, *The Conquest of Assyria: Excavations in an Antique Land* (London: Routledge, 1996), 13.

5. Larsen, *Conquest of Assyria*, 15–16.

6. "As it actually happened" (German: "wie es eigentlich gewesen") is the phrase used by the nineteenth-century German historian Leopold von Ranke

in the preface to Part 1 of his *Geschichte der romanischen und germanischen Völker von 1494 bis 1535* (Leipzig, 1824).

7. For a gripping tale of the early exploration of the Assyrian sites of northern Iraq, on which these paragraphs are based, see Larsen, *Conquest of Assyria*.

8. For details, see Grant Frame, "Lost in the Tigris," in *Neo-Assyrian Sources in Context*, ed. Shigeo Yamada (Helsinki: Neo-Assyrian Text Corpus Project, 2018), 215–238.

9. See Chapter 18.

10. See Peter T. Daniels, "Edward Hincks's Decipherment of Mesopotamian Cuneiform," in *The Edward Hincks Bicentenary Lectures*, ed. Kevin J. Cathcart (Dublin: Department of Near Eastern Languages, University College Dublin, 1994), 30–57.

11. *Inscription of Tiglath Pileser I., King of Assyria, B.C. 1150*, transl. Henry Rawlinson, Fox Talbot, Dr. Hincks, and Dr. Oppert (London: Royal Asiatic Society and J. W. Parker and Son, 1857).

12. For the notion of "the first half of history," see William W. Hallo, "Assyriology and the Canon," *American Scholar* 59, no. 1 (Winter 1990): 105–108.

13. David Damrosch, *The Buried Book: The Loss and Rediscovery of the Great Epic of Gilgamesh* (New York: Holt, 2007), 9–33.

14. For the time being, Walter Andrae, *Das wiedererstandene Assur*, 2nd ed., revised and enlarged by Barthel Hrouda (Munich: C. H. Beck, 1977), remains the best synthetic study of the city of Ashur.

15. For an overview, see Mogens Trolle Larsen, *Ancient Kanesh: A Merchant Colony in Bronze Age Anatolia* (Cambridge: Cambridge University Press, 2015).

16. For a recent synthesis of the archaeological work done on the citadel of Tell Sheikh Hamad, see Hartmut Kühne, ed., *Die Zitadelle von Dūr-Katlimmu in mittel- und neuassyrischer Zeit* (Wiesbaden: Harrassowitz, 2021).

17. Jason Ur, "Physical and Cultural Landscapes of Assyria," in *A Companion to Assyria*, ed. Eckart Frahm (Malden, MA: Wiley, 2017), 13–35.

18. Mikko Luukko and Greta Van Buylaere, "Languages and Writing Systems in Assyria," in Frahm, *Companion to Assyria*, 313–335.

19. For an edition of the treaty tablets, see SAA 2, no. 6.

20. See Beate Pongratz-Leisten, *Religion and Ideology in Assyria* (Berlin: De Gruyter, 2015), 115.

21. Nicholas Postgate, "The Bread of Aššur," *Iraq* 77 (2015): 159–172.

22. On the role and function of "portraits" of rulers in ancient Near Eastern art in general, see Paolo Matthiae, *I volti del potere: Alle origini del ritratto nell'arte dell'Oriente Antico* (Turin, Italy: Einaudi, 2020).

23. Dominique Charpin and Jean-Marie Durand, "Aššur avant l'Assyrie," *MARI* 8 (1997): 367–392.

24. For the term "mixed constitution," see Mario Liverani, "From City-State to Empire: The Case of Assyria," in *The Roman Empire in Context: Historical and Comparative Perspectives*, ed. Johann P. Arnason and Kurt A. Raaflaub (Malden, MA: Wiley-Blackwell, 2011), 251–269. For Hegel's thoughts on history, see his *Lectures on the Philosophy of History* (German: *Vorlesungen über die Philosophie der Weltgeschichte*), published after his death in 1837.

25. Wilfred G. Lambert, "The God Aššur," *Iraq* 45 (1983): 82–86.

26. For a study of Assyrian religion and royal ideology throughout history, see Pongratz-Leisten, *Religion and Ideology*.

27. See Robert Rollinger, "Assyria in Classical Sources," in Frahm, *Companion to Assyria*, 570–582; Dante, *De Monarchia* II.8.

28. See Larsen, *Ancient Kanesh*, 43, and Chapter 12 of the present book.

29. For a photo of the bull with the drawing (BM 118809b, RINAP 2, 162–171, ex. 24), see British Museum, www.britishmuseum.org/collection /object/W_1850-1228-4_1, accessed November 5, 2021. As communicated to me by Julian Reade, such board games can also be found on colossi from other locations.

30. See Karen Radner, "An Imperial Communication Network: The State Correspondence of the Neo-Assyrian Empire," in *State Correspondence in the Ancient World: From New Kingdom Egypt to the Roman Empire*, ed. Karen Radner (Oxford: Oxford University Press, 2014), 64–93.

Chapter 1: A Small Town on the Tigris

1. See Roger Matthews, *The Early Prehistory of Mesopotamia, 50,000–4,500 BC* (Turnhout, Belgium: Brepols, 2000).

2. See Jason Ur, "Physical and Cultural Landscapes of Assyria," in *A Companion to Assyria*, ed. Eckart Frahm (Malden, MA: Wiley, 2017), 13–35.

3. For the early history of Uruk, see Nicola Crüsemann, Margarete van Ess, Markus Hilgert, and Beate Salje, eds., English-language edition edited by Timothy Potts, *Uruk: First City of the Ancient World* (Los Angeles: Getty Publications, 2019).

4. For the beginnings of urban culture in northern Mesopotamia, see Jason Ur, "Early Mesopotamian Urbanism: A New View from the North," *Antiquity* 81 (2007): 585–600.

5. On prehistoric Nineveh, see Renate Vera Gut, *Das prähistorische Ninive: Zur relativen Chronologie der frühen Perioden Nordmesopotamiens* (Mainz: Von Zabern, 1995).

6. The following paragraphs, and also other sections of this chapter, draw heavily on an unpublished manuscript on "Assur Before Assyria" by Gojko Barjamovic. Originally scheduled to appear in a now aborted handbook, a

revised version of Barjamovic's manuscript is expected to be published as a monograph in the near future.

7. For the stone inscription with the earliest attestation of Shubur/Subartu on record, see Piotr Steinkeller, "An Archaic 'Prisoner Plaque' from Kiš," *Revue d'Assyriologie* 107 (2013): 131–157. For the reference to Ashur in the geographic list, see Douglas Frayne, *The Early Dynastic List of Geographic Names* (New Haven, CT: American Oriental Society, 1992), 42, 48.

8. For the archaic Ishtar temples in Ashur, see Jürgen Bär, *Die älteren Ischtar-Tempel in Assur: Stratigraphie, Architektur und Funde eines altorientalischen Heiligtums von der zweiten Hälfte des 3. Jahrtausends bis zur Mitte des 2. Jahrtausends v. Chr.* (Saarbrücken: Saarbrücker Druckerei und Verlag, 2003). For the history of the Ashur Temple, see Helen Gries, *Der Assur-Tempel in Assur: Das assyrische Hauptheiligtum im Wandel der Zeit* (Wiesbaden: Harrassowitz, 2017).

9. See Stefan M. Maul, "Assyrian Religion," in Frahm, *Companion to Assyria*, 337–338.

10. See Ignace J. Gelb, Piotr Steinkeller, and Robert M. Whiting, *Earliest Land Tenure Systems in the Near East: Ancient Kudurrus* (Chicago: Oriental Institute of the University of Chicago, 1991), no. 45.

11. For a preliminary report on the so far unpublished Old Akkadian texts from Ashur, see Hans Neumann, "Assur in altakkadischer Zeit: Die Texte," in *Assyrien im Wandel der Zeiten: XXXIXe Rencontre Assyriologique Internationale, Heidelberg 6–10. Juli 1992*, ed. Hartmut Waetzoldt and Harald Hauptmann (Heidelberg: Heidelberger Orient-Verlag, 1997), 133–138.

12. Neumann, "Assur in altakkadischer Zeit," 135.

13. The Ititi text is edited in RIMA 1, 7.

14. See Piotr Steinkeller, "Corvée Labor in Ur III Times," in *From the 21st Century BC to the 21st Century AD*, ed. Steven Garfinkle and Manuel Molina (Winona Lake, IN: Eisenbrauns, 2013), 350–351. A different view, which ascribes a greater degree of independence to Ashur during the Ur III period, was promoted by Piotr Michałowski, "Aššur During the Ur III Period," in *Here and There: Across the Ancient Near East. Studies in Honour of Krystyna Łyczkowska*, ed. Olga Drewnowska (Warsaw: Agade, 2009), 149–156. For the Zarriqum inscription, see RIMA 1, 9.

15. Exact references to the economic documents mentioned in this paragraph are found in Barjamovic's study "Assur Before Assyria."

16. See Shigeo Yamada, "The Editorial History of the Assyrian King List," *Zeitschrift für Assyriologie* 84 (1994): 11–37. The Assyrian King List is quoted in the following after A. Kirk Grayson, "Königslisten und Chroniken: B. Akkadisch," in *Reallexikon der Assyriologie und Vorderasiatischen Archäologie*, vol. 6, *Klagegesang—Königtum*, ed. D. O. Edzard (Berlin: De Gruyter, 1980), 101–115. See also Jean-Jacques Glassner, *Mesopotamian Chronicles* (Atlanta: Society of Biblical Literature, 2004), 136–145.

17. For the seal inscription from Kanesh, see RIMA 1, 12–13. The identification of Silulu with Sulili is not certain, since the King List claims that Sulili/Sulê was the son of Aminu and not of Dakiku. But the tie with Aminu may be fictitious and the result of a later alteration of the list, made with the purpose of linking Sulili/Sulê with one of the Amorite rulers of the preceding section who allegedly were "ancestors." The Old Assyrian merchant who used the seal of "Silulu son of Dakiku" some 150 years later for his own tablets probably did so because he was called Silulu son of Uku and thus shared his name with the early ruler. For the Ur III text, see Edmond Sollberger, *Royal Inscriptions, pt. 2*, Ur Excavations, Texts, vol. 8 (London: British Museum and University Museum, University of Pennsylvania, 1965), no. 14; for further discussion, see Barjamovic, "Assur Before Assyria." See also John Malcolm Russell, "Assyrian Art," in Frahm, *Companion to Assyria*, 458.

18. The seal inscription renders "Ashur" with the determinative for place-names, *ki*, which indicates the close link between the god and the city.

19. RIMA 1, 21: 35–42 (shortened). See also Mogens Trolle Larsen, *Ancient Kanesh: A Merchant Colony in Bronze Age Anatolia* (Cambridge: Cambridge University Press, 2015), 115.

20. Agnete Lassen, "The 'Bull Altar' in Old Assyrian Glyptic: A Representation of the God Assur?," in *Movement, Resources, Interaction: Studies Dedicated to Klaas Veenhof*, ed. Fikri Kulakoğlu and Gojko Barjamovic (Turnhout, Belgium: Brepols, 2017), 177–194.

21. Mogens Trolle Larsen, *The Old Assyrian City-State and Its Colonies* (Copenhagen: Akademisk Forlag, 1976), 261–262 (shortened).

22. For the bronze vagina, see Guido Kryszat, "Zur altassyrischen Votivinschrift Assur 19624a/VA 8365," *Nouvelles Assyriologiques Brèves et Utilitaires* 2017, no. 66.

23. The absolute chronology of the Old Assyrian period is still debated. This book follows the dates suggested by Barjamovic, "Assur Before Assyria."

24. Mario Liverani, "From City-State to Empire: The Case of Assyria," in *The Roman Empire in Context: Historical and Comparative Perspectives*, ed. Johann P. Arnason and Kurt A. Raaflaub (Malden, MA: Wiley-Blackwell, 2011), 251–269.

25. Larsen, *Ancient Kanesh*, 112–121.

26. Larsen, *Ancient Kanesh*, 216.

27. Larsen, *Ancient Kanesh*, 122–130.

28. Larsen, *Ancient Kanesh*, 101–111, 279.

29. This section is primarily based on Gojko Barjamovic, "Mesopotamian Economy and Trade," in *Ancient Mesopotamia Speaks: Highlights of the Yale Babylonian Collection*, ed. Agnete W. Lassen, Eckart Frahm, and Klaus Wagensonner (New Haven, CT: Yale Peabody Museum of Natural History, 2019), 82–95.

30. The estimates of the population size of Ashur are taken from Klaas Veenhof, "The Old Assyrian Period (20th–18th Century BCE)," in Frahm, *Companion to Assyria*, 62.

31. For the use of bearer checks, see Klaas Veenhof, "'Modern' Features in Old Assyrian Trade," *Journal of the Economic and Social History of the Orient* 40 (1997): 336–366.

32. Cécile Michel, *Correspondence des marchands de Kaniš au début du IIe millénaire avant J.-C.* (Paris: Cerf, 2001), nos. 176 and 177; Lassen et al., *Ancient Mesopotamia Speaks*, 220.

33. See Larsen, *Ancient Kanesh*, 197; John Huehnergard, "Reading Ancient Mail," *Journal of the American Oriental Society* 138 (2018): 691–707.

34. A. Leo Oppenheim, *Letters from Mesopotamia* (Chicago: University of Chicago Press, 1967), 84–85.

35. Cécile Michel, *Innāya dans les tablettes paléo-assyriennes* (Paris: ERC, 1991), 13–15.

36. See Jan G. Dercksen, "Adad Is King! The Sargon Text from Kültepe (with an appendix on MARV 4, 138 and 140)," *Jaarbericht Ex Oriente Lux* 39 (2005): 107–129; Gojko Barjamovic, "Contextualizing Tradition: Magic, Literacy and Domestic Life in Old Assyrian Kanesh," in *Texts and Contexts: The Circulation and Transmission of Cuneiform Texts in Social Space*, ed. Paul Delnero and Jacob Lauinger (Berlin: De Gruyter, 2015), 48–86.

37. The texts are quoted after Gianni Marchesi and Nicolò Marchetti, "A Babylonian Official at Tilmen Höyük in the Time of King Sumu-la-el of Babylon," *Orientalia Nova Series* 88 (2019): 14; RIMA 1, 18.

38. Veenhof, "Old Assyrian Period," 58.

39. For a history of Shamshi-Adad's reign, see Dominique Charpin and Nele Ziegler, *Mari et le Proche Orient à l'époque amorrite* (Paris: SEPOA, 2003), 75–168.

40. Cahit Günbattı, *Harsamna kralı Hurmeli'ye gönderilen mektup ve Kaniš kralları. The Letter Sent to Hurmeli King of Harsamna and the Kings of Kaniš* (Ankara: Türk Tarih Kurumu Yayınları, 2014).

41. Georges Dossin, *Correspondance de Šamši-Addu et ses fils* (Paris: Imprimerie nationale, 1950), 69 (shortened); Jean-Marie Durand, Christophe Nicolle, and Lionel Marti, *Le culte des pierres et les monuments commémoratifs en Syrie amorrite* (Paris: SEPOA, 2005), 1.

42. Pierre Marello, "Documents pour l'histoire du royaume de Haute-Mésopotamie IV: Lamassî-Aššur," *MARI* 7 (1993): 271–273.

43. See Nele Ziegler, "The Conquest of the Holy City of Nineveh," *Iraq* 66 (2004): 19–26.

44. The episode of the verbal attack on Ishme-Dagan is known from a letter; see Wolfgang Heimpel, *Letters to the King of Mari* (Winona Lake, IN: Eisenbrauns, 2003), 146, 399.

45. RIMA 1, 77–78.

46. The letters are edited by Andrew R. George in *Assyrian Archival Texts in the Schøyen Collection and Other Documents from North Mesopotamia and Syria* (Bethesda, MD: CDL Press, 2017), 97–100 (for the reading Atal-sharri rather than Ari-sharri, see Barjamovic, "Assur Before Assyria"). For the treaty, see Jesper Eidem, "An Old Assyrian Treaty from Tell Leilan," in *Marchands, diplomates et empereurs*, ed. Dominique Charpin and Francis Joannès (Paris: Éditions Recherche sur les Civilisations, 1991), 185–207.

47. His son, it seems, supported it too. A curious literary dialogue between Ishme-Dagan and a syncretized Ashur-Enlil, with references to the destruction of the temple of the god by fire and its projected reconstruction in a place where a white raven would land, was still copied in seventh-century BCE Ashur and Nineveh. For an edition and commentary, see Eckart Frahm, *Historische und historisch-literarische Texte*, Keilschrifttexte aus Assur literarischen Inhalts III (Wiesbaden: Harrassowitz, 2009), nos. 76 and 76a.

Chapter 2: Birth of a Kingdom

1. For an overview of what is known about this period, and additional bibliography, see Shigeo Yamada, "The Transition Period (17th to 15th Century BCE)," in *A Companion to Assyria*, ed. Eckart Frahm (Malden, MA: Wiley, 2017), 108–116. For chronological questions, some still very much unsolved, see Thomas Janssen, "Adad-nīrārī und die Erschaffung der AKL," *Nouvelles Assyriologiques Brèves et Utilitaires* 2020, no. 114.

2. Erich Neu, *Das hurritische Epos der Freilassung* (Wiesbaden: Harrassowitz, 1995). See also Eva von Dassow, "Piecing Together the Song of Release," *Journal of Cuneiform Studies* 65 (2013): 127–162. The quoted lines are strongly reminiscent of the proems of Homer's *Iliad* and *Odyssey*. Other features of the poem, which describes manifold interactions between gods, rulers, and popular assemblies preceding the liberation of a group of captives in the besieged city, bring the *Iliad* to mind as well.

3. For the evidence, see Jaume Llop, "The Creation of the Middle Assyrian Provinces," *Journal of the American Oriental Society* 131 (2011): 591–603.

4. An outline of Assyrian history between the fourteenth and eleventh centuries BCE is provided by Stefan Jakob, "The Middle Assyrian Period (14th–11th Century BCE)," in Frahm, *Companion to Assyria*, 117–142. For some of the economic changes brought about by Assyria's territorial expansion, see Bleda S. Düring, *The Imperialisation of Assyria* (Cambridge: Cambridge University Press, 2020), 65.

5. Frans A. M. Wiggerman, "A Babylonian Scholar in Assur," in *Studies in Ancient Near Eastern World View and Society Presented to Marten Stol on the*

Occasion of His 65th Birthday, ed. Robartus J. van der Spek (Bethesda, MD: CDL Press, 2008), 203–234.

6. The quotation is from William L. Moran, *The Amarna Letters* (Baltimore: Johns Hopkins University Press, 1992), 39. See also Yamada, "Transition Period," 114.

7. In Middle Assyrian, the word for king, *šarru*, had lost the final *m* it had in the Old Assyrian form *šarrum*. The same is the case below for *limmu(m)*.

8. For this view, see John Malcolm Russell, "Assyrian Art," in Frahm, *Companion to Assyria*, 463.

9. Martha T. Roth, *Law Collections from Mesopotamia and Asia Minor* (Atlanta: Scholars Press, 1997), 206 (partly restored).

10. For the Assyrian love songs, see Nathan Wasserman, *Akkadian Love Literature of the Third and Second Millennium* BCE (Wiesbaden: Harrassowitz, 2016), 206–223.

11. Editions of the coronation ritual are found in SAA 20, no. 7, and in Hanspeter Schaudig, *Staatsrituale, Festbeschreibungen und weitere Texte zum assyrischen Kult*, Keilschrifttexte aus Assur literarischen Inhalts, vol. 12 (Wiesbaden: Harrassowitz, 2020), no. 1.

12. SAA 20, no. 7: 30–36. For the medieval coronation liturgies, see Ernst Kantorowicz, *Laudes Regiae: A Study in Liturgical Acclamations and Mediaeval Ruler Worship* (Berkeley: University of California Press, 1946).

13. Moran, *Amarna Letters*, 18.

14. Harry A. Hoffner, *Letters from the Hittite Kingdom* (Atlanta: Society of Biblical Literature, 2009), 322–324.

15. Jaume Llop, "The Development of the Middle Assyrian Provinces," *Altorientalische Forschungen* 39 (2012): 107.

16. Düring, *Imperialisation*, 93–94.

17. Eva C. Cancik-Kirschbaum, *Die mittelassyrischen Briefe aus Tall Šeḫ Ḥamad* (Berlin: Dietrich Reimer, 1996), no. 3.

18. The following account (whose chronology remains debatable) follows Stefan Jakob, "Sag mir quando, sag mir wann," in *Time and History in the Ancient Near East: Proceedings of the 56th Rencontre Assyriologique Internationale, Barcelona, July 26th–30th, 2010*, ed. Lluis Feliu, J. Llop, A. Millet Albà, and Joaquin Sanmartín (Winona Lake, IN: Eisenbrauns, 2013), 509–523, and Jakob, "Middle Assyrian Period," 122–132. For "two countries divided by a common language," a phrase originally coined by George Bernard Shaw, being applied to Assyria and Babylonia, see Nicholas Postgate, "The Bread of Aššur," *Iraq* 77 (2015): 170.

19. Cancik-Kirschbaum, *Die mittelassyrischen Briefe*, no. 10. Alternatively, the unnamed Babylonian king who accompanied Tukulti-Ninurta on his tour to the west was the captive Kashtiliash.

20. Jakob, "Middle Assyrian Period," 130.

21. Benjamin R. Foster, *Before the Muses: An Anthology of Akkadian Literature*, 3rd ed. (Bethesda, MD: CDL Press, 2005), 301. For the king's titles, see Betina Faist, "Kingship and Institutional Development in the Middle Assyrian Period," in *Concepts of Kingship in Antiquity: Proceedings of the European Science Foundation Exploratory Workshop, Held in Padova, November 28th–December 1st, 2007*, ed. Giovanni B. Lanfranchi and Robert Rollinger (Padua, Italy: S.A.R.G.O.N. Editrice e Libreria, 2010), 17–18.

22. Proverbs 16:18.

23. Foster, *Before the Muses*, 319.

24. For Tukulti-Ninurta's Ishtar Temple, see Aaron Schmitt, "Verfallen und vergessen: Überlegungen zum Umgang mit dem Andenken Tukultī-Ninurtas I. anhand der Bauwerke des Herrschers in Aššur und Kār-Tukultī-Ninurta," in *Assur-Forschungen*, vol. 2, ed. Stefan M. Maul (Wiesbaden: Harrassowitz, 2020), 249–282.

25. A. Kirk Grayson, *Assyrian and Babylonian Chronicles* (Locust Valley, NY: J. J. Augustin, 1975), 176. The chronicle falsely calls the regicide Ashur-nasir-apli.

26. Jaume Llop and Andrew R. George, "Die babylonisch-assyrischen Beziehungen und die innere Lage Assyriens in der Zeit der Auseinandersetzungen zwischen Ninurta-tukulti-Aššur und Mutakkil-Nusku nach neuen keilschriftlichen Quellen," *Archiv für Orientforschung* 48/49 (2001/2002): 1–23. The letter is known through manuscripts from Ashurbanipal's seventh-century library in Nineveh.

27. For the most important areas for Assyrian trade from the Middle Assyrian period onward, see J. Nicholas Postgate, "The Economic Structure of the Assyrian Empire," in *Power and Propaganda: A Symposium on Ancient Empires*, ed. Mogens Trolle Larsen (Copenhagen: Akademisk Forlag, 1979), 197–200.

28. See Betina Faist, *Der Fernhandel des assyrischen Reiches* (Münster: Ugarit Verlag, 2001), 239–249; Nicholas Postgate, *Bronze Age Bureaucracy* (Cambridge: Cambridge University Press, 2013), 29–46.

29. Stefan M. Maul, "Assyrian Religion," in Frahm, *Companion to Assyria*, 344.

30. Düring, *Imperialisation*, 54; Marian Feldman, "Assur Tomb 45 and the Birth of the Assyrian Empire," *Bulletin of the American Schools of Oriental Research* 343 (2006): 21–43.

31. See Postgate, *Bronze Age Bureaucracy*, 61–62, with an illustration of the object, and Cornelia Wunsch, "Findelkinder und Adoption nach neubabylonischen Quellen," *Archiv für Orientforschung* 50 (2003/2004): 174–244.

32. Roth, *Law Collections*, 157, 174–175.

33. Shiyanthi Thavapalan, "Keeping Alive Dead Knowledge: Middle Assyrian Glass Recipes in the Yale Babylonian Collection," *Journal of Cuneiform Studies* 73 (2021): 158.

34. For the texts listed in the Tukulti-Ninurta Epic, see Foster, *Before the Muses*, 315.

35. A description and photos of the god list are found in Agnete W. Lassen, Eckart Frahm, and Klaus Wagensonner, eds., *Ancient Mesopotamia Speaks: Highlights of the Yale Babylonian Collection* (New Haven, CT: Yale Peabody Museum of Natural History, 2019), 46, 231–233.

36. For Rabâ-sha-Marduk, see Elena Devecchi and Irene Sibbing-Plantholt, "See Ḫattuša and Die: A New Reconstruction of the Journeys of the Babylonian Physician Rabâ-ša-Marduk," *Journal of Near Eastern Studies* 79 (2020): 305–322. The letter is edited by Daisuke Shibata, "Hemerology, Extispicy, and Ilī-padâ's Illness," *Zeitschrift für Assyriologie* 105 (2015): 139–153.

37. Eva C. Cancik-Kirschbaum, "Nebenlinien des assyrischen Königshauses in der 2. Hälfte des 2. Jts. v. Chr.," *Altorientalische Forschungen* 26 (1999): 210–222.

Chapter 3: Disruption and Recovery

1. For a comprehensive study of these events, see Eric Cline, *1177 B.C.: The Year Civilization Collapsed* (Princeton, NJ: Princeton University Press, 2014), with a translation of the letter from Ugarit on p. 9.

2. See Karen Radner, *Das mittelassyrische Tontafelarchiv von Giricano/Dunnu-ša-Uzibi* (Turnhout, Belgium: Brepols, 2004).

3. For the textual evidence, see RIMA 2, 42–44: 24–30, 67–71, and Eckart Frahm, *Historische und historisch-literarische Texte*, Keilschrifttexte aus Assur literarischen Inhalts III (Wiesbaden: Harrassowitz, 2009), no. 6. For a long time, it was believed that Ashur-bel-kala had managed to repeat the greatest feats of his father, including his campaign to the Mediterranean. But as recently established by Bieke Mahieu, "The Old and Middle Assyrian Calendars, and the Adoption of the Babylonian Calendar by Tiglath-pileser I," *State Archives of Assyria Bulletin* 24 (2018): 63–95, and further elaborated by Daisuke Shibata, "The Assyrian King of the Broken Obelisk, the Date of the Archive of Giricano, and the Timing of the Assyrian Calendar Reform," *Journal of Cuneiform Studies* 74 (2022): 109–129, the so-called Broken Obelisk, the main source for this assumption, should probably be dated to the reign of Tiglath-pileser I rather than that of Ashur-bel-kala.

4. Jean-Jacques Glassner, *Mesopotamian Chronicles* (Atlanta: Society of Biblical Literature, 2004), 188–189 (partly restored).

5. See Frahm, *Historische und historisch-literarische Texte*, no. 61.

6. Translation from Alan Lenzi, Akkadian Prayer Miscellany, http://akkpm.org/P451997.html, accessed January 28, 2022. See also Benjamin R. Foster, *Before the Muses: An Anthology of Akkadian Literature*, 3rd ed. (Bethesda, MD: CDL Press, 2005), 329.

7. For the texts mentioned in this paragraph, see RIMA 2, 133: 16–22, RIMA 3, 19: 35–38, and RIMA 2, 134–135: 60–67; 242: ii 5–36.

8. "Als alles vorbei war, ging alles weiter," from Jörg Fauser, "Kranichzüge über dem Schlachtviehhof," *Tip* 3 (1980) (reference courtesy Ambros Waibel).

9. See Ashish Sinha, Gayatri Kathayat, Harvey Weiss, Hanying Li, Hai Cheng, Justin Reuter, Adam W. Schneider, et al., "Role of Climate in the Rise and Fall of the Assyrian Empire," *Science Advances* 5, no. 11 (November 2019).

10. Thus Mario Liverani, *Assyria: The Imperial Mission* (Winona Lake, IN: Eisenbrauns, 2017), 119.

11. For this and the following, see Eckart Frahm, "The Neo-Assyrian Period (ca. 1000–609 BCE)," in *A Companion to Assyria*, ed. Eckart Frahm (Malden, MA: Wiley, 2017), 167–169. For the Katmuhu episode, see RIMA 2, 133–134.

12. RIMA 2, 134–135 (partly restored).

13. Nicholas Postgate, "Middle Assyrian to Neo-Assyrian: The Nature of the Shift," in *Assyrien im Wandel der Zeiten: XXXIXe Rencontre Assyriologique Internationale, Heidelberg 6–10. Juli 1992*, ed. Hartmut Waetzoldt and Harald Hauptmann (Heidelberg: Heidelberger Orientverlag, 1997), 159–168.

14. For royal name-giving patterns in the early Neo-Assyrian period, see Eckart Frahm, "Observations on the Name of Sargon II and on Some Patterns of Assyrian Royal Onomastics," *Nouvelles Assyriologiques Brèves et Utilitaires* 2005, no. 44. For the month names, see Shibata, "Assyrian King of the Broken Obelisk."

15. RIMA 2, 173, 176: 41–46, 90–92; Frahm, *Historische und historisch-literarische Texte*, nos. 19–20.

16. See RIMA 2, 177–178: 121–126, and 178: 133.

17. For the Banquet Stela, see RIMA 2, 292–293: 102–154. On locusts, Karen Radner, "Fressen und gefressen warden: Heuschrecken als Katastrophe und Delikatesse im Alten Vorderen Orient," *Altorientalische Forschungen* 34 (2004): 7–22, with figure 7. The recipe for Elamite blood broth is found in Gojko Barjamovic, Patricia Jurardo Gonzalez, Chelsea A. Graham, Agnete W. Lassen, Nawal Nasrallah, and Pia Sörensen, "Food in Ancient Mesopotamia: Cooking the Yale Babylonian Culinary Recipes," in *Ancient Mesopotamia Speaks: Highlights of the Yale Babylonian Collection*, ed. Agnete W. Lassen, Eckart Frahm, and Klaus Wagensonner (New Haven, CT: Yale Peabody Museum of Natural History, 2019), 124.

18. RIMA 2, 290: 40.

19. For this and the following, see Karen Radner, "The Assur–Nineveh–Arbela Triangle: Central Assyria in the Neo-Assyrian Period," in *Between the Cultures: The Central Tigris Region from the 3rd to the 1st Millennium BC*, ed. Peter A. Miglus and Simone Mühl (Heidelberg: Heidelberger Orientverlag, 2011), 321–329.

20. SAA 12, nos. 82–84. For an excellent archaeological portrait of the city of Calah, see Joan Oates and David Oates, *Nimrud: An Assyrian Imperial City Revealed* (London: British School of Archaeology in Iraq, 2001).

21. RIMA 2, 290: 36–52; 291–292: 84–101. For analysis, see Liverani, *Imperial Mission*, 69–73; Jessie DeGrado, "King of the Four Quarters: Diversity as a Rhetorical Strategy of the Neo-Assyrian Empire," *Iraq* 81 (2019): 107–125.

22. For the original colors of the palace reliefs, see Shiyanthi Thavapalan, "A World in Color," in Lassen et al., *Ancient Mesopotamia Speaks*, 193–200. Thanks to the use of visible-induced luminescence technology and other methods, it is now known that the ancient artists used clay-based ocher and orpiment to achieve shades of red, yellow, and orange; malachite for greens; chalk for whites; soot and charcoal for blacks; and a synthetic compound called Egyptian Blue—made of silica, alkali, calcium, and copper—for blues.

23. See Ömür Harmanşah, "Encounters, Interactions, and a Shared Cultural Sphere: The Assyrian Empire and the Syro-Hittite States of the Iron Age," in *The Assyrians: Kingdom of the God Aššur from Tigris to Taurus*, ed. Kemalettin Köroğlu and Selim F. Adalı (Istanbul: Yapı Kredi Yayınları, 2018), 256–275.

24. Ashurnasirpal appears to refer to those very figures when noting in one of his inscriptions that he had placed stone replicas of "beasts of the mountains and the seas" in the gates of his palace. See RIMA 2, 302: 9–10. For discussion, see Stefan M. Maul, "Der Sieg über die Mächte des Bösen: Götterkampf, Triumphrituale und Torarchitektur in Assyrien," in *Gegenwelten zu den Kulturen Griechenlands und Roms in der Antike* (Munich: Saur, 2000), 19–46.

25. Foster, *Before the Muses*, 555–578.

26. On the political implications of Ninurta mythology in Assyria, see, most recently, Beate Pongratz-Leisten, *Religion and Ideology in Assyria* (Berlin: De Gruyter, 2015), 219–270.

27. See RIMA 2, 195–196: i 32–33, and RIMA 2, 201–202: i 116–ii 1.

28. For the Assyrian war poem, see Mordechai Cogan, "'Ripping Open Pregnant Women' in Light of an Assyrian Analogue," *Journal of the American Oriental Society* 103 (1983): 755–757; Peter Dubovský, "Ripping Open Pregnant Women: Reliefs in Room L of Ashurbanipal's North Palace," *Orientalia Nova Series* 78 (2009): 394–419. The Amos quote is from Amos 1:13. For a more general discussion, see Mario Liverani, "The King and His Audience," in *From Source to History: Studies on Ancient Near Eastern Worlds and Beyond Dedicated to Giovanni Battista Lanfranchi on the Occasion of His 65th Birthday on June 23, 2014*, ed. Salvatore Gaspa, Alessandro Greco, and Daniele Morandi Bonacossi (Münster: Ugarit-Verlag, 2014), 382–383.

29. Foster, *Before the Muses*, 883–884.

30. I owe the comparison of Ishum with a psychoanalyst to Eli Tadmor, a Yale PhD student who is currently writing his dissertation on the Erra Epic.

31. See Mario Liverani, *Studies on the Annals of Ashurnasirpal II. 2: Topographical Analysis* (Rome: Università di Roma, 1992).

32. See RIMA 2, 202: ii 3–12 (with Liverani, *Imperial Mission*, 182); RIMA 2, 330: 12–14.

Chapter 4: The Crown in Crisis

1. RIMA 3, 19: ii 30–35. For analysis of Shalmaneser's western campaigns, see Shigeo Yamada, *The Construction of the Assyrian Empire: A Historical Study of the Inscriptions of Shalmaneser III (859–824 B.C.) Relating to His Campaigns in the West* (Leiden: Brill, 2000).

2. For the creation of some Neo-Assyrian "colonies" in the west and their impact on the cultural landscape, see Eckart Frahm, "The Intellectual Background of Assyrian Deportees, Colonists, and Officials in the Levant," Supplement, *Hebrew Bible and Ancient Israel* 11 (2022): 56–82.

3. See Mario Liverani, "Assyria in the Ninth Century: Continuity or Change?," in *From the Upper to the Lower Sea: Studies on the History of Assyria and Babylonia in Honour of A.K. Grayson*, ed. Grant Frame (Leiden: Netherlands Institute for the Near East, 2004), 214–217.

4. For details, see Giovanni B. Lanfranchi, "A Happy Son of the King of Assyria: Warikas and the Çineköy Bilingual (Cilicia)," in *Of God(s), Trees, Kings, and Scholars: Neo-Assyrian and Related Studies in Honour of Simo Parpola*, ed. Mikko Luukko, Saana Svärd, and Raija Mattila (Helsinki: Finnish Oriental Society, 2009), 127–150.

5. RIMA 3, 18: ii 21–24.

6. RIMA 3, 23–24: ii 89–102.

7. Shalmaneser's inscription speaks of two thousand rather than two hundred chariots provided by Ahab, but this must be a mistake.

8. See Karen Radner, "The Neo-Assyrian Empire," in *Imperien und Reiche in der Weltgeschichte*, ed. Michael Gehler and Robert Rollinger (Wiesbaden: Harrassowitz, 2014), 107–108.

9. Liverani, "Assyria in the Ninth Century," 218. For the (still somewhat uncertain) locations of the border marches, see most recently Shigeo Yamada, "Ulluba and Its Surroundings: Tiglath-pileser III's Province Organization Facing the Urartian Border," in *Neo-Assyrian Sources in Context*, ed. Shigeo Yamada (Helsinki: Neo-Assyrian Text Corpus Project, 2018), 33–37.

10. RIMA 3, 69: 141–143.

11. For the statue and its inscription, see Eckart Frahm, " 'Whoever Destroys This Image': A Neo-Assyrian Statue from Tell 'Ağāğa (Šadikanni),"

Nouvelles Assyriologiques Brèves et Utilitaires 2015, no. 51. Illicitly excavated and later probably destroyed by members of the Islamic State group, all that is left of the statue are three grainy photos posted on the Internet by the Syrian Directorate-General of Antiquities and Museums in April 2014.

12. For an attempt to reconstruct the events leading up to the death of Shalmaneser III, see Andreas Fuchs, "Der Turtān Šamšī-ilu und die große Zeit der assyrischen Großen (830–746)," *Die Welt des Orients* 38 (2008): 61–145, especially 64–68. The following paragraphs draw on this study as well, even though some of Fuchs's ideas require further corroboration.

13. The Neo-Assyrian Eponym Lists and Chronicles are edited by Alan R. Millard, *The Eponyms of the Assyrian Empire, 910–612 BC* (Helsinki: Neo-Assyrian Text Corpus Project, 1994).

14. For the most recent assessment of Sammu-ramat's political role, see Luis R. Siddall, *The Reign of Adad-nīrārī III: An Historical and Ideological Analysis of an Assyrian King and His Times* (Leiden: Brill, 2013), 86–100.

15. RIMA 3, 205: 7–18.

16. See Chapter 17.

17. RIMA 3, 233: 15–17. The Antakya inscription is edited in RIMA 3, 203–204. For the role of Shamshi-ilu in general, see Siddall, *Reign of Adad-nīrārī III*, 118–127, with earlier literature.

18. SAA 2, no. 2: v 8–9.

19. For the campaign of 765 as a possible cause of the subsequent epidemics in Assyria, see Karen Radner, "The Assyrian King and His Scholars: The Syro-Anatolian and the Egyptian Schools," in Luukko et al., *Of God(s), Trees, Kings, and Scholars*, 228–231.

20. Fuchs, "Der Turtān Šamšī-ilu."

21. See Felix Blocher, "Assyrische Würdenträger und Gouverneure des 9. und 8. Jh.: Eine Neubewertung ihrer Rolle," *Altorientalische Forschungen* 28 (2001): 298–324; Reinhard Bernbeck, "Sex/Gender/Power and Šammuramat: A View from the Syrian Steppe," in *Fundstellen: Gesammelte Schriften zur Archäologie und Geschichte Altvorderasiens ad honorem Hartmut Kühne*, ed. Dominik Bonatz, Rainer M. Czichon, and F. Janoscha Kreppner (Wiesbaden: Harrassowitz, 2008), 351–369. For the climate data, see Ashish Sinha, Gayatri Kathayat, Harvey Weiss, Hanying Li, Hai Cheng, Justin Reuter, Adam W. Schneider, et al., "Role of Climate in the Rise and Fall of the Assyrian Empire," *Science Advances* 5, no. 11 (November 2019).

22. Stephanie Dalley, "Shamshi-ilu, Language and Power in the Western Assyrian Empire," in *Essays on Syria in the Iron Age*, ed. Guy Bunnens (Leuven, Belgium: Peeters, 2000), 79–88. For the situation in Ashur in 763/762 BCE, see Eckart Frahm, "Epidemics, Climate Change, and the Birth of Empire: Assyria in the Mid-Eighth Century," in *Infecting the Ancient Mesopotamian Cosmos*, ed. Troels P. Arbøll (forthcoming). See also the next chapter.

Chapter 5: The Great Expansion

1. For the respective entries in the Eponym Chronicle, see Alan R. Millard, *The Eponyms of the Assyrian Empire, 910–612 BC* (Helsinki: Neo-Assyrian Text Corpus Project, 1994), 40–41, 58.

2. For the Mari letter, see Wolfgang Heimpel, *Letters to the King of Mari* (Winona Lake, IN: Eisenbrauns, 2003), 184–185, Text 26 17.

3. Millard, *Eponyms*, 41, 58.

4. Millard, *Eponyms*, 43, 59. For the possible connection with Gurgum, see Nadav Na'aman, "The Incirli Stela and Tiglath-pileser III's Operations on the Gurgum-Que Border," *Nouvelles Assyriologiques Brèves et Utilitaires* 2019, no. 48. SAA 12, no. 13, a royal grant dated to 762 BCE, refers on the reverse to a man with the royal name "Tukulti-apil-Esharra," that is, Tiglath-pileser. All scholars have so far assumed that the grant was issued in the name of Adad-nirari III, despite the chronological problems that this scenario poses. But it seems more likely that it was actually issued by the very Tukulti-apil-Esharra who is mentioned later in the text. If this is correct, this Tukulti-apil-Esharra must have been the rebel behind the revolt that the Eponym Chronicle claims took place in 763 and 762 in Ashur. For a variety of reasons, it is difficult to identify him with Tiglath-pileser III, but not entirely impossible. See Eckart Frahm, "Epidemics, Climate Change, and the Birth of Empire: Assyria in the Mid-Eighth Century," in *Infecting the Ancient Mesopotamian Cosmos*, ed. Troels P. Arbøll (forthcoming).

5. For editions of Tiglath-pileser III's royal inscriptions and historical notes on his reign, see Hayim Tadmor, *The Inscriptions of Tiglath-Pileser III, King of Assyria* (Jerusalem: Israel Academy of Sciences and Humanities, 1994); see also RINAP 1.

6. Andreas Fuchs, "Der Turtān Šamšī-ilu und die große Zeit der assyrischen Großen (830–746)," *Die Welt des Orients* 38 (2008): 94–96. At the same time, it must be acknowledged that Tiglath-pileser III occasionally mentions Assyrian officials in his inscriptions. For a reference to military campaigns undertaken by royal eunuchs, see, for example, RINAP 1, 44: 18–20.

7. The chronology outlined in this section follows RINAP 1, 12–13.

8. Josette Elayi, *L'Empire assyrien: Histoire d'une grande civilization de l'Antiquité* (Paris: Perrin, 2021), 100.

9. See Ashish Sinha, Gayatri Kathayat, Harvey Weiss, Hanying Li, Hai Cheng, Justin Reuter, Adam W. Schneider, et al., "Role of Climate in the Rise and Fall of the Assyrian Empire," *Science Advances* 5, no. 11 (November 2019); Canan Çakırlar and Salima Ikram, "'When Elephants Battle, the Grass Suffers': Power, Ivory and the Syrian Elephant," *Levant* 48 (2016): 167–183; Melissa S. Rosenzweig, "'Ordering the Chaotic Periphery': The Environmental Impact of the Neo-Assyrian Empire on Its Provinces," in *The Provincial*

Archaeology of the Assyrian Empire, ed. John MacGinnis, Dirk Wicke, and Tina Greenfield (Cambridge, UK: McDonald Institute for Archaeological Research, 2016), 49–58.

10. For the role of epidemics and climate change in the decline and fall of Rome, see Kyle Harper, *The Fate of Rome: Climate, Disease, and the End of Empire* (Princeton, NJ: Princeton University Press, 2017).

11. For a thorough treatment of the reign of Shalmaneser V, see Keiko Yamada and Shigeo Yamada, "Shalmaneser V and His Era, Revisited," in *"Now It Happened in Those Days": Studies in Biblical, Assyrian, and Other Ancient Near Eastern Historiography Presented to Mordechai Cogan on His 75th Birthday*, ed. Amitai Baruchi-Unnai, Tova L. Forti, Shmuel Ahituv, Israel Eph'al, and Joseph H. Tigay (Winona Lake, IN: Eisenbrauns, 2017), 2:387–442. For the letters he sent as a crown prince, see Karen Radner, "Salmanassar V. in den Nimrud Letters," *Archiv für Orientforschung* 50 (2003/2004): 95–104.

12. For a new edition of Sargon's royal inscriptions and copious notes on his reign, see RINAP 2 (with the text about Ashur on pp. 384–388). Josette Elayi, *Sargon II, King of Assyria* (Atlanta: SBL Press, 2017), provides a historical sketch of Assyria under Sargon.

13. A "western" background for Sargon II is also suggested by a Babylonian King List that makes him the first ruler of a "Dynasty of HabiGAL," the western region known in Middle Assyrian times as Hanigalbat (or Hanirabbat). For discussion, see Natalie N. May, "The Vizier and the Brother: Sargon II's Brother Sīn-aḫu-uṣur and the Neo-Assyrian Collateral Branches," *Bibliotheca Orientalis* 74 (2017): 491–527.

14. The most recent overview of Sargon's military campaigns is found in RINAP 2, 23–30.

15. For the economic consequences of the campaign against Carchemish, see Gerfrid G.W. Müller, "Gedanken zur neuassyrischen 'Geldwirtschaft,'" in *Assyrien im Wandel der Zeiten: XXXIXe Rencontre Assyriologique Internationale, Heidelberg 6–10. Juli 1992*, ed. Hartmut Waetzoldt and Harald Hauptmann (Heidelberg: Heidelberger Orientverlag, 1997), 115–121.

16. RINAP 2, 279: 18–22.

17. For the main structures and the history of Dur-Sharrukin, see Annie Caubet, ed., *Khorsabad: Le palais de Sargon II, roi d'Assyrie. Actes du colloque organisé au musée du Louvre par le Services culturel les 21 et 22 janvier 1994* (Paris: La Documentation française, 1996).

18. See May, "The Vizier and the Brother."

19. Stephen Howe, *Empire: A Very Short Introduction* (Oxford: Oxford University Press, 2002), 14–15.

20. Drawing on the example of the Roman Empire, the political theorist Michael Doyle (*Empires* [Ithaca, NY: Cornell University Press, 1986]) referred to this transition as "crossing the Augustan threshold."

21. For further discussion, see Ariel M. Bagg, *Die Assyrer und das Westland* (Leuven, Belgium: Peeters, 2011), 271–308; Mario Liverani, *Assyria: The Imperial Mission* (Winona Lake, IN: Eisenbrauns, 2017), 4–5. The term "aspirational empire" is taken from Bleda S. Düring, *The Imperialisation of Assyria* (Cambridge: Cambridge University Press, 2020), 8.

22. The numbers in this paragraph, which are to be taken with a grain of salt, are from Ariel Bagg, "The Neo-Assyrian Empire and Its Chronological and Geographical Frameworks," in *Neo-Assyrian Sources in Context*, ed. Shigeo Yamada (Helsinki: Neo-Assyrian Text Corpus Project, 2018), 27–44.

23. The following paragraphs seek to outline the Assyrian Empire's central institutions. For another recent attempt to do so, see Elayi, *L'Empire assyrien*, 100–140.

24. A king list from Ashur (A. Kirk Grayson, "Königslisten und Chroniken: B. Akkadisch," in *Reallexikon der Assyriologie und Vorderasiatischen Archäologie*, vol. 6, *Klagegesang—Königtum*, ed. D. O. Edzard [Berlin: De Gruyter, 1980], 116–121), mentions, moreover, a number of master scribes and royal advisers alongside the Neo-Assyrian kings under whom they served—but probably only because the list was composed by members of the very same scribal elite that is featured in it, and not because the scribes in question were more influential than anyone else.

25. SAA 1, nos. 22 and 26. On both letters, see also Karen Radner, "Royal Pen Pals: The Kings of Assyria in Correspondence with Officials, Clients and Total Strangers (8th and 7th Centuries BCE)," in *Official Epistolography and the Language(s) of Power*, ed. Stefan Procházka, Lucian Reinfandt, and Sven Tost (Vienna: Verlag der Akademie der Wissenschaften, 2016), 63.

26. SAA 10, nos. 196 and 207. For a slightly different translation of the second letter, see Peter Machinist, "Kingship and Divinity in Imperial Assyria," in *Text, Artifact, and Image: Revealing Ancient Israelite Religion*, ed. Gary M. Beckman and Theodore J. Lewis (Providence, RI: Brown University Press, 2006), 173–174. On *rex imago dei*, see Ernst Kantorowicz, *The King's Two Bodies: A Study in Mediaeval Political Theology* (Princeton, NJ: Princeton University Press, 1997 [1957]), 504. For further discussion and references, see Eckart Frahm, "Rising Suns and Falling Stars: Assyrian Kings and the Cosmos," in *Experiencing Power, Generating Authority: Cosmos, Politics, and the Ideology of Kingship in Ancient Egypt and Mesopotamia*, ed. Jane A. Hill, Philip Jones, and Antonio J. Morales (Philadelphia: University of Pennsylvania Press, 2013), 97–120.

27. See Davide Nadali and Lorenzo Verderame, "Neo-Assyrian Statues of Gods and Kings in Context," *Altorientalische Forschungen* 46 (2019): 234–248; Natalie N. May, " 'The True Image of the God…': Adoration of the King's Image, Assyrian Imperial Cult and Territorial Control," in *Tales of Royalty*, ed. Elisabeth Wagner-Durand and Julia Linke (Berlin: De Gruyter, 2020), 185–239. For the impact of Assyrian royal ideology on Judah, see Chapter 17.

28. See Karen Radner, "Provinz. C. Assyrien," in *Reallexikon der Assyriologie und Vorderasiatischen Archäologie*, vol. 11, *Prinz, Prinzessin–Qattara*, ed. Michael P. Streck (Berlin: De Gruyter, 2006), 42–68; Karen Radner, "Neo-Assyrian Empire," in *Imperien und Reiche in der Weltgeschichte*, ed. Michael Gehler and Robert Rollinger (Wiesbaden: Harrassowitz, 2014), 103–104.

29. Eckart Frahm, "The Neo-Assyrian Period (ca. 1000–609 BCE)," in *A Companion to Assyria*, ed. Eckart Frahm (Malden, MA: Wiley, 2017), 178.

30. Jacob Lauinger, "Esarhaddon's Succession Treaty at Tell Tayinat: Text and Commentary," *Journal of Cuneiform Studies* 64 (2012): 91–92, 112.

31. See Karen Radner, "An Imperial Communication Network: The State Correspondence of the Neo-Assyrian Empire," in *State Correspondence in the Ancient World: From New Kingdom Egypt to the Roman Empire*, ed. Karen Radner (Oxford: Oxford University Press, 2014), 71–77.

32. Radner, "Imperial Communication Network," 74.

33. Radner, "Royal Pen Pals."

34. SAA 15, nos. 288 and 289; Radner, "Imperial Communication Network," 67.

35. For the Assyrian army and Assyria at war, see Frederick Mario Fales, *Guerre et paix en Assyrie: Religion et impérialisme* (Paris: Les Editions du Cerf, 2010); Andreas Fuchs, "Assyria at War: Strategy and Conduct," in *The Oxford Handbook of Cuneiform Culture*, ed. Karen Radner and Eleanor Robson (Oxford: Oxford University Press, 2011), 380–401. The preceding and following remarks are based on these studies.

36. See RINAP 3/1, 183; SAA 16, no. 77. For analysis, see Fuchs, "Assyria at War," 381–383.

37. Katsuji Sano, *Die Deportationspraxis in neuassyrischer Zeit* (Münster: Ugarit-Verlag, 2020), 163–206.

38. SAA 19, no. 81.

39. For different viewpoints on Assyrian deportations, see (more benign) Karen Radner, "The 'Lost Tribes of Israel' in the Context of the Resettlement Programme of the Assyrian Empire," in *The Last Days of the Kingdom of Israel*, ed. Shigeo Hasegawa, Christoph Levin, and Karen Radner (Berlin: De Gruyter, 2018), 101–123, and (less so) Jonathan Valk, "Crime and Punishment: Deportation in the Levant in the Age of Assyrian Hegemony," *Bulletin of the Society of Overseas Research* 384 (2020): 77–103. For the letter, see SAA 19, no. 18.

40. Proverbs 14:28. On "bodysnatching," see Valk, "Crime and Punishment," 81.

41. See Zvi Ben-Dor Benite, *The Ten Lost Tribes: A World History* (Oxford: Oxford University Press, 2013).

42. For references and additional discussion, see Radner, "'Lost Tribes of Israel.'"

43. Avraham Faust, "The Southern Levant Under the Neo-Assyrian Empire," in *Imperial Peripheries in the Neo-Assyrian Period*, ed. Craig W. Tyson and Virginia R. Herrmann (Louisville: University Press of Colorado, 2018), 97–127.

44. See Peter Machinist, "Assyrians on Assyria in the First Millennium BC," in *Anfänge politischen Denkens in der Antike: Die nahöstlichen Kulturen und die Griechen*, ed. Kurt Raaflaub (München: R. Oldenbourg, 1993), 77–104; Frederick Mario Fales, "Ethnicity in the Assyrian Empire: A View from the Nisbe (II): 'Assyrians,'" in *Homenaje a Mario Liverani*, ed. Maria G. Biga, Joaquín M. Cordoba, Carmen del Cerro, and Elena Torres (Madrid: Centro Superior de Estudios de Oriente Próximo y Egipto, 2015), 183–204; Karen Radner, "Diglossia and the Neo-Assyrian Empire's Akkadian and Aramaic Text Production," in *Multilingualism in Ancient Contexts: Perspectives from Ancient Near Eastern and Early Christian Contexts*, ed. Louis C. Jonker, Angelika Berlejung, and Izak Cornelius (Stellenbosch, South Africa: African Sun Media, 2021), 146–181, esp. 147.

45. See Bagg, *Die Assyrer und das Westland*, 281; Samuel Boyd, "Sargon's Dūr-Šarrukīn Cylinder Inscription and Language Ideology: A Reconsideration and Connection to Genesis 11:1–9," *Journal of Near Eastern Studies* 78 (2019): 87–111.

46. For the Ashurbanipal quote, see RINAP 5/1, 41: vi 9'–13'.

Chapter 6: On the Edges of Empire

1. See Ariel Bagg, "The Neo-Assyrian Empire and Its Chronological and Geographical Frameworks," in *Neo-Assyrian Sources in Context*, ed. Shigeo Yamada (Helsinki: Neo-Assyrian Text Corpus Project, 2018), 38.

2. RINAP 3/2, 204: 1–9.

3. RINAP 4, 20: iv 53–56.

4. RINAP 3/2, 83: 74–76.

5. The following paragraphs are primarily based on Frederick Mario Fales, "Phoenicia in the Neo-Assyrian Period: An Updated Overview," *State Archives of Assyria Bulletin* 23 (2017): 181–295. See also Caroline van der Brugge and Kristin Kleber, "The Empire of Trade and the Empires of Force: Tyre in the Neo-Assyrian and Neo-Babylonian Periods," in *Dynamics of Production in the Ancient Near East, 1300–500 BC*, ed. Juan Carlos Moreno García (Oxford: Oxbow, 2016), 187–222.

6. SAA 19, no. 22. That Qurdi-Ashur-lamur was indeed a provincial governor is not completely certain.

7. SAA 2, no. 5. The quotes in the following paragraphs are from the same source.

8. For the following, see Robert Rollinger, "Assyria and the Far West: The Aegean World," in *A Companion to Assyria*, ed. Eckart Frahm (Malden, MA: Wiley, 2017), 275–285.

9. RINAP 2, 63: 117–119 (partly restored). For Qurdi-Ashur-lamur's letter, see SAA 19, no. 25.

10. See Karen Radner and Alexander Vacek, "The Site of Al-Mina, the Port of Aḫtâ and Mediterranean Trade in the Age of the Assyrian Empire," in *Der Alte Orient und die Entstehung der athenischen Demokratie*, ed. Claudia Horst (Wiesbaden: Harrassowitz, 2020), 107–171.

11. For the Orientalizing Period, see Walter Burkert, *The Orientalizing Revolution: Near Eastern Influence on Greek Culture in the Early Archaic Age* (Cambridge, MA: Harvard University Press, 1992). The quotes from the *Iliad* are from 11.531–537 and 14.201–302; the Sennacherib quote is found in RINAP 3/1, 183: vi 5–7. For discussion, see Martin L. West, *The East Face of Helicon* (Oxford: Oxford University Press, 1997), 147–148, 375–376.

12. For Homer as an Assyrian eunuch, see Raoul Schrott, *Homers Heimat: Der Kampf um Troja und seine realen Hintergründe* (Munich: Hanser, 2008), 330–336. Addikritushu is mentioned in SAA 16, no. 136. For the bowl from Amathus, and more discussion of the Greek presence in Assyria, see Rollinger, "Assyria and the Far West," 280.

13. RINAP 2, 82: 457–459.

14. Karen Radner, "The Stele of Sargon II of Assyria at Kition: A Focus for an Emerging Cypriot Identity?," in *Interkulturalität in der Alten Welt: Vorderasien, Hellas, Ägypten und die vielfältigen Ebenen des Kontakts*, ed. Robert Rollinger, Birgit Gufler, Martin Lang, and Irene Madreiter (Wiesbaden: Harrassowitz, 2010), 429–449, esp. 445.

15. RINAP 4, 23: v 54–73.

16. RINAP 4, 135: 9'–12'.

17. RINAP 1, 106–107: 19'–25'. (shortened); Eleanor Bennett, "The 'Queens of the Arabs' During the Neo-Assyrian Period" (PhD diss., University of Helsinki, 2021), 75. For general overviews of Assyro-Arab relations (on which the following remarks are based), see Israel Eph'al, *The Ancient Arabs: Nomads on the Borders of the Fertile Crescent, 9th to 5th Centuries BC*, 2nd ed. (Jerusalem: Magnes Press, 1984); Eckart Frahm, "Assyria and the Far South: The Arabian Peninsula and the Persian Gulf," in Frahm, *Companion to Assyria*, 299–310, both with additional literature and references to most of the texts mentioned below.

18. See Peter Dubovský, "Ripping Open Pregnant Women: Reliefs in Room L of Ashurbanipal's North Palace," *Orientalia Nova Series* 78 (2009); Bennett, "'Queens of the Arabs,'" 120–129, and, for the curse in the treaty, SAA 2, no. 6: 428–429.

19. For camels in early Arab history, see Martin Heide, "The Domestication of the Camel: Biological, Archaeological and Inscriptional Evidence from Mesopotamia, Egypt, Israel and Arabia, and Literary Evidence from the Hebrew Bible," *Ugarit-Forschungen* 42 (2010): 331–382.

20. RINAP 3/2, 151–156.

21. For the beads from Sheba, see RINAP 3/2, 146–150. Sabean and Assyrian sources mention only male rulers of Sheba—a historical model for the famous "Queen of Sheba," who, according to the Bible, dazzled Solomon and his royal court, is nowhere to be found. It therefore seems likely that the authors of the biblical account conflated their experience of Sabean caravans laden with exotic goods with encounters with Arab queens ruling over northern Arabian tribes.

22. The Sargon quote is found in RINAP 2, 63: 121.

23. Diodorus 2.24.5.

24. See, most recently, Romolo Loreto, "The Role of Adummatu Among the Early Arabian Trade Routes at the Dawn of the Southern Arabian Cultures," in *South Arabian Long-Distance Trade in Antiquity: "Out of Arabia,"* ed. George Hatke and Ronald Ruzicka (Newcastle upon Tyne: Cambridge Scholars Publishing, 2021), 66–110.

25. On the Ulluba campaign, see Shigeo Yamada, "Ulluba and Its Surroundings: Tiglath-pileser III's Province Organization Facing the Urartian Border," in *Neo-Assyrian Sources in Context*, ed. Shigeo Yamada (Helsinki: Neo-Assyrian Text Corpus Project, 2018). For the following, see, especially, Andreas Fuchs, "Assyria and the East: Western Iran and Elam," in Frahm, *Companion to Assyria*, 259–267, with references and additional details.

26. For more on the Medes and their role in Assyria's fall, see Chapter 14.

27. For further information on and images of some of the finds from Qalaichi, see Karen Radner, "Mannea, a Forgotten Kingdom of Iran," Assyrian Empire Builders, University College London, 2013, www.ucl.ac.uk/sargon /essentials/countries/mannea.

28. SAA 20, no. 40: rev. 23'.

29. See Andreas Fuchs, "Parsuaš," in *Reallexikon der Assyriologie und Vorderasiatischen Archäologie*, vol. 10, *Oannes–Priesterverkleidung*, ed. Michael Streck (Berlin: De Gruyter, 2003–2005), 340–342; Karen Radner, Sheler Amelirad, and Eghbal Azizi, "A First Radiocarbon Date for the Iron Age Cemetery of Sanandaj: Dating an Elite Burial in the Assyrian Province of Parsua," in *The Reach of the Assyrian and Babylonian Empires: Case Studies in Eastern and Western Peripheries*, ed. Shuichi Hasegawa and Karen Radner (Wiesbaden: Harrassowitz, 2020), 95–109.

30. Kiumars Alizadeh, "The Earliest Persians: Toponyms and Persian Ethnicity," *Dabir* 7 (2020): 16–53.

31. RINAP 4, 21–22: v 10–25.

Chapter 7: A Ghost Story

1. The story told in this chapter is based on Eckart Frahm, "Nabû-zuqup-kenu, das Gilgamesch-Epos und der Tod Sargons II," *Journal of Cuneiform Studies* 51 (1999): 73–90, where additional information and bibliographical references can be found. Only references not included in that article are provided here.

2. See Theodore Kwasman, "A Neo-Assyrian Royal Funerary Text," in *Of God(s), Trees, Kings, and Scholars: Neo-Assyrian and Related Studies in Honour of Simo Parpola*, ed. Mikko Luukko, Saana Svärd, and Raija Mattila (Helsinki: Finnish Oriental Society, 2009), 111–126.

3. For discussion, see Irving Finkel, "The Lament of Nabû-šuma-ukîn," in *Babylon: Focus mesopotamischer Geschichte, Wiege früher Gelehrsamkeit, Mythos in der Moderne*, ed. Johannes Renger (Saarbrücken: SDV, 1999), 323–341.

4. See Eckart Frahm, "New Sources for Sennacherib's First Campaign," *ISIMU* 6 (2003): 157–160.

5. Here and elsewhere in this book, Assyrian month names are accompanied by a Roman numeral that indicates their position within the year. Du'uzu, for example, was the fourth month of the year. It is not yet possible to provide exact Julian equivalents for most Assyrian dates.

6. Andrew R. George, *The Babylonian Gilgamesh Epic: Introduction, Critical Edition and Cuneiform Texts* (Oxford: Oxford University Press, 2003), 734–735 (partly restored).

7. RINAP 2, 310: 1–9.

8. RINAP 3/2, 364.

9. The text about the "Sin of Sargon" text is quoted here after SAA 3, no. 33.

10. Isaiah 14:18–19. The translation is, admittedly, not without certain problems, as shown by Saul M. Olyan, "Was the King of Babylon Buried Before His Corpse Was Exposed? Some Thoughts on Isa 14, 19," *Zeitschrift für die alttestamentliche Wissenschaft* 118 (2006): 423–426.

11. Isaiah 14:7–8.

Chapter 8: At the Gates of Jerusalem

1. 2 Kings 18:21.25.31–34. On "godnapping," the abduction of divine statues by Assyrian armies, see Shana Zaia, "State-Sponsored Sacrilege: 'Godnapping' and Omission in Neo-Assyrian Inscriptions," *Journal of Ancient Near Eastern History* 2 (2015): 19–54.

2. For the term "world event," see Seth Richardson, "The First 'World Event': Sennacherib at Jerusalem," in *Sennacherib at the Gates of Jerusalem: Story, History, and Historiography*, ed. Isaac Kalimi and Seth Richardson (Leiden: Brill, 2014), 433–505.

3. Recent studies of the campaign of 701 BCE include William R. Gallagher, *Sennacherib's Campaign to Judah: New Studies* (Leiden: Brill, 1999); Lester L. Grabbe, ed., *"Like a Bird in a Cage": The Invasion of Sennacherib in 701 BCE* (Sheffield, UK: Sheffield Academic Press, 2003); Kalimi and Richardson, *Sennacherib at the Gates of Jerusalem*; and Dan'el Kahn, *Sennacherib's Campaign Against Judah: A Source Analysis of Isaiah 36–37* (Cambridge: Cambridge University Press, 2020). Others will be referenced later in this chapter.

4. For a new edition of Sennacherib's royal inscriptions, notes on the history of his age, and references to additional studies, see RINAP 3/1 and 3/2. A historical sketch of Sennacherib's reign is provided by Josette Elayi, *Sennacherib, King of Assyria* (Atlanta: SBL Press, 2018). For the archaeology and history of Nineveh and its rural landscape, see, most recently, Lucas P. Petit and Daniele Morandi Bonacossi, eds., *Nineveh: The Great City, Symbol of Beauty and Power* (Leiden: Sidestone Press, 2017).

5. The most recent edition of the text is RINAP 3/1, 63–66.

6. For the expression "Black Pharaohs," see, for example, Robert G. Morkot, *The Black Pharaohs: Egypt's Nubian Rulers* (London: Rubicon Press, 2000). The Esarhaddon quote is found in RINAP 4, 305: 22–23. Nicolas-Christophe Grimal, *La stèle triomphale de Pi('ankhy) au Musée du Caire* (Cairo: Institut Français d'Archéologie Orientale, 1981), analyzes the literary allusions in Kushite inscriptions.

7. For Assyro-Kushite relations during this time, see Silvie Zamazalová, "Before the Assyrian Conquest in 671 B.C.E.: Relations Between Egypt, Kush and Assyria," in *Egypt and the Near East—The Crossroads*, ed. Jana Mynářová (Prague: Czech Institute of Egyptology, 2011), 297–328.

8. See RINAP 3/1, 64–65: 42–47.

9. Herodotus 2.141.

10. 2 Kings 19:9. It is possible that the reference to Taharqa is inaccurate. It might reflect a later composition date of the text, at a time when Taharqa had replaced his predecessor Shebitku as Egyptian pharaoh.

11. 2 Kings 18:13–14.

12. For photos and drawings of the reliefs, see Richard D. Barnett, Erika Bleibtreu, and Geoffrey Turner, *Sculptures from the Southwest Palace of Sennacherib at Nineveh*, vol. 2 (London: British Museum Press, 1998), Plates 322–352.

13. For the archaeology of Lachish, see David Ussishkin, "Sennacherib's Campaign to Judah: The Archaeological Perspective with an Emphasis on Lachish and Jerusalem," in Kalimi and Richardson, *Sennacherib at the Gates of Jerusalem*, 75–103, with earlier literature.

14. RINAP 3/1, 65–66: 52–58.

15. 2 Kings 18:17.

16. SAA 18, no. 98. For discussion, see Peter Dubovský, *Hezekiah and the Assyrian Spies: Reconstruction of the Assyrian Intelligence Services and Its Significance for 2 Kings 18–19* (Rome: Pontifical Biblical Institute, 2006), 163–166.

17. See Nadav Na'aman, "New Light on Hezekiah's Second Prophetic Story (2 Kings 19,9b–35)," *Biblia* 81 (2000): 393–402.

18. 2 Kings 19:35–36.

19. This is the argument made by the atmospheric and ocean scientist Carl Drews. Drews's theory was presented at great length in Chris Mooney, "No, Really: There Is a Scientific Explanation for the Parting of the Red Sea in Exodus," *Washington Post*, December 8, 2014, www.washingtonpost.com/news /wonk/wp/2014/12/08/no-really-there-is-a-scientific-explanation-for-the -parting-of-the-red-sea-in-exodus.

20. See Alan R. Millard, *The Eponyms of the Assyrian Empire, 910–612 BC* (Helsinki: Neo-Assyrian Text Corpus Project, 1994), 34–41, 57–58; Jean-Jacques Glassner, *Mesopotamian Chronicles* (Atlanta: Society of Biblical Literature, 2004), 204–205.

21. See Karen Radner, "The Assyrian King and His Scholars: The Syro-Anatolian and the Egyptian Schools," in *Of God(s), Trees, Kings, and Scholars: Neo-Assyrian and Related Studies in Honour of Simo Parpola*, ed. Mikko Luukko, Saana Svärd, and Raija Mattila (Helsinki: Finnish Oriental Society, 2009), 230–231; Margaret Barker, "Hezekiah's Boil," *Journal for the Study of the Old Testament* 95 (2001): 31–42. Note that already Josephus, with reference to Berossus, claims that it was a "pestilential distemper" that had brought Sennacherib's troops down at Jerusalem (*Jewish Antiquities* 10.21–22).

22. Stephanie Dalley, "Yabâ, Atalyā and the Foreign Policy of Late Assyrian Kings," *State Archives of Assyria Bulletin* 12 (1998): 83–98. The Atalya episode is found in 2 Kings 8:16–11:16 and 2 Chronicles 22:10–23:15. For the tombs of the Assyrian queens, see Chapter 10.

23. Henry Aubin, *The Rescue of Jerusalem: The Alliance Between Hebrews and Africans in 701 BC* (New York: Soho Press, 2002).

24. Alice Bellis, ed., *Jerusalem's Survival, Sennacherib's Departure, and the Kushite Role in 701 BCE: An Examination of Henry Aubin's Rescue of Jerusalem* (Piscataway, NJ: Gorgias Press, 2020).

25. See Jeremy Pope, "Beyond the Broken Reed: Kushite Intervention and the Limits of *l'histoire événementielle*," in Kalimi and Richardson, *Sennacherib at the Gates of Jerusalem*, 116–117.

26. See Gerfrid G.W. Müller, "Zur Entwicklung von Preisen und Wirtschaft in Assyrien im 7. Jh. v. Chr.," in *Von Sumer nach Ebla und zurück: Festschrift Giovanni Pettinato zum 27. September 1999 gewidmet von Freunden, Kollegen und Schülern*, ed. Hartmut Waetzoldt (Heidelberg: Heidelberger Orientverlag, 2004), 185–210, esp. 188.

27. John Lewis Gaddis, *On Grand Strategy* (New York: Penguin Press, 2018). For the idea that Sennacherib returned from Jerusalem to deal with the increasingly unstable situation in Babylonia, see Nazek Khalid Matty, *Sennacherib's Campaign Against Judah and Jerusalem in 701 B.C.: A Historical Reconstruction* (Berlin: De Gruyter, 2016).

28. See Richardson, "First 'World Event,'" 436–437; Eckart Frahm, *Einleitung in die Sanherib-Inschriften* (Vienna: Institut für Orientalistik, 1997), 21–28.

Chapter 9: Sennacherib's Babylonian Problem

1. For the following, see Eckart Frahm, "Assyria and the South: Babylonia," in *A Companion to Assyria*, ed. Eckart Frahm (Malden, MA: Wiley, 2017), 286–298, with additional information and references.

2. RINAP 2, 298: 314–316 (shortened).

3. "Graecia capta ferum victorem cepit et artes intulit agresti Latio" (Captive Greece took captive her savage conqueror and brought the arts to rustic Latium). Horace, *Epistles*, Book 2, Epistle 1, lines 156–157. For Sargon drawing on inscriptions of Marduk-aplu-iddina, see RINAP 2, 463 (with further literature).

4. For the animal comparisons applied to Marduk-aplu-iddina, see Andreas Fuchs, *Die Inschriften Sargons II. aus Khorsabad* (Göttingen: Cuvillier-Verlag, 1994), 334.

5. RINAP 2, 151: 141; RINAP 3/1, 34: 30–33.

6. RINAP 3/1, 36: 54.

7. RINAP 2, 139: 3–4; RINAP 3/1, 32: 4.

8. The following historical outline draws heavily on Andreas Fuchs, "Eine Flotte, zwei Versager und ein Winter: Sanherib und sein Wirken insbesondere in den Jahren 694 bis 689," in *Der Herrscher als Versager?!*, ed. Heide Frielinghaus, Sebastian Grätz, Heike Grieser, Ludger Körntgen, Johannes Pahlitzsch, and Doris Prechel (Mainz: Mainz University Press, 2019), 63–141.

9. SAA 16, no. 21.

10. For thoughts on Sennacherib's mental constitution, see Eckart Frahm, "Family Matters: Psychohistorical Reflections on Sennacherib and His Times," in *Sennacherib at the Gates of Jerusalem: Story, History, and Historiography*, ed. Isaac Kalimi and Seth Richardson (Leiden: Brill 2014), 163–222.

11. The episode of Nergal-ushezib falling from his horse is known from an epigraph recorded on a clay tablet (RINAP 3/2, 204: 14–17). The corresponding image that must have depicted the scene has not been found.

12. RINAP 3/2, 332: 39–41 (partly restored).

13. For an edition of Sennacherib's account of the Battle of Halulê, see RINAP 3/1, 181–184; for literary analysis, Elnathan Weissert, "Creating a

Political Climate: Literary Allusions to *Enūma Eliš* in Sennacherib's Account of the Battle of Halule," in *Assyrien im Wandel der Zeiten: XXXIXe Rencontre Assyriologique Internationale, Heidelberg 6–10. Juli 1992*, ed. Hartmut Waetzoldt and Harald Hauptmann (Heidelberg: Heidelberger Orientverlag, 1997), 191–202.

14. For the chronicle entry, see Jean-Jacques Glassner, *Mesopotamian Chronicles* (Atlanta: Society of Biblical Literature, 2004), 198–199; for the Nineveh text, RINAP 3/1, 226: 88–89.

15. Thus Weissert, "Creating a Political Climate."

16. Translation after RINAP 3/1, 13, n. 28.

17. SAA 21, no. 18. For discussion, see Sanae Ito, "A Letter from Assurbanipal to Enlil-bāni and the Citizens of Nippur," *Inter Faculty* 4 (2013): 19–34.

18. RINAP 3/2, 316: 47–54 (shortened).

19. For the Dilmun episode, see RINAP 3/2, 248: 36–44.

20. For the religious reforms implemented by Sennacherib and his advisers after the destruction of Babylon, see Peter Machinist, "The Assyrians and Their Babylonian Problem: Some Reflections," *Jahrbuch des Wissenschaftskollegs zu Berlin* (1984–1985): 353–364; Eckart Frahm, *Einleitung in die Sanherib-Inschriften* (Vienna: Institut für Orientalistik, 1997), 282–288; and Galo W. Vera Chamaza, *Die Omnipotenz Aššurs: Entwicklungen in der Aššur-Theologie unter den Sargoniden Sargon II., Sanherib und Asarhaddon* (Münster: Ugarit-Verlag, 2002), 71–167.

21. For an edition of the Marduk Ordeal Text, see SAA 3, nos. 34 and 35. The most detailed description of the Akitu Festival is found on clay tablets from the Hellenistic period that were recently reedited by Céline Debourse in *Of Priests and Kings: The Babylonian New Year Festival in the Last Age of Cuneiform Culture* (Leiden: Brill, 2022). Debourse argues that some of the ritual acts mentioned in the tablets may not yet have been in place in Assyrian times.

22. I owe the term "cultural cannibalism" to Eli Tadmor.

23. RINAP 3/2, 227: 1–9 (shortened).

24. RINAP 3/2, 220: obv. 19'—rev. 11.

25. RINAP 3/2, 248: 44–47. On the Assyrian Akitu Festival in general, see Beate Pongratz-Leisten, *Religion and Ideology in Assyria* (Berlin: De Gruyter, 2015), 416–427.

26. For the latest edition of *Enūma eliš*, see Wilfred G. Lambert, *Babylonian Creation Myths* (Winona Lake, IN: Eisenbrauns, 2013), 1–277. It is likely that the epic influenced the first creation account in the biblical Book of Genesis.

27. See Wilfred G. Lambert, "The Assyrian Recension of Enūma eliš," in Waetzoldt and Hauptmann, *Assyrien im Wandel der Zeiten*, 77–79.

28. RINAP 3/2, 224: 6–12 (shortened).

29. The "copy-and-paste" metaphor is taken from Fuchs, "Eine Flotte, zwei Versager," 96. For Akhenaten's religious reform, see Jan Assmann, *Ägypten: Theologie und Frömmigkeit einer frühen Hochkultur* (Stuttgart: Kohlhammer, 1991), 243–253.

30. Sennacherib's inscription is quoted after RINAP 3/2, 221: 4–5.

31. For discussion, see SAA 6, pp. xxix–xxxiv.

32. 2 Kings 19:36–37. For background, see Simo Parpola, "The Murderer of Sennacherib," in *Death in Mesopotamia*, ed. Bendt Alster (Copenhagen: Akademisk, 1980), 171–182. It must be admitted that the scenario outlined here is not universally accepted. Asking the *cui bono* question, several scholars, among them most recently Andrew Knapp, in "The Murderer of Sennacherib, Yet Again," *Journal of the American Oriental Society* 140 (2020): 165–181; and Stephanie Dalley and Louis R. Siddall, in "A Conspiracy to Murder Sennacherib? A Revision of SAA 18 100 in the Light of a Recent Join," *Iraq* 83 (2021): 45–56, have suggested that it was actually Esarhaddon who was behind Sennacherib's murder. All things considered, though, it still seems more likely that Urdu-Mullissu was the culprit.

33. The episode is described in the letter SAA 18, no. 100 (new edition: Dalley and Siddall, "Conspiracy"). The letter's first line is probably to be translated as "[...] of the goodness of the king (?) [...]."

34. RINAP 4, 13–14: i 53–ii 11. The Babylonian Chronicle gives a slightly later date for Esarhaddon's accession. For the flight of the brothers, presumably to the land of Urartu, see Nadav Na'aman, "Sennacherib's Sons' Flight to Urartu," *Nouvelles Assyriologiques Brèves et Utilitaires* 2006, no. 5.

35. See Aristotle, *Politics* 2.1269b.

Chapter 10: Mother Knows Best

1. SAA 9, no. 1, 1.8.

2. For a comprehensive study of Naqia's life and career, and editions of the texts mentioning her, see Sarah C. Melville, *The Role of Naqia/Zakutu in Sargonid Politics* (Helsinki: Neo-Assyrian Text Corpus Project, 1999).

3. For Naqia's possible connection with Harran, see Erle V. Leichty, "Esarhaddon's Exile: Some Speculative History," in *Studies Presented to Robert D. Biggs, June 4, 2004*, ed. Martha Roth, Walter Farber, and Matthew W. Stolper (Chicago: Oriental Institute of the University of Chicago, 2007), 189–191.

4. RINAP 3/2, 42–43: 44"–50".

5. See Eckart Frahm, "Family Matters: Psychohistorical Reflections on Sennacherib and His Times," in *Sennacherib at the Gates of Jerusalem: Story, History, and Historiography*, ed. Isaac Kalimi and Seth Richardson (Leiden: Brill 2014), 215–217. For a skeptical view of this idea, see Natalie N. May, "Neo-Assyrian Women, Their Visibility, and Their Representation in Written

and Pictorial Sources," in *Studying Gender in the Ancient Near East*, ed. Saana Svärd and Agnès Garcia-Ventura (University Park, PA: Eisenbrauns, 2018), 218. But note that May's reading *il-te* rather than *al-te* in a key text needs additional verification.

6. SAA 16, no. 95. The interpretation of this difficult letter is uncertain, as is its exact date.

7. Julian Reade, "Was Sennacherib a Feminist?," in *La femme dans le Proche-Orient antique*, ed. Jean-Marie Durand (Paris: Éditions Recherche sur les Civilisations, 1987), 139–145.

8. RINAP 4, 315–318.

9. RINAP 4, 318–322.

10. For the relief, see RINAP 4, 323–324, with further literature; for the letter, SAA 13, no. 61.

11. SAA 10, no. 244.

12. SAA 18, no. 85.

13. Recent studies on Assyrian royal women include Sarah C. Melville, "Neo-Assyrian Royal Women and Male Identity: Status as a Social Tool," *Journal of the American Oriental Society* 124 (2004): 37–57; Sherry L. Macgregor, *Beyond Hearth and Home: Women in the Public Sphere in Neo-Assyrian Society* (Helsinki: Neo-Assyrian Text Corpus Project, 2012); Saana Svärd, *Power and Women in Neo-Assyrian Palaces* (Helsinki: Neo-Assyrian Text Corpus Project, 2015); and May, "Neo-Assyrian Women." For the harems in different Assyrian cities, see Simo Parpola, "The Neo-Assyrian Royal Harem," in *Leggo! Studies Presented to Frederick Mario Fales on the Occasion of His 65th Birthday*, ed. Giovanni B. Lanfranchi, Daniele Morandi Bonacossi, Cinzia Pappi, and Simonetta Ponchia (Wiesbaden: Harrassowitz, 2012), 613–626. The use of the term "harem" in connection with the women's quarters of ancient Mesopotamian royal courts has occasionally been criticized as anachronistic, but no better one is at hand.

14. See Saana Teppo, "The Role and the Duties of the Neo-Assyrian *šakintu* in the Light of the Archival Evidence," *State Archives of Assyria* 16 (2007): 257–272; François Joannès, "Women and Palaces in the Neo-Assyrian Period," *Orient* 51 (2016): 29–46.

15. For the Ashurbanipal quote, see RINAP 5/1, 236–237: ii 63–80. The later Greek Ashurbanipal tradition is covered in Chapter 17.

16. For more discussion, see Walter Scheidel, "Sex and Empire: A Darwinian Perspective," in *The Dynamics of Ancient Empires: State Power from Assyria to Byzantium*, ed. Ian Morris and Walter Scheidel (Oxford: Oxford University Press, 2009), 255–324. For a concrete example of how foreign women abducted in war became the property of Assyrian citizens, see Chapter 13.

17. For the chronicle entry, see Jean-Jacques Glassner, *Mesopotamian Chronicles* (Atlanta: Society of Biblical Literature, 2004), 208–209. Even

though the deceased queen mentioned in it is not named, it is very likely that she can be identified with Esharra-hammat. For an edition of the letter, see SAA 10, no. 188.

18. Thus Natalie N. May, "The Vizier and the Brother: Sargon II's Brother Sīn-aḫu-uṣur and the Neo-Assyrian Collateral Branches," *Bibliotheca Orientalis* 74 (2017): 514–515. For the document mentioning Abi-ramu, see SAA 6, no. 252. Although not without reservations, I wonder whether the biblical figure of Abram/Abraham—who had come from Ur in southern Babylonia and had lived in Harran, and thus in Hanigalbat, until he was seventy-five years old—might not have had some historical connection with Naqia's sister Abi-ramu, with whom he shares his name. Given that the reign of Esarhaddon provided the setting for quite a number of other popular tales, many known from Aramaic texts and Demotic papyri from ancient Egypt (see Kim Ryholt, "The Assyrian Invasion of Egypt in Egyptian Literary Tradition," in *Assyria and Beyond: Studies Presented to Mogens Trolle Larsen*, ed. Jan G. Dercksen [Leiden: Netherlands Institute for the Near East, 2004], 483–510), the possibility, though unprovable, should not be discarded out of hand. In a similar vein, it is hard to deny that the story of Esarhaddon's rise to power bears some conspicuous similarities with the story of another biblical patriarch closely associated with Harran, Abraham's great-grandson Joseph. Both Esarhaddon and Joseph rose to great power despite the fact that they were younger sons born to junior wives (with family ties to Harran); both were, against all odds, favorites of their respective fathers; both received divine signs of encouragement; and both became, in the end, and each in his own way, rulers of Egypt. For more discussion, see Eckart Frahm, "'And His Brothers Were Jealous of Him': Surprising Parallels Between Joseph and King Esarhaddon," *Biblical Archaeology Review* 42, no. 3 (2016): 43–64.

19. For detailed information on the "queens' tombs" in Calah, see John E. Curtis, Henrietta McCall, Dominique Collon, and Lamia Al-Gailani Werr, eds., *New Light on Nimrud: Proceedings of the Nimrud Conference, 11th–13th March 2002* (London: British Institute for the Study of Iraq, in association with the British Museum, 2008), and Muzahim M. Hussein's lavishly illustrated volume *Nimrud: The Queens' Tombs* (Chicago: Oriental Institute of the University of Chicago, 2016). On the gender of the unidentified body, see p. 9 in the same volume.

20. Farouk N.H. Al-Rawi, "Inscriptions from the Tombs of the Queens of Assyria," in Curtis et al., *New Light on Nimrud*, 124.

21. See Chapter 4.

22. For a detailed assessment of Hamâ's bodily remains and the funerary gifts she received, see Tracy L. Spurrier, "Finding Hama: On the Identification of a Forgotten Queen Buried in the Nimrud Tombs," *Journal of Near Eastern Studies* 76 (2017): 149–174.

23. A golden bowl inscribed with the name of Shamshi-ilu was found in a second bronze sarcophagus from the antechamber of Tomb III. The sarcophagus held, inter alia, the bones of an adult woman, whom one could identify with Hadianu's daughter as well.

24. Al-Rawi, "Inscriptions," 119–124. It should be noted that there is still some uncertainty about the identification of the skeletons found in the sarcophagus in Tomb II. Tracy Spurrier will deal with the issues at stake in a forthcoming article.

25. See Chapter 8. Objects from the sarcophagus mention the name of what appears at first glance to be yet another queen, Banitu ("The Beautiful"), who is said to have been the "Palace Woman of Shalmaneser." Since only two bodies were found in the sarcophagus, it has been suggested that Banitu was actually identical with Yabâ, a name that could mean "beautiful" as well. If this is accurate, Yabâ would have kept her title of "Palace Woman" under Shalmaneser V. It is also possible, however, that Banitu was the wife of an earlier Shalmaneser (III or IV), and that Yabâ or Atalya had inherited the objects from that woman. I am grateful to Tracy Spurrier for discussing these possibilities with me.

26. Frahm, "Family Matters," 179.

27. SAA 6, no. 143.

28. SAA 4, no. 20.

29. SAA 16, no. 28. For a different interpretation of the letter, see Alasdair Livingstone, "Ashurbanipal: Literate or Not?," *Zeitschrift für Assyriologie* 97 (2007): 105.

30. SAA 3, no. 8 (partly restored and shortened).

31. For the role of Sherua-etirat ("Saritra") in the Demotic tale, and further thoughts on the princess, see, most recently, Frederick Mario Fales, "Saritra and the Others: A Neo-Assyrian View of Papyrus Amherst 63," in *Città e parole, argilla e pietra: Studi offerti à Clelia Mora*, ed. Maria E. Balza, Paola Cotticelli Kurras, Lorenzo D'Alfonso, Mauro Giorgieri, Federico Giusfredi, and Alfredo Rizza (Bari, Italy: Edipuglia, 2020), 225–251. For a more detailed account of her mission in the four-year war that started in 652, see Chapter 12.

32. SAA 4, no. 321 (shortened). SAA 4, no. 322 is a very similar oracle query. In both queries, the author is not named, but since Libbali-sharrat was one of presumably not that many Neo-Assyrian royal women capable of writing in cuneiform, it is likely that she was the one who composed them. Lahar (if read correctly) may be an esoteric name of the sun god.

Chapter 11: 671 BCE

1. Eckart Frahm, "Hochverrat in Assur," in *Assur-Forschungen: Arbeiten aus der Forschungsstelle "Edition literarischer Keilschrifttexte aus Assur" der*

Heidelberger Akademie der Wissenschaften, ed. Stefan M. Maul and Nils P. Heeßel (Wiesbaden: Harrassowitz, 2010), 89–139.

2. Balaam's star vision is found in Numbers 24:17. It is noteworthy that in Numbers 22:5 and Deuteronomy 23:4, Balaam is said to have come from Pethor, a place that may be identical with the Aramaean-Assyrian city of Pitru in the Middle Euphrates region. Pitru had been conquered by Shalmaneser III, who settled Assyrian colonists in the city and referred to it by the Assyrian name Ana-Ashur-uter-asbat.

3. For a recent edition of Esarhaddon's royal inscriptions, see RINAP 4. In *Images, Power, and Politics: Figurative Aspects of Esarhaddon's Babylonian Policy* (Philadelphia: American Philosophical Society, 1993), Barbara N. Porter studies Esarhaddon's Babylonian politics. For the king's military campaigns, see, most recently, Josetter Elayi, *L'Empire assyrien: Histoire d'une grande civilization de l'Antiquité* (Paris: Perrin, 2021), 213–219.

4. Jean-Jacques Glassner, *Mesopotamian Chronicles* (Atlanta: Society of Biblical Literature, 2004), 201–202.

5. Esarhaddon's apology is edited in RINAP 4, 11–14. For the historical context, see Andrew Knapp, "The *Sitz im Leben* of Esarhaddon's Apology," *Journal of Cuneiform Studies* 68 (2016): 181–195.

6. SAA 2, no. 6; Jacob Lauinger, "Esarhaddon's Succession Treaty at Tell Tayinat: Text and Commentary," *Journal of Cuneiform Studies* 64 (2012): 87–123.

7. SAA 10, no. 185.

8. RINAP 4, 231–236: i 7–ii 18 (shortened).

9. See SAA 10, nos. 348 and 24.

10. Simo Parpola, *Letters from Assyrian Scholars to the Kings Esarhaddon and Assurbanipal*, Part II, *Commentary and Appendices* (Kevelaer: Butzon und Bercker, 1983), 229–236. For the Urad-Nanaya letter, see SAA 10, no. 315.

11. See SAA 10, nos. 43 and 196.

12. See Karen Radner, "Esarhaddon's Expedition from Palestine to Egypt in 671 BCE: A Trek Through Negev and Sinai," in *Fundstellen: Gesammelte Schriften zur Archäologie und Geschichte Altvorderasiens ad honorem Hartmut Kühne*, ed. Dominik Bonatz, Rainer M. Czichon, and F. Janoscha Kreppner (Wiesbaden: Harrassowitz, 2008), 305–314; Elayi, *L'Empire assyrien*, 225. Despite the skepticism of others, it seems likely to me that the Sha-amile in the Babylonian Chronicle entry for 674 (Glassner, *Mesopotamian Chronicles*, 208–209) is Silé, and not the city with the same name in southern Babylonia.

13. See RINAP 4, 87–88, and Herodotus 2.75, 3.109. My interpretation of these two passages follows Karen Radner, "The Winged Snakes of Arabia and the Fossil Site of Makhtesh Ramon in the Negev," *Wiener Zeitschrift für die Kunde des Morgenlandes* 97 (2007): 353–365.

14. Migdol is mentioned in Exodus 14:2. Herodotus 2.159 calls the town Magdalos.

15. The reference about tearing out the roots of Kush is found in RINAP 4, 185–186: rev. 45–46.

16. RINAP 4, 54–56. See also Marian H. Feldman, "Nineveh to Thebes and Back: Art and Politics Between Assyria and Egypt in the Seventh Century BCE," *Iraq* 66 (2004): 141–150, and Karen Radner, "The Assyrian King and His Scholars: The Syro-Anatolian and the Egyptian Schools," in *Of God(s), Trees, Kings, and Scholars: Neo-Assyrian and Related Studies in Honour of Simo Parpola*, ed. Mikko Luukko, Saana Svärd, and Raija Mattila (Helsinki: Finnish Oriental Society, 2009).

17. RINAP 4, 182: obv. 13–16. For later Egyptian stories about the event, see Kim Ryholt, "The Assyrian Invasion of Egypt in Egyptian Literary Tradition," in *Assyria and Beyond: Studies Presented to Mogens Trolle Larsen*, ed. Jan G. Dercksen (Leiden: Netherlands Institute for the Near East, 2004), 483–510.

18. See SAA 10, no. 347, and Parpola, *Letters from Assyrian Scholars*, xxii–xxxii.

19. The killing of the substitute king is described in the letter SAA 10, no. 350.

20. For discussions of the rebellions of 671 BCE, see Martti Nissinen, *References to Prophecy in Neo-Assyrian Sources* (Helsinki: Neo-Assyrian Text Corpus Project, 1998), 107–153; Karen Radner, "The Trials of Esarhaddon: The Conspiracy of 670 BC," *ISIMU* 6 (2003): 165–184; Frahm, "Hochverrat in Assur."

21. The promises made by Sîn and Nusku are known from SAA 10, no. 174. The Nabû-rehtu-usur letter is edited in SAA 16, no. 59 (the translation of the last line, which is partly restored, is not completely certain). SAA 16, nos. 60 and 61, deal with the Harran insurgency as well.

22. SAA 10, no. 179.

23. Radner, "Trials of Esarhaddon," 168.

24. SAA 2, no. 6, §10. The John le Carré quote is from his 1974 novel *Tinker, Tailor, Soldier, Spy*.

25. For the Nabû-ahhe-eriba letter, see SAA 10, no. 68; for the letter from Guzana, SAA 16, no. 63. In the classical world "drawing down the moon" was associated with witchcraft as well. See Vergil, *Eclogues*, 8.69: "Carmina vel caelo possunt deducere Lunam" (Charms can even bring the moon down from heaven).

26. Thus first Nissinen, *References to Prophecy*, 144–150.

27. For the chronicle entry, see Glassner, *Mesopotamian Chronicles*, 202–203.

28. SAA 10, no. 316.

29. For a text that seems to describe Esarhaddon's funeral, see Theodore Kwasman, "A Neo-Assyrian Royal Funerary Text," in Luukko et al., *Of God(s), Trees, Kings, and Scholars*, 111–126.

Chapter 12: Scholar, Sadist, Hunter, King

1. Jamie Novotny, *Selected Royal Inscriptions of Ashurbanipal* (Helsinki: Neo-Assyrian Text Corpus Project, 2014), 96.

2. Andrew R. George, *The Babylonian Gilgamesh Epic: Introduction, Critical Edition and Cuneiform Texts* (Oxford: Oxford University Press, 2003), 538–539. See Beate Pongratz-Leisten, *Herrschaftswissen in Mesopotamien* (Helsinki: Neo-Assyrian Text Corpus Project 1999), 312.

3. Novotny, *Selected Inscriptions of Ashurbanipal*, 97 (shortened); RINAP 5/1, 232: i 41–51.

4. René Labat, "Un prince éclairé: Assurbanipal," *Comptes rendus des séances de l'Académie des Inscriptions et Belles-Lettres* 116, no. 4 (1972): 670–676; Sebastian Fink, "Assurbanipal, der Wirtschaftsweise: Einige Überlegungen zur mesopotamischen Preistheorie," in *Emas non quod opus est, sed quod necesse est*, ed. Kai Ruffing and Kerstin Droß-Krüpe (Wiesbaden: Harrassowitz, 2018), 131–142; Sanae Ito, "Assurbanipal the Humanist? The Case of Equal Treatment," *State Archives of Assyria Bulletin* 23 (2017): 67–90.

5. This and the following paragraphs draw on RINAP 5/1, 14–26, a concise overview of the Assyrian military campaigns that took place under Ashurbanipal. Gareth Brereton, ed., *I Am Ashurbanipal, King of the World, King of Assyria* (New York: Thames and Hudson, 2018), sheds new light on a variety of aspects of the reign of Ashurbanipal and includes numerous images of artwork and texts from his time.

6. RINAP 5/1, 61: ii 30–34. For the Roman spoliation of Egyptian obelisks, see Susan Sorek, *The Emperors' Needles: Egyptian Obelisks and Rome* (Exeter: Bristol Phoenix Press, 2010).

7. Psamtik's linguistic experiments are known from Herodotus 2.2. Based on the observation of two newborn babies who had no human interlocutors, they established Phrygian as the earliest language ever spoken.

8. The episode is described in RINAP 5/1, 41: vi 9'–13'. A new edition of this difficult passage, based on some recently identified new manuscripts, is provided by Tonio Mitto and Jamie Novotny in "'Ashurbanipal, the King Who Is Resplendent Like a Bright Light': Gyges' Dream in Ashurbanipal's E Prisms Revisited," *State Archives of Assyria Bulletin* 27 (2021): 133–158. According to this study, it was most likely a professional translator who conveyed the meaning of Gyges's message to the Assyrians, but the gap in the text has still not been restored. Plato talks about Gyges and his ring in the second book of his *Republic*; Gog is mentioned in Ezekiel 38.

9. The chronology of these events is not entirely certain and an earlier date for the Til Tuba campaign, possibly 663 BCE, not excluded. See Julian E. Reade and Christopher B. F. Walker, "Some Neo-Assyrian Royal Inscriptions," *Archiv für Orientforschung* 28 (1982): 120–122. For the Egyptianizing features of the Til Tuba reliefs, see Marian H. Feldman, "Nineveh to Thebes and Back: Art and Politics Between Assyria and Egypt in the Seventh Century BCE," *Iraq* 66 (2004): 141–150.

10. RINAP 5/1, 69–70: v 49–72 (shortened).

11. For details, see Chapter 17.

12. On mimetic desire and its potential to breed conflict, see René Girard, *La violence et le sacré* (Paris: Grasset, 1972).

13. See Shana Zaia, "My Brother's Keeper: Assurbanipal versus Šamaš-šuma-ukīn," *Journal of Ancient Near Eastern History* 6 (2018): 19–52; Shana Zaia, "Going Native: Šamaš-šuma-ukīn, Assyrian King of Babylon," *Iraq* 81 (2019): 247–268. For one of Shamash-shumu-ukin's flawed Sumerian inscriptions, see Thorkild Jacobsen, "Abstruse Sumerian," in *Ah, Assyria... Studies in Assyrian History and Ancient Near Eastern Historiography Presented to Hayim Tadmor*, ed. Mordechai Cogan and Israel Eph'al (Jerusalem: Magnes Press, 1991), 279–291.

14. SAA 21, no. 3 (shortened). The letter is known from a dated archival copy found at Nineveh. For a detailed historical account of the conflict, see Grant Frame, *Babylonia, 689–627 B.C.: A Political History* (Leiden: Netherlands Institute for the Near East, 1992), 131–190.

15. My summary of the tale is based on Frederick Mario Fales, "Saritra and the Others: A Neo-Assyrian View of Papyrus Amherst 63," in *Città e parole, argilla e pietra: Studi offerti à Clelia Mora*, ed. Maria E. Balza, Paola Cotticelli Kurras, Lorenzo D'Alfonso, Mauro Giorgieri, Federico Giusfredi, and Alfredo Rizza (Bari, Italy: Edipuglia, 2020), 225–251.

16. RINAP 5/1, 174–175: viii 3'''–16''''.

17. RINAP 5/1, 249–261: v 126–x 39.

18. For this and the following, see Elnathan Weissert, "Royal Hunt and Royal Triumph in a Prism Fragment of Ashurbanipal (82-5-22,2)," in *Assyria 1995*, ed. Simo Parpola and Robert Whiting (Helsinki: Neo-Assyrian Text Corpus Project, 1997), 339–358; Julian E. Reade, "The Assyrian Royal Hunt," in *I Am Ashurbanipal, King of the World, King of Assyria*, ed. Gareth Brereton (New York: Thames and Hudson, 2018), 52–79.

19. Weissert, "Royal Hunt," 355.

20. For more information on Ceaușescu's bear hunts, see David Quammen, "The Bear Slayer," *Atlantic*, July/August 2003, www.theatlantic.com /magazine/archive/2003/07/the-bear-slayer/302768.

21. RINAP 5/1, 77: viii 13–15.

22. RINAP 5/1, 58: i 35–36; SAA 3, no. 25. The modern equivalents given for the ancient measurements presuppose that Ashurbanipal used the "light" rather than the "heavy" standard, which is not certain.

23. SAA 10, no. 100.

24. Gerfrid G.W. Müller, "Zur Entwicklung von Preisen und Wirtschaft in Assyrien im 7. Jh. v. Chr.," in *Von Sumer nach Ebla und zurück: Festschrift Giovanni Pettinato zum 27. September 1999 gewidmet von Freunden, Kollegen und Schülern*, ed. Hartmut Waetzoldt (Heidelberg: Heidelberger Orientverlag, 2004), 209. For the document from Calah, see Suzanne Herbordt, Raija Mattila, Barbara Parker, John Nicholas Postgate, and Donald J. Wiseman, *Documents from the Nabu Temple and from Private Houses on the Citadel*, Cuneiform Texts from Nimrud 6 (London: British Institute for the Study of Iraq, 2019), no. 66.

25. Austen Henry Layard, *Discoveries in the Ruins of Nineveh and Babylon* (London: John Murray, 1853), 345. For the following, see, most recently, Irving Finkel, "Assurbanipal's Library: An Overview," in *Libraries Before Alexandria: Ancient Near Eastern Traditions*, ed. Kim Ryholt and Gojko Barjamovic (Oxford: Oxford University Press, 2019), 367–389.

26. For an introduction to the Mesopotamian art of divination, see Stefan Maul, *Die Wahrsagekunst im Alten Orient: Zeichen des Himmels und der Erde* (Munich: Beck, 2013).

27. Wilfred H. van Soldt, *Solar Omens of Enuma Anu Enlil: Tablets 23 (24)–29 (30)* (Leiden: Netherlands Institute for the Near East, 1995), 46–47: ii 1–2. For cuneiform commentaries in general, see Eckart Frahm, *Babylonian and Assyrian Commentaries: Origins of Interpretation* (Münster: Ugarit-Verlag, 2011).

28. See "The Poor Man of Nippur—World's First Film in Babylonian," YouTube, posted by Cambridge Archaeology, November 26, 2018, www.youtube .com/watch?v=pxYoFlnJLoE.

29. Grant Frame and Andrew R. George, "The Royal Libraries of Nineveh: New Evidence for King Ashurbanipal's Tablet Collecting," *Iraq* 67 (2005): 265–284 (the quote, shortened here, is on p. 275). See also Eckart Frahm, "On Some Recently Published Late Babylonian Copies of Royal Letters," *Nouvelles Assyriologiques Brèves et Utilitaires* 2005, no. 43.

30. For the quote and its relevance for Ashurbanipal's image, see Eckart Frahm, "The Exorcist's Manual: Structure, Language, Sitz im Leben," in *Sources of Evil: Studies in Mesopotamian Exorcistic Lore*, ed. Greta Van Buylaere, Mikko Luukko, Daniel Schwemer, and Avigail Mertens-Wagschal (Leiden: Brill, 2018), 39 (shortened).

31. The quote from the Ashurbanipal letter is from Frame and George, "Royal Libraries," 275: lines 28–32. The letter is known from a Late Babylonian

copy that may or may not accurately reflect what Ashurbanipal had originally written. For Tukulti-Ninurta's "booknapping," see Chapter 2.

32. This is the thesis of David Brown in *Mesopotamian Planetary Astronomy-Astrology* (Groningen, Netherlands: Styx, 2000).

33. On Ashurbanipal's stylus, see Ursula Seidl, "Assurbanipals Griffel," *Zeitschrift für Assyriologie* 97 (2007): 119–124. Balasî's and Nabû-ahhe-eriba's letters are published in SAA 10, nos. 44 and 58, and SAA 16, no. 19. For the question of how well Ashurbanipal could read and write, see Alasdair Livingstone, "Ashurbanipal: Literate or Not?," *Zeitschrift für Assyriologie* 97 (2007): 98–118 (quote on p. 107).

34. RINAP 5/1, 129–130: vii 47–47'; 255: viii 11–13.

35. RINAP 5/1, 243: iv 28–29; Rykle Borger, *Beiträge zum Inschriftenwerk Assurbanipals* (Wiesbaden: Harrassowitz, 1996), 333–334. The beard metaphor is, admittedly, also known from a few texts from other times.

36. That the head in the tree is Teumman's is the most widely held opinion, but see Natalie N. May, "Neo-Assyrian Women: Their Visibility, and Their Representation in Written and Pictorial Sources," in *Studying Gender in the Ancient Near East*, ed. Saana Svärd and Agnès Garcia-Ventura (University Park, PA: Eisenbrauns, 2018), 260, for a different view.

37. See RINAP 5/1, 30–31.

38. For the Greek Sardanapallus legend, see Chapter 17.

Chapter 13: Everyday Life in the Empire

1. SAA 15, no. 4.

2. For the pits near Khinis, see Kawa Omar, "Wine Press Dating Back 2,700 Years Discovered in Northern Iraq," Reuters, November 1, 2021, www .reuters.com/world/middle-east/wine-press-dating-back-2700-years -discovered-northern-iraq-2021-11-01. For Sennacherib's attempts to cultivate cotton, see, for example, RINAP 3/1, 142: vii 56.

3. See Karen Radner, "How Did the Neo-Assyrian King Perceive His Land and Its Resources?," in *Rainfall and Agriculture in Northern Mesopotamia*, ed. Remko M. Jas (Leiden: Netherlands Institute for the Near East, 2000), 233–246.

4. Andrew R. George and Junko Taniguchi, "The Dogs of Ninkilim, Part Two: Babylonian Rituals to Counter Field Pests," *Iraq* 72 (2010): 85.

5. SAA 1, no. 104. See Karen Radner, "Fressen und gefressen werden: Heuschrecken als Katastrophe und Delikatesse im Alten Vorderen Orient," *Altorientalische Forschungen* 34 (2004): 17–18.

6. SAA 13, nos. 19 and 20.

7. For the domestic architecture of Ashur, see Peter Miglus, *Das Wohngebiet von Assur: Stratigraphie und Architektur* (Berlin: Gebrüder Mann, 1996);

for the "Red House" in Dur-Katlimmu, Janoscha Kreppner, "Neuassyrische palatiale Architektur urbaner Eliten: Das Rote Haus von Dūr-Katlimmu," in *Der Palast im antiken und islamischen Orient*, ed. Dirk Wicke (Wiesbaden: Harrassowitz, 2019), 91–108.

8. See Karen Radner, *Die neuassyrischen Privatrechtsurkunden als Quelle für Mensch und Umwelt* (Helsinki: Neo-Assyrian Text Corpus Project, 1997), 14–18.

9. Heather D. Baker, *Neo-Assyrian Specialists: Crafts, Offices, and Other Professional Designations* (Helsinki: Neo-Assyrian Text Corpus Project, 2017).

10. See Karen Radner, "Diglossia and the Neo-Assyrian Empire's Akkadian and Aramaic Text Production," in *Multilingualism in Ancient Contexts: Perspectives from Ancient Near Eastern and Early Christian Contexts*, ed. Louis C. Jonker, Angelika Berlejung, and Izak Cornelius (Stellenbosch, South Africa: African Sun Media, 2021), 161–162, 170.

11. Nahum 3:16.

12. Karen Radner, "Economy, Society, and Daily Life in the Neo-Assyrian Period," in *A Companion to Assyria*, ed. Eckart Frahm (Malden, MA: Wiley, 2017), 224–226.

13. SAA 16, no. 89.

14. The Urad-Gula quote is from SAA 10, no. 294 (shortened).

15. Gershon Galil, *The Lower Stratum Families in the Neo-Assyrian Period* (Leiden: Brill, 2007).

16. Andrew R. George, "The Assyrian Elegy: Form and Meaning," in *Opening the Tablet Box: Near Eastern Studies in Honor of Benjamin R. Foster*, ed. Sarah Melville and Alice Slotsky (Leiden: Brill, 2010), 203–216. George's translation, faithfully reproduced here, is less literal than the one offered in SAA 3, no. 15.

17. SAA 10, no. 187.

18. Walter Farber, *Lamaštu: An Edition of the Canonical Series of Lamaštu Incantations and Rituals and Related Texts from the Second and First Millennia B.C.* (Winona Lake, IN: Eisenbrauns, 2014), 157.

19. See Nils P. Heeßel, *Pazuzu: Archäologische und philologische Untersuchungen zu einem altorientalischen Dämon* (Leiden: Brill, 2002). While Pazuzu's iconography seems to have been inspired by that of Bes (who is likewise associated with birth-giving), Pazuzu's name and character may have inner-Mesopotamian roots, for which see Eckart Frahm, "A Tale of Two Lands and Two Thousand Years: The Origins of Pazuzu," in *Mesopotamian Medicine and Magic: Studies in Honor of Markham J. Geller*, ed. Strahil V. Panayotov and Luděk Vacín (Leiden: Brill, 2018), 272–291.

20. For an edition of the Mesopotamian "lullabies," see Walter Farber, *Schlaf, Kindchen, schlaf! Mesopotamische Baby-Beschwörungen und -Rituale* (Winona Lake, IN: Eisenbrauns, 1989).

21. Markham J. Geller, "Freud and Mesopotamian Magic," in *Mesopotamian Magic: Textual, Historical, and Interpretive Perspectives*, ed. Tzvi Abusch and Karel Van Der Toorn (Leiden: Brill, 1999), 54. For a new edition of the Mesopotamian potency rituals, see Gioele Zisa, *The Loss of Male Sexual Desire in Ancient Mesopotamia: "Niš Libbi" Therapies* (Berlin: De Gruyter, 2021).

22. Ulla Koch-Westenholz, *Babylonian Liver Omens* (Copenhagen: Museum Tusculanum Press, 2000), 33, 106.

23. Wilfred G. Lambert, *Babylonian Wisdom Literature* (Oxford: Oxford University Press, 1960), 146–147.

24. In Latin: *domum servavit, lanam fecit.*

25. SAA 10, no. 191.

26. See Heather Baker, "Slavery and Personhood in the Neo-Assyrian Empire," in *On Human Bondage: After Slavery and Social Death*, ed. John Bodel and Walter Scheidel (Malden, MA: Wiley-Blackwell, 2017), 15–30, esp. 21–24; Radner, "Economy, Society, and Daily Life," 223–224. For slaves in the Neo-Assyrian period in general, see also Simonetta Ponchia, "Slaves, Serfs, and Prisoners in Imperial Assyria (IX to VII Cent. BC): A Review of Written Sources," *State Archives of Assyria Bulletin* 23 (2017): 157–179.

27. SAA 15, no. 74.

28. SAA 16, no. 105.

29. See Erica Reiner, " 'Runaway—Seize Him,' " in *Assyria and Beyond: Studies Presented to Mogens Trolle Larsen*, ed. Jan G. Dercksen (Leiden: Netherlands Institute for the Near East, 2004), 475–482.

30. See Ponchia, "Slaves, Serfs, and Prisoners," 173; SAA 1, no. 21.

31. Greta Van Buylaere, "The Secret Lore of Scholars," in *Leggo! Studies Presented to Frederick Mario Fales on the Occasion of His 65th Birthday*, ed. Giovanni B. Lanfranchi, Daniele Morandi Bonacossi, Cinzia Pappi, and Simonetta Ponchia (Wiesbaden: Harrassowitz, 2012), 859–860.

32. Sally M. Freedman, *If a City Is Set on a Height: The Akkadian Omen Series šumma ālu ina mēlê šakin*, vol. 1, *Tablets 1–21* (Philadelphia: University of Pennsylvania Museum, 1998), 33–34 (translation not absolutely certain), and vol. 3, *Tablets 41–46* (Winona Lake, IN: Eisenbrauns, 2017), 41–49; Eckart Frahm, *Babylonian and Assyrian Commentaries: Origins of Interpretation* (Münster: Ugarit-Verlag, 2011), 41.

33. Gojko Barjamovic, Patricia Jurardo Gonzalez, Chelsea A. Graham, Agnete W. Lassen, Nawal Nasrallah, and Pia Sörensen, "Food in Ancient Mesopotamia: Cooking the Yale Babylonian Culinary Recipes," in *Ancient Mesopotamia Speaks: Highlights of the Yale Babylonian Collection*, ed. Agnete W. Lassen, Eckart Frahm, and Klaus Wagensonner (New Haven, CT: Yale Peabody Museum of Natural History, 2019), 113. See, moreover, Georges Contenau, *La vie quotidienne à Babylone et en Assyrie* (Paris: Hachette, 1950), 309

(in the original the quote reads, "On ne voit pas rire le Mésopotamien; il ne semble pas connaître le délassement"); Enrique Jiménez, "Two Foxy Notes," in *The Third Millennium: Studies in Early Mesopotamia and Syria in Honor of Walter Sommerfeld and Manfred Krebernik*, ed. Ilya Arkhipov, Leonid Kogan, and Natalia Koslova (Leiden: Brill, 2020), 333–334; and Maddalena Rumor, "There's No Fool Like an Old Fool: The Mesopotamian *Aluzinnu* and Its Relationship to the Greek *Alazôn*," *Kaskal* 14 (2017): 187–210.

34. Barjamovic et al., "Food in Ancient Mesopotamia," 111–113.

35. See Stefan M. Maul, "Der Kneipenbesuch als Heilverfahren," in *La circulation des biens, des personnes et des idées dans le Proche-Orient ancien. Actes de la XXXVIIIe Rencontre Assyriologique Internationale (Paris, 8–10 juillet 1991)*, ed. Dominique Charpin and François Joannès (Paris: Éditions Recherche sur les Civilisations, 1992), 389–396; SAA 16, no. 115; SAA 1, no. 154.

36. SAA 3, no. 30; translation after Nicla De Zorzi, "Rude Remarks Not Fit to Smell," in *Sounding Sensory Profiles in the Ancient Near East*, ed. Annette Schellenberg and Thomas Krüger (Atlanta: SBL Press), 227.

37. See Karen Radner, "The Reciprocal Relationship Between Judge and Society in the Neo-Assyrian Period," *Maarav* 12 (2005): 41–68; Betina Faist, *Assyrische Rechtsprechung im 1. Jahrtausend v. Chr.* (Münster: Zaphon, 2020).

38. SAA 13, no. 26.

39. For an overview of the main units of the Neo-Assyrian army, and how they changed over time, see Tamás Dezsö, *The Assyrian Army*, vol. 2, *Recruitment and Logistics* (Budapest: Eötvös University Press, 2016).

40. Henry Stadhouders and Strahil V. Panayotov, "From Awe to Audacity: Stratagems for Approaching Authorities Successfully. The Istanbul Egalkura Tablet A 373," in *Mesopotamian Medicine and Magic: Studies in Honor of Markham J. Geller*, ed. Strahil V. Panayotov and Luděk Vacín (Leiden: Brill, 2018), 632–633. The petitioner had to recite this incantation three times before entering the palace.

Chapter 14: Imperial Twilight

1. See David Stronach, "Notes on the Fall of Nineveh," in *Assyria 1995*, ed. Simo Parpola and Robert M. Whiting (Helsinki: Neo-Assyrian Text Corpus Project, 1997), 307–324; Diana Pickworth, "Excavations at Nineveh: The Halzi Gate," *Iraq* 67 (2005): 295–316. The UC Berkeley team assumed that it was the Halzi Gate they had excavated, but Julian E. Reade, in "The Gates of Nineveh," *State Archives of Assyria Bulletin* 22 (2016): 39–93, esp. 58–72, has argued that the gate in question is actually the Shamash Gate (even though he calls it the "Enlil Gate," to distinguish it from the elaborately restored next gate farther north, which has been known as the Shamash Gate since the 1960s).

2. Garelli's remark reads, in full, "L'écroulement de l'Empire assyrien, qui suit de près le triomphe de son plus grand souverain, est souvent considéré comme un scandale historique." Paul Garelli and André Lemaire, *Le Proche-Orient asiatique*, vol. 2, *Les Empires mésopotamiens, Israël*, 3rd ed. (Paris: Presses Universitaires de France, 1997), 123.

3. Rocío Da Riva, *The Inscriptions of Nabopolassar, Amēl-Marduk, and Neriglissar* (Berlin: De Gruyter, 2013), 81.

4. The Babylonian Chronicle is quoted in the following after A. Kirk Grayson, *Assyrian and Babylonian Chronicles* (Locust Valley, NY: J. J. Augustin, 1975), 87–98, and Jean-Jacques Glassner, *Mesopotamian Chronicles* (Atlanta: Society of Biblical Literature, 2004), 214–225.

5. For Ashurbanipal's last years, see Chapter 12; for the Scythian raids, Karl Jansen-Winkeln, "Psametik I., die Skythen und der Untergang des Assyrerreiches," *Orientalia Nova Series* 88 (2019): 238–266, esp. 247–250, and further discussion below.

6. SAA 12, nos. 35 and 36 (shortened). The following account draws primarily on Andreas Fuchs, "Die unglaubliche Geburt des neubabylonischen Reiches oder: Die Vernichtung einer Weltmacht durch den Sohn eines Niemand," in *Babylonien und seine Nachbarn in neu- und spätbabylonischer Zeit*, ed. Manfred Krebernik and Hans Neumann (Münster: Ugarit-Verlag, 2014), 26–71, and John MacGinnis, "The Fall of Assyria and the Aftermath of the Empire," in *I Am Ashurbanipal, King of the World, King of Assyria*, ed. Gareth Brereton (New York: Thames and Hudson, 2018), 276–285.

7. Glassner, *Mesopotamian Chronicles*, 214–215.

8. For another Assyrian chief eunuch trying, unsuccessfully, to seize royal power, see Chapter 11.

9. Michael Jursa, "Die Söhne Kudurrus und die Herkunft der neubabylonischen Dynastie," *Revue d'Assyriologie* 101 (2006): 125–136.

10. Rocío Da Riva, "The Figure of Nabopolassar in Late Achaemenid and Hellenistic Historiographic Tradition: BM 34793 and CUA 90," *Journal of Near Eastern Studies* 76 (2017): 83 (shortened).

11. Da Riva, "Figure of Nabopolassar," 82. As the murdered enemy is identified only by his title, not by his name, it is not completely certain that the passage is really about Sîn-shumu-lishir. Some scholars have suggested that Sîn-shumu-lishir had already died by 627 BCE.

12. Given that the kingdoms involved were no nation-states in the modern sense, the term is, admittedly, slightly anachronistic.

13. For the political organization of the Medes, see, most recently, Robert Rollinger, "The Medes of the 7th and 6th c. BCE: A Short-Term Empire or Rather a Short-Term Confederacy?," in *Short-Term Empires in World History*, ed. Robert Rollinger, Julian Degen, and Michael Gehler (Wiesbaden: Springer Fachmedien, 2020), 189–213.

14. See Stuart C. Brown, "Media and Secondary State Formation in the Neo-Assyrian Zagros: An Anthropological Approach to an Assyriological Problem," *Journal of Cuneiform Studies* 38 (1986): 107–119.

15. See Peter Miglus, "Die letzten Tage von Assur und die Zeit danach," *ISIMU* 3 (2000): 85–99; Peter Miglus, "Assyrien im Untergang: Das Jahr 614 v. Chr. und der archäologische Befund," in *Befund und Historisierung: Dokumentation und ihre Interpretationsspielräume*, ed. Sandra Heinsch, Walter Kuntner, and Robert Rollinger (Turnhout, Belgium: Brepols, 2021), 7–19.

16. The presence of Arabs is suggested by Diodorus 2.24.5; for the role of Elamites in the conquest of Nineveh, see Fuchs, "Unglaubliche Geburt," 49.

17. Pamela Gerardi, "Declaring War in Mesopotamia," *Archiv für Orientforschung* 33 (1986): 30–38 (partly restored and shortened).

18. For the Sîn-sharru-ishkun letter, see Wilfred G. Lambert, "Letter of Sîn-šarra-iškun to Nabopolassar," in *Cuneiform Texts in the Metropolitan Museum of Art II: Literary and Scholastic Texts of the First Millennium B.C.*, ed. Ira Spar and Wilfred G. Lambert (New York: Metropolitan Museum of Art and Brepols, 2005), 203–210. Both letters will be reedited in a forthcoming study by Mary Frazer.

19. Rykle Borger, *Beiträge zum Inschriftenwerk Assurbanipals* (Wiesbaden: Harrassowitz, 1996), 54–55, K 3062+; Fuchs, "Unglaubliche Geburt," 49.

20. Joan Oates and David Oates, *Nimrud: An Assyrian Imperial City Revealed* (London: British School of Archaeology in Iraq, 2001), 65–68, 103–104.

21. Simo Parpola, "Cuneiform Texts from Ziyaret Tepe (Tušḫan) 2002–2003," *State Archives of Assyria Bulletin* 17 (2008): 86–87 (partially restored and shortened).

22. For the last days of Tushhan and thoughts on Mannu-ki-Libbali's letter, see Karen Radner, "An Imperial Communication Network: The State Correspondence of the Neo-Assyrian Empire," in *State Correspondence in the Ancient World: From New Kingdom Egypt to the Roman Empire*, ed. Karen Radner (Oxford: Oxford University Press, 2014), 83, 225; John MacGinnis, "Middle and Neo-Assyrian Texts from Anatolia," in *The Assyrians: Kingdom of the God Aššur from Tigris to Taurus*, ed. Kemalettin Köroğlu and Selim F. Adalı (Istanbul: Yapı Kredi Yayınları, 2018), 215–221.

23. See Karen Radner, "Late Emperor or Crown Prince Forever? Aššur-uballiṭ II of Assyria According to Archival Sources," in *Neo-Assyrian Sources in Context*, ed. Shigeo Yamada (Helsinki: Neo-Assyrian Text Corpus Project, 2018), 135–142. A document from Dur-Katlimmu that was drafted after the loss of the Assyrian heartland refers to the "covenant of the crown prince" rather than, as would have been customary, the "covenant of the king," and a text from the same time period from Guzana reveals that Ashur-uballit's field marshal bore the name Nabû-mar-sharri-usur, which means "O Nabû, protect the crown prince." The name must have been assigned to him, with

reference to Ashur-uballit II, shortly after the latter had assumed his office in Harran.

24. For an edition of the document, see Koray Toptaş and Faruk Akyüz, "A Neo-Assyrian Sale Contract from the Province of the Chief Cupbearer (*rab-šāqê*) Kept at the Hasankeyf Museum (Batman)," *Zeitschrift für Assyriologie* 111 (2021): 77–87. For the identification of Ubakisteri as the Median ruler, see Michael Roaf, "Cyaxares in Assyria," *Nouvelles Assyriologiques Brèves et Utilitaires* 2021, no. 118.

25. For the term "World War" for the events that led to the fall of the Assyrian Empire, see Karen Radner, "Neo-Assyrian Empire," in *Imperien und Reiche in der Weltgeschichte*, ed. Michael Gehler and Robert Rollinger (Wiesbaden: Harrassowitz, 2014), 111.

26. See John Curtis, "The Assyrian Heartland in the Period 612–539 BC," in *Continuity of Empire (?): Assyria, Media, Persia*, ed. Giovanni B. Lanfranchi, Michael Roaf, and Robert Rollinger (Padua, Italy: S.A.R.G.O.N. Editrice e Libreria, 2003), 157–168. A clay tablet inscribed in cuneiform with what seems to be an astronomical almanac was found by Japanese archaeologists in a Hellenistic context at Tell Fisna, some 40 kilometers (25 miles) north of Mosul. See Jeremy Black, "Hellenistic Cuneiform Writing from Assyria: The Tablet from Tell Fisna," *Al-Rafidan* 18 (1997): 229–238. Rather than testimony to a continued tradition of cuneiform writing in the north, though, it should probably be regarded as an import from southern Babylonia, as is argued by David Brown in "Increasingly Redundant: The Growing Obsolescence of the Cuneiform Script in Babylonia from 539 BC," in *The Disappearance of Writing Systems*, ed. John Baines, John Bennet, and Stephen Houston (London: Equinox, 2008), 96–97. For the survival of certain features of Assyrian culture, and memories of the Assyrian collapse in later tradition, see Chapters 15 and 17.

27. Adam W. Schneider and Selim Adalı, " 'No Harvest Was Reaped': Demographic and Climatic Factors in the Decline of the Neo-Assyrian Empire," *Climatic Change* 127 (2014): 435–346.

28. Ashish Sinha, Gayatri Kathayat, Harvey Weiss, Hanying Li, Hai Cheng, Justin Reuter, Adam W. Schneider, et al., "Role of Climate in the Rise and Fall of the Assyrian Empire," *Science Advances* 5, no. 11 (November 2019).

29. Jansen-Winkeln, "Skythen," drawing on Herodotus 1.103–106.

30. For details, see Chapter 5.

31. For the evidence from economic documents, see Gerfrid G.W. Müller, "Zur Entwicklung von Preisen und Wirtschaft in Assyrien im 7. Jh. v. Chr.," in *Von Sumer nach Ebla und zurück: Festschrift Giovanni Pettinato zum 27. September 1999 gewidmet von Freunden, Kollegen und Schülern*, ed. Hartmut

Waetzoldt (Heidelberg: Heidelberger Orientverlag, 2004), 189, as well as Chapter 12. For the situation in Ashur, see Miglus, "Die letzten Tage von Assur," 89.

32. For an edition of the Shulgi text, see Eckart Frahm, "Schulgi Sieger über Assur und die Skythen?," *Nouvelles Assyriologiques Brèves et Utilitaires* 2006, no. 25.

33. For the law of "diminishing returns" in politics, see Joseph Tainter, *The Collapse of Complex Societies* (Cambridge: Cambridge University Press, 1988).

34. Radner, "Neo-Assyrian Empire," 109. For the eponyms, see RINAP 5/1, 31–32, and Raija Mattila, "The Chief Singer and Other Late Eponyms," in *Of God(s), Trees, Kings, and Scholars: Neo-Assyrian and Related Studies in Honour of Simo Parpola*, ed. Mikko Luukko, Saana Svärd, and Raija Mattila (Helsinki: Finnish Oriental Society, 2009), 159–166. Additional analysis is found in Chapters 11, 12, and 17.

35. For the term "empire without mission," see Ariel Bagg, "Palestine Under Assyrian Rule: A New Look at the Assyrian Imperial Policy in the West," *Journal of the American Oriental Society* 133 (2013): 129–132.

Chapter 15: Assyria's Legacy on the Ground

1. Anabasis 2.4.28, 3.4.7–9 (shortened), and 3.4.10–11.

2. For details on the post-imperial settlements in the Assyrian heartland, see Julian E. Reade, "Greco-Parthian Nineveh," *Iraq* 60 (1998): 65–83, and John Curtis, "Nineveh in the Achaemenid Period," in *Nineveh the Great City: Symbol of Power and Beauty*, ed. Lucas D. Petit and Daniele Morandi Bonacossi (Leiden: Sidestone Press, 2017), 253–255. The Calachene is mentioned, inter alia, by Strabo (16.1.1). In "The Terms 'Assyria' and 'Syria' Again," *Journal of Near Eastern Studies* 65 (2006): 283–287, Robert Rollinger discusses the origins of the toponym "Syria." The Tennyson quote is from his poem "Ulysses."

3. For the term "post-imperial," see Stefan R. Hauser, "Post-Imperial Assyria," in *A Companion to Assyria*, ed. Eckart Frahm (Malden, MA: Wiley, 2017), 229–246, esp. 229. For the period in general and additional bibliographical references, see ibid., passim.

4. Michael Jursa, "Observations on the Problem of the Median 'Empire' on the Basis of Babylonian Sources," in *Continuity of Empire (?): Assyria, Media, Persia*, ed. Giovanni B. Lanfranchi, Michael Roaf, and Robert Rollinger (Padua, Italy: S.A.R.G.O.N. Editrice e Libreria, 2003), 173.

5. For the archaeology of Temple A, see Peter Miglus, "Das letzte Staatsarchiv der Assyrer," in *Von Uruk nach Tuttul—Eine Festschrift für Eva Strommenger*, ed. Bartel Hrouda, Stephan Kroll, and Peter Z. Spanos (Munich: Profil Verlag, 1992), 135–142.

6. Thus Eckart Frahm, *Historische und historisch-literarische Texte*, Keilschrifttexte aus Assur literarischen Inhalts III (Wiesbaden: Harrassowitz, 2009), 9.

7. Karen Radner, "Assur's 'Second Temple Period': The Restoration of the Cult of Aššur, c. 538 BC," in *Herrschaftslegitimation in vorderorientalischen Reichen der Eisenzeit*, ed. Christoph Levin and Reinhard Müller (Tübingen: Mohr Siebeck, 2017), 77–96. The (shortened) quote from the Cyrus Cylinder (lines 30–32) is from Hanspeter Schaudig, "Zum Tempel 'A' in Assur: Zeugnis eines Urbizids," in *Grenzüberschreitungen: Studien zur Kulturgeschichte des Alten Orients*, ed. Kristin Kleber, Georg Neumann, and Susanne Paulus (Münster: Zaphon, 2018), 624–625. For more on the Assyrians in Uruk, see Chapter 16.

8. Schaudig, "Tempel 'A' in Assur," 621–636.

9. Hauser, "Post-Imperial Assyria," 234–235. See also Chapter 14.

10. For the governor of Guzana, see Jursa, "Observations," 173; for the situation in Edessa, Lucinda Dirven, "The Exaltation of Nabû," *Die Welt des Orients* 28 (1997): 113n71. I analyzed the Assyrian traditions preserved in Nappigi/Hierapolis in "Of Doves, Fish, and Goddesses: Reflections on the Literary, Religious, and Historical Background of the Book of Jonah," in *Sibyls, Scriptures, and Scrolls: John Collins at Seventy*, ed. Joel Baden, Hindy Najman, and Eibert J.C. Tigchelaar (Leiden: Brill, 2016), 432–450, esp. 443–447. For additional discussion, see Chapters 4 and 16.

11. Bisitun, Persian ii.90.

12. Hauser, "Post-Imperial Assyria," 230–231, with additional literature.

13. See Reade, "Greco-Parthian Nineveh"; Julian Reade, "More About Adiabene," *Iraq* 63 (2001): 188–193.

14. The Pliny quote is from his *Naturalis Historia* 5.13.

15. See Simo Parpola, "National and Ethnic Identity in the Neo-Assyrian Empire and Assyrian Identity in Post-Empire Times," *Journal of Assyrian Academic Studies* 18, no. 2 (2004): 18–21; Karen Radner, *Ancient Assyria: A Very Short Introduction* (Oxford: Oxford University Press, 2015), 19–20. That Ashur was called Labbana in Parthian times remains disputed, as the old name of the city, rendered *'twr*, is still found in Syriac sources. For discussion and literature, see Michał Marciak, *Sophene, Gordyene, and Adiabene: Three Regna Minora of Northern Mesopotamia Between East and West* (Leiden: Brill, 2017), 316–317, with n. 326.

16. For the personal names, see Alasdair Livingstone, "Remembrance at Ashur: The Case of the Dated Aramaic Memorials," in *Of God(s), Trees, Kings, and Scholars: Neo-Assyrian and Related Studies in Honour of Simo Parpola*, ed. Mikko Luukko, Saana Svärd, and Raija Mattila (Helsinki: Finnish Oriental Society, 2009), 151–158, esp. 153–154. For evidence of linguistic continuity in

post-imperial Assyria, see Frederick Mario Fales, "Neo-Assyrian," in *History of the Akkadian Language*, ed. Juan-Pablo Vita (Leiden: Brill, 2021), 2:1347–1395, esp. 1348, with additional literature.

17. Livingstone, "Remembrance at Ashur," 155. The relevant texts were edited by Klaus Beyer, *Die aramäischen Inschriften aus Assur, Hatra und dem übrigen Ostmesopotamien (datiert 44 v. Chr. bis 238 n. Chr.)* (Göttingen: Vandenhoeck and Ruprecht, 1998), 11–25. For the Akitu Festival in Neo-Assyrian Ashur, see Chapter 9.

18. Livingstone, "Remembrance at Ashur," 155–157.

19. Hauser, "Post-Imperial Assyria," 241.

20. For an up-to-date history of Adiabene, see Marciak, *Sophene, Gordyene, and Adiabene*, 257–418.

21. Marciak, *Sophene, Gordyene, and Adiabene*, 285–286, with additional literature. For Ashurbanipal relying on a prophetic message sent by Ishtar of Arbela, see Chapter 12.

22. Tawny L. Holm, "Memories of Sennacherib in Aramaic Tradition," in *Sennacherib at the Gates of Jerusalem: Story, History, and Historiography*, ed. Isaac Kalimi and Seth Richardson (Leiden: Brill, 2014), 315–317.

23. Holm, "Memories of Sennacherib," 319–322.

24. For an up-to-date history of the Church of the East, see Christine Chaillot, *L'Église assyrienne de l'Orient—Histoire bimillénaire et géographie mondiale* (Paris: Editions L'Harmattan, 2020). For Lâbasi, see Chapter 14.

25. Austen Henry Layard, *Nineveh and Its Remains* (London: John Murray, 1849), 1:215–216. For analysis, see Aaron M. Butts, "Assyrian Christians," in Frahm, *Companion to Assyria*, 599–612.

26. For the events that led to the decimation of Turkey's Christian minorities between 1894 and 1924, see Benny Morris and Dror Ze'evi, *The Thirty-Year Genocide: Turkey's Destruction of Its Christian Minorities* (Boston: Harvard University Press, 2019).

27. For a photo of the statue, see also Butts, "Assyrian Christians," 606. Although some clearly are, not all claims regarding direct links between ancient and modern Assyrians are based on evidence. For the "Wikipedia wars" between adherents of the modern "Assyrianism" movement, which stresses the continuity between past and present, and more skeptical voices, see, inter alia, "Talk: Assyrian Continuity," Wikipedia, https://en.wikipedia.org/wiki/Talk:Assyrian_continuity, accessed December 31, 2020. That central theological concepts of Christianity, such as the idea of the Trinity or the salvation of the soul, have roots in the official religion of imperial Assyria (thus Simo Parpola, *Assyrian Prophecies* [Helsinki: Helsinki University Press, 1997], XIII–CVIII) seems unlikely.

Chapter 16: A Model Empire

1. Mario Liverani, *Assyria: The Imperial Mission* (Winona Lake, IN: Eisenbrauns, 2017), 258.

2. Peter Bedford, "The Neo-Assyrian Empire," in *The Dynamics of Ancient Empires*, ed. Ian Morris and Walter Scheidel (Oxford: Oxford University Press, 2009), 47.

3. For an up-to-date overview of the world's empires from antiquity to the present, see Peter F. Bang, C. A. Bayly, and Walter Scheidel, eds., *The Oxford World History of Empire*, 2 vols. (Oxford: Oxford University Press, 2021).

4. See Rocío Da Riva, "Assyrians and Assyrian Influence in Babylonia (626–539 BCE)," in *From Source to History: Studies on Ancient Near Eastern Worlds and Beyond Dedicated to Giovanni Battista Lanfranchi on the Occasion of His 65th Birthday on June 23, 2014*, ed. Salvatore Gaspa, Alessandro Greco, and Daniele Morandi Bonacossi (Münster: Ugarit-Verlag, 2014), 99–125.

5. For details, see Chapter 14.

6. Michael Jursa, "Der neubabylonische Hof," in *Der Achämenidenhof—The Achaemenid Court*, ed. Bruno Jacobs and Robert Rollinger (Wiesbaden: Harrassowitz, 2010), 67–106. The word *mašennu* originally entered the Assyrian language from Hurrian.

7. Rocío Da Riva, "A Lion in the Cedar Forest: International Politics and Pictorial Self-Representations of Nebuchadnezzar II (605–562 BC)," in *Studies on War in the Ancient Near East: Collected Essays on Military History*, ed. Jordi Vidal (Münster: Ugarit-Verlag, 2010), 165–185. For the lion hunt in Assyria, see Chapter 12.

8. Paul-Alain Beaulieu, "Nebuchadnezzar's Babylon as World Capital," *Journal of the Canadian Society for Mesopotamian Studies* 3 (2008): 8–9.

9. For Assyrians doing work for the temple of Shamash in Sippar, see John MacGinnis, "Assyrians After the Fall: The Evidence from the Ebabbar Temple in Sippar," in *At the Dawn of History: Ancient Near Eastern Studies in Honour of J. N. Postgate*, ed. Yağmur Heffron, Adam Stone, and Martin Worthington (Winona Lake, IN: Eisenbrauns, 2017), 781–796. For Assyrians serving as bureaucrats in Babylon, see Olof Pedersén, "Neo-Assyrian Texts from Nebuchadnezzar's Babylon: A Preliminary Report," in *Of God(s), Trees, Kings, and Scholars: Neo-Assyrian and Related Studies in Honour of Simo Parpola*, ed. Mikko Luukko, Saana Svärd, and Raija Mattila (Helsinki: Finnish Oriental Society, 2009), 193–199.

10. Eckart Frahm, *Babylonian and Assyrian Commentaries: Origins of Interpretation* (Münster: Ugarit-Verlag, 2011), 165.

11. Paul-Alain Beaulieu, "The Cult of AN.ŠÁR/Aššur in Babylonia After the Fall of the Assyrian Empire," *State Archives of Assyria Bulletin* 11 (1997): 55–73; Angelika Berlejung, "Innovation als Restauration in Uruk und

Jehud: Überlegungen zu Transformationsprozessen in vorderorientalischen Gesellschaften," in *Reformen im Alten Orient und der Antike. Programme, Darstellungen und Deutungen*, ed. Ernst-Joachim Waschke (Tübingen: Mohr Siebeck, 2009), 71–111.

12. For the seal, see Ronald Wallenfels, "The Impression of an Inscribed Middle Assyrian Cylinder Seal on a Late Babylonian Cuneiform Tablet," *Nouvelles Assyriologiques Brèves et Utilitaires* 2019, no. 26. For the Ashurbanipal tablet and its possible implications, see, most recently, Paul-Alain Beaulieu, "The Afterlife of Assyrian Scholarship in Hellenistic Babylonia," in *Gazing on the Deep: Ancient Near Eastern and Other Studies in Honor of Tzvi Abusch*, ed. Jeffrey Stackert, Barbara Nevling Porter, and David P. Wright (Bethesda, MD: CDL Press, 2010), 1–18.

13. For references, see Hanspeter Schaudig, *Die Inschriften Nabonids von Babylon und Kyros' des Großen* (Münster: Ugarit-Verlag, 2001), 708–711. For additional discussion, see Paul-Alain Beaulieu, "Assyria in Late Babylonian Sources," in *A Companion to Assyria*, ed. Eckart Frahm (Malden, MA: Wiley, 2017), 551, and Mary Frazer and Selim Adalı, " 'The Just Judgements that Ḥammu-rāpi, a Former King, Rendered': A New Royal Inscription in the Istanbul Archaeological Museums," *Zeitschrift für Assyriologie* 111 (2021): 253–254.

14. Ashurbanipal's jasper seal is mentioned in RINBE 2, 70–71: x 32'–51'. For discussion, see Thomas E. Lee, "The Jasper Cylinder Seal of Aššurbanipal and Nabonidus' Making of Sîn's Statue," *Revue d'Assyriologie* 87 (1993): 131–136.

15. Adda-guppi's inscription is edited in RINBE 2, 223–228.

16. See Yuval Levavi, "The Neo-Babylonian Empire: The Imperial Periphery as Seen from the Centre," *Journal of Ancient Near Eastern History* 7 (2020): 59–84, with further literature.

17. Jursa, "Der neubabylonische Hof," 96–97.

18. On Babylon's urban landscape during the sixth century, see Beaulieu, "Nebuchadnezzar's Babylon," 8–11.

19. The numbers, which must be taken as very rough approximations, are from Walter Scheidel, "The Scale of Empire: Territory, Population, Distribution," in Bang et al., *Oxford World History of Empire*, 93. For a history of the Persian Empire, see Pierre Briant, *Histoire de l'Empire Perse* (Paris: Fayard, 1996).

20. See Matt Waters, "The Far Side of the Long Sixth Century: Mesopotamian Political Influences on Early Achaemenid Persia," in *In the Shadow of Empire: Israel and Judah in the Long Sixth Century*, ed. Pamela Barmash and Mark W. Hamilton (Atlanta: SBL Press, 2021), 139–160.

21. For an edition of the Cyrus Cylinder, see Schaudig, *Inschriften Nabonids*, 550–556.

22. See Beaulieu, "Assyria in Late Babylonian Sources," 552; Matt Waters, "Ashurbanipal's Legacy: Cyrus the Great and the Achaemenid Empire," in *Iran and Its Histories: From the Beginnings Through the Achaemenid Empire*, ed. Touraj Daryaee and Robert Rollinger (Wiesbaden: Harrassowitz, 2021), 149–161, esp. 157–159. For analysis of the Cyrus Cylinder and its Assyrian resonances, see also Robartus J. van der Spek, "Cyrus the Great, Exiles, and Foreign Gods: A Comparison of Assyrian and Persian Policies on Subject Nations," in *Extraction and Control: Studies in Honor of Matthew W. Stolper*, ed. Michael Kozuh, Wouter F.M. Henkelman, Charles E. Jones, and Christopher Woods, Studies in Ancient Oriental Civilization (SAOC 68) (Chicago: Oriental Institute of the University of Chicago, 2014), 233–264. For the date formulas of tablets from the beginning of Cyrus's reign, see Caroline Waerzeggers, "The Day Before Cyrus Entered Babylon," in *Individuals and Institutions in the Ancient Near East: A Tribute to Ran Zadok*, ed. Uri Gabbay and Shai Gordin (Berlin: De Gruyter, 2021), 79–88.

23. See Alireza Askari Chaverdi, Pierfrancesco Callieri, and Emad Matin, "The Monumental Gate at Tol-e Ajori, Persepolis (Fars): New Archeological Data," *Iranica Antiqua* 52 (2017): 205–258, and, for discussion and further literature, David S. Vanderhooft, "Babylon as Cosmopolis in Israelite Texts and Achaemenid Architecture," *Hebrew Bible and Ancient Israel* 9 (2020): 57–61.

24. See John Curtis, "Nineveh in the Achaemenid Period," in *Nineveh the Great City: Symbol of Power and Beauty*, ed. Lucas D. Petit and Daniele Morandi Bonacossi (Leiden: Sidestone Press, 2017), 255, with further literature.

25. Waters, "Far Side of the Long Sixth Century," 142–143.

26. For discussion, see Salvatore Gaspa, "State Theology and Royal Ideology of the Neo-Assyrian Empire as a Structuring Model for the Achaemenid Imperial Religion," in *Persian Religion in the Achaemenid Period*, ed. Wouter Henkelman and Céline Redard (Wiesbaden: Harrassowitz, 2017), 125–184.

27. See Muhammad Dandamayev, "Assyrian Traditions in Achaemenid Times," in *Assyria 1995*, ed. Simo Parpola and Robert Whiting (Helsinki: Neo-Assyrian Text Corpus Project, 1997), 41–48.

28. See Waters, "Ashurbanipal's Legacy," 151; Gaspa, "State Theology," 137–138.

29. Waters, "Ashurbanipal's Legacy," 158–159.

30. Jennifer Finn, "Persian Collections: Center and Periphery at Achaemenid Imperial Capitals," *Studia Orientalia Electronica* 9, no. 2 (2021): 154–173, esp. 158–159.

31. This and the following two paragraphs draw heavily on Liverani, *Imperial Mission*, 249–250.

32. For Assyria and the notion of *translatio imperii*, see Robert Rollinger, "Assyria in Classical Sources," in Frahm, *Companion to Assyria*, 570–575.

Chapter 17: Distorted Reflections

1. A poorly preserved astronomical almanac from Uruk has recently been declared to be from 79/80 CE, which would make it even later than the text from 75 CE. See Hermann Hunger and Teije de Jong, "Almanac W22340a from Uruk: The Latest Datable Cuneiform Tablet," *Zeitschrift für Assyriologie* 104 (2014): 182–194. Given the fragmentary state of the tablet, though, some serious doubts remain about the accuracy of this dating.

2. See Mogens Trolle Larsen, *The Conquest of Assyria: Excavations in an Antique Land* (London: Routledge, 1996), 164.

3. The Delitzsch quote is from Friedrich Delitzsch, *Die große Täuschung* (Stuttgart: Deutsche Verlags-Anstalt, 1920/1921), 1:95, translated by Mogens Trolle Larsen in "The 'Babel/Bible' Controversy," in *Civilizations of the Ancient Near East*, ed. Jack Sasson (New York: Scribner, 1995), 104–105. On the Babel/Bible controversy in general, see, most recently, Eva Cancik-Kirschbaum and Thomas L. Gertzen, eds., *Der Babel-Bibel-Streit und die Wissenschaft vom Judentum* (Münster: Zaphon, 2021).

4. See Chapter 8.

5. See Eckart Frahm, "Text, Stories, History: The Neo-Assyrian Period and the Bible," in *Stones, Tablets, and Scrolls: Periods of the Formation of the Bible*, ed. Peter Dubovský and Federico Giuntoli (Tübingen: Mohr Siebeck, 2020), 166–171, with further literature.

6. The quote is from 2 Kings 19:35.

7. Nahum 3:1–5.

8. Genesis 10:10–12. Many Bible translators assume that it was Nimrod and not Ashur who founded Assyria, but this seems unlikely.

9. The quotes are from Isaiah 10:14 and 6:3.

10. For an edition of the Tayinat treaty, see Jacob Lauinger, "Esarhaddon's Succession Treaty at Tell Tayinat: Text and Commentary," *Journal of Cuneiform Studies* 64 (2012): 87–123. For additional discussion, see Frederick Mario Fales, "After Ta'yinat: The New Status of Esarhaddon's *adê* for Assyrian Political History," *Revue d'Assyriologie* 106 (2012): 133–158.

11. See Deuteronomy 28:28–30 and SAA 2, no. 6, §§39–42. The sequence of these deities is governed by genealogical considerations and therefore not random.

12. See SAA 2, no. 6, §24; Deuteronomy 6:5; Deuteronomy 17:14–20. Assyrian rulers had notably seized horses and chariot troops from Samaria in 722 and royal women, silver, and gold from Judah in 701 BCE.

13. See SAA 2, no. 6, §10; Deuteronomy 13:1–11.

14. See, inter alia, Hans Ulrich Steymans, *Deuteronomium 28 und die adê zur Thronfolgeregelung Asarhaddons* (Fribourg: Academic Press Fribourg; Göttingen: Vandenhoeck and Ruprecht, 1995).

15. See Eckart Otto, *Gottes Recht als Menschenrecht: Rechts- und literaturhistorische Studien zum Deuteronomium* (Wiesbaden: Harrassowitz, 2002), esp. 167–194.

16. For Isaiah 14, see Chapter 7, for the story of Joseph, Chapter 10, note 18.

17. For an overview and additional bibliography, see Robert Rollinger, "Assyria in Classical Sources," in *A Companion to Assyria*, ed. Eckart Frahm (Malden, MA: Wiley, 2017), 570–582.

18. For thoughts on the early history of the Semiramis legend, see Eckart Frahm, "Of Doves, Fish, and Goddesses: Reflections on the Literary, Religious, and Historical Background of the Book of Jonah," in *Sibyls, Scriptures, and Scrolls: John Collins at Seventy*, ed. Joel Baden, Hindy Najman, and Eibert J.C. Tigchelaar (Leiden: Brill, 2016), 432–450 (with further literature); for Sammu-ramat, see Chapter 4.

19. Diodorus 2.4–20.

20. For references, see Kerstin Droß-Krüpe, *Semiramis, de qua innumerabilia narrantur* (Wiesbaden: Harrassowitz, 2020), 51, 70–71. The statement about "the most renowned of all women" is found in Diodorus 2.4.1.

21. See Ronald Wallenfels, *Uruk: Hellenistic Seal Impressions in the Yale Babylonian Collection I. Cuneiform Tablets* (Mainz: Philipp von Zabern, 1994), no. 23.

22. For references, see Frahm, "Of Doves, Fish, and Goddesses," 436.

23. The quotes are from Diodorus 2.23.1–3.

24. Quoted after Rollinger, "Assyria in Classical Sources," 577.

25. For the full quote as well as bibliographical references, see Chapter 12.

26. See Chapter 12. Ashurbanipal's letter to the scholars of Borsippa is edited in SAA 21, no. 13.

27. "Models of exceptionality" is taken from Julia M. Asher-Greve, "From 'Semiramis of Babylon' to 'Semiramis of Hammersmith,'" in *Orientalism, Assyriology, and the Bible*, ed. Steven W. Holloway (Sheffield, UK: Sheffield Phoenix Press, 2006), 322–373.

28. Juvenal, Satire 10 (transl. Lewis Evans, *Satires of Juvenal, Persisus, Sulpicia, and Lucilius* (New York: Harper, 1861). For Delacroix's Sardanapallus painting as a coded representation of the modern artist, see Christine Tauber, *Ästhetischer Despotismus: Eugène Delacroix' "Tod des Sardanapal" als Künstlerchiffre* (Konstanz: UVK Universitätsverlag, 2006).

29. Rainer Bernhardt, "Sardanapal—Urbild des lasterhaften orientalischen Despoten: Entstehung, Bedeutung für die griechisch-römische Welt und Nachwirkung," *Tyche* 24 (2009): 1–25.

30. For the Orosius quote, see Rollinger, "Assyria in Classical Sources," 575. The passages from Dante are from *Paradiso* XV:107–108, *Inferno* V:52–60, and *Purgatorio* XII:52–54 (transl. C. H. Sisson, *Dante Alighieri: The Divine Comedy* [Oxford: Oxford University Press, 1998]).

31. Droß-Krüpe, *Semiramis*.

32. John Oldham, *Sardanapalus: An Ode*, quoted after Rachel J. Weil, "Sometimes a Scepter Is Only a Scepter: Pornography and Politics in Reformation England," in *The Invention of Pornography, 1500–1800: Obscenity and the Origins of Modernity*, ed. Lynn Hunt (New York: Zone Books, 1993), 125–153, esp. 128–129. I owe the reference to this poem to Ann Guinan.

33. It is noteworthy, though, that Hitler, an artist by trade, had remarked in a dinner conversation in 1942 that "someone who has no heir for his house would do best to have himself burned there, with everything inside, as if on a magnificent funerary pyre." See Eckart Frahm, "Images of Ashurbanipal in Later Tradition," *Eretz Israel* 27 (2003): 47*, for further discussion and references.

Chapter 18: The Second Destruction

1. Other names include the Islamic State of Iraq and the Levant (ISIL) or Islamic State of Iraq and al-Sham (i.e., the Levant), as well as its Arabic acronym, Daesh.

2. See Aaron Tugendhaft, *The Idols of ISIS: From Assyria to the Internet* (Chicago: University of Chicago Press, 2020), 1–3, from where the translations are taken. Selected video footage of the attack on the bull colossus and the devastation of the Mosul Museum can be found at "ISIS Video Purports to Show Militants Smashing Ancient Iraq Artifacts," NBC, February 26, 2015, www.nbcnews.com/storyline/isis-terror/isis-video-purports-show-militants-smashing-ancient-iraq-artifacts-n313636.

3. "Nous n'aurons point tout démoli si nous ne démolissons même les ruines!" The words are from a line introducing Jarry's 1900 play.

4. For an overview of the sites destroyed by ISIS in Syria and Iraq, see "Destruction of Cultural Heritage by the Islamic State," Wikipedia, https://en.wikipedia.org/wiki/Destruction_of_cultural_heritage_by_the_Islamic_State, accessed May 21, 2022. For details on the Tell Ajaja sculptures, see Eckart Frahm, "'Whoever Destroys This Image': A Neo-Assyrian Statue from Tell 'Ağāğa (Šadikanni)," *Nouvelles Assyriologiques Brèves et Utilitaires* 2015, no. 51.

5. For the situation at Nineveh in the 1990s, see John M. Russell, *The Final Sack of Nineveh* (New Haven, CT: Yale University Press, 1998). Sadly, the title of Russell's study would have been more appropriate for a book written about Nineveh some twenty years later.

6. An excellent resource for information on the attacks by ISIS on cultural heritage sites in northern Iraq is Christopher Jones's *Gates of Nineveh* website at https://gatesofnineveh.wordpress.com, accessed January 24, 2022.

7. The Arabic document is quoted after a translation by Lamia Al-Gailani, posted on the Agade Mailing List in 2016.

8. The case is documented at US District Attorney's Office, US Department of Justice, www.justice.gov/usao-dc/press-release/file/918536/download, accessed January 20, 2022.

9. Resolution GA/11646, see United Nations, "Expressing Outrage over Attacks on Cultural Heritage of Iraq, General Assembly Unanimously Adopts Resolution Calling for Urgent Action," 69th General Assembly, 91st Meeting (AM), GA/11646, May 28, 2015, www.un.org/press/en/2015/ga11646.doc.htm. For the Bokova quote, see Irina Bokova, "Fighting Cultural Cleansing: Harnessing the Law to Preserve Cultural Heritage," *Harvard International Review* 36 (2015): 40–45.

10. *Dabiq* 8 (2015): 22. Unlike others in this issue of *Dabiq*, the article is not attributed to a specific author.

11. Among the passages in the Quran about the smashing of images is Surah 21:51–58.

12. For a discussion of the composite nature of Assyrian bull colossi, see Chapter 3.

13. For the Islamic Nimrud legend, see Heinrich Schützinger, *Ursprung und Entwicklung der arabischen Abraham-Nimrod-Legende* (Bonn: Selbstverlag des Orientalischen Seminars, 1961). In the aftermath of the attacks of September 11, 2001, the Islamic Studies scholar Patrick Franke suggested, in an article in the *Frankfurter Allgemeine Zeitung* ("Der Turm und die Mücke: Allahs Strafgericht gegen Nimrod," September 13, 2001), that the mosquito episode in the Nimrud legend might have inspired the terrorists who flew planes into the Twin Towers in New York.

14. The religious underpinnings of ISIS's cultural politics are emphasized in a much-quoted article by Graeme Wood ("What ISIS Really Wants," *Atlantic* 315, no. 2 [March 2015]: 78–94, www.theatlantic.com/magazine /archive/2015/03/what-isis-really-wants/384980). For a thorough discussion of the group's media strategy for advertising its attacks on archaeological sites, see Tugendhaft, *Idols of ISIS*, esp. 75–96. The toppling and disfiguring of ancient statues, in the Mosul Museum and elsewhere, might also have been inspired by widely broadcast scenes of residents knocking down a statue of Saddam Hussein in Baghdad in April 2003 (Tugendhaft, *Idols of ISIS*, 65–67). For ancient ruins in the Quran, see, for example, Surah 22:45–46.

15. For an image of the medal, see "Second Empire, Les Fouilles de Ninive (Mésopotamie), 1853 Paris," iNumis, www.inumis.com/shop/second-empire -les-fouilles-de-ninive-mesopotamie-1853-paris-1303679, accessed January 22, 2022. For Western explorers of Iraq in the nineteenth century, see the introduction to this book.

16. For the relationship between archaeology and politics in modern Iraq, see Magnús T. Bernhardsson, *Reclaiming a Plundered Past: Archaeology and Nation Building in Modern Iraq* (Austin: University of Texas Press, 2005).

17. For this and the following, see, most recently, András Bácskay, "Elements of Ancient Mesopotamian Cultures in the National Ideology of Iraq," in *The Collapse of Empires in the 20th Century: New States and New Identities*, ed. Samvel Poghosyan, Garik Galstyan, and Edgar Hovhannisyan (Yerevan: Armenian State Pedagogical University, 2020), 305–316; Umberto Livadiotti, Andrea Ercolani, Marco Bonechi, and Silvia Alaura, "Evocazioni filateliche fra orientalismo e propaganda: Il Vicino Oriente antico nei francobolli di Turchia, Siria, Libano e Iraq," in *Digging in the Archives: From the History of Oriental Studies to the History of Ideas*, ed. Silvia Alaura (Rome: Edizioni Quasar, 2020), 437–496.

18. The events accompanying the conference included a lavish display of dresses inspired by Mesopotamian art—the only fashion show the present writer, who had the opportunity to attend, ever saw in his life.

19. For an illustration of the billboards set up near Nineveh, see Tugendhaft, *Idols of ISIS*, 64. Saddam's novel is discussed by David Damrosch in *The Buried Book: The Loss and Rediscovery of the Great Epic of Gilgamesh* (New York: Holt, 2007), 254–272.

20. The text on the stamp mistakenly identifies the site as Nineveh. See Livadiotti et al., "Evocazioni filateliche," 482.

21. Livadiotti et al., "Evocazioni filateliche," 486.

22. For a photo, see the artist's website at www.michaelrakowitz.com/the-invisible-enemy-should-not-exist-lamassu-of-nineveh, accessed January 22, 2022.

23. For a comprehensive survey of the operation that led to the liberation of Mosul, see "Battle of Mosul (2016–2017)," Wikipedia, https://en.wikipedia.org/wiki/Battle_of_Mosul_(2016%E2%80%932017), accessed January 22, 2022. Information on the Nahrein Network is found at "The Nahrein Network," University College London, www.ucl.ac.uk/nahrein/nahrein-network, accessed January 22, 2022.

24. See Stefan Maul and Peter Miglus, "Erforschung des *ekal mašarti* auf Tell Nebi Yunus in Ninive 2018–2019," *Zeitschrift für Orient-Archäologie* 13 (2020): 128–213.

Epilogue

1. Jo Ann Scurlock, Review of *Guerre et paix en Assyrie*, by Frederick Mario Fales, *Journal of the American Oriental Society* 132 (2012): 312.

2. "Assour était son dieu, le pillage sa morale, les jouissances matérielles son idéal, la cruauté et la terreur ses moyens" (Jacques de Morgan, *Les premières civilisations* [Paris: E. Leroux, 1909], cited after René Labat, "Un prince éclairé: Assurbanipal," *Comptes rendus des séances de l'Académie des Inscriptions et Belles-Lettres* 116, no. 4 [1972]: 670). For the other statements

referenced in this paragraph, see Susan Pollock, "The Subject of Suffering," *American Anthropologist* 118 (2016): 726–741, esp. 737; Jonathan Jones, "Demons, Mummies, and Ancient Curses," *The Guardian*, March 24, 2014, www .theguardian.com/artanddesign/jonathanjonesblog/2014/mar/27/british -museum-assyrian-gallery-cuneiform-auction; Larry R. Gonick, *Cartoon History of the Universe*, vol. 1 (San Francisco: Rip Off Press, 1978), n.p.

3. See Seneca, *Epistolae morales*, 95.30, and, for violence and war in ancient Rome in general, Gabriel Baker, *Spare No One: Mass Violence in Roman Warfare* (Lanham, MD: Rowman and Littlefield, 2021). For the Assyrians as Nazis *avant la lettre*, see Jonathan Jones, " 'Some of the Most Appalling Images Ever Created': I Am Ashurbanipal Review," *The Guardian*, November 6, 2018, www.theguardian.com/artanddesign/2018/nov/06/i-am-ashurbanipal-review -british-museum: "Just as Hannah Arendt argued that the Holocaust was perpetrated by characterless paper-pushers, not flamboyant sadists, so we find here that Assyrian atrocities—including the forced resettlement of thousands of Israelites—were not the product of random mayhem but diligent organization."

4. Walter Benjamin, *Über den Begriff der Geschichte* IX, in *Gesammelte Schriften*, 7 vols., ed. Rolf Tiedemann and Hermann Schweppenhäuser (Frankfurt am Main: Suhrkamp, 1972–1989), I/2:697–698 (transl. Harry Zohn). The passage is also quoted in Eckart Frahm, "Images of Assyria in Nineteenth- and Twentieth-Century Western Scholarship," in *Orientalism, Assyriology and the Bible*, ed. Steven W. Holloway (Sheffield, UK: Sheffield Phoenix Press, 2006), 93–94, and Pollock, "Subject of Suffering," 737–738.

5. Frahm, "Images of Assyria," 94.

Index

INDEX

Akitu Festival, 214–215, 224–226, 229, 361–362

Akitu House, 226, 228–231, 362, 364–365

Akkad (city and state), 37–39, 51–52, 75, 80–81, 133, 136–137, 214, 257–258, 263, 274, 320

Akkadian language, 320

Akko (city), 159

Akkulanu (astrologer), 290

Aleppo (city and kingdom), 109, 119

Alexander the Great, 3, 148, 358–359, 402

Alexandria, 296

Al-Lat (Arab goddess), 169

Al-Mina (site), 161. *See also* Ahtâ

Aluzinnu Text (cuneiform parody), 317–318

Amanus, Mount, 99

Amar-Suen (king of Ur), 39

Amarna correspondence, 63

Amathus (site), 162

Ambaris (ruler in Tabal), 178, 249

Amel-Marduk (Babylonian king), 180, 377

Ammon (kingdom), 103, 196

Amorites (ethnic group), 40, 44, 51, 54, 56, 378

Amos (prophet), 103, 390

Amurru (god), 231

Amurru (kingdom), 74

Anatolia, central, 47, 59, 107, 132, 134, 154, 178, 249

Anchiale (city), 402

Andrae, Walter, 14

animal husbandry, 31–32, 302

AN.ŠÁR (god), 373–374

Anshan (region), 379

Anu (god), 332, 373–374

Anu-Adad Temple (Ashur), 332

Anzû bird and Anzû Epic, 101, 119, 283

Apollo Smintheus (Greek god), 206

Apqu (city), 260

Apsû (primeval god), 161–162, 229

Apum (city), 55

aqueducts, 194, 302

Arabs, Arabian Peninsula

  Assyrian influence on material and political culture, 170–172

  desert caravan trade, 167–168

  ethnogenesis, 85

  inscribed beads, 175

  leadership role of women, 165–166

  military incursion into, 154, 168–170

  post-imperial Mesopotamia, 360–361

Aramaean peoples and cultures, 19, 85–90, 93–94, 99–100, 104, 108, 128, 144, 147, 217

Aramaic language, 17–18, 27, 109, 151, 173, 241, 248, 251, 305–306, 358, 361, 379, 394, 399–400

Arbaces (legendary Median ruler), 402

Arbela (city), 33, 36–37, 54, 61, 70, 88, 91, 97, 235, 279, 358–360, 363–365, 384

archaeological excavations

  at Ashur, 14–15, 36–37, 64–65, 354–356

  Calah temples, 98–99

  Calah tombs, 244–249

  at Dur-Katlimmu, 15–16

  early exploration of Assyrian cities, 6–10

  fieldwork following ISIS destruction, 422–423

  Iraqi excavations at Nineveh, 412–413

  ISIS destruction of monuments and artifacts, 409–413

  at Kanesh, 15

  transporting artifacts to the West, 9–10

  wine production installations, 302–303

  See also Calah/Nimrud; cuneiform; Nineveh

Ardashir (Sasanian king), 362

Argishti (Urartian king), 119

Aribua (city), 105

Aristobulos (Greek historian), 402

Arpad (city-state), 117, 119–120, 128–129, 133, 192, 204, 214

Arrabu (exorcist), 295

Arrapha (city), 53, 61–62, 93, 114, 126, 146, 302, 329–332

Artabanus IV (Parthian king), 362

Artaxerxes II (Persian ruler), 351, 382, 397

arts and culture

  Akkadian influences on Assyria, 37–38

  Ashurbanipal's cultural ambitions, 273–275

  Assyrian influence on Arab material and political culture, 170–172

  Babylonian monumental art, 372

  Babylonization of, 57–58

  influence of Assyria on the Zagros region, 173–174

  ISIS mass destruction and looting, 409–416, 418

  literary culture of Neo-Assyrians, 317–318

  Middle Assyrian period, 78–79

  Neo-Babylonian interest in Assyrian culture, 374–376

  Persian Empire, 380–382, 384

  Wadi Brisa relief, 372

  Semiramis and Sardanapallus, 404–408

Arukku (son of Kurash I), 175, 384

Arwad (island-city), 86, 156, 196, 241

490

Eckart Frahm is professor of Assyriology in the Department of Near Eastern Languages and Civilizations at Yale. One of the world's foremost experts on the Assyrian Empire, he is the author or coauthor of six books on ancient Mesopotamian history and culture. He lives in New Haven, Connecticut.